Educating Children with Autism

Committee on Educational Interventions for Children with Autism

Catherine Lord and James P. McGee, editors

Division of Behavioral and Social Sciences and Education

National Research Council

NATIONAL ACADEMY PRESS
Washington, DC

NATIONAL ACADEMY PRESS 2101 Constitution Avenue, N.W. Washington, DC 20418

NOTICE: The project that is the subject of this report was approved by the Governing Board of the National Research Council, whose members are drawn from the councils of the National Academy of Sciences, the National Academy of Engineering, and the Institute of Medicine. The members of the committee responsible for the report were chosen for their special competences and with regard for appropriate balance.

The study was supported by Contract No. H324F980001 between the National Academy of Sciences and the U.S. Department of Education. Any opinions, findings, conclusions, or recommendations expressed in this publication are those of the author(s) and do not necessarily reflect the view of the organizations or agencies that provided support for this project.

Library of Congress Cataloging-in-Publication Data

Educating children with autism / Committee on Educational Interventions for Children with Autism, Division of Behavioral and Social Sciences and Education, National Research Council.
    p. cm.
Includes bibliographical references (p.   ) and index.
    ISBN 0-309-07269-7 (cloth)
    1. Autistic children—Education (Early childhood)—United States. 2. Autism in children—United States. I. National Research Council (U.S.). Committee on Educational Interventions for Children with Autism.
    LC4718 .E39 2001
    371.94—dc21

                        2001003875

Additional copies of this report are available from National Academy Press, 2101 Constitution Avenue, N.W., Washington, DC 20418. Call (800) 624-6242 or (202) 334-3313 (in the Washington metropolitan area). This report is also available online at http://www.nap.edu

Printed in the United States of America

Suggested citation: National Research Council (2001) *Educating Children with Autism*. Committee on Educational Interventions for Children with Autism. Catherine Lord and James P. McGee, eds. Division of Behavioral and Social Sciences and Education. Washington, DC: National Academy Press.

First Printing, October 2001
Second Printing, April 2002
Third Printing, August 2002
Fourth Printing, November 2002

THE NATIONAL ACADEMIES

National Academy of Sciences
National Academy of Engineering
Institute of Medicine
National Research Council

The **National Academy of Sciences** is a private, nonprofit, self-perpetuating society of distinguished scholars engaged in scientific and engineering research, dedicated to the furtherance of science and technology and to their use for the general welfare. Upon the authority of the charter granted to it by the Congress in 1863, the Academy has a mandate that requires it to advise the federal government on scientific and technical matters. Dr. Bruce M. Alberts is president of the National Academy of Sciences.

The **National Academy of Engineering** was established in 1964, under the charter of the National Academy of Sciences, as a parallel organization of outstanding engineers. It is autonomous in its administration and in the selection of its members, sharing with the National Academy of Sciences the responsibility for advising the federal government. The National Academy of Engineering also sponsors engineering programs aimed at meeting national needs, encourages education and research, and recognizes the superior achievements of engineers. Dr. Wm. A. Wulf is president of the National Academy of Engineering.

The **Institute of Medicine** was established in 1970 by the National Academy of Sciences to secure the services of eminent members of appropriate professions in the examination of policy matters pertaining to the health of the public. The Institute acts under the responsibility given to the National Academy of Sciences by its congressional charter to be an adviser to the federal government and, upon its own initiative, to identify issues of medical care, research, and education. Dr. Kenneth I. Shine is president of the Institute of Medicine.

The **National Research Council** was organized by the National Academy of Sciences in 1916 to associate the broad community of science and technology with the Academy's purposes of furthering knowledge and advising the federal government. Functioning in accordance with general policies determined by the Academy, the Council has become the principal operating agency of both the National Academy of Sciences and the National Academy of Engineering in providing services to the government, the public, and the scientific and engineering communities. The Council is administered jointly by both Academies and the Institute of Medicine. Dr. Bruce M. Alberts and Dr. Wm. A. Wulf are chairman and vice chairman, respectively, of the National Research Council.

COMMITTEE ON EDUCATIONAL INTERVENTIONS FOR CHILDREN WITH AUTISM

CATHERINE LORD (*Chair*) Department of Psychology, University of Michigan
MARIE BRISTOL-POWER, Mental Retardation and Developmental Disabilities Branch, National Institutes of Health
JOANNE M. CAFIERO, Graduate School of Education, Johns Hopkins University
PAULINE A. FILIPEK, Departments of Pediatrics and Neurology, University of California at Irvine College of Medicine
JAMES J. GALLAGHER, School of Education, University of North Carolina at Chapel Hill
SANDRA L. HARRIS, Graduate School of Applied and Professional Psychology, Rutgers University
ALAN M. LESLIE, Department of Psychology and Center for Cognitive Science, Rutgers University
GAIL G. MCGEE, Department of Psychiatry and Behavioral Sciences, Emory University
SAMUEL L. ODOM, Wendell Wright School of Education, Indiana University
SALLY J. ROGERS, Department of Psychiatry, University of Colorado Health Sciences Center
FRED R. VOLKMAR, School of Medicine, Yale University
AMY M. WETHERBY, Department of Communication Disorders, Florida State University

JAMES P. McGEE, *Study Director*
NATHANIEL TIPTON, *Senior Project Assistant*

Preface

John Brian Harley, a British geographer, described the process of making a map as the social construction of knowledge to facilitate understanding. In many ways, the preparation of this report seemed like that of making a map, not to direct, but to organize and represent information to help progress through the many scientific findings and unknowns in the field of early education in autism. At the request of the U.S. Department of Education's Office of Special Education Programs, this project was undertaken by the National Research Council to consider the state of the scientific evidence of the effects of early educational intervention on young children with autistic spectrum disorders. In any such project, the questions become as important as the answers. Our committee represented many different fields—including clinical and developmental psychology, special education, speech and language pathology, psychiatry, and child neurology—and we elected to organize our report around the questions that we defined as most important for our areas of inquiry; these questions demand multidisciplinary attention. We attempted to provide a "map" for each of these questions that represented scientific literature from our respective fields.

The questions cover epidemiology, family support, diagnosis and screening, assistive technology, characteristics of autism, features of intervention programs, and how instructional strategies have been put together in comprehensive programs. The questions also include issues in public policy, personnel preparation, and future research.

In elementary school, children are first taught the scientific principles of experimentation and replication. Experimental methods are at the core of the systematic collection and evaluation of knowledge that is science. Yet as Richard Horton recently said, in an article about the future of academic medicine, ". . . straightforward observations rather than intricate experimentation often produce the significant step forward," steps that could then be tested through experimental methods. Our committee believed strongly that we needed to consider the insights provided by systematic observations, as long as the methods for such observations were detailed sufficiently enough to permit us to consider factors that might influence interpretations of the results. Similar to the recent criteria for evaluating treatment guidelines proposed by the American Psychological Association, we elected to focus on convergence and divergence of findings and to evaluate strengths and biases of sources of information, to best represent the current questions and state of evidence concerning the effectiveness of early education in autism.

This report presents the results of the committee's deliberations. We hope it will have a broad audience, including educators and other professionals who work with and who carry out research with children with autistic spectrum disorders and their families, parents and family members, legislators and other policy makers, and advocates.

Many individuals have made contributions to the panel's thinking and to various sections of this report by serving as presenters, advisers, and liaisons to useful sources of information. The committee is grateful to Gail Houle, at the Department of Education's Office of Special Education Programs, for her continuous support, encouragement, and generous sharing of information most useful to the committee; and to Louis Danielson, at the Department of Education, for his workshop presentation of relevant data.

The committee thanks the following authors, who prepared commissioned papers and presented them at workshops sponsored by the committee: Grace Baranek, University of North Carolina; Eric Fombonne, King's College London; Howard Goldstein, Florida State University; Myrna Mandlawitz; Scott McConnell, University of Minnesota; Pat Mirenda, University of British Columbia; Marian Sigman, University of California-Los Angeles; Rutherford Turnbull, University of Kansas; Robert Horner, University of Oregon; Phillip Strain, University of Colorado-Denver; Edward Carr, State University of New York at Stony Brook; Connie Kasari, University of California-Los Angeles; Joicey Hurth, Donald Kates, and Kathy Whaley, NECTAS; and Mark Wolery, University of North Carolina. The papers prepared by these authors are available through the National Research Council's unit on Behavioral, Cognitive, and Sensory Sciences and Education.

The committee also thanks the following program directors who responded to our request for data concerning their programs: Glen Dunlap and Lise Fox, Center for Autism and Related Disorders, University of

South Florida; Stanley Greenspan, George Washington University Hospital; Lynn Koegel and Robert Koegel, Graduate School of Education, University of California, Santa Barbara; O. Ivar Lovaas, University of California-Los Angeles; Gary Mesibov, TEACCH, University of North Carolina; Raymond Romanczyk, Institute for Child Development, Children's Unit for Treatment and Evaluation, State University of New York at Binghamton; and Phillip Strain, Professor of Educational Psychology, University of Colorado-Denver.

We also thank the following invited participants who attended the committee's workshops and offered valuable input to its proceedings: Doris Allen, JCC on the Palisades Therapeutic Nursery; Gina Green, Eunice Kennedy Shriver Center; Cathy Pratt, Indiana Resource Center for Autism; Serena Wieder, Interdisciplinary Council on Developmental Disorders; and Isabelle Rapin, Albert Einstein College of Medicine.

This report has been reviewed in draft form by individuals chosen for their diverse perspectives and technical expertise, in accordance with procedures approved by the Report Review Committee of the National Research Council (NRC). The purpose of this independent review is to provide candid and critical comments that will assist the institution in making the published report as sound as possible and to ensure that the report meets institutional standards for objectivity, evidence, and responsiveness to the study charge. The review comments and draft manuscript remain confidential to protect the integrity of the deliberative process.

We thank the following individuals for their participation in the review of this report: H. Carl Haywood, Departments of Psychology and Neurology (emeritus), Vanderbilt University; Susan Hyman, Strong Center for Developmental Disabilities, University of Rochester; Linda J. Lotspeich, Division of Child and Adolescent Psychiatry and Child Development, Stanford University School of Medicine; Edwin W. Martin, Division for Learning Disabilities, Council for Exceptional Children, Arlington, VA; Nancy Minshew, Department of Psychiatry, University of Pittsburgh; Michael Rutter, Social, Genetic, and Developmental Psychiatry Research Center, Institute of Psychiatry, London, England; Stephen R. Schroeder, Schiefelbusch Institute for Life Span Studies, University of Kansas; and Linda R. Watson, Division of Speech and Hearing Sciences, Department of Allied Health Sciences, University of North Carolina at Chapel Hill.

Although the reviewers listed above have provided many constructive comments and suggestions, they were not asked to endorse the conclusions or recommendations nor did they see the final draft of the report before its release. The review of this report was overseen by Richard Wagner, Department of Psychology, Florida State University, and Eleanor Maccoby, Department of Psychology, Stanford University (emerita). Appointed by the National Research Council, they were responsible for making certain that an independent examination of this report was carried out in accordance with institutional procedures and that all review comments were carefully considered. Responsibility for the final content of this report rests entirely with the authors.

This report is the collective product of the entire panel, and each member took an active role in drafting sections of chapters, leading discussions, and reading and commenting on successive drafts. In particular, Marie Bristol-Power assumed major responsibility for the chapter on problem behaviors, Pauline Filipek on sensory and motor development, James Gallagher on public policy and personnel preparation, Sandra Harris on the role of families, Gail McGee on comprehensive programs and adaptive behavior, Samuel Odom on research methodology and problem behaviors, Sally Rogers on social development and instructional strategies, Fred Volkmar on diagnosis and prevalence, and on cognitive development, and Amy Wetherby on development of communication. Joanne Cafiero contributed significant sections on assistive technology, and Alan Leslie added key discussions on cognitive development. Fred Volkmar also performed detailed reviews of the report drafts, contributing additional valuable insights and information.

Staff at the National Research Council made important contributions to our work in many ways. We express our appreciation to Christine Hartel, director of the Board on Behavioral, Cognitive, and Sensory Sciences, for her valuable insight, guidance, and support; and to Alexandra Wigdor, former director of the Division on Education, Labor, and Human Performance, for establishing the groundwork and direction of the project. We offer major thanks to Nathaniel Tipton, the panel's project assistant, who was indispensable in organizing meetings, arranging travel, compiling agenda materials, conducting extensive outreach with the interested community, copyediting and formatting the report, and managing the exchange of documentation among the committee members. We are deeply indebted to Eugenia Grohman, who significantly improved the report by dedicated application of her extraordinary editing skills. We also thank Amanda Taylor, at the University of Chicago, for her untiring and competent support of many aspects of the activities of the committee Chair.

Catherine Lord, *Chair*
James P. McGee, *Study Director*
Committee on Educational Interventions for
Children with Autism

Contents

EXECUTIVE SUMMARY   1
    Committee's Charge, 2
    Diagnosis, Assessment, and Prevalence, 2
    Role of Families, 4
    Goals for Educational Services, 5
    Characteristics of Effective Interventions, 6
    Public Policies, 7
    Personnel Preparation, 7
    Research , 8

1   INTRODUCTION   11
    Features of Autism, 11
    The Challenge of Educating Children with Autism, 12
    The Committee's Work, 13
    Organization of the Report, 19

I GOALS FOR CHILDREN WITH AUTISM AND THEIR FAMILIES

2   DIAGNOSIS, ASSESSMENT, AND PREVALENCE   23
    Multidisciplinary Perspectives, 23
    Prevalence of Autism and Related Conditions, 24
    Screening Instruments, 25
    Assessment, 26
    Medical Considerations, 30
    Implications for Intervention, 31

3   FAMILY ROLES   32
    Special Demands on Parents, 33
    Teaching Parents Needed Skills, 35
    The Advocacy Role, 36
    Support for Families, 37
    From Research to Practice, 39

4   GOALS FOR EDUCATIONAL SERVICES   40
    Interventions as Paths to Goals, 41
    Outcomes, 43

    II   CHARACTERISTICS OF EFFECTIVE INTERVENTIONS

5   DEVELOPMENT OF COMMUNICATION   47
    Core Communication Deficits, 48
    Planning for Intervention, 50
    Intervention Approaches, 52
    From Research to Practice, 63

6   SOCIAL DEVELOPMENT   66
    Developmental Constructs and Theory, 66
    Commonalties and Individual Differences, 69
    Planning for Intervention, 71
    Interventions Used to Teach Social Behavior, 75
    From Research to Practice, 81

7   COGNITIVE DEVELOPMENT   82
    Cognitive Abilities in Infants and Very Young Children, 83
    Stability and Uses of Tests of Intelligence, 84
    General Issues in Cognitive Assessment, 87
    Theoretical Models of Cognitive Dysfunction in Autism, 88
    Academic Instruction and Outcomes, 90
    From Research to Practice, 92

8   SENSORY AND MOTOR DEVELOPMENT   93
    Constructs and Deficits, 94
    Intervention Techniques, 98
    Sensory and Motor Development and Educational
    Programming, 101
    From Research to Practice, 102

9 ADAPTIVE BEHAVIORS   103
    Background, 103
    Developmental Constructs and Theory, 105
    Form of Adaptive Behaviors, 106
    Assessing Adaptive Behavior and Planning for Intervention, 107
    Intervention Studies, 110
    Intervention Programs, 112
    From Research to Practice, 113

10 PROBLEM BEHAVIORS   115
    Nature and Persistence of Behavior Problems, 116
    Preventive Interventions, 118
    After the Fact: Teaching Alternative Behaviors, 121
    Other Interventions, 127
    From Research to Practice, 131

11 INSTRUCTIONAL STRATEGIES   133
    Types of Instructional Strategies, 133
    Individual Versus Group Instruction, 137
    The Use of Peers as Instructors, 138
    The Roles of Selected Disciplines, 138

12 COMPREHENSIVE PROGRAMS   140
    Selection and Overview of Model Programs, 140
    Theoretical Orientations of Program Models, 147
    Convergence and Variability of Program Dimensions, 149
    Intervention Studies, 166

          III   POLICY, LEGAL, AND RESEARCH CONTEXT

13 PUBLIC POLICY AND LEGAL ISSUES   175
    Legislation, 176
    Adequacy of Services and Resources, 181

14 PERSONNEL PREPARATION   183
    Need for a Support Infrastructure, 183
    Kinds of Personnel, 186
    Providers of Personnel Preparation, 188
    Content of Personnel Preparation Programs, 188
    Resources, 190

15 METHODOLOGICAL ISSUES IN RESEARCH ON
   EDUCATIONAL INTERVENTIONS   193
   Separate Literatures, 194
   Early Screening and Diagnosis, 195
   Description of Participants of Studies, 197
   Methodological Issues, 199
   From Research to Practice, 209

16 CONCLUSIONS AND RECOMMENDATIONS   211
   Diagnosis, Assessment, and Prevalence, 211
   Role of Families, 214
   Goals for Educational Services, 216
   Characteristics of Effective Interventions, 218
   Public Policies, 222
   Personnel Preparation, 224
   Needed Research, 227

REFERENCES   231

BIOGRAPHICAL SKETCHES   290

INDEX   295

Educating Children with Autism

Executive Summary

Autistic spectrum disorders are present from birth or very early in development and affect essential human behaviors such as social interaction, the ability to communicate ideas and feelings, imagination, and the establishment of relationships with others. Although precise neurobiological mechanisms have not yet been established, it is clear that autistic spectrum disorders reflect the operation of factors in the developing brain. Autistic disorders are unique in their pattern of deficits and areas of relative strengths. They generally have lifelong effects on how children learn to be social beings, to take care of themselves, and to participate in the community. The autism spectrum occurs along with mental retardation and language disorder in many cases. Thus, educational planning must address both the needs typically associated with autistic disorders and needs associated with accompanying disabilities.

Education, both directly of children, and of parents and teachers, is currently the primary form of treatment for autistic spectrum disorders. The education of children with autistic disorders was accepted as a public responsibility under the Education of All Handicapped Children Act in 1975. Despite the federal mandate, however, the goals, methods and resources available vary considerably from state to state and school system to school system. In the last few years, due to a confluence of factors, courts have become increasingly active in determining the methods and resources allocated by school systems for the education of young children with autistic spectrum disorders.

COMMITTEE'S CHARGE

At the request of the U.S. Department of Education's Office of Special Education Programs, the National Research Council formed the Committee on Educational Interventions for Children with Autism and charged the committee to integrate the scientific, theoretical, and policy literature and create a framework for evaluating the scientific evidence concerning the effects and features of educational interventions for young children with autism. The primary focus of the charge was early intervention, preschool, and school programs designed for children with autism from birth to age 8. The charge included specific suggestions to examine several issues pertaining to education of children with autism: early intervention, diagnosis and classification, the rights of children with autism under the Individuals with Disabilities Education Act, inclusion, and assistive technology.

The committee's key conclusions and recommendations are summarized below, organized by the significant issues relevant to educational interventions for young children with autistic spectrum disorders. Each section begins with the key questions the committee addressed. The final chapter of this report presents the committee's complete conclusions and recommendations.

DIAGNOSIS, ASSESSMENT, AND PREVALENCE

What is the role of diagnosis, classification, and assessment in providing appropriate educational services to young children with autistic spectrum disorders? Are the specific deficits associated with a diagnosis or educational classification of autistic spectrum disorder important to planning and implementing educational interventions?

Autistic spectrum disorders vary in severity of symptoms, age of onset, and the presence of various features, such as mental retardation and specific language delay. The manifestations of autistic spectrum disorders can differ considerably across children and within an individual child over time. Even though there are strong and consistent commonalities, especially in social deficits, there is no single behavior that is always typical of autism or any of the autistic spectrum disorders and no behavior that would automatically exclude an individual child from diagnosis of autistic spectrum disorder. Because of the continuity across autistic spectrum disorders, this report addresses both autistic disorder specifically (referring to the more narrowly defined syndrome) and autistic spectrum disorder, (including autistic disorder, pervasive developmental disorder-not otherwise specified [PDD-NOS], Asperger's Disorder, and

Childhood Distintegrative Disorder). Because of its special characteristics, Rett's syndrome is not specifically considered in this report, though
children with Rett's syndrome may require similar services to children
with autism in some circumstances.

It is clear that autistic spectrum disorders have effects on development in ways that affect children's educational goals and the appropriate
strategies to reach them. It is also clear that deficits in language development, nonverbal communication, cognitive abilities, and other areas have
distinct effects on behavior and outcome in ways that have implications
for the educational goals of children with autistic spectrum disorders, as
well as other children. However, it is not yet clear the degree to which
specific educational goals and strategies are associated with particular
diagnoses within the autism spectrum, such as Asperger's Disorder,
Childhood Disintegrative Disorder, or PDD-NOS, once factors such as
language development and cognitive abilities are taken into account. Although experienced clinicians and educators can reliably identify the constellation of behaviors that define autistic spectrum disorders even in
very young children, distinctions among "classical" autism and atypical
autism, PDD-NOS, and Asperger's Disorder are not nearly as reliable.
Thus, though the identification of categories within the autism spectrum
is necessary for some research purposes and is an important area for
research, the educational and clinical benefit of making such distinctions
is not yet clear. Altogether, the most important considerations in devis-
ing educational programs for children with autistic spectrum disorders
have to do with recognition of the autism spectrum as a whole, with the
concomitant implications for social, communicative, and behavioral development and learning, and with the understanding of the strengths and
weaknesses of the individual child across areas of development. A child
who receives a diagnosis of any autistic spectrum disorder should be
eligible for special educational programming under the educational category "autism" regardless of the specific diagnostic category within the
autism spectrum.

The committee recommends that children with any autistic spectrum
disorder (autistic disorder, Asperger's disorder, atypical autism, PDD-
NOS, childhood distintegrative disorder), regardless of level of severity
or function, be eligible for special education services within the category
of autism.

With adequate time and training, the diagnosis of autism can be made
reliably in 2-year-olds by professionals experienced in the diagnostic assessment of young children with autistic spectrum disorders, and children are beginning to be referred even before age two years. Many families express concern about their children's behavior, usually to health

professionals, even before this time, and more children are being referred for specific educational interventions for autistic spectrum disorders. However, diagnostic and screening instruments effective with children under age 2 have not yet been identified. Although children with autistic spectrum disorders share some disabilities with children with other developmental disorders, they offer unique challenges to families, teachers, and others who work with them, particularly in nonverbal and verbal communication and behavioral problems.

The committee recommends that the National Institutes of Health and the Department of Education's Office of Special Education Programs, in cooperation with professional organizations and through support for research and training, promote early identification, appropriate screening, and multidisciplinary assessment for young children with autistic spectrum disorders, as is done for children with vision or hearing problems. In addition, because of variability in early diagnosis and test scores, young children with autistic spectrum disorders should always receive an appropriate follow-up diagnostic and educational assessment within 1-2 years after initial evaluation.

ROLE OF FAMILIES

What are the needs of families of children with autistic spectrum disorders and how can they effectively participate in education and intervention?

Having a child with an autistic spectrum disorder is a challenge for any family. Involvement of families in the education of young children with autistic spectrum disorders can occur at multiple levels. Parents can learn to successfully apply skills to changing their children's behavior. Parents' use of effective teaching methods, support from within the family and the community, and access to balanced information about autistic spectrum disorders and the range of appropriate services can contribute to successful child and family functioning. It is crucially important to make information available to parents to ensure their active role in advocacy for their children's education.

The committee recommends that families' participation should be supported in education through consistent presentation of information by local school systems, through ongoing consultation and individualized problem solving, and through the opportunity to learn techniques for teaching their children new skills and reducing behavioral problems. Although families should not be expected to provide the majority of educational programming for their child, the parents' concerns and perspectives should actively help shape educational planning.

GOALS FOR EDUCATIONAL SERVICES

What are appropriate goals for educational services provided to young children with autistic spectrum disorders, and how are the goals best measured as outcomes in scientific studies, so that effectiveness of various programs may be determined?

At the root of questions about the most appropriate educational interventions for autistic spectrum disorders are differences in assumptions about what is possible and what is important to give students with these disorders through education. The appropriate goals for educational services for children with autistic spectrum disorders are the same as those for other children: personal independence and social responsibility. These goals imply progress in social and cognitive abilities, verbal and nonverbal communication skills, and adaptive skills; reduction of behavioral difficulties; and generalization of abilities across multiple environments.

A large body of research has demonstrated substantial progress in response to specific intervention techniques in relatively short periods of time (e.g., several months) in many specific areas, including social skills, language acquisition, nonverbal communication, and reductions in challenging behaviors. Longitudinal studies over longer periods of time have documented changes in IQ scores and in core deficits (e.g., joint attention), in some cases related to treatment, that are predictive of longer-term outcomes. However, children's outcomes are variable, with some children making substantial progress and others showing very slow gains. Although there is evidence that interventions lead to improvements, there does not appear to be a clear, direct relationship between any particular intervention and children's progress. Thus, while substantial evidence exists that treatments can reach short-term goals in many areas, gaps remain in addressing larger questions of the relationships between particular techniques and specific changes.

The committee recommends that ongoing measurement of treatment objectives and progress be documented frequently across a range of skill areas in order to determine whether a child is benefiting from a particular intervention and that the intervention be adjusted accordingly. Appropriate objectives should be observable, measurable behaviors and skills. These objectives should be able to be accomplished within a year and be anticipated to affect a child's participation in education, the community, and family life.

CHARACTERISTICS OF EFFECTIVE INTERVENTIONS

What are the characteristics of effective interventions in educational programs for young children with autistic spectrum disorders?

There is general agreement across comprehensive intervention programs about a number of features of effective programs. However, practical and, sometimes, ethical considerations have made well-controlled studies with random assignment (e.g., studies of treatments that systematically vary only one dimension) almost impossible to conduct. In several cases, features have been identified through correlational or comparative analyses and then assumed to be factors of importance in intervention programs, without further direct evaluation.

The consensus across programs is generally strong concerning the need for: early entry into an intervention program; active engagement in intensive instructional programming for the equivalent of a full school day, including services that may be offered in different sites, for a minimum of 5 days a week with full-year programming; use of planned teaching opportunities, organized around relatively brief periods of time for the youngest children (e.g., 15- to 20-minute intervals); and sufficient amounts of adult attention in one-to-one or very small group instruction to meet individualized goals. Overall, effective programs are more similar than different in terms of levels of organization, staffing, ongoing monitoring, and the use of certain techniques, such as discrete trials, incidental learning, and structured teaching periods. However, there are real differences in philosophy and practice that provide a range of alternatives for parents and school systems.

The committee recommends that educational services begin as soon as a child is suspected of having an autistic spectrum disorder. Those services should include a minimum of 25 hours a week, 12 months a year, in which the child is engaged in systematically planned, and developmentally appropriate educational activity toward identified objectives. What constitutes these hours, however, will vary according to a child's chronological age, developmental level, specific strengths and weaknesses, and family needs. Each child must receive sufficient individualized attention on a daily basis so that adequate implementation of objectives can be carried out effectively. The priorities of focus include functional spontaneous communication, social instruction delivered throughout the day in various settings, cognitive development and play skills, and proactive approaches to behavior problems. To the extent that it leads to the acquisition of children's educational goals, young children with an autistic spectrum disorder should receive specialized instruction in a setting in which ongoing interactions occur with typically developing children.

PUBLIC POLICIES

What public policies at the local, state, and federal level will best ensure that individual children with autistic spectrum disorders and their families have access to appropriate education?

The Individuals with Disabilities Education Act contains the necessary provisions for ensuring rights to appropriate education for children with autistic spectrum disorders. Yet the implementation and specification of these services are uncertain. The treatment of autistic spectrum disorders often involves many disciplines and agencies, which confuses lines of financial and intellectual responsibility and complicates assessment and educational planning. However, a number of states have successfully addressed some of these challenges and can provide model approaches for doing so.

The committee recommends that coordination across services and funding at federal and state levels should be encouraged through several mechanisms: the creation of a federal joint agency task-force on autistic spectrum disorders; state monitoring of coordination among service delivery systems; minimum standards for personnel in educational and early intervention settings for children with autistic spectrum disorders; and the availability of ombudspersons within school systems who are knowledgeable about autistic spectrum disorders and are independent of the school program. Coordinated, systematic strategies should be developed to fund the interventions that are necessary in local communities for children under age 3 years and in local schools so that this cost is not borne totally by parents or local school systems.

PERSONNEL PREPARATION

How should personnel who work with children with autistic spectrum disorders be prepared and trained to guarantee a sufficient number of well-qualified specialists and regular teachers and administrators?

The nature of autistic spectrum disorders and other disabilities that frequently occur with them has significant implications for approaches to education and intervention at schools, in homes, and in communities. Approaches that emphasize the use of specific one-size-fits-all packages of materials and methods may understate the multiple immediate and long-term needs of individual students for behavioral support and for instruction across areas. Teachers and other professionals and paraprofessionals who often provide the bulk of service to very young children need familiarity with the course of autistic spectrum disorders and the range of possible outcomes and with the many methods that fit into best practices. Specific problems in generalization and maintenance of behaviors also affect the kind of training needed, as does the wide range of IQs and verbal skills associated with autistic spectrum disorders, from profound mental retardation and severe language impairments to high intelligence.

Multiple exposures, opportunities to practice, and active involvement are all important aspects of learning for teachers and other professionals. Technical assistance consisting of ongoing consultation, hands-on opportunities to practice skills, and building on the knowledge of teachers as they acquire experience with children with autistic spectrum disorders are crucial. Administrative attitudes and support are critical in improving schools, as are explicit strategies for keeping skilled personnel within the field. Providing knowledge about autistic spectrum disorders to special education and regular education administrators as well as to specialized providers with major roles in early intervention (e.g., speech language pathologists) are also critical in proactive change.

The committee recommends that the relevant state and federal agencies, including the Office of Special Education Programs, should accelerate their personnel preparation funds for 5 years for those who work with, and are responsible for, children with autistic spectrum disorders and their families. These efforts should be part of a larger effort to coordinate and collaborate with the already established infrastructure for special education, including regional resource centers and technical assistance programs.

RESEARCH

What research and further scientific investigations of effective education for young children with autistic spectrum disorders are needed?

A number of comprehensive programs report results on their effects, but interpretations of these results have been limited by several factors: practical and ethical difficulties in randomly assigning children and families to treatment groups; problems in selecting contrast groups; inadequate description of the children and families who participated in the studies; and lack of fidelity of treatment or generalization data. There is little evidence concerning the effectiveness of discipline-specific therapies, and there are no adequate comparisons of different comprehensive treatments. However, there is substantial research supporting the effectiveness of many specific therapeutic techniques and of comprehensive programs in contrast to less intense, nonspecific interventions. Research would yield more valuable information if there were minimal standards in design and description of intervention projects.

The committee recommends that all intervention studies provide adequate information on the children and families who participated and those who chose not to participate or withdrew from participation, describe the intervention in sufficient detail so that an external group could replicate it, measure fidelity of treatment, and include objective measures of short-term and long-term outcomes that are assessed by independent examiners. The federal agencies involved in autism initiatives—including the Office of Special Education Programs, the Office of Educational Research and Improvement, the National Institute of Child Health and Human Development, the National Institute of Mental Health, the National Institute on Deafness and Other Communication Disorders, and the National Institute of Neurological Disorders and Stroke—should establish a joint task force and call for proposals for longitudinal and other intervention studies that assess the relative effectiveness of treatments and that investigate the effectiveness of different educational and treatment models for children, with individual differences defined either according to broadly delineated categories (e.g., children with autistic spectrum disorders with average or greater intelligence) or according to continuous dimensions (e.g., chronological age), and that consider the effects of selection or assignment. Competitively funded initiatives in early intervention in autistic spectrum disorders should routinely provide sufficient funding for short- and long-term assessment of program efficacy. Complementary research on the development of more specific, precise measures of outcome, educational skills, and sequences should be supported to assess the effects of interactions between family variables, child factors, and responses to interventions, and to identify the active ingredients and mediating variables that influence effects of treatment.

In summary, education at home, at school, and in community settings remains the primary treatment for young children with autistic spectrum disorders. Many specific techniques and several comprehensive programs have clear effects on important aspects of these children's learning. Yet links between interventions and improvements are also dependent on characteristics of the children and aspects of the treatments that are not yet fully understood. The challenges are to ensure implementation of what is already known so that every child benefits from this knowledge and to work from existing research to identify more effective educational interventions for all children with autistic spectrum disorders.

1

Introduction

FEATURES OF AUTISM

Autism is a disorder that is present from birth or very early in development that affects essential human behaviors such as social interaction, the ability to communicate ideas and feelings, imagination, and the establishment of relationships with others. It generally has life-long effects on how children learn to be social beings, to take care of themselves, and to participate in the community. Autism is a developmental disorder of neurobiological origin that is defined on the basis of behavioral and developmental features. Although precise neurobiological mechanisms have not yet been established, it is clear that autism reflects the operation of factors in the developing brain. As yet, known direct links between pathophysiology and behavior in autism are still rare and have not yet had great influence on treatments or diagnoses (see Rumsey et al., 2000). Nevertheless, current biologic research, such as in genetics, may already have important implications for families of children with autistic spectrum disorders.

Autism is best characterized as a spectrum of disorders that vary in severity of symptoms, age of onset, and associations with other disorders (e.g., mental retardation, specific language delay, epilepsy). The manifestations of autism vary considerably across children and within an individual child over time. There is no single behavior that is always typical of autism and no behavior that would automatically exclude an individual child from a diagnosis of autism, even though there are strong and consistent commonalities, especially in social deficits.

A number of years ago, the concept of pervasive developmental disorder (PDD) was introduced to provide an umbrella term for autism and other disorders that include similar impairments in basic social skills but vary in severity or the presence of communication delay and repetitive behaviors. Because of the continuity across autistic disorders, this report addresses both the more narrowly defined disorder of *autism* and the broader range of *autistic spectrum disorder* including pervasive developmental disorder—not otherwise specified (PDD-NOS), Asperger's disorder, and childhood disintegrative disorder. Autistic spectrum disorders are unique in their pattern of deficits and areas of relative strengths. Because of the special characteristics of Rett's syndrome (i.e., its onset and pattern of deficits), it is not specifically considered in this report. Children with Rett's syndrome, however, may require similar services to children with autism in some circumstances.

THE CHALLENGE OF EDUCATING CHILDREN WITH AUTISM

Education, both directly of children, and of parents and teachers, is currently the primary form of treatment in autism. For the purposes of this report, *education* is defined as the fostering of acquisition of skills or knowledge—including not only academic learning, but also socialization, adaptive skills, language and communication, and reduction of behavior problems—to assist a child to develop independence and personal responsibility. Education includes services that foster acquisition of skills and knowledge, offered by public and private schools; infant, toddler, preschool and early education programs; and other public and private service providers. *Young children* are defined here as children 8 years or younger. Because children with autism are at high risk for other impairments, educational planning must address both the needs typically associated with autistic spectrum disorders and needs associated with accompanying disabilities.

Education of children with autism was accepted as a public responsibility as part of the Education Act of All Handicapped Children in 1975. Yet today, 25 years later, despite the federal mandate for appropriate education and intervention services, the goals, methods, and resources available vary considerably from state to state and from school system to school system. In the last few years, courts have become increasingly active forces in determining the methods applied and the resources allocated by school systems for the education of children with autistic spectrum disorders.

Although there is a very substantial body of research on the treatment and education of these children (Rumsey et al., 2000), this work has not often been clearly integrated into educational decision-making and policy at local or state levels. For example, many treatment approaches and demonstration projects have disseminated information, yet most have not yet provided appropriate, scientifically rigorous documentation of effectiveness and efficiency. While research in developmental psychology, child psychiatry, and pediatric neurology has become increasingly well integrated, there is a need for more effective communication between professionals in these disciplines and the educators and other professionals who carry out the bulk of treatment and intervention-oriented research.

THE COMMITTEE'S WORK

Charge

At the request of the U.S. Department of Education's Office of Special Education Programs, the National Research Council formed the Committee on Educational Interventions for Children with Autism and charged the committee to integrate the scientific, theoretical, and policy literature and create a framework for evaluating the scientific evidence concerning the effects and features of educational interventions for young children with autism. The primary focus of the charge was early intervention, preschool, and school programs designed for children with autism from birth to age 8. The charge included specific suggestions to examine several issues pertaining to education of children with autism: early intervention, diagnosis and classification, the rights of children with autism under IDEA, mainstreaming, and assistive technology.

To carry out its charge, the committee examined the scientific literature; commissioned papers addressing science and policy issues; examined solicited reports provided by leaders of model intervention programs; and conducted two workshops at which researchers, educators, administrators, practitioners, advocates of individuals with autism, and other interested participants presented to the committee information and perspectives on approaches to address the educational needs of children with autism. The committee also solicited and reviewed written statements, provided by individuals and organizations, summarizing their perceptions of the educational needs of young children with autism. The committee also addressed a specific charge to survey the developing field of assistive technology for young children with autism. Thus, the committee's activities served as a forum for interdisciplinary discussion of theory and scientific research concerning the evaluation of educational needs of, and methods used with, young children with autism.

The committee conceptualized its task as the integration and evaluation of existing information from multiple sources in order to provide recommendations regarding educational policies affecting families with young children with autism. These policies are carried out in school systems and state and federal programs. The committee applied strict standards to assess the quality of the large body of information that it assembled. The committee considered arguments of legal rights and documentation of public policy, and current practices in well-established programs, as well as empirical data concerning the effectiveness of various techniques. Within its evaluation of the current scientific literature, the committee's goal has been to interpret findings as broadly as possible in terms of their implications for early educational practices, while retaining scientific integrity and perspective in considering the strengths and limitations of various bodies of work.

Committee's Process for Evaluating Evidence

Science is a systematic way of gathering, analyzing, and assessing information. One of the strengths of the field of autism is the many disciplines and areas of scientific inquiry within which it has been addressed. The committee's approach was to gather information from as wide a range of sources as possible, to assess the strengths and limitations of different sources of information, and to assess the results with an eye toward convergence, particularly from independent sources, of descriptive data, inferential data, and theory.

For example, within the field of autism, there are many approaches to intervention that are widely disseminated but little researched. Some approaches have been greeted with great enthusiasm initially, but have relatively quickly faded out of general use, in part because of their failure to demonstrate worthwhile effects. Other approaches have withstood the test of time across sites and the children and families they serve, though they continue to be largely supported by clinical descriptions of effectiveness, rather than by formal evaluations. Yet wide use and respect cannot be interpreted as clear evidence of effectiveness; therefore, the committee elected to consider information about these approaches in light of more empirically oriented studies.

To achieve a systematic and rigorous assessment of research studies, the committee established guidelines for evaluating areas of strength, limitations, and the overall quality of the evidence; these guidelines are presented in Box 1-1. They are based on approaches used by scientific societies and in recent publications, including: the American Academy of Neurology (Filipek et al., 2000); the American Psychological Association (American Psychological Association, 2000; Barlow, 1996; Chambless and Hollon, 1998); the Society for Clinical Child Psychology (Lonigan et al., 1998); and the New York State Department of Health (1999). A number of comprehensive reviews concerning early intervention in autism also provided examples of ways to systematize information (Dawson and Osterling, 1997; Howlin, 1998; Rogers, 1998; Rumsey et al., 2000). These

---

BOX 1-1 Guidelines Used to Evaluate Studies

Every research report considered by the committee was assigned to one category (I-IV) for each area (A, B, and C).

A. Internal Validity: Control for nonspecific factors, such as maturation, expectancy, experimenter artifacts

 I. Prospective study comparing the intervention to an alternative intervention or placebo in which evaluators of outcome are blind to treatment status
 II. Multiple baseline, ABAB design, or reversal/withdrawal with measurement of outcome blind to treatment conditions or pre-post design with independent evaluation
 III. Pre-post or historical designs or multiple baseline, ABAB, reversal/ withdrawal not blind to treatment conditions
 IV. Other

B. External Validity/Selection Biases

 I. Random assignment of well-defined cohorts and adequate sample size for comparisons
 II. Nonrandom assignment, but well-defined cohorts with inclusion/ exclusion criteria and documentation of attrition/failures; additionally, adequate sample size for group designs or replication across three or more subjects in a single-subject design
 III. Well-defined population of three or more subjects in single-subject designs or sample of adequate size in group designs
 IV. Other

C. Generalization

 I. Documented changes in at least one natural setting outside of treatment setting (includes social validity measures)
 II. Generalization to one other setting or maintenance beyond experimental intervention in natural setting in which intervention took place
 III. Intervention occurred in natural setting or use of outcome measures with documented relationship to functional outcome
 IV. Not addressed or other

---

guidelines were used by both committee members and commissioned paper authors in their reviews of the literature. Figures 1-1, 1-2, and 1-3 present summarized data from journal articles cited within the areas addressed during the workshops (communication, social development, problem behaviors, intervention methods, and sensorimotor develop-

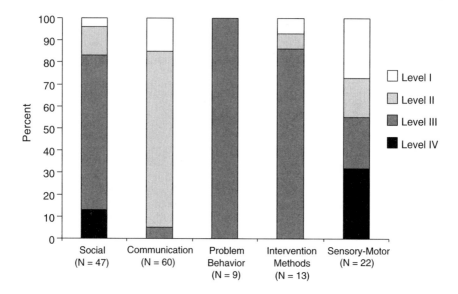

FIGURE 1-1   Internal validity.
NOTES: Level I represents the strongest methodological controls and IV the least strong (see Box 1-1); N is the number of studies.
SOURCES: For social studies, McConnell (1999); for communication studies, Goldstein (1999); for problem behavior studies, Horner (2000); for intervention studies, Kasari (2000); for sensory-motor studies (Baranek, 1999).

ment), in terms of percentages of studies falling into different levels of rigor with respect to internal validity, external validity, and generalization. This information is discussed in more detail in Chapter 15 and in the chapters describing those content areas. (For details on the coding of individual studies, see the appendices of the papers cited in the figures.)

One of the difficulties in interpreting research, particularly longitudinal studies, is that standards for scientific research within different theoretical perspectives have changed enormously in the last 20 years, and they continue to evolve. Twenty years ago, behavioral researchers were not as concerned with rigorously standardizing measures or diagnoses, maintaining independence between intervention and assessment, or analyzing the effects of development. Similarly, group designs based on a clinical trials model were not expected to monitor treatment fidelity, equate participants for intellectual or language level, address generalization or maintenance of effects, or justify measures by their clinical value. Therefore, particularly when depicting outcomes from longitudinal studies, reviewers of the literature often have to piece together information

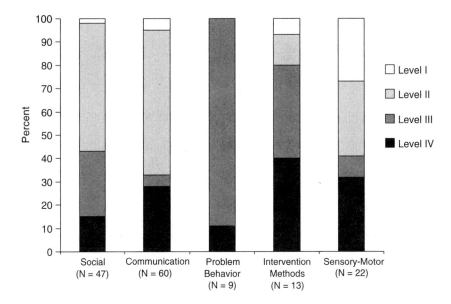

FIGURE 1-2   External validity.
NOTES: Level I represents the strongest methodological controls and IV the least strong (see Box 1-1); N is the number of studies.
SOURCES: For social studies, McConnell (1999); for communication studies, Goldstein (1999); for problem behavior studies, Horner (2000); for intervention studies, Kasari (2000); for sensory-motor studies (Baranek, 1999).

fragmented across studies. Today, that information would have been an expected component of a research design from the start.

Clinical research always involves compromises based on such factors as access to populations and acknowledgment of clinical needs; often, expense is also considered. Even today, there are very different standards across journals and across research communities as to what are considered unacceptable compromises and what is deemed a necessary part of dealing with complex questions. One of the goals that arose from this review was to identify ways of bridging gaps between perspectives in setting guidelines for research about autism. The committee recognized that a range of emphases and designs is important for different questions. Because of the varied nature of the research, the guidelines presented in Box 1-1 were used to characterize the research reviewed. In this way, the strengths and limitations of individual studies could be considered when deriving conclusions based on the consistencies and inconsistencies observed across investigations and theories.

Evidence concerning the effectiveness of instructional and comprehensive programs, strategies, and approaches to intervention for young

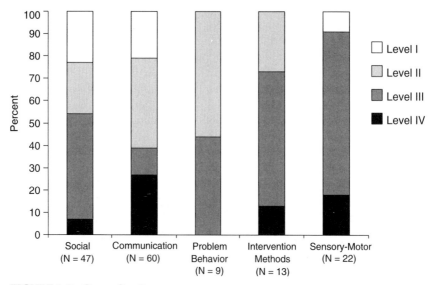

FIGURE 1-3 Generalization.
NOTES: Level I represents the strongest methodological controls and IV the least strong (see Box 1-1); N is the number of studies.
SOURCES: For social studies, McConnell (1999); for communication studies, Goldstein (1999); for problem behavior studies, Horner (2000); for intervention studies, Kasari (2000); for sensory-motor studies (Baranek, 1999).

children with autism was considered. The committee's strategy in assessing the effectiveness of components of intervention programs and approaches was to consider, along with the findings of individual research papers, the methodological challenges that many clinical studies face in attempting to control for nonspecific factors, selection biases, and the difficulty in measuring meaningful, generalizable outcomes. Some aspects of interventions, particularly short-term, problem-focused treatments, are much more easily researched than longer-term interventions aimed at more multifaceted concerns (American Psychological Association, 2000). The committee summarized results across areas of interest and approaches to intervention, taking these factors into account. The goal was to integrate this information into a coherent picture of appropriate educational interventions for young children within the autism spectrum, and to acknowledge points of convergence and points of controversy to be addressed in future educational research, practice, and policy. There are no strong studies that compare one comprehensive intervention program with another. Because programs are evolving (and better approaches may be developed in the future), the committee chose to focus on discussion of the effective components and features of each program—

identified on the basis of theory, empirical reports, and consensus across representative programs—rather than to attempt any ranking of specific programs.

There are several related areas the committee hoped to address but, because of limited resources and time, did not. Two issues we did not address are the feasibility and costs of various programs and treatments. Because feasibility and cost-effectiveness formulations involve not only short-term costs to school systems but also short- and long-term costs to health systems and society as a whole, and this information and its analysis are not readily available, it was felt that it would be inappropriate for us to analyze these questions in a superficial way. However, this information is much needed. We were also interested in more directly addressing ways of implementing the changes we recommended, but we were unable within the constraints of this project to acquire sufficient information and expertise about strategies for educational change. Because discrepancies in the kind of programs provided are so great across the United States (Hurth et al., 2000; Mandlawitz, 1999), questions concerning implementation are also crucial.

ORGANIZATION OF THE REPORT

The report is organized according to relationships among issues that, the committee believes, represent the key areas pertaining to educational interventions for young children with autism. Part I addresses the general issue of goals for children with autistic spectrum disorders and their families. Within Part I, Chapter 2 describes how autistic spectrum disorders are diagnosed and assessed and prevalence estimates, Chapter 3 considers the impact on and the role of families, and Chapter 4 discusses appropriate goals for educational services.

Part II presents the characteristics of effective interventions and educational programs. Chapters 5 through 10 discuss fundamental areas of development and behavior that must be addressed by such programs: communication; social, cognitive, sensory and motor development; and adaptive and problem behaviors. Chapter 11 analyzes the characteristics of representative instructional strategies, and Chapter 12 analyzes the features of ten model comprehensive programs and approaches to intervention.

Part III examines the policy and research contexts within which interventions are developed, implemented, and assessed: Chapter 13 presents an overview of public policy and legal issues pertaining to education for children with autism, Chapter 14 addresses the needs for personnel preparation to implement policies, and Chapter 15 identifies the experimental design and methodological issues that should be considered by future researchers in educational interventions for children with autism.

Our final chapter summarizes the committee's findings and presents conclusions about the state of the science in early intervention for children with autism and its recommendations for future intervention strategies, programs, policy, and research.

1
Goals for Children with Autism and Their Families

2

Diagnosis, Assessment, and Prevalence

MULTIDISCIPLINARY PERSPECTIVES

The diagnosis of autism and related autistic spectrum disorders in young children is often relatively straightforward but can, at times, be challenging (Lord, 1997). Complexities in diagnosis and evaluation relate to the range of syndrome expression in these conditions along various dimensions such as language abilities and associated mental handicap (Volkmar et al., 1997); differential diagnosis, particularly in children younger than 3 years (Lord and Schopler, 1989); concerns regarding labeling (Hobbs, 1975) and diagnostic terminology within school systems; and lack of expertise in assessment and diagnosis among some educational professionals (Siegel et al., 1988).

In general, the perspectives of various professionals are required as part of the diagnostic process. This may involve the efforts of special educators, general educators, psychologists, speech pathologists, occupational and physical therapists, and physicians. The need for a multidisciplinary or transdisciplinary perspective can create challenges for local educational authorities. Although the mandate of the local education authority (LEA) and state-funded developmental disability programs is to provide appropriate education, the services of non-LEA specialists are required for initial identification, diagnosis, and clinical services related to the presence of additional handicapping conditions. A LEA and state services may need to form relationships with individuals and centers with such expertise. Although various rating scales and checklists have been developed to aid in the process of assessment, these do not replace the need for a thoughtful and comprehensive diagnostic assessment (discussed below)—this is particularly true for preschool children, for whom issues of diagnosis can be complicated.

PREVALENCE OF AUTISM AND RELATED CONDITIONS

Epidemiological studies of autism have important implications for both research and clinical service, for example, through helping to plan for the need for special services and selecting samples for research studies. Fombonne (1999) has recently summarized the available research on this topic and systematically reviewed more than 20 studies conducted in ten countries. As he notes, although important details were sometimes lacking in the studies, the total population base included in the review was approximately 4 million children surveyed.

Studies have typically employed a two-stage design, with an initial screening followed by more systematic assessment. Complexities in interpreting the available data include variations in approaches to diagnosis of autism and differences in screening methods. In the studies surveyed, approximately 80 percent of individuals with autism also exhibited mental handicap (i.e., mental retardation). Studies have also consistently identified more boys with autism than girls (three to four boys for every girl). In addition, girls with autism are more likely than boys to also exhibit mental handicaps.

The epidemiology of autism has recently become quite controversial. In the United States, increased demand for autism-specific services (Fombonne, 1999) has drawn attention to growing numbers of children with the educational categorization of autism. Large, systematic epidemiologic studies have reported increases in prevalence from the estimated rate of 2-5 per 10,000 in the 1970s to 6-9 per 10,000. Fombonne (1999) considers a rate of 7.5 per 10,000 to best reflect the result of studies conducted since 1987. Those studies also report a rate of 12.5 per 10,000 individuals for atypical autism/pervasive developmental disorders, producing an overall rate of about 20 cases per 10,000. Rates for Asperger's disorder, excluding individuals who also met criteria for autism, were low, at 1-2 per 10,000. Because the studies did not consider individuals with less-pronounced variants of autistic spectrum disorder, it is possible that the figures for atypical autism/pervasive developmental disorder and Asperger's disorder are underestimates.

Two simple reasons explain the difference in current and historical rates: more complete diagnoses and a broader definition of autistic spectrum disorders (Fombonne, 1999). However, there are a number of recent studies, most with small samples, and several reports from school systems that found even higher rates of autism (Centers for Disease Control and Prevention, 2000; Arvidsson et al., 1997; Baird et al., 2000; Kadesjoe et al., 1999; California Department of Developmental Services, 2000). Studies reporting much higher rates were from relatively small samples or from state surveys, in which an educational label of autism was associated with provision of intensive services and thus highlight the need for further, well-designed investigations. For example, the Department of Education's Office of Special Education Programs (OSEP) could support a research study examining the prevalence and incidence of autism, using OSEP data gathered for school-age children since the autism category was recognized in 1991. This study could investigate in particular whether the dramatic increases in numbers of children served with autistic spectrum disorders are offset by commensurate decreases in categories in which children with autism might have previously been misclassified.

SCREENING INSTRUMENTS

The symptoms of autism are often measurable by 18 months of age (Charman et al., 1997; Cox et al., 1999; Lord, 1995; Stone et al., 1999; Baird et al., 2000). The main characteristics that differentiate autism from other developmental disorders in the 20-month to 36-month age range involve behavioral deficits in eye contact, orienting to one's name, joint attention behaviors (e.g., pointing, showing), pretend play, imitation, nonverbal communication, and language development (Charman et al., 1997; Cox et al., 1999; Lord, 1995; Stone et al., 1999). There are three published screening instruments in the field that focus on children with autism: the Checklist for Autism in Toddlers (Baird et al., 2000), the Autism Screening Questionnaire (Berument et al., 1999), and the Screening Test for Autism in Two Year Olds (Stone et al., 2000).

The Checklist for Autism in Toddlers (CHAT) (Baron-Cohen et al., 1992; 1996) is designed to screen for autism only at 18 months of age. From both the initial study of siblings of children with autistic disorder and from a larger epidemiological study involving a population study of 16,000 18-month-old infants (excluding children with suspected developmental delays), virtually all the children failing the five item criterion on the CHAT administered twice (one month apart, the second time by an experienced clinician and including other sources of information) were found to have autistic disorder when diagnosed at 20 and 42 months (Baron-Cohen et al., 1992; Baron-Cohen et al., 1996; Charman et al., 1998; Cox et al., 1999). However, the CHAT was less sensitive to milder symptoms of autism; children later diagnosed with other autistic spectrum disorders did not routinely fail the CHAT at 18 months. Follow-up of the cases at age 7 revealed that this instrument had a high specificity (98%) but relatively low sensitivity (38%) (Baird et al., 2000), suggesting that it is not appropriate for screening.

The Autism Screening Questionnaire is a new 40-item screening scale that has good discriminative validity between autistic spectrum and other disorders, including nonautistic mild or moderate mental retardation, in children age 4 years and older; it has not yet been tested with very young children. A score of 1 is given for an item if the abnormal behavior is present and a score of 0 if the behavior is absent. The cutoff for consideration of a diagnosis of autism is a score of 15 or higher. Further reliability studies and validation studies in younger children are ongoing. The recently published Screening Test for Autism in Two-Year Olds (Stone et al., 2000) is a direct observational scale; it showed good discrimination between children with autism and other developmental disorders in a small sample of two-year-old children.

Several additional instruments are currently undergoing validation studies. The Australian Scale for Asperger's Syndrome (Garnett and Attwood, 1998) is a parent or teacher rating scale for high-functioning older children on the autistic spectrum who remain undetected at school-age. The Pervasive Developmental Disorders Screening Test-II (PDDST-II) is a clinically derived parent questionnaire designed in three formats: Stage 1 is aimed for use in the primary care setting, Stage 2 for use in developmental clinics, and Stage 3 for use in autism clinics. The Modified Checklist for Autism in Toddlers (M-CHAT) expands the CHAT into a 23-item checklist that a parent can fill out in about 10 minutes (Robins et al., 1999). Other approaches are being developed.

ASSESSMENT

Developmentally based assessments of cognitive, communicative, and other skills provide information important for both diagnosis and program planning for children with autism and related conditions. Careful documentation of a child's unique strengths and weaknesses can have a major impact on the design of effective intervention programs and is particularly critical, because unusual developmental profiles are common. Given the multiple areas of difficulty, the efforts of professionals from various disciplines are often needed (e.g., psychology, speech and language pathology, neurology, pediatrics, psychiatry, audiology, physical and occupational therapy). The level of expertise required for effective diagnosis and assessment may require the services of individuals, or a team of individuals, other than those usually available in a school setting (Sparrow, 1997). In some cases, psychological and communication assessments can be performed by existing school staff, depending on their training and competence in working with children with autism. However, other services (e.g., genetic testing, drug therapy, management of seizures) are necessarily managed in the health care sector. Some children may fall between systems and therefore not be served well.

Several principles underlie assessment of a young child with autism or autistic spectrum disorder (Sparrow, 1997):

1. Multiple areas of functioning must typically be assessed, including current intellectual and communicative skills, behavioral presentation, and functional adjustment.

2. A developmental perspective is critical. Given the strong association of mental retardation with autism, it is important to view results within the context of overall developmental level.

3. Variability of skills is typical, so it is important to identify a child's specific profile of strengths and weaknesses rather than simply present an overall global score. Similarly, it is important not to generalize from an isolated or "splinter" skill to an overall impression of general level of ability, since such skills may grossly misrepresent a child's more typical abilities.

4. Variability of behavior across settings is typical. Behavior of a child will vary depending on such aspects of the setting as novelty, degree of structure provided, and complexity of the environment; in this regard, observation of facilitating and detrimental environments is helpful.

5. Functional adjustment must be assessed. Results of specific assessments obtained in more highly structured situations must be viewed in the broader context of a child's daily and more typical levels of functioning and response to real-life demands. The child's adaptive behavior (i.e., capacities to translate skills into real world settings) is particularly important.

6. Social dysfunction is perhaps the most central defining feature of autism and related conditions, so it is critical that the effect of a child's social disability on behavior be considered.

7. Behavioral difficulties also must be considered, since they affect both the child's daily functioning and considerations for intervention.

Various diagnostic instruments can be used to help structure and quantify clinical observations. Information can be obtained through observation (e.g., the Autism Diagnostic Observation Scale, Lord et al., 2000) as well as the use of various diagnostic interviews and checklists, e.g., Autism Diagnostic Interview-Revised (Lord et al. 1994); Childhood Autism Rating Scale (Schopler et al., 1980); Autism Behavior Checklist (Krug et al., 1980); Aberrant Behavior Checklist (Aman and Singh, 1986). An adequate assessment will involve both direct observation and interviews of parents and teachers.

The range of syndrome expression in autism and autistic spectrum disorders is quite broad and spans the entire range of IQ (Volkmar et al., 1997). A diagnosis of autism or autistic spectrum disorder can be made in a child with severe or profound mental retardation as well as in a child who is intellectually gifted. In addition, individuals vary along a number of other dimensions, such as levels of communicative ability and degree of behavioral difficulties. As a result, in working with a child with an autistic spectrum disorder, considerable expertise is required of the various evaluators. Evaluators must consider the quality of the information obtained (both in terms of reliability and validity), the involvement of parents and teachers, the need for interdisciplinary collaboration, and the implications of results for intervention. Coordination of services, including specialized assessment services, is important, as is facilitating discussion between members of assessment and treatment teams and parents (Filipek et al., 1999; Volkmar et al., 1999).

A range of components should be part of a comprehensive educational evaluation of young children with autism. These include obtaining a thorough developmental and health history, a psychological assessment, a communicative assessment, medical evaluation, and, in some cases, additional consultation regarding aspects of motor, neuropsychological, or other areas of functioning (Filipek et al., 1999; Volkmar et al., 1999). This information is important both to diagnosis and differential diagnosis and to the development of the individual educational intervention plan.

The psychological assessment should establish the overall level of cognitive functioning as well as delineate a child's profiles of strengths and weaknesses (Sparrow, 1997). This profile should include consideration of a child's ability to remember, solve problems, and develop concepts. Other areas of focus in the psychological assessment include adaptive functioning, motor and visual-motor skills, play, and social cognition. Children will usually need to be observed on several occasions during more and less structured periods.

The choice of assessment instruments is a complex one and depends on the child's level of verbal abilities, the ability to respond to complex instructions and social expectations, the ability to work rapidly, and the ability to cope with transitions in test activities (the latter often being a source of great difficulty in autism). Children with autism often do best when assessed with tests that require less social engagement and less verbal mediation. In addition to the formal quantitative information provided, a comprehensive psychological assessment will also provide a considerable amount of important qualitative information (Sparrow, 1997). It is important that the psychologist be aware of the uses and limitations of standardized assessment procedures and the difficulties that children with autism often have in complying with verbal instructions and social reinforcement. Operant techniques may be helpful in facilitating assessment.

Difficulties in communication are a central feature of autism, and they interact in complex ways with social deficits and restricted patterns of behavior and interests in a given individual. Accurate assessment and understanding of levels of communicative functioning is critical for effective program planning and intervention. Communication skills should be viewed in a broad context of an individual's development (Lord and Paul, 1997; Prizant and Schuler, 1997); standardized tests constitute only one part of the assessment of communication abilities in younger children with autism and related conditions. The selection of appropriate assessment instruments, combined with a general understanding of autism, can provide important information for purposes of both diagnostic assessment and intervention.

In addition to assessing expressive language, it is very important to obtain an accurate assessment of language comprehension. The presence of oral-motor speech difficulties should be noted. In children with autism, the range of communicative intents may be restricted in multiple respects (Wetherby et al., 1989). Delayed and immediate echolalia are both common in autism (Fay, 1973; Prizant and Duchan, 1981) and may have important functions. In addition, various studies have documented unusual aspects even of very early communication development in autism (Ricks and Wing, 1975; Tager-Flusberg et al., 1990).

In assessing language and communication skills, parent interviews and checklists may be used, and specific assessment instruments for children with autistic spectrum disorders have been developed (Sparrow, 1997). For children under age 3, scores on standardized tests may be particularly affected by difficulties in assessment and by the need to rely on parent reports and checklists. For preverbal children, the speech-communication assessment should include observation of a child's level of awareness of communication "bids" from others, the child's sense of intentionality, the means used for attempting communication, and the quality and function of such means, sociability, and play behaviors. The evaluator should be particularly alert to the child's capacity for symbolic behavior, because this has important implications for an intervention program (Sparrow, 1997). There are also several standardized instruments that provide useful information on the communication and language development of preverbal children with autism; these include the Communication and Symbolic Behavior Scales, the Mullen Scales of Early Learning, and the MacArthur Communicative Development Inventory. For children with some verbal ability, social and play behaviors are still important in terms of clinical observation but various standardized instruments are available as well, particularly when a child exhibits multiword utterances. Areas to be assessed include receptive and expressive vocabulary, expressive language and comprehension, syntax, semantic relations, morphology, pragmatics, articulation, and prosody.

The choice of specific instruments for language-communication assessment will depend on the developmental levels and chronological age of the child. For higher functioning individuals with autism or Asperger's syndrome, additional observations may address aspects of topic management and conversational ability, ability to deal with nonliteral language, and language flexibility. As with other aspects of assessment, an evaluator should be flexible and knowledgeable about the particular concerns related to assessment of children with autism.

Motor abilities in autism may, at least in the first years of life, represent an area of relative strength for a child, but as time goes on, the development of motor skills in both the gross and fine motor areas may be compromised, and motor problems are frequently seen in young children with autism. Evaluations by occupational and physical therapists are often needed to document areas of need and in the development of an intervention program (Jones and Prior, 1985; Hughes, 1996). Standardized tests of fine and gross motor development and a qualitative assessment of other aspects of sensory and motor development, performed by a professional in motor development, may be helpful in educational planning.

MEDICAL CONSIDERATIONS

For very young children, there may be concerns about the child recognized or first expressed in the context of well-child care. The education of physicians, nurses, and others regarding warning signs for autistic spectrum disorders is very important. After initial referral for assessment and diagnosis, consultations with other medical professionals may be indicated, depending on the context (Filipek et al., 1999; Volkmar et al., 1999), for example, to developmental and behavioral pediatricians, child psychiatrists, geneticists, and pediatric neurologists. When this consultation is relevant to the educational program, reimbursement may appropriately be made by the local education authority.

The available literature has clearly documented that children with autism are at risk for developing seizure disorders throughout the developmental period (Deykin and MacMahon, 1979; Volkmar and Nelson, 1990). Seizure disorders in autism are of various types and may sometimes present in unusual ways. Although not routinely indicated, an electroencephalogram (EEG) and/or neurological consultation is indicated if any symptoms suggestive of seizures, such as staring spells, are present. The presence of a family history of developmental delay or unusual aspects of a child's history or examination may suggest the need for genetic or other consultation. In some cases, autism may be associated with other conditions—notably fragile X syndrome and tuberous sclerosis (Dykens and Volkmar, 1997).

A child's hearing should be tested, but behavioral problems may sometimes complicate assessment. Definitive documentation of adequate hearing levels should then be obtained through other methods, such as auditory brainstem evoked responses (BSERs) (Klin, 1993). Certain features, such as the abrupt behavioral and developmental deterioration of a child who was previously developing normally, may suggest the importance of extensive medical investigations (Volkmar et al., 1999).

In some cases, the use of psychotropic medications may be indicated for young children (see Chapter 10). Although not curative, such medications may help to reduce levels of associated maladaptive behaviors and help children profit from educational programming. The use of such agents requires careful consideration of potential benefits and risks and the active involvement of parents and school staff (see Volkmar et al., 1999 for a review).

IMPLICATIONS FOR INTERVENTION

Many aspects of the procedures, curricula, and educational programs relevant to other children are readily applicable to children with autism and related conditions. As for all children, an intervention program must be individualized and tailored to the specific needs, strengths, and weaknesses of the individual child. In addition, children with autistic spectrum disorders often present special challenges for intervention.

From the time of Kanner's (1943) definition of autism, social deficits have been consistently identified as an, if not the, essential feature of the condition. Social interaction requires careful attention to multiple, shifting strands of information; an ability to perceive the thoughts, feelings, and intentions of others; and coping with novel situations on a regular basis. In children with autistic spectrum disorders, social difficulties persist over time, although the nature of the social difficulties may change with age and intervention (Siegel et al., 1990). These social difficulties, as reflected in relationships with teachers and particularly in relationships with peers, are different from those seen in all other developmental disorders and present special difficulties for programming. For a child with an autistic spectrum disorder to be able to be included in mainstream settings, the child must be able to manage social experiences. This requires careful consideration on the part of school staff. While children with an autistic spectrum disorder can be served within many school environments, even for more cognitively able individuals this can be a challenge. The characteristic difficulties in social interaction require special teacher training and support beyond knowledge concerning general developmental delays or other learning disabilities.

3

Family Roles

Parents of young children with autism play multiple roles in their children's life. Often they are the first people to recognize a developmental problem, and they must pursue their concern until they receive a satisfactory diagnosis and find or develop appropriate services for their child. Once they find a suitable treatment program, parents typically are active partners in their child's education to ensure that skills learned in the educational program transfer to the home setting and to teach their child the many behaviors that are best mastered in the home and community. As members of the individualized education plan (IEP) team, parents may also be active advocates for the child, ensuring that the educational process goes forward appropriately.

These many demands on parents occur in the context of family life, including the needs of other children, the parents as individuals and as a couple, and family needs as a whole. In addition, the parents of young children may confront sadness, anger, disappointment, or other complex emotions that can accompany the initial discovery that one's child has a significant developmental problem and the ongoing need to make sacrifices to serve the needs of their child. Most families cope effectively with these demands, but some may encounter very substantial stress as they raise their child with autism.

In the 1950s and 1960s the psychodynamic explanation of autism held sway in the United States (Bettelheim, 1974). That perspective, now clearly counter to a large body of research on the biological roots of autism, had important implications for treatment. Fortunately, today we hold a far different view of the role of parents in the treatment of autism. We recognize that parents are partners in an educational process that requires close collaboration between home and school (e.g., Lovaas et al., 1973; Schopler and Reichler, 1971).

In order to provide an appropriate education for their child, parents of children with autism need specialized knowledge and skills and scientifically based information about autism and its treatment. Prime among these are the mastery of specific teaching strategies that enable them to help their child acquire new behaviors and an understanding of the nature of autism and how it influences their child's learning patterns and behavior. Parents also need to be familiar with special education law and regulations, needed and available services, and how to negotiate on behalf of their child. In addition, some parents need help coping with the emotional stress that can follow from having a child with a significant developmental disorder.

SPECIAL DEMANDS ON PARENTS

The identification of parents as serving a key role in effective treatment of their child has great benefit for the child. However, it is a role that is not without costs, and the implications for family life are considerable. Many parents of children with autism face multiple, demanding roles. These include serving as teacher and advocate as well as loving parent and family member. Gallagher (1992) points out the complex demands this places on parents and the need to support family decision-making and control, while providing sufficient professional expertise to enable their choices.

Research suggests that while many families cope well with these demands, the education of a child with autism can be a source of considerable stress for some families (see, e.g. Bristol et al., 1988; Harris, 1994). In general, mothers report more stress than do fathers, often describing issues related to time demands and personal sacrifice (e.g., Konstantareas et al., 1992). Among specific concerns expressed by mothers are worry about their child's welfare in the years ahead, the child's ability to function independently, and the community's acceptance of their child (Koegel et al., 1992). Mothers of children with autism also report more stress in their lives than do mothers of children with other disabilities (e.g., Rodrigue et al., 1990).

Fathers of children with autism or Down syndrome report more disruption of planning family events and a greater demand on family finances than do fathers whose children are developing typically. These three groups of men do not differ, however, on measures of perceived competence as a parent, marital satisfaction, or social support (Rodrigue et al., 1992).

In a study of families who had a son with autism under the age of 6 years referred to the TEACCH (Treatment and Education of Autistic and Related Communication Handicapped Children) program, Bristol and colleagues (1988) found that, while fathers assumed some role in children's care, mothers carried a much greater burden. This difference was not due solely to employment outside of the home. Bristol et al. (1988) reported that mothers who worked in jobs outside of the home still had greater child care burdens than their employed husbands. These authors also found that expressive support from one's partner was an important predictor of the quality of parenting in the home.

The time spent working with a child with autism is sometimes stressful and demanding, but it also has the potential to reduce family distress and enhance the quality of life for the entire family including the child with autism (Gallagher, 1991). Techniques such as individualized problem solving, in-home observations and training, and didactic sessions have been employed with families. Mothers who learned skills based on the TEACCH model of education for their child showed a decrease in depressive symptoms over time in comparison with a group of mothers not given this training (Bristol et al., 1993). Koegel et al. (1996) reported that teaching parents how to use pivotal response training as part of their applied behavioral analysis instruction resulted in happier parent-child interactions, more interest by the parents in the interaction, less stress, and a more positive communication style. The use of effective teaching methods for a child with autism can have a measurable positive impact on family stress. As a child's behavior improves and his or her skills become more adaptive, families have a wider range of leisure options and more time for one another (Koegel et al., 1984). To realize these gains, parents must continue to learn specialized skills enabling them to meet their child's needs.

Professionals serving children with autism and their families in the United States must also be sensitive to the cultural context of service delivery (see e.g., Harris, 1996; Heller et al., 1994). That cultural sensitivity means providing services in a language in which parents are fluent (e.g., Preito-Bayard and Baker, 1986; Shapiro and Simonsen, 1994; Smith and Ryan, 1987). It also means understanding that a child's autism means different things in different cultures. For example, for some ethnic, racial, or socioeconomic groups, having a child with a disability may carry implications of shame about one's failure as a parent and blame for parents and the extended family (e.g., Hanson et al., 1990). Some cultures may encourage an expectation of a magical cure for a developmental disorder (Stahl, 1991). If teachers and other professionals fail to understand what a child's autism means to a family, it will be difficult to establish the kind of collaborative relationship between school and home that is so essential to the education of young children with autism. While existing research suggests that it is important to be sensitive to the family's cultural context to provide effective services, there is a need for more research to understand how socioeconomic status, race, and ethnicity impact services.

TEACHING PARENTS NEEDED SKILLS

Because of the nature of autism, young children with this disorder need a consistent and supportive environment to make optimal educational progress. For example, children with autistic spectrum disorders often have problems transferring a skill learned in one setting to another place or time. This process of generalization of learning needs to be anticipated and supported, and so parents of children with autism need to be more closely involved in the educational process than do parents of children with many other childhood disorders. For example, early research on the benefits of applied behavior analysis by Lovaas and his colleagues (1973) showed that children with autism who returned to a home prepared to support their learning maintained their treatment gains better than children who went to institutional settings that failed to carry over the treatment methods.

Parents can learn techniques for teaching adaptive skills and managing the behavior of their child with autism. Such intervention maximizes the child's learning, improves the quality of family life, and may enable parents to sustain their efforts with their child over time. Based on that early observation of the importance of the home environment (Lovaas et al., 1973), several behavior analysts developed techniques for teaching parents the fundamentals of applied behavior analysis and making them integral members of the educational team. That research documented that parents could master the basics of applied behavior analysis, and many became highly skilled teachers (e.g., Baker, 1989; Harris, 1983; Koegel et al., 1984) who expressed satisfaction with the benefits of training (e.g., Harris, 1983; Kolko, 1984). The proponents of applied behavior analysis have carried the role of parental involvement farther than other approaches, and in some cases it is parents who provide much of the oversight and management of home-based applied behavioral analysis programs, with an outside consultant offering periodic input (e.g., Lovaas, 1987).

Although the bulk of the research on teaching parents to work with their child in the home has been done using applied behavior analysis, Ozonoff and Cathcart (1998) reported a study in which parents of young children with autism were taught to use TEACCH instructional methods in the home. In contrast with a no-treatment control group, the children whose parents used TEACCH methods in the home showed greater improvement in a variety of skills over a 4-month interval. The children in

Support by training parents and supporting their effort @ home (handwritten margin note)

both groups were simultaneously receiving day treatment from a variety of settings.

It is important for schools to recognize that parents need both initial training and on-going support for trouble shooting if they are to sustain their effort at home teaching (Harris, 1986). Simply providing a basic training course in teaching principles is often insufficient to ensure the long-term ability of many parents to solve new problems as they arise.

Our review of the practices of the most frequently cited programs serving children with autism indicates that all of them offer training to parents in the teaching methods used in the programs (see Chapters 11 and 12). Their expectations for parental involvement range from the assumption of a major role on a daily basis to a less central but still essential role of ensuring that a child can transfer material from school to the home and community.

Most studies of parents as teachers were carried out when parents had an auxiliary role in supporting school based programs. There has been a dearth of studies of the role of parents in intensive home-based programs. Today, though it is not uncommon for parents to have the central function in a home-based program, little is known about the most effective ways to help them master the skills they need for this role or about the stress this role may bring to family life.

THE ADVOCACY ROLE

In addition to supporting their child's learning at home and in the community, parents are also cast in the role of advocate for their child with autism. Like parents of children with other disorders, these parents need to serve as effective members of the IEP or Individual Family Service Plan (IFSP) team, helping to ensure that appropriate educational programs are in place for their children (Seligman and Darling, 1997). Being an effective advocate means that parents understand the legal rights of their child according to federal and state law and regulations. For most families the advocacy role focuses mainly on the needs of their own child. There will also be some parents for whom that role may encompass work at the local, state, or national level to advocate on behalf of policies to meet the needs of all children and adults with autism.

Although some parents may resort to legal processes to obtain the educational resources needed by their children, for most families the advocacy process is a much less adversarial one. Being a good advocate means being an effective collaborator with the professionals who serve a child. That entails learning the vocabulary of education, understanding the characteristics of autism and how those are related to a child's educational needs, and appreciating how treatment techniques work. It also means learning how to disagree and resolve differences within a constructive atmosphere and being supportive of the professionals who work with one's child. Public school systems and advocacy groups can offer training in advocacy skills, including conflict resolution, to parents and school staff to ensure both groups are well informed and to ease tensions that may arise in their interactions.

Although the role of parent as advocate is compatible with current legislation and consistent with many people's views of the roles of parents, there are no high quality studies examining either the most effective ways to train parents to be advocates on behalf of their children with autism or how effective parents are in this role. Such research might be useful in determining how best to prepare parents for advocacy and when additional support from others may be most useful in the advocacy process.

SUPPORT FOR FAMILIES

In addition to research specifically on the support needs of families of children with autism, there is a valuable tradition of research in the early intervention literature that explores the needs of families who have children with a range of developmental and physical disorders. Both of these bodies of research have the potential to make important contributions to serving and empowering children with autism and their families (Dunst, 1999; Seligman and Darling, 1997), including parents, siblings, and members of their extended families.

The perception of the meaning of having a child with autism and of family support can have an impact on how well parents cope. For example, Bristol (1987) found that mothers who feel they are to blame for their child's disability, or who experience the child's needs as a catastrophe for the family, tend to make less effective adaptations than those who hold a less critical view. Fong (1991) demonstrated that negative expectations can color one's perception of relatively neutral events concerning the performance of a child with autism. In a study of mothers of children with autism whose husbands assumed a share of child care, Milgram and Atzil (1988) reported enhanced life satisfaction from that sharing of responsibilities. Similarly, perceived social support and psychological hardiness both tended to buffer mothers of children with autism from the effects of stress (Gill and Harris, 1991).

Family needs change over time (Bristol and Schopler, 1983; DeMyer and Goldberg, 1983). For example, parents of young children typically are focused on understanding their child's diagnosis, dealing with the emotions that are stirred by encountering a serious problem in their child's development, finding services, and working intensively on behalf of their child. For parents of an older child, there is the growing realization that their child's needs will continue over a lifetime— that they must consider their child's educational program in relation to a chronic disability and that they will need to continue to cope in the face of unrelenting demands. Family needs also vary according to the severity of the child's autistic disorder. Younger children and those who are less impaired have a better prognosis than those who are older or have very severe autism. It is useful for school personnel to be sensitive to these different problems and to work closely with parents to provide family support and help them find the resources that fit the developmental needs of the child and the family as whole.

Many families benefit from the availability of both formal and informal social support to handle the complex demands in their lives. A family-centered approach emphasizes addressing the needs and desires of individual families, rather than providing predefined services. This philosophy is often practiced in other fields within early childhood special education and has been applied implicitly to the field of autism. Potential sources of support include classroom teachers; IEP team members, including representatives of the local education authority (LEA); pediatricians; and other professionals who evaluate and treat children with autism. Although the schools can provide a number of formal supports to families of children with autism, there are also other valuable resources for parents to access. These informal supports are found through networking with other parents, membership in support groups, and from families and neighbors. Bristol (1987) found a positive relationship between adequacy of social support, the use of active coping behaviors, and family adaptation for parents of children enrolled in the TEACCH program. Lack of financial resources and of access to information can be significant barriers to families seeking needed support.

In serving families, it is important not to overlook siblings, whose lives can be disrupted in serious ways, but who also benefit from their brothers or sisters with autism as well (Konidaris, 1997). These children experience more feelings of sadness and worry than do other children, although for the most part these differences do not reflect significant psychopathology (e.g., Rodrigue et al., 1993). Brothers and sisters need support as they come to understand autism and its impact on a sibling who has the disorder, and these needs change over time (Glasberg, 2000). Often siblings will be enrolled at the same school: a sensitive teacher can help a child respond to questions about a sibling's autism and be alert to the impact on the child's peer relationships of having a brother or sister who is markedly different from most other children in the school. The LEA can offer sibling support groups to provide factual information, teach play skills, and provide peer group support for brothers or sisters (Celiberti and Harris, 1993; Lobato, 1990; McHale and Harris, 1992).

Research on the genetics of autism suggests that siblings are at a greater risk for having autism or a related milder disorder than are other children (e.g., Bailey et al., 1998; Szatmari et al., 1998). For this reason, discussion of recurrence risks should be part of the overall delivery of services, and it is important that younger siblings of children with an autistic spectrum disorder be followed carefully after birth to determine whether they show any indication of a disorder on the autism spectrum. Careful tracking would enable very early intervention with this group of youngsters.

FROM RESEARCH TO PRACTICE

In general, the research literature examining methods of training parents to be teachers has been of somewhat higher quality and more systematic than the work looking at the effects of raising a child with autism on the quality of family life. One of the common flaws in a number of studies of family stress been the failure to include two comparison groups, one of typically developing children of the same developmental level and the other of children with a different disability. Both of these groups are important because raising any child affects parents, and most serious chronic disabilities of childhood are likely to influence the quality of family life. There is also a striking lack of research examining how socioeconomic status, ethnicity, and race influence vulnerability to stress, which forms of support and training that are most helpful when and for whom, and the most effective modalities for service delivery (Wolery and Garfinkle, 2000). Although researchers tend to look where the light is brightest (i.e., the easiest places to find research participants), if we are to fully appreciate the impact of autism on families and become expert at teaching parents how to work with and advocate on behalf of their child, we need to understand different kinds of families. Research has also not paid sufficient attention to interactions between child factors—such as degree of cognitive and language impairment, severity of autistic involvement, and specific diagnosis on the spectrum of autism—and family characteristics that may influence both the ease with which parents can teach their child and the stress level in the household.

4

Goals for Educational Services

There are many different goals for the education of young children with autism. At the root of these goals are societal desires and expectations about the benefits of education for all children, and assumptions about what is important and what is possible to teach children with autistic spectrum disorders. Education provides opportunities for the acquisition of knowledge and skills that support personal independence and social responsibility (Kavale and Forness, 1999). For a child with an autistic spectrum disorder or any other developmental disability, how independence and responsible participation in a social world are manifested may include different behaviors from those targeted as goals for more typical children, though often the similarities are greater than the differences. For the purposes of this report, in which we are concerned with children 8 years of age and younger, independence and responsibility are defined in terms of age-appropriate participation in mainstream school and social activities to the extent possible, rather than as vocational or residential independence.

There are many behaviors that ordinary children learn without special teaching, but that children with autism may need to be taught (Klin, 1992). A preschool child with autism may have learned to count backwards on his own, but may not learn to call to his mother when he sees her at the end of the day without special teaching. A high school student with autism may have excellent computer skills but not be able to decide when she needs to wash her hair. Educational goals for these students, as part of addressing independence and social responsibility, often need to address language, social, and adaptive goals that are not part of standard curricula. Now, both academic and nonacademic goals must be considered against the background of "standards-based educational reform," according to which educators will increasingly become accountable for establishing and meeting goals that are challenging for students at all levels of disability, while allowing for individual adaptations for students with significant cognitive disabilities (see National Research Council [1997] for a detailed discussion of the implications of standards-based reform for students with disabilities).

As discussed in Chapter 12, most comprehensive early education programs for children with autistic spectrum disorders share similar goals across a range of areas (Handleman and Harris, 2000), though the emphasis placed by the different programs may differ. These areas include social and cognitive development, verbal and nonverbal communication, adaptive skills, increased competence in motor activities, and amelioration of behavior difficulties. Specific issues within each of these areas are discussed in individual chapters of this report. However, often areas overlap. For example, communication involves both social and representational skills. In addition, priorities change as children develop. Yet challenges in making skills truly useful in terms of spontaneity and generalizability across environments are significant across all areas.

INTERVENTIONS AS PATHS TO GOALS

Research on the effectiveness of early interventions and on the course of development of autistic spectrum disorders provides some insight into the complexities of the selection of appropriate goals for education in autism. For example, is a therapy addressing a reasonable goal if its primary aim is getting a child with autism to play or to match similar objects? Is it worth the expense and time of the child and parent to drive across town once a week or the disruption for a child to be taken out of class by a therapist in order to meet either of these goals? Generally, outcome research has studied the effectiveness of programs, not the appropriateness of various goals. Thus, the question of whether play or matching can be taught is different from—and can be more easily answered than—the question of whether or when they should or should not be taught.

Educational objectives must be based on specific behaviors targeted for planned interventions. However, one of the questions that arises repeatedly, both on a theoretical and on a clinical basis, is how specific a link has to be between a long-term goal and a behavior targeted for intervention. Some targeted behaviors, such as toilet training or acquisition of functional spoken language, provide immediately discernible practical benefits for a child and his or her family. However, in many other cases, both in regular education and specialized early intervention, the links between the objectives used to structure what a child is taught and the child's eventual independent, socially responsible functioning are much less obvious. This is particularly the case for preschool children, for whom play and manipulation of toys (e.g., matching, stacking of blocks) are primary methods of learning and relating to other children.

Often, behaviors targeted in education or therapy are not of immediate practical value but are addressed because of presumed links to overall educational goals. The structuring of activities in which a child can succeed and feel successful is an inherent part of special education. Sometimes the behavior is one component of a series of actions that comprise an important achievement. Breaking down a series of actions into components can facilitate learning. Thus, a preschool child may be taught to hold a piece of paper down with one hand while scribbling with another. This action is a first step in a series of tasks designed to help the child draw and eventually write.

Other behaviors, or often classes of behaviors, have been described as "pivotal behaviors" in the sense that their acquisition allows a child to learn many other skills more efficiently (Koegel et al., 1999; Pierce and Schreibman, 1997). Schreibman and the Koegels and their colleagues have proposed a specific treatment program for children with autism: pivotal response treatment. It includes teaching children to respond to natural reinforcers and multiple cues, as well as other "pivotal" responses. These are key skills that allow better access to social information. The idea of "pivotal skills" to be targeted as goals may also hold for a broad range of behaviors such as imitation (Stone, 1997; Rogers and Pennington, 1991), maintaining proximity to peers (Hanson and Odom, 1999), and learning to delay gratification (understanding "first do this, then you get to do that"). Longitudinal research has found that early joint attention, symbolic play, and receptive language are predictors of long-term outcome (Sigman et al., 1999). Although the research to date has been primarily correlational, one inference has been that if interventions succeed in modifying these key behaviors, more general improvements will occur as well (Kasari, 2000); another explanation is that these behaviors are early indicators of the child's potential developmental trajectory.

Sometimes goals for treatment and education involve attempting to limit and treat the effects of one aspect of autism, with the assumption that such a treatment will allow a child to function more competently in a range of activities. For example, a number of different treatment programs emphasize treating the sensory abnormalities of autism, with the implication that this will facilitate a child's acquisition of communication or social skills (e.g., auditory integration; sensory integration). For many interventions, supporting these links through research has been difficult. There is little evidence to support identifiable links between general treatment of a class of behaviors (e.g., sensory dysfunction) and improvements in another class of behaviors (e.g., social skills), especially when the treatment is carried out in a different context from that in which the targeted behaviors are expected to appear.

However, there are somewhat different examples in other areas of education and medicine in which interventions have broad effects on behavior. One example is the effect of vigorous exercise on general behavior in autism (Kern et al., 1984). In addition, both desensitization (Cook et al., 1993) and targeted exercise in sports medicine and physical therapy often involve working from interventions carried out in one context to generalization to more natural circumstances. Yet, in both of these cases, the shift from therapeutic to real-life contexts is planned explicitly to occur within a relatively brief period of time. At this time, there is no scientific evidence of this kind of link between specifically-targeted therapies and general improvements in autism outside the targeted areas. Until information about such links becomes available, this lack of findings is relevant to goals, because it suggests that educational objectives should be tied to specific, real-life contexts and behaviors with immediate meaning to the child.

OUTCOMES

Because the range of outcomes for children with autistic spectrum disorders is so broad, the possibility of relatively normal functioning in later childhood and adulthood offers hope to many parents of young children. Although recent literature has conveyed more modest claims, the possibility of permanent "recovery" from autism, in the sense of eventual attainment of language, social and cognitive skills at, or close to, age level, has been raised in association with a number of educational and treatment programs (see Prizant and Rubin, 1999). Natural history studies have revealed that there are a small number of children who have symptoms of autism in early preschool years who do not have these symptoms in any obvious form in later years (Szatmari et al., 1989). Whether these improvements reflect developmental trajectories of very mildly affected children or changes in these trajectories (or more rapid movement along a trajectory) in response to treatment (Lovaas, 1987) is not known.

However, as with other developmental disabilities, the core deficits in autism have generally been found to persist in some degree in most persons with autistic spectrum diagnoses. There is no research base explaining how "recovery" might come about or which behaviors might mediate general change in diagnosis or cognitive level. Although there is evidence that interventions lead to improvements and that some children shift specific diagnoses within the spectrum and change in severity of cognitive delay in the preschool years, there is not a simple, direct relationship between any particular current intervention and "recovery" from autism. Because there is always room for hope, recovery will often be a goal for many children, but in terms of planning services and programs, educational objectives must describe specific behaviors to be acquired or changed.

Research on outcomes (or whether goals of independence and responsibility have been attained) can be characterized by whether the goal of an intervention is broadly defined (e.g., "best outcome") or more narrowly defined (e.g., increasing vocabulary, increasing peer-directed social behavior); whether the study design involves reporting results in terms of individual or group changes; and whether goals are short term (i.e., to be achieved in a few weeks or months) or long term (i.e., often several years). A large body of single-subject research has demonstrated that many children make substantial progress in response to specific intervention techniques in relatively short time periods (e.g., several months). These gains occur in many specific areas, including social skills, language acquisition, nonverbal communication, and reductions of challenging behaviors. Often the most rapid gains involve increasing the frequency of a behavior already in the child's repertoire, but not used as broadly as possible (e.g., increasing use of words) (Watson et al., 1989). In single-subject reports, changes in some form are almost always documented within weeks, if not days, after the intervention has begun. Studies over longer periods of time have documented that joint attention, early language skills, and imitation are core deficits that are the hallmarks of the disorder, and are predictive of longer-term outcome in language, adaptive behaviors, and academic skills. However, a causal relationship between improvements in these behaviors as a result of treatment and outcomes in other areas has not yet been demonstrated.

Many treatment studies report postintervention placement as an outcome measure. Successful participation in regular education classrooms is an important goal for some children with autism. However, its usefulness as an outcome measure is limited because placement may be related to many variables other than the characteristics of a child (such as prevailing trends in inclusion, availability of other services, and parents' preferences).

The most commonly reported outcome measure in group treatment studies of children with autism have been IQ scores. Studies have reported substantial changes in IQ scores in a surprisingly large number of children in intervention studies and in longitudinal studies in which children received nonspecific interventions. These are discussed in more detail in Chapter 7. However, even in the treatment studies that have shown the largest gains, children's outcomes have been variable, with some children making great progress and others showing very small gains. Overall, while much evidence exists that education and treatment can help children attain short-term goals in targeted areas, gaps remain in addressing larger questions of the relationship between particular techniques and both general and specific changes.

II
Characteristics of
Effective Interventions

5

Development of Communication

Major advances have been made over the past two decades in delineating and understanding the communication and language difficulties of children with autism. The characterization of communication deficits in the diagnostic criteria for autism has changed dramatically. Until about 1980, peculiar speech patterns were emphasized, such as echolalia, pronoun reversal, and unusual intonation (Baltaxe and Simmons, 1975; American Psychiatric Association, 1980). Now, verbal and nonverbal communication are considered a core deficit in the diagnostic criteria for autistic spectrum disorders (American Psychiatric Association, 1987; 1994). This change highlights the recognition that children with autistic spectrum disorders not only have difficulty in the acquisition of speech and language, but also have difficulty understanding and using nonverbal behavior in communicative interactions.

The level of communicative competence attained by individuals with autism has been found to be an important predictor of outcome (Garfin and Lord, 1986; McEachin et al., 1993). The presence of fluent speech (using multiword combinations spontaneously, communicatively, and regularly) before the age of 5 continues to be a good prognostic indicator of IQ scores, language measures, adaptive skills, and academic achievement in adolescence (Venter et al., 1992). Moreover, the severity of the communicative impairment may be one of the greatest sources of stress for families (Bristol, 1984).

There is much heterogeneity in the speech, language and communication characteristics of children with autistic spectrum disorders. Language impairments in autistic spectrum disorders range from failure to develop any functional speech to the development of functional but idio-syncratic use of spontaneous speech and language (Lord and Paul, 1997). One-third (Bryson, 1996) to one-half (Lord and Paul, 1997) of children and adults with autism do not use speech functionally. For both verbal and nonverbal individuals, impairments in social or pragmatic aspects of language and related cognitive skills are the most salient (Wetherby et al., 1997).

CORE COMMUNICATION DEFICITS

Research over the past decade has identified core communication deficits in children with autism that fall into two major areas: joint attention and symbol use (Dawson et al., 1990; Kasari et al., 1990; McArthur and Adamson, 1996; Mundy et al., 1990; Sigman and Ruskin, 1999; Stone et al., 1997; Wetherby et al., 1998). Joint attention reflects difficulty coordinating attention between people and objects and is evident by deficits in orienting and attending to a social partner; shifting gaze between people and objects; sharing affect or emotional states with another person; following the gaze and point of another person; and being able to draw another persons' attention to objects or events for the purpose of sharing experiences.

Symbol use reflects difficulty learning conventional or shared meanings for symbols and is evident in deficits in using conventional gestures; learning conventional meanings for words; and using objects functionally and in symbolic play.

Joint attention has been found to be a significant predictor of language outcome. Mundy et al. (1990) found that measures of gestural joint attention (e.g., showing or pointing to direct attention) at initial testing were a significant predictor of language development 1 year later for preschool children with autism. The failure to acquire gestural joint attention appears to be a critical milestone that impairs language development and an important target for early communication intervention.

Similarly, children with autism do not compensate for their lack of verbal skills with gestures; they show limited gestural use, both in quantity and quality. They predominantly use primitive motoric gestures to communicate (i.e., leading, pulling or manipulating another's hand). They lack the use of many conventional gestures, such as showing, waving, pointing, nodding the head and symbolic gestures depicting actions (Loveland and Landry, 1986; McHale et al., 1980; Stone and Caro-Martinez, 1990; Stone et al., 1997; Wetherby et al., 1998; Wetherby et al., 1989).

Moreover, in this population, there is much variability in the capacity to use vocal communication which likely contributes to the wide range of verbal skills. Some children with autism have been found to use a limited

limited

consonant inventory and less complex syllabic structure, while others show adequate complexity of vocalizations (McHale et al., 1980; Stone and Caro-Martinez, 1990; Wetherby and Prutting, 1984; Wetherby et al., 1989).   *normal but must move beyond*

The vast majority of those who do learn to talk go through a period of using echolalia, the imitation of speech of others, which may be immediate or delayed (Prizant et al., 1997). An echolalic utterance is usually equivalent to a single word or a label for a situation or event. Many children learn to use echolalia purposefully in communicative interactions, and eventually are able to break down the echolalic chunks into smaller meaningful units as part of the process of transitioning to a rule-governed, generative language system (Prizant and Rydell, 1993).

Children with autism who progress beyond echolalia usually acquire more advanced aspects of grammar: that is, they develop grammatical skills in the same general progression as typically developing children, but show persisting problems in following the social rules and shifting between speaker and listener roles of conversation (Baltaxe, 1977; Tager-Flusberg, 1996), which are the pragmatic aspects of language.

In lieu of conventional means of communicating, children with autism may develop idiosyncratic, unconventional, or inappropriate behaviors to communicate, such as self-injurious behavior, aggression, or tantrums. Despite the fact that at least 50 percent of individuals with autism display some functional speech and language skills (Lord and Paul, 1997), challenging behaviors such as aggression, tantrums, and self-injury are often used to procure attention, to escape from a task or situation, to protest against changes of schedule and routine, or to regulate interactions in a predictable manner. Carr and Durand (1985) reported that aggression, tantrums, and self-injury were more likely to occur in situations with a high level of task difficulty and a low level of adult attention. Challenging behaviors need to be considered relative to the child's repertoire of verbal and nonverbal communicative behaviors and may reflect limitations in symbolic capacity.

Further evidence of a deficit in the symbolic capacity in autism is the limited ability to develop symbolic or pretend play. Although play is a social-cognitive skill, a lack of varied, spontaneous make-believe play is one of the four possible features of the impairment in communication in the most recent Diagnostic and Statistical Manual (DSM-IV) (American Psychiatric Association, 1994). Children with autism show significant deficits in symbolic or make-believe play (i.e., using pretend actions with objects) and limited abilities in functional play (i.e., using objects functionally) (Dawson and Adams, 1984; Sigman and Ungerer, 1984; Wetherby and Prutting, 1984; Wing et al., 1977). Functional and symbolic play skills have been found to be significantly correlated with receptive and expressive language (Mundy et al., 1987; Sigman and Ruskin, 1999). In contrast to deficits in functional object use and symbolic play, children with autism often perform at similar or sometimes even higher levels on nonsocial constructive play (e.g., using objects in combination to create a product, such as putting puzzles together) in comparison with typically developing children or children with language delays at the same language stage (Wetherby and Prutting, 1984; Wetherby et al., 1998).

Exploring developmental patterns in communication and symbolic abilities has contributed to better understanding of the nature of these problems in autism. Stone et al. (1997) and Wetherby et al. (1998) compared the developmental profiles of 2- to 4-year-old children with autistic spectrum disorders with that of children with delayed language who were at the same language stage. Using similar strategies for gathering communication samples, both researchers reported a similar profile in children with autistic spectrum disorders, characterized by a distinct constellation of strengths and weaknesses in parameters of communication. Specifically, the children with autistic spectrum disorders showed comparable use of communication to request and protest, but significantly less use of gaze shifts, shared positive affect, conventional gestures, and communication for joint attention. They performed at comparable levels of constructive play but significantly poorer levels of language comprehension and symbolic play. Correlational findings from the Wetherby et al. (1998) study showed that children who displayed a greater capacity to coordinate attention and affect were more likely to communicate for more social reasons, to use a larger repertoire of conventional gestures, to have a higher rate of communicating, and to employ better repair strategies. These findings underscore the importance of addressing these core deficits in interventions for children with autism and have important implications for predicting which children will benefit from specific intervention approaches.

PLANNING FOR INTERVENTION

Goals

Researchers and educators have debated the question of how communication goals and objectives for children with autism and related disabilities should be derived. The perspective espoused by traditional behavioral programs has been to establish goals and objectives a priori (e.g., Lovaas, 1981). Behavioral discrete-trial programs begin with general compliance training to get a child to sit in a chair, look at the clinician, and imitate nonverbal behavior in response to verbal commands. Speech is taught as a verbal behavior, and objectives are targeted beginning with verbal imitation, following one-step commands, receptive discrimination of body parts, objects, person names and pictures, and expressive labeling in response to questions. Later, language objectives include prepositions, pronouns, same/different and yes/no.

More contemporary behavioral approaches have developed goals for outcomes from a functional assessment. Goals and objectives are individualized, based on a child's repertoire of communicative behaviors, teaching functional equivalents of challenging behavior, and addressing the child's individual needs. The functional emphasis focuses on goals that affect a child's access to choices of activities in which to participate, opportunities for social interaction, and community settings (Brown et al., 1979; Horner et al., 1990). Contemporary behavioral programs emphasize teaching communication skills so that greater access is provided to a variety of people, places and events, thereby enhancing the quality of life of children with autistic spectrum disorders.

The perspective espoused by developmentally oriented approaches has been to focus on the communicative meaning of behaviors and to target goals and objectives that enhance a child's communicative competence by moving the child along a developmental progression (Lahey, 1988). Contemporary developmentalists begin with social-communicative goals, including gaze to regulate interaction, sharing positive affect, communicative functions, and gestural communication. Language goals are mapped onto social communication skills and are guided by a developmental framework (Greenspan and Wieder, 1997; Klinger and Dawson, 1992; Wetherby et al., 1997).

Goal-setting in an augmentative and alternative communication (AAC) intervention is usually guided by a developmental perspective. Beukelman and Mirenda (1998) state that the goals of an AAC intervention are to assist individuals with severe communication disorders to become communicatively competent in the present, with the view toward meeting their future communication needs.

Assessment Strategies

One major purpose of communication assessment is to document change as an outcome measure of treatment. However, most formal or standardized language assessment measures focus primarily on language form and rely on elicited responses. Because language impairments associated with autism are most apparent in social-communicative or pragmatic aspects of language, formal assessment instruments can provide information about only a limited number of aspects of communication for children with autism (Schuler et al., 1997; Prizant et al., 1997; Wetherby and Prizant, 1999). Formal language measures are especially imprecise in measuring nonverbal aspects of communication and therefore are not sufficient, particularly for low-functioning children with autism. In many situations, the tests used for pre- and post-assessment are different, due to the child's increasing age, making interpretation of results difficult.

Another major purpose of assessment is to provide information for educational planning that can be directly translated into goals, strategies, and outcome measures for communication enhancement. Several communication abilities have been identified as important to assess for children with autism: use of eye gaze and facial expression for social referencing and to regulate interaction, range of communicative functions expressed, rate of communicating, use of gestures and vocal/verbalizations, use of repair strategies, understanding of conventional meanings, and ability to engage in conversation (Schuler et al., 1997; Wetherby et al., 2000). Wetherby et al. (1997) point out that communicative abilities of children with autism should be documented in natural communicative exchanges, with a child's symbolic abilities serving as a developmental frame of reference. To supplement formal measures, the systematic use of informal procedures to assess language and communication is needed. In order to gather an accurate picture of the communication and symbolic abilities of children with autism, a combination of assessment strategies has been recommended, including interviewing significant others (i.e., parents, teachers) and observing in everyday situations to find out how a child communicates in the home, classroom, and other daily settings (Wetherby and Prizant, 1999).

INTERVENTION APPROACHES

Although there is consensus on the importance of enhancing communication abilities for children with autism, intervention approaches vary greatly, and some even appear to be diametrically opposed. The methodological rigor in communication intervention studies in terms of internal and external validity and measures of generalization has been stronger than in many other areas of autism intervention studies. Nevertheless, there have been relatively few prospective studies with controls for maturation, expectancy, or experimenter artifacts. The strongest studies in terms of internal validity have been multiple baseline, ABAB, or similar designs that have included controls for blindness of evaluations (see Figure 1-1 in Chapter 1). There have been almost no studies with random assignment, although about 70 percent of the studies included well-defined cohorts of adequate sample size or replication across three or more subjects in single subject designs (see Figure 1-2 in Chapter 1). A substantial proportion of communication interventions have also included some assessment of generalization, though most often not in a natural setting (see Figure 1-3 in Chapter 1).

In order to examine the critical elements of treatment programs that affect the speech, language, and communication skills of children with autism, it is useful to characterize the active ingredients of treatment approaches along a continuum—from traditional, discrete trial approaches to more contemporary behavioral approaches that used naturalistic language teaching techniques to developmentally oriented approaches (Prizant and Wetherby, 1998; Anderson and Romanczyk, 1999; Prizant and Rubin, 1999). The earliest research efforts at teaching speech and language to children with autism used massed discrete trial methods to teach verbal behavior by building labeling vocabulary and simple sentences. Lovaas (1977, 1981) provided the most detailed account of the procedures for language training using discrete trial approaches. Outcomes of discrete trial approaches have included improvements in IQ scores, which are correlated with language skills, and improvements in communication domains of broader measures, such as the Vineland Adaptive Behavior Scales (McEachin et al., 1993). A limitation of a discrete trial approach in language acquisition is the lack of spontaneity and generalization. Lovaas (1977) stated that "the training regime . . . its use of 'unnatural' reinforcers, and the like may have been responsible for producing the very situation-specific, restricted verbal output which we observed in many of our children" (p. 170). In a review of research on discrete trial approaches, Koegel (1995) noted that "not only did language fail to be exhibited or generalize to other environments, but most behaviors taught in this highly controlled environment also failed to generalize" (p. 23).

There is now a large body of empirical support for more contemporary behavioral approaches using naturalistic teaching methods that demonstrate efficacy for teaching not only speech and language, but also communication. These approaches include natural language paradigms (Koegel et al., 1987), incidental teaching (Hart, 1985; McGee et al., 1985; McGee et al., 1999), time delay and milieu intervention (Charlop et al., 1985; Charlop and Trasowech, 1991; Hwang and Hughes, 2000; Kaiser, 1993; Kaiser et al., 1992), and pivotal response training (Koegel, 1995; Koegel et al., 1998). These approaches use systematic teaching trials that have several common active ingredients: they are initiated by the child and focus on the child's interest; they are interspersed and embedded in the natural environment; and they use natural reinforcers that follow what the child is trying to communicate. Only a few studies, all using single-subject designs, have compared traditional discrete trial with naturalistic behavioral approaches. These studies have reported that naturalistic approaches are more effective at leading to generalization of language gains to natural contexts (Koegel et al., 1998; Koegel et al., 1992; McGee et al., 1985).

There are numerous intervention approaches based on a developmental framework (e.g., Greenspan and Wieder, 1997; Klinger and Dawson, 1992; Wetherby et al., 1997; Prizant and Wetherby, 1998). While there are many different developmental programs, a common feature of developmental approaches is that they are child-directed. The environment is arranged to provide opportunities for communication, the child initiates the interaction or teaching episode, and the teacher or communicative partner follows the child's lead by being responsive to the child's communicative intentions, and imitating or expanding the child's behavior. Although the empirical support for developmental approaches is more limited than for behavioral approaches, there are several treatment studies that provide empirical support for language outcomes using specific strategies built on a developmental approach (Lewy and Dawson, 1992; Hwang and Hughes, 2000; Rogers and DiLalla, 1991; Rogers and Lewis, 1989) and many case studies, with Greenspan and Wieder (1997) providing the largest case review. Developmental approaches share many common active ingredients with contemporary naturalistic behavioral approaches and are compatible along most dimensions (Prizant and Wetherby, 1998).

Teaching Speech and Language

Gains in speech and language outcomes for children with autism have been documented using a variety of behavioral and developmental intervention approaches. Numerous studies have investigated methods of teaching specific receptive and expressive language skills. Most of these studies have used a behavioral method ranging from discrete-trial to naturalistic. Studies have reported good outcomes for teaching specific language content, such as single-word vocabulary, describing objects and pictures, responding to questions, and increasing speech intelligibility (see Goldstein, 1999; Koegel et al., 1998; Krantz et al., 1981). Very positive outcomes have been reported by McGee and colleagues (1999) through natural reinforcers of vocalization, speech shaping, and incidental teaching. They reported that 36 percent of the toddlers studied used verbalizations at program entry with a mean age of 2 years 5 months, and 82 percent were verbalizing meaningful words 1 year later. Most other programs have reported about children entering at 3 years of age or later, and therefore, the impressive treatment outcomes may be related to the young age at entry of treatment.

Teaching Communication

Research that has documented changes in the communication skills of children with autism falls into three major categories organized by the goal of the intervention: functional communication training to replace challenging behavior, increases in initiation of verbal and nonverbal communication, and increases in the core communication skills.

There is strong empirical support for the efficacy of functional communication training to replace challenging behaviors. This approach includes a functional assessment of the particular behavior to determine its function for a child (e.g., desire for tangible or sensory item, attention, or to escape a situation or demand) and teaching communication skills that serve efficiently and effectively as functional equivalents to challenging behaviors, a method that has been documented to be the most effective for reductions in challenging behavior (Horner et al., 1990; see Horner et al., 2000).

There are also some findings concerning the use of augmentative communication strategies. In a literature review of the functional communication training research, Miranda (1997) found that eight children with autism, three of whom were under 8 years of age, were able to learn to use AAC to replace challenging behaviors. Their problem behaviors included self-injurious behavior, aggression, crying, screaming, property destruction, tantrums, non-compliance, and self-stimulatory behaviors. These children were systematically taught to use AAC with messages congruent with the function of the behavior, such as "Look at me" (attention); "I want__" (tangible); "I need a break" (escape). This intervention resulted in a substantial and immediate decrease in the problem behaviors, and the use of AAC for functional communication training was maintained over the course of a year. Naturalistic behavioral language interventions leading to improved communicative skills have also been associated with reductions in disruptive behavior (Koegel et al., 1992) and provide further evidence supporting the relationship between communication and behavior.

There is a growing body of research on increasing the initiation of communication in children with autism. Initiation of communication has been described as a pivotal behavior: the more often a child initiates communication, the more often it will trigger responses from others, which will in turn enhance and expedite the improvement of other communication and language skills (Koegel, 1995). Two important findings have been reported (Koegel et al., 1999). First, children who show more spontaneous, self-initiated communication at the beginning of treatment show more favorable language treatment outcomes. Second, in specific contexts, self-initiated communication can be taught to children with autism who show few or no spontaneous communication and has been associated with favorable treatment outcomes (Charlop et al., 1985; Charlop and Trasowech, 1991). In general, truly spontaneous, self-initiated, socially directed behaviors are much more difficult, though not impossible, to teach (Watson et al., 1989) and require a combination of developmental and naturalistic teaching methods.

In spite of the large number of studies documenting the core communication deficits associated with autism (i.e., joint attention and symbolic capacity), there are only a few studies that have documented intervention effects on these core deficits. Most of the comprehensive programs do not present data targeting improvement in these skills. Exceptions are Rogers and Lewis (1989), who documented improvements in symbolic play as a result of a structured, developmentally based program (see Chapter 6) and studies of symbolic play with pivotal response treatment (Thorp and Schreibman, 1995; Stahmer, 1995). Other studies that have documented improvement in these core communication deficits have demonstrated increases in gaze to regulate interaction, shared positive affect, use of conventional gestures, and joint attention. Lewy and Dawson (1992) compared the effects of a child-directed teaching strategy in which the adult imitated the child's behavior with an adult-directed teaching strategy in a group comparison study. They demonstrated that the imitation strategy improved gaze, turn-taking, object use, and joint attention in children with autism, while the adult-directed strategy did not lead to these communicative gains. More recent studies have used single-subject designs to provide systematic evidence of naturalistic language teaching techniques that improve joint attention skills in children with autism (Buffington et al., 1998; Hwang and Hughes, 2000; Pierce and Schriebman, 1995). Thus, naturalistic behavioral or structured developmental methods appear to be an effective way to address the core communication deficits of autism.

Augmentative and Alternative Communication and Assistive Technology

For children with autism who do not acquire functional speech or have difficulty processing and comprehending spoken language, augmentative and alternative communication (AAC) and assistive technology (AT) can be useful components of an educational program. There is disagreement about whether to use AAC to train speech and language for young children with autistic spectrum disorders. There is relatively little rigorous, systematic research to elucidate characteristics of children and the components of AAC and AT that may interact to produce effective (or ineffective) intervention. However, available findings are summarized in some detail here to provide a snapshot of this emerging area.

AAC is defined as "an area of clinical practice that attempts to compensate (either temporarily or permanently) for the impairment and disability patterns of individuals with severe expressive communication disorders" (American Speech-Language-Hearing Association, 1989:7). AAC may involve supporting existing speech or developing independent use of a nonspeech symbol system, such as sign language, visual symbols (pictures and words) displayed on communication boards, and voice output devices with synthesized and digitized speech. AT is any commercial, hand-made, or customized device or service used to support or enhance the functional capabilities of individuals with disabilities. AT includes computer-assisted instruction, mobility devices, high and low technology adaptations and AAC.

The methods and tools of AAC interventions, properly applied, are tailored to unique strengths and needs of individuals with autism. AAC includes the use of visual language systems, such as visual icons or words representing specific communicative units, which capitalize on strong visual processing of many children with autism. The visual information is static and predictable, and enables the child with autism to rely on recognition rather than recall memory to receive language input or generate language output. AAC provides a motorically simple way to communicate needs and may preempt the development of challenging coping behaviors. Low-technology AAC tools, such as picture systems, can be relatively simple and inexpensive to implement (Hodgdon, 1995).

Relationship Between AAC and Speech and Language Development

There is empirical evidence that systematic teaching of speech using a naturalistic behavioral approach is efficacious for many children, particularly if treatment can begin by 2-1/2 years of age (McGee et al., 1999). However, a substantial proportion of children fail to make meaningful gains in speech (with failure rates ranging from about 20 percent to 40 percent). For those children who do acquire speech, the degree of spontaneity and complexity of language is not clearly reported in most research studies. There is now a body of research on AAC and speech and language acquisition in children with autism that is important to consider, particularly for those children who make slow or minimal gains in other programs.

There is a dearth of research on communication assessment strategies for children with autism using AAC. In one case study of a child with autism (Light et al., 1998), the AAC assessment principles of the Communication Participation Model (Beukelman and Mirenda, 1998) were implemented to gather information needed for an effective AAC intervention. Based on this participation plan and a variety of informal assessments, a comprehensive multimodal AAC intervention (speech, pointing, a communication book, a laptop computer with synthesized speech) was implemented, increasing the level of communication and participation for this child.

There have been numerous experimental studies of the efficacy of teaching sign language to children with autism (see Goldstein, 1999). These studies have demonstrated that total communication (speech plus sign language) training resulted in faster and more complete receptive and expressive vocabulary acquisition than speech training alone for many children with autism (Barrera et al., 1980; Barrera and Sulzer-Azaroff, 1983; Carr and Dores, 1981; Layton, 1988; McIlvane et al., 1984; Yoder and Layton, 1988). These findings support several conclusions for children with autism:

1. There is no evidence that use of AAC systems as collaterals to language instruction results in delays in the acquisition of speech, though specifying the advantages and disadvantages of using AAC in support of the development of speech in different populations remains a research question.
2. There is evidence that sign language enhances the use of speech for some children.
3. There is no evidence to suggest that sign language interferes with the development of speech.
4. Children with good verbal imitation skills demonstrate better speech production than those with poor verbal imitation skills, with or without AAC.
5. Children with poor verbal imitation skills are the best candidates for an AAC system, such as sign language, because they are likely to make poor progress in speech acquisition without AAC.

Seal and Bonvillian (1997) analyzed sign language formation of 14 low-functioning students with autism and found that the size of the sign vocabulary and accuracy of sign formation were highly correlated with measures of fine motor abilities and tests of apraxia, which is a neurogenic impairment of planning, executing, and sequencing movements (LaPointe and Katz, 1998). These findings support the role of a motor impairment in the level of competence attained in sign language and speech acquisition for children with autism, in addition to their social-communication and symbolic deficits. It is important to note that simple signs may be a support for children learning to speak or an additional mode of communication for children who have no speech or limited speech. However, it is very rare to find a child with autism who learns to sign fluently (in sentences) and flexibly. Signing is not generally an entry point into a complex, flexible system.

The use of visual symbol systems has received attention recently because of the limited outcomes with signs and the visual strengths of many children with autistic spectrum disorders. Picture Communication Symbols are the most commonly used line drawings for augmenting spoken language. Other visual symbols used include tangible or real objects, photographs, rebus symbols and several commercial symbol-to-word computer programs, such as Picture-It, Pix-writer, and Writing with Symbols 2000. Visual symbols have been used successfully with children with autism to increase compliance, enhance communicative initiations and responses, and decrease verbal prompt dependence (Mirenda and Santogrossi, 1985; Steibel, 1999). Communication partner training in using visual symbols, with parents, practitioners, and peers has been shown to be relatively simple (Steibel, 1999; Garrison-Harrell et al., 1997; Cafiero, 1995).

Because children with autism have difficulty pointing and show strengths in using contact gestures, they may benefit from using a giving gesture to make choices or indicate a selection from an array of objects or visual symbols. The most widely used exchange system, the Picture Exchange Communication System (PECS) (Frost and Bondy, 1994), is a structured program that teaches the exchange of symbols for communication. PECS is a systematic behavioral program that teaches a child to initiate communicative requests by approaching the communication partner and exchanging the symbol for the desired object. It includes protocols for expanding communication from single to multiple words and for increasing communicative function from requesting to labeling and commenting. Bondy and Frost (1994) reported a case review of a group of preschoolers with autism who were taught PECS. Of 19 children who used PECS for less than 1 year, only two (10%) acquired independent speech, while five used speech with PECS, and 12 children used PECS as their sole communication. Of 66 children using PECS for 2 years, 39 (59%) developed independent speech, 20 developed speech as they used PECS, and 7 used only PECS. Thus, for most preschoolers introduced to PECS, it took more than 1 year after initiating PECS to observe independent speech, and many continued to have very limited spontaneous use of language. Speech tended to develop once the children were able to use 30-100 symbols to communicate (Frost and Bondy, 1994). Furthermore, the overall communication development of the children was strongly related to their overall level of intellectual functioning.

The only other published study using PECS was reported by Schwartz et al., (1998) on 11 children with autistic spectrum disorders who attended an integrated preschool. These children required an average of 11 months to exchange "I want + symbol" sentence strips with adults and 14 months with peers. In this study, 6 (55%) of the 11 children developed functional and complex speech, and the 5 who did not were able to use PECS effectively to communicate. The authors state, however, that their study did not control for maturation or the effects of other components of their school program. Whether comparable outcomes with PECS and the concomitant development of speech would be expected without the specific intervention or with older children is not known.

There is even less research on the effectiveness of other AAC systems used by children with autism. A voice output communication aid (VOCA) is a portable AAC device that produces synthesized or digitized (recorded) speech. Particular messages can be accessed through visual-graphic symbols, words, or letters on the VOCA display. A VOCA can range from a single switch device that delivers a limited number of voice messages to a more complex VOCA that delivers a series of communicative units or messages, often related to a specific theme or activity, and has the capability for thousands of messages. Dynamic display devices are VOCAs in which a child points to a particular generic symbol, such as "lunch", and a new "lunch specific" board instantly opens up with the vocabulary needed for the child to make requests, interact, comment, and question within the lunch context. Some highly sophisticated VOCAs have large capacities for storing complex spoken and written text and can operate with personal computers.

A possible advantage of a VOCA over a low-technology symbol board is the ability to facilitate more normalized, natural interactions and provide verbal models for speech development due to the voice output. Four preschool children with autism with little or no functional speech were taught to use VOCAs with line drawing displays to make requests. Using a naturalistic behavioral teaching method, all four of the children successfully learned to use their VOCAs to request, make social comments, and respond to questions in a contextually appropriate and spontaneous manner in 1 to 3 months (Schepis et al., 1998). These findings are preliminary but suggest the potential value of VOCAs to support communicative interactions of children with autism.

In addition to using visual symbols for communicative output, AAC interventions have also used visual symbols to augment communicative input from others. Recently, this equally important "input" aspect of AAC is being recognized, and several case studies demonstrate the effectiveness of augmented input for young children with autism (Hodgdon, 1995; Quill, 1997; Peterson et al., 1995). One of the most widely used AAC input techniques is the use of visual schedules. The visual schedule enables a child with autism to understand the sequence of an activity through the visual input. The TEACCH (Treatment and Education of Autistic and Related Communication Handicapped Children) program, developed and implemented in North Carolina for almost 30 years, has utilized visual schedules and protocols to promote independence, self-management, and task completion (Schopler et al., 1983; Marcus et al., 2000; see Chapter 12). A few studies have demonstrated independent task engagement and completion through pictorial representation of the task components, called "within-task" schedules (Hall et al., 1995; Mirenda et al., in press; Pierce and Schreibman, 1994). Schedules that provide predictability as students transition from one activity or environment to another are called "between-task" schedules and are also being implemented with young children with autism; however, evidence of success is only in case study format.

There is some preliminary evidence for AAC systems for both generating and receiving communication that have demonstrated increases in language and social participation for children with autism. Aided language stimulation is receptive language training in natural environments in which the communication partner highlights or touches pictures while speaking the corresponding words (Elder and Goossens, 1994; Goossens et al., 1995). Aided language stimulation is an interactive, generative use of visual symbols, using a developmental, rather than a behavioral approach. The natural aided language approach, an analog of aided language stimulation, uses visual language as a second language in the child's environment (Cafiero, 1995; 2000). In natural aided language, every environment has a corresponding language board with the vocabulary needed to provide receptive language stimulation and opportunities for communicative interaction and expressive language. Although there are no published investigations of these AAC approaches used by children with autism to date, there have been two unpublished doctoral dissertations that have demonstrated significant increases in verbal and picture communicative initiations and responses and increases in utterance length (Cafiero, 1995; Dexter, 1998).

The System for Augmenting Language (SAL) (Romski and Sevcik, 1996) is another AAC system that provides augmented input and output with a VOCA. The VOCA has a communication board overlay of visual-graphic symbols; communication partners augment their verbal input with the VOCA as they interact with their nonverbal communication partner. Romski and Sevcik (1996) conducted a 2-year longitudinal study of SAL with 13 students with moderate or severe intellectual disabilities, including a 7-year-old participant with autism. They reported that all of the students used referential and social-regulatory symbols and that seven of the children, including the child with autism, produced messages with multiple symbols, recognized some printed words paired with their corresponding symbols, and increased the proportion of intelligible spoken words.

Facilitated Communication

Facilitated Communication (FC) is a method for providing support to individuals with severe communication problems as they convey typed messages. Supports consist of emotional (encouragement); physical (stable physical context, supporting the forearm or wrist, pulling back the communicator's hand, helping isolate the index finger); and communicative (ignoring stereotypic behaviors and utterances, using structured questions) components to stimulate communication (Biklen, 1993). FC differs in critical ways from typical AAC interventions. In traditional AAC, practitioners may guide or systematically prompt a communicator. Only when a communicator is independently accessing the word board, picture board, or keyboard is the communication considered under the authorship of that individual. Because FC involves continued support, within the AAC paradigm FC is considered to be a teaching strategy and motor access mode that is intended to be faded. The essential issue in FC authorship is whether the communication is under the authorship of the child with autism, the facilitator, or the communicator, or is it a collaboration (see Calculator et al., 1995; Shane, 1994).

There are over 50 research studies of FC with 143 communicators. Based on these research studies, the American Speech-Language-Hearing Association (1994) has stated that there is a lack of scientific evidence validating FC skills and a preponderance of evidence of facilitator influence on messages attributed to communicators (ASHA Technical Report, 1994). Thus, there is now a large body of research indicating that FC does not have scientific validity. Therefore, any significant message communicated by a child through FC should be validated through qualitative and experimental analysis.

While quantitative studies reveal no validation for FC, there are several qualitative studies indicating that some children with autism have developed independent communication skills through training in FC. Beukelman and Mirenda (1998) state that there are a small number of individuals with autism around the world who were communicating through FC and are now independent typists. In these cases, it is quite clear that they are the authors of their messages.

The lack of validation of FC with most individuals with autism and the growing body of research supporting the use of AAC with children with autism suggest that FC should only be considered in relation to broader AAC practices by a team that evaluates a child's progress in achieving independence in communication. The goal of any AAC system for children with autism is independent functional communication without physical support from a communication partner. The development of keyboarding skills, not simply for literacy learning, but for communicative output, is providing considerable promise in the field of autism. Past research that invalidates FC should not preempt research and practice in keyboarding, literacy learning, and AAC as a communication modality for children with autistic spectrum disorders. However, it draws attention to the need for continued evaluation of independence and functional value in using new techniques.

Assistive Technology, Literacy, and Communication

In AAC/AT and autism research, a link is emerging between literacy learning and functional communication, due to the visual nature of reading and writing and the strong visual-spatial strengths characteristic of the cognitive and processing styles of children with autistic spectrum disorders. Reading skills have been successfully used as the mode to teach spontaneous verbal communication skills. Systematic instruction in the use of written scripts that focus on commenting and questioning revealed that when scripts were faded, children spontaneously and appropriately verbalized those scripts (Krantz and McClannahan, 1998).

Computer-assisted instruction (CAI) includes the use of computer delivered prompts, systematic learning programs, technology based curricular adaptations, writing programs with word prediction, and virtual reality. In a study of four children with autism, Chen and Bernard-Opitz (1993) found more motivation and fewer aberrant behaviors during CAI than during human instruction, though there was variance in the comparative efficacy of these techniques across children. Heimann et al. (1995) conducted an investigation of CAI using an interactive multimedia reading and language software program with 11 children with autism. They documented significant gains in reading, phonological awareness, verbal behavior, and motivation over 5 months. In an investigation of CAI with synthesized speech, Parsons and LaSorte (1993) demonstrated substantial increases in spontaneous utterances when the speech was turned on, compared with when it was turned off and when there was no computer used.

Computer software, such as Boardmaker, enables practitioners to create child-centered, environmentally specific visual language tools for language boards or VOCA displays. Other software programs, such as Picture-It, Pix-Writer, and Writing with Symbols 2000 provide iconic representations for phrases and sentences and can be used to create social stories and adapted curricular materials to augment ordinary auditory and textual information input. To date, there are no published studies on the efficacy of these tools and strategies, although they are gaining popularity among practitioners and parents trained in AAC. In addition, there are no systematic evaluations of computer software that targets children with autism.

FROM RESEARCH TO PRACTICE

Advances in the understanding of autism indicate that the core deficits in communication and language abilities involve joint attention and symbolic capacity. The effectiveness of communication and language intervention programs needs to be documented relative to these core deficits and relative to the target goal of communicative competence in natural language learning environments, with the emphasis on acquisition of functional skills that support successful communicative interactions. The efficacy of communication intervention should be determined by meaningful outcome measures in social communicative parameters, not just the acquisition of verbal behaviors. Intervention research is needed that helps predict which specific intervention programs or approaches work best with which children. Such research will help families and educators to determine what goals are important and to implement specific teaching strategies designed to best meet those goals.

There is empirical support demonstrating the effectiveness of a range of approaches for enhancing communication skills of children with autism, along a continuum from behavioral to developmental, that differ in both underlying philosophy and specific teaching strategies (Dawson and Osterling, 1997; Rogers, 1996; Prizant and Wetherby, 1998). Single-subject design studies have found that naturalistic behavioral approaches are effective at leading to generalization of language gains to natural environments; generalization has been more limited for traditional discrete trial approaches (Koegel, et al., 1998; Koegel et al., 1992; McGee, et al., 1985). However, there are no group design studies directly comparing the effectiveness of two or more different approaches using randomly assigned, matched control samples (Dawson and Osterling, 1997; Sheinkopf and Siegel, 1998).

Intervention research is not yet available to predict which specific intervention approaches or strategies work best with which children. No one approach is equally effective for all children, and not all children in outcome studies have benefited to the same degree (see Dawson and Osterling, 1997; Rogers, 1996). The most positive outcomes that have been reported have been for 58 percent and 47 percent of the children (Greenspan and Wieder, 1997; McEachin et al., 1993), which means that a large minority of the children did not benefit to this extent. Educators and clinicians could provide extremely useful data by documenting the effectiveness of intervention programs on a child-by-child basis. Based on the available research with this population, progress on language and communication goals should be evident within 2 to 3 months, or different teaching approaches should be considered. In order to determine whether an individual child is benefiting from a particular educational program, measurement of that child's progress using methods of single-subject design research are helpful.

Shonkoff et al. (1988) propose going beyond traditional measures of language skills to include "ecologically compelling child characteristics" that include more meaningful measures such as a child's use of core communication skills in natural environments. Since learning in natural environments is the most desirable approach to working with children with autistic spectrum disorders, and spontaneous, initiated language and communicative behavior is of greater value than cue-dependent responding, spontaneity and generalization are particularly important research issues.

The application of functional communication training to the management of behavioral problems, and the integration of this approach into overall communication programming remains an area in which continued research can produce value for practice. As work with younger and younger children is undertaken, research that targets goals and documents progress for the core communication skills becomes even more essential, because these skills provide the underpinnings for later social and linguistic competence (Wetherby et al., 2000).

More rigorous research in developmental interventions and interventions that combine or compare naturalistic teaching, focused behavioral and developmental approaches for different aspects of communication and language would contribute valuable perspectives and could contribute ideas for innovative educational techniques. For example, Greenspan and Wieder (1997) suggested that the capacity for complex gestural interaction with shared positive affect was an important predictor to success in their intervention. Future research examining the predictive value of a child's capacity for joint attention and symbol use could help refine decision-making in treatment and contribute to better understanding of the role of motor functioning in communication and language outcomes.

Studies in autism have focused primarily on child variables and child outcomes. Family variables, considered to be critical to general early intervention research (such as socioeconomic level, stress, supports available, and parents' involvement in a child's development), have not been addressed in outcome studies of children with autism (Gresham and MacMillan, 1997). Seminal research on efficacy of early intervention for children with a range of disabilities (Shonkoff et al., 1992) demonstrated that family variables were strong predictors of outcome. Studies of the relationships between family factors and the development and use of communication and language, and the ways in which those factors interact with interventions, would help address this significant gap in understanding.

6

Social Development

Difficulties with social relationships and interactions have been one of the hallmarks of autism from its first description (Kanner, 1943), and efforts to understand the nature of the social difficulties in autism, and to find effective treatments, have driven research and clinical and educational practice for the past 40 years. Several theoretical and developmental approaches to the social difficulties in autism have had significant effects on intervention strategies offered over the years. This chapter describes these approaches, as well as the main intervention techniques and the empirical support for such techniques.

DEVELOPMENTAL CONSTRUCTS AND THEORY

Kanner's (1943) original description of autism suggested that the basis for the social difficulties lay in a child's inability to form emotional ties ("affective contact") with parent(s). This view reflected two long-held assumptions in psychology: that one's initial relationship with parents forms a blueprint for all other relationships and that maternal-infant relations grow from an affective bond rather than from the feeding experience. Kanner suggested that a child with autism was biologically impaired in this capacity—a view that was echoed by many of the early autism theorists and practitioners (Rimland, 1964; DesLauriers and Carlson, 1969). Early approaches to intervention focused diffusely on a child's social and affective experience with others (Mahler, 1952; DesLauriers and Carlson, 1969; Bergman and Escalona, 1949), trying to

66

provide a normalized social-emotional experience that would set development in this domain on a more typical path, in the hope that once righted, it would flourish.

Attachment Constructs

Attachment constructs, first influenced by psychoanalytic principles, offer an orientation to the nature and treatment of social difficulties in autism that conceptualizes attachment relations as the most important social-emotional accomplishment of infancy and early childhood. Attachment theory grew out of the integrative work of John Bowlby (1969), who drew from early cross-species work and theory on infant-maternal relations to propose that the attachment relationship was a biological-behavioral control system. This control system, present in both caregivers and infants across the mammalian species, served to maintain proximity between infants and caregivers and thus to assure infant protection and care. Bowlby's theoretical work was carried forward in empirical studies begun by Mary Ainsworth and colleagues, and it represents one of the most thoroughly studied areas of infant development at the present time. For our purposes, two of the most important findings for autism from the body of attachment literature have to do with the role of parental sensitivity and responsivity to child cues in fostering secure attachments and the association between early attachment to parents and later peer relations in typically developing children.

For a long period of time, it was assumed that autism represented a failure of the attachment process, and this view continues to pervade many people's understanding of autism. However, a series of laboratory studies of attachment behavior in autism in the 1980s and early 1990s yielded the very surprising finding that children with autism met standard criteria for secure attachment patterns with their caretakers (Capps et al., 1994; Rogers et al., 1991, 1993; Shapiro et al., 1987). Furthermore, in comparison with children with other kinds of developmental delays of similar age and cognitive levels, children with autism did *not* demonstrate greater insecurity or lack of attachment relations in these settings. Two separate studies demonstrated that maternal sensitivity and responsivity affect attachment security in autism, as they do in typical development (Capps et al., 1994; Wehner et al., 1998) . However, several researchers have questioned the validity of the attachment construct in autism: more general measures of social reciprocity (Lord and Pickles, 1996; Tanguay et al., 1998; Kasari et al., 1990) indicate that some children with autism differ from other populations in many aspects of relationships with their parents and others, even though their performance on specific attachment measures may not differ.

Behavioral Constructs

The behavioral approach to the social difficulties in autism has also been present in psychology since the 1960s. The behavioral tradition emphasizes description of actual behavioral deficits and excesses, rather than underlying constructs about the nature of development (Lovaas et al., 1965). Behavioral interventions use the powerful tools of operant learning to treat symptoms of autistic spectrum disorders. This approach, which treated each social symptom as a separate entity, was radically different from the social relations traditions described above, which considered all social behavior as emanating from one main construct. As we review below, interventions based on behavioral approaches have consistently demonstrated short-term success at teaching individual social behaviors and establishing social motivators.

Overarousal Theories of Autism

The third developmental theory to address the social deficits in autism, "withdrawal," goes back to the beginnings of interest in autism. This theory, first articulated by Bergman and Escalona (1949), studied experimentally by Hutt and Hutt (1964), and developed further by ethologists (Tinbergen and Tinbergen, 1972), postulates that children with autism find social interaction with others aversive. This is generally attributed to overly narrow thresholds or overly sensitive central nervous systems that cannot tolerate the arousing qualities of emotional engagement or sensory stimulation. Children's response to these aversive exchanges is to withdraw from them, seeking to reduce overarousal through repetitive activities with their bodies and objects. DesLauriers and Carlson (1969) suggested that there was also an "underaroused" subgroup in autism, for whom typical levels of social engagement were not arousing enough to be registered. The result of the ongoing and increasing withdrawal is a lack of opportunity to learn appropriate behavior and skills from other people. This theory continues today, expressed quite strongly in sensory integration approaches to understanding and treating autism (Ayres and Tickle, 1980). It has also been suggested by researchers and clinicians who focus on social engagement (Greenspan et al., 1997; Dawson and Lewy, 1989).

There is little empirical research to support an overarousal theory of autism. While the findings are not uniform (James and Barry, 1980), a variety of studies have failed to find evidence of overarousal to sensory stimuli (Bernal and Miller, 1971; Miller et al., 2000). In fact, the more typical finding is under-arousal, in comparison with other groups. Corona et al. (1998) examined overarousal in a social paradigm. Using psychophysiological measures of arousal in the face of strong adult affective displays in a naturalistic paradigm, Corona and colleagues found no evidence that children with autism have higher levels of arousal than other children. In fact, in reaction to adult affect, there was much less response, both behaviorally and physiologically, from the children with autism than from carefully matched controls.

This study, and other research from Sigman's laboratory, emphasized the lack of social orienting to other's faces. Other investigators have also have begun to ask whether social orienting is particularly impaired in autism (Dawson et al., 1998). The social orienting question is currently compelling because of possible links to particular brain structures that play a very specific role in orientation to other people, including awareness of eye contact and directionality of gaze (as reviewed in Baron-Cohen et al., 1999). Whether social orienting represents one of a variety of social behaviors that are impaired in autism, or whether it represents the pivotal social behavior that leads to the development of a much wider social repertoire, remains to be seen.

COMMONALTIES AND INDIVIDUAL DIFFERENCES

Given that children with autism, as a group, demonstrate widely differing levels of skills and of severity of symptoms, discussion of commonalties must occur at a general level. By definition, children with autism demonstrate impairments in relationships to peers, the use of nonverbal communicative behaviors within their social exchanges, the use of imitation, and symbolic or dramatic play. Peer interactions, and indeed social interactions in general, are characterized by low rates of both initiation and response. This is most marked in interactions for the purpose of sharing experiences and establishing joint foci of attention (Peterson and Haralick, 1977; Mundy et al., 1990; Mundy et al., 1987; Wetherby and Prutting, 1984; Corona et al., 1998). The use of nonverbal communication, including gestures and emotional expressions, is affected in young children, both expressively and receptively. As described in these papers, children with autism use fewer nonverbal gestures and a more limited range of facial expressions in their communications than children with other types of developmental disabilities of the same developmental and chronological age. Children with autism appear to pay less attention to other people's emotional displays than do comparison groups and to demonstrate fewer acts of empathy or shared emotion. Children with autism also demonstrate less imitation of other people's actions, movements, and vocalizations (DeMyer et al., 1972; Stone et al., 1997).

Yet there are wide-ranging differences within the group of children with autism in their social interests and behaviors. In terms of general sociability, Wing and Gould (1979) suggested three subgroupings of children with autism based on social interests: aloof, passive, and active but odd. Aloof was defined as indifferent in all situations, particularly marked with other children, though approaching to get needs met and often enjoying physical interactions. The passive group involved children who made few social initiations but responded positively to the approaches of others, both adults and peers. The active but odd group made initiations and responded to others: these children were interested in interactions and sought them out, but their ways of carrying out the interactions were unusual in their odd language, obsessional topics, and lack of understanding of others.

Clearly, the descriptions of these groups also connote developmental differences, and, in fact, IQ scores and language levels correlate with these groupings (Wing and Gould, 1979) as do differences in patterns of brain function (Dawson et al., 1995) and differences in context (for example, a child may be aloof with peers but passively responsive to adults [Lord and Hopkins, 1986]). However, characterizing the patterns in this way may be useful to educators and clinicians, because it may help to focus interventions and set priorities. In a related vein, differences in temperament and amount of negative affect and behavior displayed in social interactions vary considerably within autism and may well figure in what differentiates children in the aloof and passive groups (Kasari and Sigman, 1997).

Mundy and Sigman's work on social responses demonstrated that continuing pleasurable social routines and regulating others' behavior to get needs met were types of social interaction that were not specifically affected by autism (Mundy et al., 1987). In a related vein, Dawson and colleagues demonstrated that an adult's imitation of a child's behavior elicited social orienting, interest, and engagement (Dawson and Galpert, 1990). Other affectively based approaches also target this early level of social involvement (Rogers, 2000; Greenspan et al., 1997). These affectively rich, simple dyadic interactions may provide an effective starting point for social interventions for the aloof group, who do not yet demonstrate much social interest.

There are also wide-ranging differences in the levels of play skills seen in young children with autism, again related to language and IQ levels, as well as age. Among toddlers with autism, Charman and colleagues (1998) reported that functional play and other object play was not impaired relative to clinical controls. Only the production of symbolic play acts was markedly deficient. However, when older children are studied, sensorimotor play also appears to be affected, with more repetitive and immature play seen in children with autism than in children with other developmental delays matched to the same developmental level (Libby et al., 1998; Stone et al., 1990). Several investigators have reported successful interventions for stimulating symbolic play development in preschoolers with autism (Thorp et al., 1995; Goldstein et al., 1988; Stahmer, 1995; Rogers and Lewis, 1989; see also Chapters 11 and 12).

Given the importance of symbolic play for normal development (Vygotsky, 2000; Piaget, 1962), this is an important target of early education for children with autism.

Communication is the means by which people carry out social interactions. The wide-ranging differences in communication skills that exist in young children with autism and their intervention needs are described in Chapter 5. Although it might appear that communication skills are a necessary prerequisite for building peer interactions, the large body of research in peer-mediated methods for socially engaging young children with autism suggests that no particular level of communicative ability is needed in order to work on social interventions (Lord and Hopkins, 1986). However, the form of the intervention strategy needs to be selected so that it fits with a child's current communicative abilities. Strategies that teach peers to initiate and persist in physical engagement (Odom and Strain, 1986) are quite important for preverbal children with autism, while strategies that teach a child with autism to make verbal initiations to peers (Krantz and McClannahan, 1993) target children with some speech.

PLANNING FOR INTERVENTION

The individual differences in autism most often linked to predicting outcomes have typically included developmental variables. Past research has indicated that IQ scores and level of language skill at age 5 are very strong indicators of future performance (Lotter, 1978; Lord and Schopler, 1989; Sigman and Ruskin, 1999). Even in some intervention studies, initial developmental rate appears to be related to level of attainment after intervention (Lovaas, 1987; Sheinkopf and Siegel, 1998; Smith et al., 2000).

However, there is some evidence that autism-specific behaviors also predict outcomes. Parents' reports of autism-specific characteristics of language and severity of repetitive and restricted behavior, gathered through interviews by or before the time their children turned 5, significantly predicted adaptive behavior scores 8 years later in a large sample of high-functioning persons with autism (Venter et al., 1992). Similarly, severity of social symptoms assessed from parental report was the strongest concurrent predictor of adult adaptive functioning in that study.

Setting Goals for Social Development

The process of education involves assessment of existing skills, defining what skills will be taught (setting goals and objectives), planning how the skills will be taught (teaching strategies), implementing the teaching plan, assessing student progress, and adapting the teaching strategy so that a student acquires the target skill (Cipani and Spooner, 1994). Most educational programs and approaches for young children with autism fall into one of two theoretical frameworks: developmental or behavioral.

The developmental approach uses a model of typical development to guide the educational process involving assessment, goal setting, and teaching. When carried out in an optimal way, this approach involves assessing each developmental area—motor, cognition, communication, and social development, among others—and using a child's successes, emerging skills, and failures to determine a child's zone of proximal development (Vygotsky, 2000). This zone indicates the set of skills that a child appears to be ready to learn next, based on his or her assessed performance. Those skills are then targeted for teaching. The developmental approach is widely used in early childhood education of both typically developing children and those with special needs.

Some advantages of a developmental approach are the ease with which it is conducted in early childhood settings, the many developmentally based curriculum assessment and teaching materials that are available, and the developmental training of those professionals typically involved in young children with special needs. Some drawbacks, when looking at education of children with autism, involve the fact that these children do not demonstrate typical patterns of development in several key areas (communication, language and speech development, social development). Nor do they necessarily learn through developmentally typical teaching practices (verbal instruction, imitation of teachers and peers, and independent learning), because these strategies are often dependent on a child's internal motivation to learn, to be like others, and to gain competence.

In a behavioral approach, a child's behavioral repertoire is evaluated according to the presence of behavioral excesses—presence of abnormal behaviors or of an abnormal frequency of certain behaviors—and behavioral deficits—absence or low frequency of typical skills (Lovaas, 1987). Behavioral teaching strategies are then designed to increase a child's performance of deficit skills and decrease the behavioral excesses. These strategies involve identifying the target of teaching, determining the appropriate antecedent and consequence for the target behavior, and using systematic instruction and assessment to teach the target behavior and assess student progress.

Some advantages of the behavioral research on changing social skills have been the measurement of generalization and maintenance, attention to antecedents and consequences, and use of systematic strategies to teach complex skills by breaking them down into smaller, teachable parts. Some drawbacks of traditional behavioral approaches are the complex data systems that often accompany them and that may impede their use in more typical settings, as well as the lack of training in their use that most staff members on early childhood teams receive. Personnel may sometimes apply the strategies in highly artificial ways, particularly in extended one-on-one interactions, which prevents their easy use in group settings and inclusive settings. Newer behavioral approaches such as incidental teaching and pivotal response training stress naturalistic delivery, are used in group settings, and allow easier coordination with inclusion (Prizant and Wetherby, 1998; Anderson and Romanczyk, 1999). These strategies have demonstrated very effective outcomes, but are not as well known to the public, either parents or professionals.

Developing Goals for Improving Social Interactions with Adults

For very young children with autism, goals for specific social behaviors or skills identified in interactions with adults may focus on early prelinguistic behaviors, such as joint attention, turn taking, imitation, responding by gaze to adult initiations, and initiating social interactions with adults (Wetherby and Prizant, 1993). These interactions occur within a play context, so establishing and supporting toy play with an adult may be a goal for some children. As children grow older, interactions with adults may more often occur in classroom contexts. Although such classroom-based interactions may also occur in a play context, the nature of adult-child interactions will extend to behaviors necessary for participating and functioning independently in the classroom. Social skills–such as responding to adult directions, independently participating in the routines of the classroom, expressing needs to adults (e.g., need to go to the bathroom), and requesting assistance of the adult—all become important functional skills necessary for children to be successful in classroom settings.

Developing Goals for Peer Interactions

Interaction with peers is another dimension of children's social development that becomes increasingly important for children beginning at the age of 3. To identify potential intervention target behaviors for young children with severe handicaps (including autism), Strain (1983) observed groups of preschool children with and without disabilities who received high and low sociometric ratings from their peers. Children with high sociometric ratings engaged in more play organizers (i.e., suggesting a play idea, sharing, affection, and social initiations that involved assisting others) and responded more to peer social bids than children with low peer ratings. These social initiations have been used as targets or goals for interventions with young children with autism in a range of studies (see Odom and Ogawa, 1992). Other investigators (Goldstein et al., 1992) have used prelinguistic social-communicative behaviors, such as joint attention and pragmatic communicative forms (e.g., requesting, comments, and nonverbal responses directed toward peers), as outcomes for peer-mediated interventions. Such skills may well be appropriate goals for many children with autism who have limited communicative abilities.

Assessment Strategies for Developing Social Goals

In assessing the social repertoire and social needs of young children with autism, early childhood professionals need to turn to several different sources. Social development has not been as thoroughly researched as language development, and different aspects of social development require different approaches to assessment. One set of tools that provide a very global assessment of social development are adaptive behavior scales like the Vineland Adaptive Behavior Scales (Sparrow et al., 1984) or the Scales of Independent Behavior-Revised (SIB-R), (Bruininks et al., 1996). These tools are best used in setting general goals for the social domain, since they provide an overview of social functioning in various areas, but not a detailed look at social skill repertoires.

More detail about social development can be gathered with preschool curriculum assessments, most of which contain a social subscale. Some scales are standardized so that average levels are determined for children of different ages. Others are criterion-referenced, so they compare performance to a practical standard for particular behaviors. Such instruments include the Battelle Developmental Inventory (Newborg et al., 1984), the Learning Accomplishment Profile (LAP) (LeMay et al., 1983), the Michigan Scales (Rogers et al., 1979), and the Assessment, Evaluation, and Programming System (AEPS) (Bricker, 1993). These tools assess behaviors seen in typically developing children of various ages, and thus may be helpful in determining what skills a child already has, and what should be taught next from a developmental perspective.

For assessing social abilities within the context of parent-infant interactions, one may turn to traditional rating scales of parent-infant interactions (see Munson and Odom, 1996, for a review), measures of early symbolic communication and behavior (e.g., Wetherby and Prizant, 1993), or criterion referenced assessment of early development (e.g., the AEPS by Bricker, 1993). Since communication is the process by which people carry out social relationships, children's communication skills and needs are part and parcel of social development. Developing social goals and objectives needs to be carried out hand in hand with developing communication goals and objectives. Thus, assessing communication abilities and needs and making sure that teaching strategies for communication are integrated with social teaching strategies are crucial for developing skills that are functional and adaptive for a child.

Play, like communication, is an important social activity in early childhood. Play skills and needs, like communication, must be assessed and considered within the social domain. Developmental sequences of play have been published in various sources (Wetherby and Prizant, 1993;

Rogers et al., 1987; Fewell, 1994; Gowen et al., 1992). A recent study demonstrated that even when using a behavioral paradigm to teach symbolic play, children's learning was enhanced when the play skills taught were those that were developmentally appropriate next steps for a child (Lifter et al., 1993). Development of more mature play skills in both independent play and social play is important for the social development and peer interaction of young children with autism, since play is the glue that holds together peer interactions in early childhood (Nadel and Peze, 1993).

Social assessment needs to be carried out in ecologically valid situations. Observing the social repertoire of a young child with autism in a setting with familiar typical peers provides information about a child's current social repertoire that is unavailable in any other way. Assessing a child's actual behaviors with other children—including initiations, responses, length of rounds, interest in others, proximity to others, and level of social play—provides an important baseline against which to measure the degree to which interventions are having ecologically valid effects. Observational, sociometric, rating scale, and criterion-referenced measures are available for identifying specific goals and instructional target behaviors for young children with autism (a detailed review of these assessment instruments and techniques can be found in Odom and Munson, 1996). This assessment information, when paired with information about priorities, parents' concerns, the skills needed to be successful in the current educational settings, and the skills needed to be successful in the next educational setting, can serve as a basis for selecting functional social outcomes that practitioners could select for young children with autism.

INTERVENTIONS USED TO TEACH SOCIAL BEHAVIOR

Since social development is an extremely important aspect of education for children with autistic spectrum disorders, a child's social behavior with both adults and peers needs to be targeted for intervention, and intervention should take into account both specific evaluation of a child's current social skills and specific teaching goals and plans that address the social area.

The methods demonstrated to be effective are complex to deliver and require careful attention to delivery, maintenance, and generalization, as well as skill acquisition. Furthermore, as in any instructional area, objective data need to be gathered during the teaching process to assure skill acquisition, maintenance, and generalization (Krantz and McClannahan, 1998; Rogers, 2000). Studies of interventions aimed at improving social interaction for young children with autistic spectrum disorders have generally had significant methodological limitations, as indicated by comprehensive ratings of individual articles by McConnell (1999) according to our guidelines (see Box 1-1 in Chapter 1). Almost all studies were pre-post designs or multiple baseline or ABAB designs without procedures to ensure blindness of evaluators to condition, as shown in Figure 1-1 in Chapter 1. About 60 percent of samples were well defined and included samples of sufficient size or replication across several subjects (see Figure 1-2 in Chapter 1). About 50 percent of the social intervention studies addressed generalization or maintenance across contexts, with 30 percent showing generalization from the teaching context to another natural situation (see Figure 1-3 in Chapter 1). This pattern reflects the commitment of most social interventions to changing behaviors in "real world" contexts, but also the difficulties of doing so with random assignments and independent evaluators blind to the intervention.

Intervention Techniques

Child-Parent Social Interactions

Dawson and Galpert (1990) described a pre-post study of 14 children aged 20 to 66 months and their mothers. The intervention involved teaching the parent to imitate a child in play with toys for 20 minutes each day for 2 weeks. Follow-up after 2 weeks demonstrated significant increases in the child's gaze to mother's face, increased number of toys played with, and increased number of play schemas used, as well as generalization to novel toys. Rogers and colleagues (1986, 1989) used a similar pre-post design to assess changes in child behavior of 13 pre-schoolers following 6 or more months of intensive intervention in a daily preschool program that emphasized positive adult-child interactions, play, and communication. Improvements in social-communicative play levels with a familiar adult, increases in child positive affect and social initiations, and decreased negative responses to mother's initiations during mother-child play were found. The changes were interpreted as demonstrating generalization of effects from the day program. Improvement in social interactions was demonstrated across three separate measures and with various partners, adding convergent validity to the impact of this model on social development in young children with autism.

Child-Adult Interactions

Two approaches for increasing interactions with teachers or other therapists have been demonstrated using multiple baseline approaches. One approach comes from the work of Laura Schreibman, Robert Koegel, and colleagues, using pivotal response training (PRT; see Chapter 12). Stahmer (1995) compared two interventions, symbolic play training and language training, using pivotal response techniques with seven verbal preschool-aged children with autism. The children demonstrated increases in the targeted symbolic play skills and increased positive responses to adult initiations and in initiations to adults during the play training, but not during the language training, with maintenance for 3 months and generalization across settings and other adults.

Krantz and McClannahan (1998) used a script-fading procedure to increase social initiations to a teacher. The technique involved using a one-word written stimulus embedded in a child's independent play schedule. The stimulus prompted the child to approach an adult and initiate a joint attention request (look, watch me, etc.). The adult responded with comments but without any other reinforcing consequence. Three verbal preschoolers learned the procedure and maintained and increased initiations after the stimuli were faded. Furthermore, generalization was demonstrated through spontaneous use of unscripted initiations, as well as by generalization across new adults and new activities.

Child-Child Interactions

Peer Mediated Techniques for Increasing Interaction and Responses to Peers In the peer-mediated approach, developed over the past 20 years by Phillip Strain, Samuel Odom, Howard Goldstein, and their associates, typical peers are taught to repeatedly initiate "play organizers" such as sharing, helping, giving affection, and praise. Peers learn the strategies through role-play with adults and then are cued by adults to use those strategies with children with autism. Peers are reinforced by adults for their efforts, and the reinforcements are systematically and carefully reduced. The power of these strategies to increase social interactions of young children with autism, as well as generalization and maintenance, has been demonstrated in inclusive preschool classes, as reported in many published multiple baseline studies (Hoyson et al., 1984; Strain et al., 1979; Strain et al., 1977; Goldstein et al., 1992).

Variables found to be important in maintenance and generalization include the characteristics of the peers, methods of prompting and reinforcing peers, fading reinforcers, ages of children, and characteristics of the setting, as well as the use of multiple peer trainers (Brady et al., 1987; Sainato et al., 1992). Self-monitoring systems for the peers have also been used successfully (Strain et al., 1994). These interventions have been found most powerful when delivered in inclusive preschools, but they have also been used successfully by parents and siblings in homes (Strain and Danko, 1995; Strain et al., 1994).

Oke and Schreibman (1990) extended the use of play organizers in a case study involving one child, a high-functioning 5-year-old. They added two procedures to the peer-mediated techniques: they trained a typical peer to discriminate between and differentially attend to parallel play and interactive play, which increased and stabilized responding of the target child. They also trained the target child to use peer-initiating procedures. The second addition had four important effects: maintenance of high rates of social engagement during the reversal phase, a decrease in inappropriate behaviors, normalization of child affect, and maintenance and generalization across peers (but not across settings).

An important feature of these peer-mediated procedures is the use of typical peers rather than adults, because studies have demonstrated that interactions established between children with autism and adults do not easily generalize to peer partners (Bartak and Rutter, 1973). Though they can be highly effective, peer-mediation approaches are complex to deliver, requiring socially skilled typical peers and precise adult control during training of peers, managing and fading reinforcement, and monitoring ongoing child interaction data. However, these approaches are manualized (Danko et al., 1998) and well described in many publications.

Peer Tutoring Using Incidental Teaching McGee and colleagues (1992) trained and reinforced typical peers in an inclusive classroom to use teaching techniques and take turns with their peers with autism in 5-minute teaching segments. The multiple baseline design included both the implementation phase and two fading periods, in which adult prompts to the peer tutors were systematically withdrawn. Results for three children with autism demonstrated long-term (5-month) increases in reciprocal social behavior and social initiations, as well as higher peer acceptance. The typical peers also maintained greatly increased rates of social initiations toward the children with autism across the fading of adult prompts. However, these gains generalized to other times during the preschool day for only one of the three children.

Adult Instruction in Social Games Goldstein and colleagues (1988) taught sociodramatic scripts to two trios of preschool children consisting of two typical peers and a child with social, communicative, and behavioral problems (presumably, autism). Each child was trained in each of three related social role scripts (e.g., cook, customer, and waiter in a restaurant). Following training, child interaction and generalization across settings and other behaviors improved during free play periods at preschool. However, the effects depended on continued teacher prompts in role-playing activities, and they did not result in general increases in social exchanges across the preschool day.

Social Stories Developed by Gray and Garand (1993), social stories involve written narratives about certain social situations that are difficult for the child involved. Since this technique involves the use of print, it is generally targeted for older children with reading skills. The effectiveness of this technique with young children has not yet been established (Norris and Dattilo, 1999).

Comprehensive Early Intervention Models for Teaching Social Interactions

Behaviorally Based Programs

Although the various programs based on behavioral treatment differ in a number of ways, behavioral work in the social arena is based on similar approaches. This grouping includes the program at the University of California at Los Angeles (Lovaas, 1987) and its various replications, as well as the Princeton program (McClannahan and Krantz, 1994). The first social interventions involve responses to a teacher, with interventions generally focusing on eye contact, imitation, and response to language. Play skills with toys are also taught. As children master speech and a number of other basic skills and appear ready to learn in group settings, behavioral techniques from the "shadow" teacher support interactions with peers. In these approaches, social skills are taught directly, like any other skill, through establishment of an antecedent-behavior-consequence chain.

Neobehavioral Approaches

More recently developed approaches, like the Walden Program (McGee et al., 1999) and the Learning Experiences, Alternative Program (LEAP) approach (Kohler et al., 1997; Strain et al., 1996) have used more naturalistic behavioral teaching to develop peer interactions and communication skills. Both approaches, as well as the pivotal response training approach described by Koegel and colleagues (1999), carefully apply behavioral teaching paradigms embedded in natural or naturalistic social interactions to focus on social development as the primary thrust of the intervention.

Interactive Approaches

In Greenspan and Wieder's Developmental Intervention model (Greenspan et al., 1997) interventions are built on "circles of communication," reciprocal social interactions with adults that over time increase the length and complexity of social interactions. These are child-centered—built on children's spontaneous behavior and adult responses that are carefully fit to children's current developmental and communicative capacities. Positive emotional valence is highly valued. This model has been evaluated in one large review of records (Greenspan et al., 1997).

Denver Model

In the Denver approach, social interactions with adults are taught in two ways. Initiation and maintenance are taught through the use of "sensory social exchanges." These exchanges are naturalistic child-centered social activities in which a child makes choices, initiates pleasurable interactions with an adult, and continues them through several rounds, using whatever communicative behavior a child has available. Social responses are taught through adult-directed interactions, as are toy play skills. Imitation of peers' and adults' motor actions and object actions is taught through direct teaching and through prompting in typical social exchanges. Peer interactions are taught in inclusive preschool settings, in which both typical peers and children with autism are prompted to initiate object actions with each other (e.g., giving, taking, and passing objects); to imitate each other in play; and to engage in social routines like circle games, songs, and similar activities. Pre- and post-testing demonstrated significant gains in social skills after participation in the Denver program (see Rogers et al., 2000) for a detailed discussion of the Denver model).

TEACCH

The TEACCH (Treatment and Education of Autistic and Related Communication Handicapped Children) approach emphasizes individual functioning in a group setting, and its focus on social interaction comes particularly through communication training, participating in group activities, following instructions and routines with others, and taking turns (Watson et al., 1989). In a TEACCH classroom, the staff teaches many toy play skills, games, and object skills, which can in turn be used to facilitate social interaction (Schopler et al., 1995).

Convergence of Techniques Across Program Models

The various techniques used can be grouped into three strategies: (1) adult-directed instruction of specific components of social interactions, like eye contact, response to gestures, toy play skills, and social speech; (2) child-centered approaches in which adults follow children's leads, stimulate and continue interactions, and in general scaffold higher level and longer rounds of interaction; and (3) peer strategies in which either adults or typical peers prompt and sustain social engagement. Each technique has demonstrated success in teaching some aspects of social interaction. Comprehensive programs that heavily emphasize social development make use of some or all of these strategies in various ways.

The choice of strategies, in addition to reflecting the theoretical orientation of the intervenor, must also reflect individual differences among children. For children who exhibit very little appropriate spontaneous behavior, adult-directed instruction may be the most effective approach to acquiring new behaviors, with more child-centered and peer strategies used to build fluency, generalization, and maintenance. For children who generate more appropriate behavior in the face of new stimuli, child-centered approaches may be as effective as (or more effective than) adult instruction in building a wider repertoire of skills. The need to tailor instruction to the individual learning styles and needs of each child requires that educators of children with autism be fluent in a wide range of educational strategies across various theoretical traditions. In this way, the educator can maximally individualize instruction and achieve the best results possible. It is axiomatic that methods that do not result in educational gains should be replaced by other approaches.

FROM RESEARCH TO PRACTICE

More empirical data are available to support the efficacy of behavioral interventions than developmental interventions. However, no comparative studies have been published that support one methodology over another. The field has very little data on effectiveness of developmental approaches for social development in early autism. Given the popularity of developmentally appropriate practices in other areas of early childhood education, empirical studies of the effectiveness of developmentally based interventions are needed to determine their relative value for stimulating growth in young children with autistic spectrum disorders.

Comparative studies of varying approaches are needed. Given the current debates about the appropriateness of various approaches and their relative effectiveness in modifying social behaviors, the field needs comparative studies of the social outcomes achieved by various approaches to intervention for young children with autism. Informative studies would include very careful control of independent variables so that the approaches themselves, and not the hours or child/adult ratios, are compared.

Studies that examine interactions of learner characteristics and rate of progress under varying educational methodologies are also needed. The social strengths and needs of young children with autism vary widely. No one approach would be expected to be appropriate for all children. There is a need for sophisticated studies that carefully examine the interactions among program variables and child variables in the social domain, so that real individualization can be achieved.

7

Cognitive Development

In his original paper, Kanner (1943) commented on the intelligent appearance of children with autism and observed that they did well on some parts of tests of intelligence. This view led to the impression that children with autism did not suffer from cognitive delay. Observed difficulties in assessment and low test scores were attributed to "negativism" or "untestability" (Brown and Pace, 1969; Clark and Rutter, 1977). As time went on, it became apparent that, although some areas of intellectual development were often relatively strong, many other areas were significantly delayed or deviant in their development and that probably a majority of children with autism functioned in the mentally retarded range. Various investigators (e.g., Rutter, 1983) began to emphasize the centrality of cognitive-communicative dysfunction.

As noted by Sigman and colleagues (1997), studies of normal cognitive development have generally focused either on the process of acquisition of knowledge (emphasizing theories of learning and information processing) or on symbolic development, concept acquisition, and skill acquisition (a combined line of work often based on the theories of Piaget), as well as questions concerning the nature of intelligence. Various authors have summarized the large and growing literature on these topics in autism (e.g. DeMyer et al., 1981; Fein et al., 1984; Prior and Ozonoff, 1998). The interpretation of this literature is complicated by the association of autism with mental retardation in many individuals, by developmental changes in the expression of autism, and by the strong interdependence of various lines of development. For example, deficits in aspects of symbolic functioning may be manifest in problems with play at one time, and in language at a later time. In addition, individuals with autism may attempt compensatory strategies, either spontaneously or through instruction, so profiles of ability may also change over time.

Children with autistic spectrum disorders have unique patterns of development, both as a group and as individuals. Many children with autistic spectrum disorders have relative strengths that can be used to buttress their learning in areas that they find difficult. For example, a child with strong visual-spatial skills may learn to read words to cue social behavior. A child with strong nonverbal problem-solving skills may be motivated easily by tasks that have a clear endpoint or that require thinking about how to move from one point to another. A child with good auditory memory may develop a repertoire of socially appropriate phrases from which to select for specific situations.

Autistic spectrum disorders are disorders that affect many aspects of thinking and learning. Cognitive deficits, including mental retardation, are interwoven with social and communication difficulties, and many of the theoretical accounts of autistic spectrum disorders emphasize concepts, such as joint attention and theory of mind, that involve components of cognition, communication, and social understanding. Thus, educational interventions cannot assume a typical sequence of learning; they must be individualized, with attention paid to the contribution of each of the component factors to the goals most relevant for an individual child.

COGNITIVE ABILITIES IN INFANTS AND VERY YOUNG CHILDREN

Early studies on development in autism focused on basic capacities of perception and sensory abilities. Although children with autistic spectrum disorders appear to be able to perceive sensory stimuli, their responses to such stimuli may be abnormal (Prior and Ozonoff, 1998). For example, brainstem auditory evoked response hearing testing may demonstrate that the peripheral hearing pathway is intact, although the child's behavioral response to auditory stimuli is abnormal. In infants and very young children, the use of infant developmental scales is somewhat limited, since such tests have, in general, relatively less predictive value for subsequent intelligence. Indeed, the nature of "intelligence" in this period may be qualitatively different than in later years (Piaget, 1952).

Several studies have investigated sensorimotor intelligence in children with autism. The ability to learn material by rote may be less impaired than that involved in the manipulation of more symbolic materials (Klin and Shepard, 1994; Losche, 1990). Attempts made to employ traditional Piagetian notions of sensorimotor development have revealed generally normal development of object permanence, although the capacities to imitate gesture or vocalization may be deficient (Sigman and Ungerer, 1984b; Sigman et al., 1997). The difficulties in imitation begin early (Prior et al., 1975) and are persistent (Sigman and Ungerer, 1984b; Otah, 1987). The specificity of these difficulties has been the topic of some debate (Smith and Bryson, 1994), although it is clear that children with autism usually have major difficulties in combining and integrating different kinds of information and their responses (Rogers, 1998).

Although sensorimotor skills may not appear to be highly deviant in some younger children with autism, aspects of symbolic play and imagination, which typically develop during the preoperational period, are clearly impaired (Wing et al., 1977; Riquet et al., 1981). Children with autism are less likely to explore objects in unstructured situations (Kasari et al., 1993; Sigman et al., 1986). Younger children with autism do exhibit a range of various play activities, but the play is less symbolic, less developmentally sophisticated, and less varied than that of other children (Sigman and Ungerer, 1984a). These problems may be the earliest manifestations of what later will be seen to be difficulties in organization and planning ("executive functioning") (Rogers and Pennington, 1991). Thus, younger children with autism exhibit specific areas of deficiency that primarily involve representational knowledge. These problems are often most dramatically apparent in the areas of play and social imitation. As Leslie has noted (e.g., Leslie, 1987), the capacity to engage in more representational play, especially shared symbolic play, involves some ability for metarepresentation. Shared symbolic play also involves capacities for social attention, orientation, and knowledge, which are areas of difficulty for children with autism.

STABILITY AND USES OF TESTS OF INTELLIGENCE

IQ scores have been important in the study of autism and autistic spectrum disorders. To date, scores on intelligence tests, particularly verbal IQ, have been the most consistent predictors of adult independence and functioning (Howlin, 1997). IQ scores have generally been as stable for children with autism as for children with other disabilities or with typical development (Venter et al., 1992). Though fluctuations of 10-20 points within tests (and even more between tests) are common, within a broad range, nonverbal IQ scores are relatively stable, especially after children with autism enter school. Thus, nonverbal intelligence serves, along with the presence of communicative language, as an important prognostic factor. Epidemiological studies typically estimate that about 70 percent of children with autism score within the range of mental retardation, although there is some suggestion in several recent studies that this proportion has decreased (Fombonne, 1997). This change may be a function of more complete identification of children with autism who are not mentally retarded, a broader definition of autism that includes less impaired individuals, and greater educational opportunities for children with autism in the past two decades in many countries. It will be important to consider the effects of these possible shifts on interventions.

In school-age children, traditional measures of intelligence are more readily applicable than in younger (and lower functioning) individuals. Such tests have generally shown that children with autism exhibit problems both in aspects of information processing and in acquired knowledge, with major difficulties in more verbally mediated skills (Gillies, 1965; McDonald et al., 1989; Lockyer and Rutter, 1970; Wolf et al., 1972; Tymchuk et al., 1977). In general, abilities that are less verbally mediated are more preserved, so that such tasks as block design may be areas of relative strength. Tasks that involve spatial understanding, perceptual organization, and short-term memory are often less impaired (Hermelin and O'Connor, 1970; Maltz, 1981) unless they involve more symbolic tasks (Minshew et al. 1992). There may be limitations in abilities to sequence information cross modally, particularly in auditory-visual processing (Frith, 1970, 1972; Hermelin and Frith, 1971). There is also some suggestion that in other autistic spectrum disorders (e.g., Asperger's syndrome) different patterns may be noted (Klin et al., 1995). In addition, the ability to generalize and broadly apply concepts may be much more limited in children with autism than other children (Tager-Flusberg, 1981; Schreibman and Lovaas, 1973). As for other aspects of development, programs have been implemented to maximize generalization of learning (Koegel et al., 1999), but this process cannot be assumed to occur naturally.

In autism research, IQ scores are generally required by the highest quality journals in descriptions of participants. These scores are important in characterizing samples and allowing independent investigators to replicate specific findings, given the wide variability of intelligence within the autism spectrum. IQ is associated with a number of other factors, including a child's sex, the incidence of seizures, and the presence of other medical disorders, such as tuberous sclerosis. Several diagnostic measures for autism, including the Autism Diagnostic Interview-Revised, are less valid with children whose IQ scores are less than 35 than with children with higher IQs (Lord et al., 1994). Diagnostic instruments often involve quantifying behaviors that are not developing normally. This means that it is difficult to know if the frequency of autism is truly high in severely to profoundly mentally retarded individuals, or if the high scores on diagnostic instruments occur as the result of "floor" effects due to the general absence of more mature, organized behaviors (Nordin and Gillberg, 1996; Wing and Gould, 1979).

IQ scores have been used as outcome measures in several studies of treatment of young children with autism (Lovaas, 1993; Sheinkopf and

Siegel, 1998; Smith et al., 2000). IQ is an important variable, particularly for approaches that claim "recovery," because "recovery" implies intellectual functioning within the average range. However, these results are difficult to interpret for a number of reasons. First, variability among children and variability within an individual child over time make it nearly impossible to assess a large group of children with autism using the same test on numerous occasions. Within a representative sample of children with autism, some children will not have the requisite skills to take the test at all, and some will make such large gains that the test is no longer sufficient to measure their skills. This is a difficulty inherent in studying such a heterogeneous population as children with autistic spectrum disorders.

The challenge to find appropriate measures and to use them wisely has direct consequences in measuring response to treatment. For example, there is predictable variation in how children perform on different tests (Lord and Schopler, 1989a). Children with autism tend to have the greatest difficulty on tests in which both social and language components are heavily weighted and least difficulty with nonverbal tests that have minimum demands for speed and motor skills (e.g., the Raven's Coloured Progressive Matrices [Raven, 1989]). Comparing the same child's performance on two tests, given at different times—particularly a test that combines social, language, and nonverbal skills, or a completely nonverbal test – does not provide a meaningful measure of improvement. Even within a single test that spans infant to school-age abilities, there is still variation in tasks across age that may differentially affect children with autism; this variation is exemplified in many standard instruments such as the Stanford-Binet Intelligence Scales (Thorndike et al., 1986) or Mullen Scales of Early Development (Mullen, 1995).

Generally, IQ scores are less stable for children first tested in early preschool years (ages 2 and 3) than for those tested later, particularly when different tests are used at different times. In one study (Lord and Schopler, 1989a), mean differences between test scores at 3 years or younger and 8 years and older were greater than 23 points. These findings have been replicated in other populations (Sigman et al., 1997). Thus, even without special treatment, children first assessed in early preschool years are likely to show marked increases in IQ score by school age (Lord and Schopler, 1989b), also presumably reflecting difficulties in assessing the children and limitations of assessment instruments for younger children.

Studies with normally developing children have indicated that there can be practice effects with developmental and IQ tests, particularly if the administration is witnessed by parents who may then, not surprisingly, subsequently teach their children some of the test items (Bagley and McGeein, 1989). Examiners can also increase scores by varying breaks, motivation, and order of assessment (Koegel et al., 1997). There are difficulties analyzing age equivalents across different tests because of lack of equality in intervals (Mervis and Robinson, 1999). Deviation IQ scores may not extend low enough for some children with autism, and low normative scores may be generated from inferences based on very few subjects. In the most extreme case, a young child tested with the Bayley Scales at 2 years and a Leiter Scale at 7 years might show an IQ score gain of over 30 points. This change might be accounted for by the change in test (i.e., its emphasis and structure), the skill of the examiner, familiarity with the testing situation, and practice on test measures—all important aspects of the measurement before response to an intervention can be interpreted.

Because researchers are generally expected to collect IQ scores as descriptive data for their samples, the shift to reporting IQ scores as outcome measures is a subtle one. For researchers to claim full "recovery," measurement of a posttreatment IQ within the average range is crucial and easier to measure than the absence of autism-related deficits in social behavior or play. IQ scores, at least very broadly, can predict school success and academic achievement, though they are not intended to be used in isolation. Indeed, adaptive behavior may be a more robust predictor of some aspects of later outcomes (Lord and Schopler, 1989b; Sparrow, 1997). Furthermore, an IQ score is a composite measure that is not always easily dissected into consistent components. Because of the many sources for their variability and the lack of specific relationship between IQ scores and intervention methods, IQ scores on their own provide important information but are not sufficient measures of progress in response to treatment and certainly should not be used as the sole outcome measure.

Similar to findings with typically developing children, tests of intellectual ability yield more stable scores as children with autistic spectrum disorders become older and more varied areas of intellectual development can be evaluated. Although the process of assessment can be difficult (Sparrow, 1997), various studies have reported on the reliability and validity of appropriately obtained intelligence test scores (Lord and Schopler, 1989a). Clinicians should be aware that the larger the sampling of intellectual skills (i.e., comprehensiveness of the test or combination of tests), the higher will be the validity and accuracy of the estimate of intellectual functioning (Sparrow, 1997).

GENERAL ISSUES IN COGNITIVE ASSESSMENT

There are several important problems commonly encountered in the assessment of children with autism and related conditions. First, it is common to observe significant scatter, so that, in autism, verbal abilities may be much lower than nonverbal ones, particularly in preschool and school-age children. As a result, overall indices of intellectual functioning may be misleading (Ozonoff and Miller, 1995). Second, correlations reported in test manuals between various assessment batteries may not readily apply, although scores often become more stable and predictive over time (Lord and Schopler, 1989a; Sparrow, 1997). Third, for some older children with autism standard scores may fall over time, reflecting the fact that while gains are made, they tend to be at a slower rate than expected given the increase in chronological age. This drop may be particularly obvious in tests of intelligence that emphasize aspects of reasoning, conceptualization, and generalization.

Approximately 10 percent of children with autism show unusual islets of ability or splinter skills. These abilities are unusual either in relation to those expected, given the child's overall developmental level, or, more strikingly, in relation to normally developing children. The kinds of talents observed include drawing, block design tasks, musical skill, and other abilities, such as calendar calculation (Treffert, 1989; Shah and Frith, 1993; Prior and Ozonoff , 1998). Hermelin and colleagues (e.g., Hermelin and Frith, 1991) noted that these unusual abilities may be related to particular preoccupations or obsessions. Such abilities do not seem to be based just on memory skills; they may reflect other aspects of information processing (Pring et al., 1995).

In summary, general measures of intellectual functioning, such as IQ scores, are as stable and predictive in children with autistic spectrum disorders as in children with other developmental disorders, but this does not mean that these measures do not show individual and systematic variation over time. Because IQ scores provide limited information and there are complex implications of test selection across ages and developmental levels, IQ scores should not be considered a primary measure of outcome, though they may be one informative measure of the development of the children who participate in an intervention program. Specific cognitive goals, often including social, communicative, and adaptive domains, are necessary to evaluate progress effectively. Direct evaluations of academic skills are also important if children are learning to read or are participating in other academic activities.

THEORETICAL MODELS OF COGNITIVE DYSFUNCTION IN AUTISM

Various theoretical notions have been advanced to account for the cognitive difficulties encountered in autism. The "theory of mind" hypothesis proposes that individuals with autism are not able to perceive or understand the thoughts, feelings, or intentions of others; i.e., they lack a theory of mind and suffer from "mind blindness" (Leslie and Frith, 1987;

Leslie, 1992; Frith et al., 1994). Various experimental tasks and procedures used to investigate this capacity generally indicate that many somewhat more able (e.g., verbal) children with autism do indeed lack the capacity to infer mental states. This capacity is viewed as one aspect of a more general difficulty in "metarepresentation" (Leslie, 1987) that is presumed to be expressed in younger children by difficulties with understanding communicative gesture and joint attention (Baron-Cohen, 1991). While not all children with autistic spectrum disorders entirely lack a theory of mind (Klin et al., 1992), they may be impaired to some degree (Happe, 1994). There appear to be strong relationships between verbal ability and theory of mind capacities in autism (e.g., Ozonoff et al., 1991), though many language-impaired non-autistic children can normally acquire these skills (Frith et al., 1991). The theory of mind hypothesis has been a highly productive one in terms of generation of research, and in focusing increased attention on the social aspects of autism, including deficits in joint attention, communication, and pretense play (see Happe, 1995, for a summary). However, specific behaviors that evidence a deficit in theory of mind are not by themselves sufficient to yield a diagnosis of autism, which can be associated with other cognitive deficits. In addition, research in which theory of mind concepts were taught to individuals with autism did not result in general changes in social behavior, suggesting that links between theory of mind and sociability are not simple (Hadwin et al., 1997).

A second body of work has focused on deficits in executive functioning, that is, in forward planning and cognitive flexibility. Such deficits are reflected in difficulties with perseveration and lack of use of strategies (see Prior and Ozonoff, 1998). Tests such as the Wisconsin Card Sort (Heaton, 1981) and the Tower of Hanoi (Simon, 1975) have been used to document these difficulties. In preschool children, the data on executive functioning deficits are more limited. McEvoy and colleagues (1993) used tasks that required flexibility and response set shifting, and noted that younger children with autism tended to exhibit more errors in perseveration than either mentally or chronologically age-matched control children. More recently, others did not find that the executive functioning in preschoolers with autistic spectrum disorders differed from that in other children (Griffith et al., 1999; Green et al., 1995).

A third area of theoretical interest has centered on central coherence theory, in which the core difficulties in autism are viewed as arising from a basic impairment in observing meaning in whole arrays or contexts (Frith, 1996; Jarrold et al., 2000). As Frith (1996) has noted, it is likely that a number of separate cognitive deficits will be ultimately identified and related to the basic neurobiological abnormalities in autism.

Neuropsychological assessments are sometimes of help in documenting sensory-perceptual, psychomotor, memory, and other skills. The utility of more traditional neuropsychological assessment batteries in children, especially in young children, is more limited than for adults. Extensive neuropsychological assessments may not provide enough useful information to be cost-effective. However, selected instruments may be helpful in answering specific questions, particularly in more able children. Exploring a child's visual-motor skills or motor functioning can be of value for some children whose learning and adaptation appear to be hindered by deficits in these skills. (Motor and visual motor skills are discussed in detail in Chapter 8.)

ACADEMIC INSTRUCTION AND OUTCOMES

In addition to interventions that have been designed to improve intellectual performance (e.g., scores on IQ tests), there is a small literature on instructional strategies designed to promote the academic performance of young children with autism. Academic performance, for this discussion, refers to tasks related to traditional reading and mathematics skills. This literature consists primarily of single-subject design, quasi-experimental design, and descriptive observational research, rather than randomized clinical trials. The studies have usually included children with autism at the top of the age range covered in this report (i.e., ages 5-8), and the participant samples often include older children with autistic spectrum disorders as well. Notwithstanding these caveats, there is evidence that some young children with autistic spectrum disorders can acquire reading skills as a result of participation in instructional activities. There is very limited research on instructional approaches to promoting mathematics skills.

A range of instructional strategies have involved children with autistic spectrum disorders. In early research, Koegel and Rincover (1974) and Rincover and Koegel (1977) demonstrated that young children with autism could engage in academic tasks and respond to academic instruction as well in small-group instructional settings as they did in one-to-one instruction with an adult. Kamps and colleagues replicated and extended these findings on small-group instruction of academic tasks to a wider range of children within the autism spectrum and other developmental disabilities (Kamps et al., 1990; Kamps et al., 1992).

In another study, Kamps and colleagues (1991) first performed descriptive observational assessment of children with autism in a range of classroom settings. They used these data to identify the following commonly used instructional approaches:

1. Incorporate naturally occurring procedures into intervention groups across classrooms.
2. Include three to five students per group.

3. Use individual sets of materials for each student.
4. Use combination of verbal interaction (discussion format) and media.
5. Use five-minute rotations of media/concept presentation.
6. Use a minimum of three sets of materials to teach each concept.
7. Use frequent group (choral) responding.
8. Use fast-paced random responding.
9. Use serial responding—three to five quick responses per student.
10. Use frequent student-to-student interactions.

They then conducted a series of single-subject designs that demonstrated experimentally (with treatment fidelity measures documenting implementation) the relationship between the instructional measures and the children's performance on criterion-referenced assessments of academic tasks. This combination of instructional strategies (choral responding, student-to-student responding, rotation of materials, random student responding) was also found to be effective in teaching language concepts to elementary-aged children with autism in a later study (Kamps et al., 1994a). In their subsequent research, Kamps and colleagues (1994b) have examined the use of classwide peer tutoring (i.e., classmates provide instruction and practice to other classmates) with young children with autistic spectrum disorders. In a single-subject design study, these researchers found increased reading fluency and comprehension for children who received peer tutoring, as compared with those who received traditional reading instruction.

Other strategies have also appeared in the literature. Using an incidental teaching technique, McGee and colleagues (1986) embedded sight-word recognition tasks in toy play activities and found that two children with autism acquired sight-word recognition skills and generalized those skills to other settings. Cooperative learning groups are another instructional approach. Provided tutoring by peers, a group of children with autistic spectrum disorders practiced reading comprehension and planned an academic game; the children increased their academic engagement in reading (Kamps et al., 1995).

There is also some evidence that children with autism might benefit from computer-assisted instruction (CAI) in reading. Using a single-subject design, Chen and Bernard-Optiz (1993) compared delivery of academic tasks by an instructor or through a computer monitor and found higher performance and more interest from children in the CAI than the adult-delivered intervention. In a study conducted in Sweden, Heimann and colleagues (1995) used a CAI program and a traditional instructional approach to present lessons to students. Children with autism made significant gains in the CAI program (compared with traditional instruction), while typically developing children progressed similarly in both settings. These two studies suggest that a CAI format for presenting instruction to young children with autism may be useful, but the results are far from conclusive and require further study.

FROM RESEARCH TO PRACTICE

There is need for research on the development of more specific measures of important areas of outcome in cognition, including the acquisition and generalization of problem-solving and other cognitive skills in natural contexts (e.g., the classroom and the home) and the effects of these skills on families and other aspects of children's lives. There is also a need for research to define appropriate sequences of skills that should be taught through educational programs for young children with autistic spectrum disorders, as well as methods for selecting those sequences, while developing programs for individual children.

8

Sensory and Motor Development

Paucity of Evidence for Treatment / Therapy for Success

There are fewer empirical studies about sensory and motor development in children with autism than studies of other aspects of development. However, the evidence converges to confirm the existence of sensory and motor difficulties for many children with autism at some point in their development, although there is much variability in the specific symptoms or patterns expressed (Dawson and Watling, 2000). In this chapter, the terms "sensory" and "sensory-perceptual" are used to refer *Def.* to responses to basic sensations and perceptions, including touch, taste, sight, hearing, and smell. Because much of the research is based on parental reports or natural observation, the characterization of these behaviors as sensory-perceptual is based on inference, which, in the long run, must be tested.

Unusual sensory-perceptual reactions appear to be manifest in some children with autism as early as the first year of life (Baranek, 1999a; Dawson and Watling, 2000). These types of behaviors appear neither universal nor specific to the disorder of autism, and there are no longitudinal studies systematically documenting developmental trajectories of these behaviors from infancy through childhood. However, though not well understood, sensory processing and motor patterns may be related to other aberrant behaviors and core features of the disorder; thus, these patterns may have implications for early diagnosis and intervention.

CONSTRUCTS AND DEFICITS

Developmental Constructs

The majority of infants with autism attain basic motor milestones essentially "on time" (Johnson et al., 1992; Lord et al., 1997; Rapin, 1996a). Although parental report of motor delays in infants with autism was low (9%), reports of motor delays and clumsiness in more complex skills increased to 18 percent during the preschool and school years (Ohta et al., 1987).

Some recent evidence suggests that, based on parents' reports, sensory-perceptual abnormalities may be among some of the first signs of autism. Lack of responsiveness to certain sounds, hypersensitivity to the taste of foods, and insensitivities to pain are more commonly seen in infants with autism than in typical infants or infants with other developmental disorders (Hoshino et al., 1982). More recently, retrospective parents' reports of the presence of unusual sensory behaviors (e.g., strange response to sounds, atypical interest in visual stimuli, overexcitement when tickled, unusual visual behavior), and some play behaviors (e.g., play limited to hard objects), discriminated between children with autistic spectrum disorders and typical children during infant and toddler ages (Dahlgren and Gillberg, 1989; Gillberg et al., 1990).

Converging evidence, based on retrospective home video studies, demonstrates very early nonspecific sensory and motor difficulties in infants later diagnosed with autism. Stereotypic behaviors, under- and overreactions to auditory stimuli, unusual postures, and unstable visual attention were found to be characteristic of infants with autism, compared with those with other developmental disorders or with typical children. In addition, autistic symptoms observed during the first year persisted into the second year of life (Adrien et al., 1992, 1993). In another study, poor responsiveness to visual stimuli in the environment, excessive mouthing behaviors, decreased responsiveness to sound (e.g., name being called), and aversion to social touches were found to be characteristic of infants with autism. However, unusual motor posturing and repetitive motor behaviors were not more common in children with autism than in other children, and visual fixations, reduced level of affective range, and stereotyped object play were more generally characteristic of the group with other developmental disorders than of the children with autism, contrary to original hypotheses (Baranek, 1999b). Other researchers using retrospective videotape analyses have not found early sensorimotor abnormalities in children with autistic spectrum disorders (Mars et al., 1998; Osterling and Dawson, 1999; Werner et al., 2000).

Sensorimotor Deficits in Autism

Several recent studies comparing children with autism and children with other developmental disorders have concluded that the prototypical developmental profile for children with autism is one of motor skills that are relatively more advanced than social skills, even when all are delayed (DeMyer et al., 1972; Klin et al., 1992; Stone et al., 1999). Early hand-eye coordination significantly predicted later vocational skills and independent functioning, while earlier fine motor skills predicted later leisure skills (Martos-Perez and Fortea-Sevilla, 1993).

Although the basic motor skills of children with autism are often reported to be an area of relative strength, numerous studies also provide evidence that motor problems may sometimes be quite significant. Specific deficits have been reported, including in motor imitation, balance, coordination, finger-to-thumb opposition, speech articulation, and the presence of hypotonia. No significant differences were found in tactile perception or gait, beyond that accounted for by cognitive level (Jones and Prior, 1985; Rapin, 1996b; Stone et al., 1990).

Imitation skills have been a focus of study in autism. They have been consistently found to be impaired in children with autism, and deficits in imitation were found in more than 60 percent of a large longitudinal cohort (Rapin, 1996b). Imitation of body movements was more impaired than object imitation skills in young children with autism; imitation of body movements predicted later expressive language skills, and imitation of actions with objects was associated with later play skills (Stone et al., 1997). Specific gesture imitation was deficient in children with autistic spectrum disorders, although it did not account for all of the motor coordination deficits. Vocabulary size and accuracy of sign language in autistic children correlated highly with their performance on two measures of apraxia and with their fine motor age scores (Seal and Bonvillian, 1997). In addition, praxis deficits may also be present in children with autism during goal-directed motor tasks that do not require imitation (Hughes and Russel, 1993; Smith and Bryson, 1998). Deficits in oral-motor praxis, including poor range of movements, isolation of movement, and awkward execution, were also noted in children with autism given both verbal and imitative prompts (Adams, 1998; Rapin, 1996b)

Adolescents with Asperger's Disorder and high-functioning autism showed average to above average performance in simple motor tasks, but had impairments in skilled motor tasks (Minshew et al., 1997). Both groups showed similar problems with coordination (Ghaziuddin et al., 1994). the performance of children with autism on goal-directed motor tasks was better in purposeful contexts than in nonpurposeful conditions (Hughes and Russel, 1993; Rogers et al., 1996; Stone et al., 1997).

Muscle Tone, Postural Stability, and Motor Control

Although one study by Jones and Prior (1985) found no significant differences in muscle tone between older children with autism and mental-age-matched typical children, other researchers have reported such differences in children with autism spectrum disorders (Rapin, 1996b). Children with autism were posturally more unstable than typical children, and they were less sensitive to visually perceived environmental motion. They also displayed unusual reactions to vestibular tasks (Gepner et al., 1995; Kohen-Raz et al., 1992). Children with autism relied on proprioceptive feedback over visual feedback to modulate goal-directed motor actions, including reaching and placing objects under conditions that required adaptation to the displacement of a visual field by prisms. This finding might be indicative of a perceptual deficit resulting in poor visual control and visual sequential processing (Masterton and Biederman, 1983). Although vestibular mechanisms may be generally intact and postural responses adequate under some conditions, postural mechanisms may be more compromised in children with autism when integration of visual-proprioceptive, vestibular functions, and motor skills is required.

Prevalence of Atypical Sensory Responses and Motor Stereotypies

Standardized behavioral examinations demonstrated that the overwhelming majority of children with autistic spectrum disorders displayed atypical sensorimotor behaviors at some point during the toddler or preschool years, including both heightened sensitivities or reduced responsiveness across sensory modalities, and motility disturbances such as stereotypies (Ermer and Dunn, 1998; Kientz and Dunn, 1997; Rapin, 1996b). Unusual sensory and motor behaviors included but were not limited to failing to respond to sounds (81%), heightened sensitivity to loud noises (53%), watching hands or fingers (62%), and arm flapping (52%) (Volkmar et al., 1986). Hand-finger mannerisms, whole body mannerisms other than rocking, and unusual sensory interests, as recorded on the Autism Diagnostic Interview, discriminated children with autism from those with other developmental delays (Le Couteur et al., 1989; Lord et al., 1994). A pattern of atypical sensory modulation and motor behaviors, including rubbing surfaces, finger flicking, body rocking, and absence of responses to stimuli, was present in almost 60 percent of one cohort (in 15% to a severe degree) (Rapin, 1996b). This pattern similarly distinguished children with autistic spectrum disorders from children with other developmental disorders, even those with very low developmental levels (Adrien et al., 1987; Rapin, 1996b).

Some studies report pronounced individual differences and suggest subtypes based on patterns that include unusual sensory or motor behaviors, in addition to social and communicative differences (Eaves et al.,

1994; Greenspan and Wieder, 1997; Stone and Hogan, 1993; Wing and Gould, 1979). In general, attempts have not yet been made to replicate these findings across studies. However, the variability in motor and sensory processing symptoms in children with autism, like other domains of development, may be related to developmental factors such as age or developmental stage. For example, few stereotypies are reported by parents of very young children with autism. Repetitive behaviors and mannerisms became more common in the same children after age 3 (Cox et al., 1999; Lord, 1995; Stone et al., 1997). Others have found no differences in sensory manifestations across ages or autism severity levels in school-aged children with autism (Kientz and Dunn, 1997). Maturational factors may affect sensory responses differently at varying developmental periods in children with autism.

Sensory and Arousal Modulation

Some of the unusual sensory processing and motor patterns seen in autism have been thought to result from problems in arousal modulation or habituation that result in withdrawal, rejection, or lack of response to sensory stimuli. Both physiological overarousal to novel events and underarousal and slower rates of habituation have been reported in children with autism (Hutt et al., 1964; James and Barry, 1984; Kinsbourne, 1987; Kootz and Cohen, 1981; Kootz et al., 1982; Rimland, 1964; Zentall and Zentall, 1983). A pattern of sensory rejection of external stimuli was associated with higher levels of arousal on measures of blood pressure, heart rate, and peripheral vascular resistance in children with autism, which was greatest in lower functioning children; this finding was attributed to problems in filtering and modulating responses to novelty (Cohen and Johnson, 1977; Kootz et al., 1982). It has been theorized that unpredictable and complex tasks may increase arousal modulation difficulties in both social and nonsocial situations (Dawson and Lewy, 1989).

Some studies suggest that physiological abnormalities relate to the bizarre behavioral symptoms seen in children with autism, particularly the need to preserve sameness. The children may be more sensitive to the environment and may use behavioral strategies, such as avoiding environmental change and social interaction, as methods of reducing further disorganizing experiences. In particular, tactile hypersensitivies were found to be related to behavioral rigidities (Baranek et al., 1997). Other studies have found no evidence of overarousal, and some have found evidence of underarousal (James and Barry, 1980; Corona et al., 1998). The overall circadian regulation of cortisol production, a physiologic marker of response to stress, was not found to be significantly different in autistic children; however, a tendency toward cortisol hypersecretion during school hours was found, and it appeared to be an environmental stress response (Richdale and Prior, 1992).

Visual and Auditory Systems

The presence of unusual visual or auditory behaviors has been consistently reported in children with autism (Dahlgren and Gillberg, 1989; Gillberg et al., 1990). Even though visual-spatial skills (e.g., completing complex puzzles) are a relative strength, many children with autism demonstrate unusual visual-spatial behaviors, such as visual stereotypies, atypical interest in visual stimuli, or unusual visual gaze behavior. Many children with autism exhibit exaggerated sensitivity to common environmental noises, such as dishwashers, hairdryers, and garbage disposals. This hypersensitivity is also evident when children are in a busy or crowded area, such as an amusement park.

INTERVENTION TECHNIQUES

There is little rigorous research on intervention techniques for the sensory symptoms of children with autistic spectrum disorders. In general, the quality of research in the existing assessments of the efficacy of sensorimotor interventions for autistic spectrum disorders has been relatively strong in external validity and the selection and definition of samples (see Figure 1-2 in Chapter 1) in comparison with studies in other areas. Because this area is small, the few published studies that included random assignment represent a relatively high proportion of the literature. Criteria for internal validity, including the use of prospective methods and evaluation of blind procedures, were also met for a higher proportion of published studies in the sensorimotor area than any other area than communication (as shown in Figure 1-1 in Chapter 1), though, as in other areas, 50 percent of studies did not meet fairly minimal standards in this area (see Box 1-1 in Chapter 1). Studies that included measures of generalization were very rare (see Figure 1-3 in Chapter 1). The limited consideration of generalization is also of concern, but one that holds true, though to a lesser extent, for other areas of research. Overall, it is clear that high quality research can be done in this area, but that it is very rare, and many widely publicized treatments have not received careful, systematic study. Thus, the following discussion of these methods must be primarily descriptive (see Dawson and Watling [2000] and Goldstein [1999] for a recent review and commentary).

Sensory Integration Therapy

By focusing a child on play, sensory integration therapy emphasizes the neurological processing of sensory information as a foundation for learning of higher-level skills (Ayres, 1972). The goal is to improve subcortical (sensory integrative) somatosensory and vestibular functions by providing controlled sensory experiences to produce adaptive motor responses. The hypothesis is that, with these experiences, the nervous system better modulates, organizes, and integrates information from the environment, which in turn provides a foundation for further adaptive responses and higher-order learning. Other components of the classical sensory integration model include a child-centered approach, providing a just-right challenge (scaffolding) with progressively more sophisticated adaptive motor responses and engaging the child in meaningful and appropriate play interactions.

There is a paucity of research concerning sensory integration treatments in autism. In one retrospective study, children with autism who had average to hyperresponse patterns to sensory stimuli tended to have better outcomes from sensory integration therapy than did those with a hyporesponsive pattern (Ayres and Tickle, 1980). Recently, some children with autistic spectrum disorders studied prospectively during sensory integration therapy showed significant improvements in play and demonstrated less "non-engaged" play. Only one child had significant improvements with adult interactions, and none had improved peer interactions (Case-Smith and Bryan, 1999).

Other approaches based on sensory integration therapy include the "sensory diet," in which the environment is filled with sensory-based activities to satisfy a child's sensory needs. The "alert program'" (usually with higher-functioning individuals) combines sensory integration with a cognitive-behavioral approach to give a child additional strategies to improve arousal modulation. No empirical studies of these approaches were identified for children with autism or related populations.

Sensory stimulation techniques vary but usually involve passive sensory stimulation; they are incorporated within the broader sensory integration programs or used in isolation. The underlying proviso is that a given sensory experience may facilitate or inhibit the nervous system and produce behavioral changes, such as arousal modulation. Examples of this approach include "deep pressure" to provide calming input by massage or joint compression or using an apparatus such as a weighted vest. Vestibular stimulation, another example, is often used to modulate arousal, facilitate postural tone, or increase vocalizations. These interventions have also not yet been supported by empirical studies.

Auditory Integration Therapy

Auditory integration therapy for autism has received much media attention in recent years. Proponents of auditory integration therapy suggest that music can "massage" the middle ear (hair cells in the cochlea), reduce hypersensitivities and improve overall auditory processing ability. Two philosophical approaches to auditory integration therapy exist: Tomatis and Berard (the latter is more common in the United States). In both approaches, music is input through earphones with selected frequencies filtered out. Although improved sound modulation is one goal of treatment, other behaviors, including attention, arousal, language, and social skills, are also hypothesized to be enhanced. In children with learning disabilities given the Tomatis approach to therapy, no positive gains were noted in comparison with a placebo approach (Kershner et al., 1990). In a pilot study of the Berard auditory integration therapy method, children with autism demonstrated fewer auditory problems and aberrant behaviors than children who received no treatment, and there was no evidence of a reduction in sound sensitivity after treatment (Rimland and Edelson, 1995).

More recent studies noted no differences in responses to auditory integration therapy in children with autism or controls (Best and Miln, 1997; Gillberg et al., 1997). One study noted significant but equal amounts of improvement on all measures for children with autism and for a control group who listened to music (Bettison, 1996). In that study, treatment effects were not related to auditory integration therapy but may have been related to general auditory desensitization or simply to placebo effects. A recent review noted that for children treated with auditory integration therapy, objective electrophysiologic measures failed to demonstrate differences in hearing sensitivity between children with autism and controls, thereby questioning the overall premise of auditory integration therapy (Gravel, 1994).

A variation of auditory training programs applied to autism includes acoustic intervention: by using human voice instead of music, in theory, the stimulation alternatively challenges and relaxes the middle ear muscles to improve speech perception (Porges, 1998). Although acoustic intervention is currently undergoing some scientific experiments in children with autism, no empirical data are available to support this approach.

In summary, auditory integration therapy has received more balanced investigation than has any other sensory approach to intervention, but in general studies have not supported either its theoretical basis or the specificity of its effectiveness.

Vision Therapy

A variety of visual therapies (including oculomotor exercises, colored filters, i.e., Irlen lenses, and ambient prism lenses) have been used with children with autism in attempts to improve visual processing or visual-spatial perception. There are no empirical studies regarding the efficacy of the use of Irlen lenses or oculomotor therapies specifically in children with autism. Prism lenses are purported to produce more stable visual perception and improved behavior or performance by shifting the field of vision through an angular displacement of 1 to 5 degrees (base up or base down). Only one study investigated the use of prism lenses in children with autism, almost half of whom also had strabismus (Kaplan et al., 1996; Kaplan et al., 1998). Results indicated some short-term positive behavioral effects with less improvement at later follow-up. Performance on orientation and visual-spatial tasks was not significantly different between conditions. As with auditory integration therapy, studies have not provided clear support for either its theoretical or its empirical basis.

SENSORY AND MOTOR DEVELOPMENT AND EDUCATIONAL PROGRAMMING

Motor development plays an important role in learning—young children typically use motor skills to explore the environment, engage in social interactions, engage in physical activities, and develop basic academic skills, such as handwriting. Unusual sensory responses (e.g., hypo- and hyperresponses, preoccupations with sensory features of objects, paradoxical responses to sensory stimuli) are common concerns in children with autistic spectrum disorders. Given that most educational environments involve many sensory demands (e.g., the noise level of a regular classroom) and stimuli that may seem unpredictable (e.g., fire alarms), interventions may need to address the individualized sensory processing needs of children who have such difficulties. However, exactly how this should be done has not been addressed in scientific investigations.

Praxis is an area of particular interest; several studies note that both younger and older children with autism may demonstrate difficulties with aspects of motor planning. These difficulties are exaggerated in tasks that require execution of a social imitation, either motor or object related, but they may also be present in non-imitated, simple, goal-directed motor tasks. Such difficulties would affect many daily aspects of early childhood, such as games and sports (e.g., throwing a ball, riding a bicycle), crafts (e.g., using scissors), and performing gestures. Although it is possible that the formulation of motor plans is deficient in children with autistic spectrum disorders, it is also possible that simple motor planning is intact but that the use of externally guided visual feedback is diminished. If so, the quality of motor control, postural stability, and effective sequencing would all be affected.

Classical sensory integration therapy provides a child-centered and playful approach that is often appealing to even the most unmotivated or disengaged child. In the case of the other treatments based on sensory integration, a child must be able to tolerate various sensory applications or physical manipulations. For some children with autism, structure and repetition are positive factors whereas passive application of stimulation may not be.

In general, interventions based in natural environments that teach or attempt to change behaviors in the context in which they would typically occur have been found to be most effective (see Chapters 10, 11, and 12). Thus, ways of helping children with autistic spectrum disorders cope with unusual sensory responses within their ordinary environments or modifications to these environments might be expected to have more effects than would specific, one-to-one therapies (e.g., individual sensory integration treatment or individual sensory diets) or group treatments with unique stimuli (e.g., auditory integration therapy). This is particularly likely, given the many questions that arise about the theoretical bases for these sensory interventions. However, even if the results of sensory approaches are not specific, children may benefit from techniques that elicit social engagement, attention, and the use of toys and other materials at home and within classroom settings.

FROM RESEARCH TO PRACTICE

There is no consistent evidence that sensory-based treatments have specific effects; in many cases, the theories underlying such approaches have not withstood careful consideration (Dawson and Watling, 2000; Goldstein, 1999). A lack of empirical data does not necessarily demonstrate that a treatment is ineffective, but only that efficacy has not been objectively demonstrated (Rogers, 1998). There were some nonspecific positive findings in the studies of interventions reviewed, and there is a need to address at least functional aspects of motor difficulties, particularly as they affect social, adaptive, and academic functioning.

Future research in these areas needs to include well controlled, systematic studies of effectiveness. Only such research can answer not only what is effective, but with whom and under what conditions. Because most sensory- and motor-oriented interventions augment comprehensive educational programs, it is critical to know whether or not these approaches facilitate progress as additional interventions or hinder it by taking away valuable instruction time. It will be important to investigate to what degree specific treatments can be altered to fit an inclusive education model while still retaining their essential therapeutic elements and purported benefits. Comparisons of such treatments need to be systematically investigated in future efficacy research.

9

Adaptive Behaviors

BACKGROUND

Adaptive behavior refers to a person's social responsibility and independent performance of daily activities. One of the first publications of intervention with a child with autism was an application of then new behavior analysis procedures to the problem of teaching a young boy to wear his glasses (Wolf et al., 1964). Since that time, behavioral interventions have been applied to building a wide variety of adaptive skills with varied populations of children and adults with developmental disabilities.

Toilet training and associated issues have been the focus of a broad range of early behavioral interventions. For example, behavioral interventions for toilet training have been based upon principles of both operant and classical conditioning (Azrin et al., 1971; Azrin and Foxx, 1971, 1974; Mahoney et al., 1971). The problem of nocturnal enuresis has been addressed with urine detection devices that serve to awaken children so they can get out of bed when wet, as well as with systematic behavioral procedures involving practice, rewards, and clean-up requirements (Hansen, 1979). Interventions have also been developed and evaluated to address encopresis (O'Brien et al., 1986).

Adaptive skills are usually taught through a process that begins with a task analysis, which breaks down a skill into its component parts (Haring and Kennedy, 1988). Instruction then proceeds through a process of teaching each component skill in small steps, and ultimately chaining the sequence of behaviors together. This approach has been evaluated through

103

the use of single-subject designs across many applications. A number of interventions have demonstrated that adolescents or adults with autism can be taught purchasing skills and other community living skills, such as ordering food in a restaurant (Haring et al., 1987). However, most applications of instruction in community living skills have been developed for children and adults with mental retardation. Daily living skills targeted have ranged from appropriate mealtime behaviors (O'Brien et al., 1972; Wilson et al., 1984), to eating in public places (van den Pol et al., 1981). Proactive approaches to promoting community access include instruction in clothing selection skills (Nutter and Reid, 1978), pedestrian safety (Page et al., 1976), nondisruptive bus riding (Neef et al., 1978), vending machine use (Sprague and Horner, 1984), and coin summation (Lowe and Cuvo, 1976; Miller et al., 1977; Trace et al., 1977). Additionally, procedures for teaching leisure skills have targeted independent walking (Gruber et al., 1979) and soccer (Luyben et al., 1986).

Another area of widespread application is found in investigations on the remediation of eating disorders. For example, various approaches have been documented as effective in controlling rumination, or persistent vomiting (Kohlenberg, 1970; Rast et al., 1981; Sajwaj et al., 1974), pica (Mace and Knight, 1986), and diurnal bruxism (Blount et al., 1982). Skill-based interventions have been aimed at promoting oral hygiene (Singh et al., 1982) and food acceptance by a child with a gastrointestinal feeding tube (Riordan et al., 1984). A simple procedure of requiring placement of the fork down between bites was shown to reduce the pacing and quantity of food intake by obese children (Epstein et al., 1976).

Behavioral medicine, or the application of behavioral principles to medical problems, includes an experimental case study with a child with autism, whose seizure disorder was ameliorated by a technique involving interruption early in an identified behavioral chain (Zlutnick et al., 1975). Procedures that have been developed for teaching generalized toy play skills to children with mental retardation should translate to use with children with autism (Haring, 1985). Of additional relevance to children with autism are applications of operant procedures to the assessment of hearing in persons with profound mental retardation (Woolcock and Alferink, 1982), as well as the assessment of visual acuity in nonverbal children (Macht, 1971; Newsom and Simon, 1977).

The bulk of the literature cited above was derived from research in which the subjects were described as having mental retardation, and early applications of behavior analysis were conducted primarily with adults in residential settings. However, it is likely that some of the subjects in these early applications also had undiagnosed autism. There was little attention to diagnostic precision in the early behavioral research, though the brief subject descriptions provided often mentioned behaviors com-

that's quite an assumption

monly associated with autism (e.g., self-stimulatory behaviors, self-injury, echolalia, etc.).

There has been an assumption that behavioral interventions documented as effective in teaching adaptive skills to adults with developmental disabilities will apply equally well to child populations. For example, although written as a commercial self-help guide for toilet training normal children, the procedures in *Toilet Training in Less Than a Day* (Azrin and Foxx, 1974) involved rather minor modifications of the procedures previously developed for adults in residential settings (Foxx and Azrin, 1973). Similarly, faded guidance procedures that were evaluated for teaching adolescents with disabilities to brush their teeth (Horner and Keilitz, 1975) bear marked resemblance to procedures described for teaching independent daily living skills to toddlers with autism (McGee et al., 1999). In other words, many procedures for teaching self-care skills to adults with mental retardation have been extended to younger children. Yet there have been relatively few direct empirical tests of adaptations to young children with autism. This situation may partially result from the lack of emphasis on publishing systematic replications, as well as from the cost- and time-efficiency of simply using existing procedures that prove to be clinically effective.

DEVELOPMENTAL CONSTRUCTS AND THEORY

An issue of considerable relevance to understanding autism is whether associated impairments are simply developmental delays or developmental irregularities. Pertinent to this question are findings that suggest that children with autism show uneven patterns between developmental domains (Burack and Volkmar, 1992). Depending on how broadly developmental domains are defined, children with autism have also been found to show scatter within certain domains. Specifically, children with autism were found to show deviant and not just delayed development in the social and communication domains represented on the Vineland Adaptive Behavior Scales (Sparrow et al., 1984), although not necessarily in domains of daily living skills that can be more easily taught (VanMeter et al., 1997).

Several studies have queried parents on the developmental progress of their children with autism. In a survey of 100 parents of children with autism between the ages of 9 and 39 years, 48 percent of the children were still wearing diapers after the age of 3 (Dalrymple and Ruble, 1992). In addition, 25 percent of the parents surveyed reported past or present problems with their children eliminating in inappropriate places, such as outdoors or in the bedroom. Although the average reported age for urine control was 3.85 years and 3.26 for bowel continence, 22 percent of children and adults with autism continued to wet their beds at night. Five adults, at an average age of 24, were still not toilet-trained. Health-related problems included constipation (13%) and severe diarrhea (13%). Behavioral issues included stuffing toilets with paper or items, continual flushing, smearing of feces, playing in toilets, and refusing to use a variety of toilets.

A substantially larger sample of children and adults with autism (1,442) was compared with people with mental retardation (24,048) in terms of their motor, daily living, social, and academic skills, using a database of the New York Developmental Disabilities Information System (Jacobson and Ackerman, 1990). Comparisons were made between age groupings of children (5-12 years of age), adolescents (13-21), and adults (21-35 years). Although the children with autism functioned at higher levels than did the children who had mental retardation without autism, these differences were no longer evident when examining the skill levels of adolescents. The advantage of children with autism was reversed in the groups of adults, with people with autism functioning at lower levels in academic and social skills although they continued to maintain an advantage in gross motor skills.

FORM OF ADAPTIVE BEHAVIORS

A subjective account of 25 Irish mothers of children with autism between the ages of 3 to 14 years of age presents an array of perceived difficulties in the day-to-day management of a child with autism and the consequent effects on the child's family (O'Moore, 1978). Among the difficulties reported were parental problems in managing housework, due to the extra time needed to feed, toilet train, dress, engage, and put their children with autism to sleep. Parents often felt uncertain regarding effective behavior management techniques, and most reported the use (although not approval) of corporal punishment. Both the children with autism and the overall family had restricted levels of contact in the community, due to either the fear or reality of increased behavioral problems during community outings. Another study compared the breastfeeding patterns of children with autism with a matched group of children with more general developmental delays, and findings were that the mothers of children with autism reported no significant differences in the offering or acceptance of breastfeeding (Burd et al., 1988).

Although the range of adaptive behaviors can be defined more or less broadly, virtually all categorizations include a focus on self-care skills related to basic biological functions. In addition to issues of toileting, eating and sleep disorders are frequently reported in children with autism (Richdale and Prior, 1995). However, most research on irregularities in biological functions has been based on parental report, which can be influenced by the behavioral characteristics of autism. For example, in a study of sleep patterns of 22 children with autism, aged 3 through 22, parental responses on a questionnaire were compared to direct measurement of ambulatory behavior with an actigraphic device (Hering et al., 1999). More than half of the parents reported that their children had sleep problems, including difficulty in getting to sleep, early morning awakening, and multiple night arousals. However, direct measures of non-sleep activity suggested fewer differences between the children with autism and a comparison group of normally developing children. Children with autism, on average, tended to awaken approximately 1 hour earlier than the typical children. The investigators speculated that parents of children with autism might be more sensitive to sleep issues with their children. Other studies have reported rates of sleep disorders that equal or exceed those of children with other developmental disorders (Dahlgren and Gillberg, 1989, Thompson et al., 1994).

Other adaptive behaviors pertain to home and community living skills, with applicable areas for young children including dressing, grooming, and safety-related behaviors. A broader perspective on adaptive behaviors may expand to school-related skills, such as academic behaviors (McGee et al., 1986), play skills (Haring, 1985), or overall engagement with work materials or the social environment (McGee et al., 1997). For example, children with autism often need to be directly taught how to request help when facing challenging tasks (Carr and Durand, 1985). Finally, most views of adaptive behaviors also cover domains of language, social, and motor skills, which are reviewed in other sections of this report.

Not surprisingly, there are correlations between levels of adaptive skills and intellectual ability (Carter et al., 1996). For example, lower cognitive and verbal levels are highly correlated with age of accomplishment of bowel and urine training (Dalrymple and Ruble, 1992). However, successful use of toileting intervention procedures based on operant and classical conditioning may be more related to physical maturity and social responsiveness than to cognitive level (Azrin and Foxx, 1971). There is some evidence that levels of adaptive behavior predict future independent functioning more accurately than measures of cognitive or academic functioning (Carter et al., 1996).

ASSESSING ADAPTIVE BEHAVIOR AND PLANNING FOR INTERVENTION

The aim of assessment of adaptive skills is to obtain a measure of the child's typical functioning in familiar environments such as the home and the school. Such measures provide clinicians with an estimate of the degree to which the child can meet the demands of daily life and respond appropriately to environmental demands. A significant discrepancy between IQ and the level of adaptive skills or between observed performance in a highly structured situation and in more typical situations indicates that an explicit focus on acquisition and generalization of adaptive skills is important. For a diagnosis of mental retardation, assessment of adaptive level is required.

Assessment of adaptive functioning is particularly important for children with autism for several reasons. First, measures of a child's typical patterns of functioning in familiar and representative environments, such as the home and the school, can be obtained. Assessment of adaptive skills provides a measure of a child's ability to generalize teaching across settings; given the nature of the cognitive difficulties in generalization in autistic spectrum disorders, such assessments are especially important. As with other children with developmental difficulties, acquisition of basic capacities for communication, socialization, and daily living skills are important determinants of outcome. Significant discrepancies, for example, between performance in a highly structured setting and in less structured settings, or between intellectual skills and adaptive abilities, indicate the importance of including an explicit focus on teaching such skills and encouraging their generalization across settings. Adaptive skills may be in marked contrast to a child's higher ability to perform in one-on-one teaching situations or in highly structured behavioral programs.

Second, assessment of adaptive behaviors can be used to target areas for skills acquisition. Third, there is some suggestion that relatively typical patterns of performance in autistic spectrum disorders can be identified and that some aspects of adaptive assessment (e.g., of social skills) can contribute to a diagnostic evaluation (Carter et al., 1998; Loveland and Kelley, 1991). This can be especially important in high-functioning children, in whom IQ scores may not reflect the ability to function independently in natural environments. Fourth, assessment of adaptive skills, as well as of intellectual ability, is essential in documenting the prevalence of associated mental retardation and, thus, eligibility for some services (Sparrow, 1997).

The Vineland Adaptive Behavior Scales (Sparrow et al., 1984) are the most widely used instruments to assess adaptive skills (Harris and Handleman, 1994). The Vineland assesses capacities for self-sufficiency in various domains such as communication (receptive, expressive and written language), daily living skills (personal, domestic and community skills), socialization (interpersonal relationships, play and leisure time and coping skills), and motor skills (gross and fine). A semistructured interview is administered to a parent or other primary caregiver; the Vineland is available in four editions: a survey form to be used primarily as a diagnostic and classification tool for normal to low-functioning children or adults, an expanded form for use in the development of individual education or rehabilitative planning, a classroom edition to be used by teachers, and a preschool form. Particularly for children with autistic spectrum disorders, the expanded or preschool form may be most helpful since it can be used to derive goals that can be directly translated in an individualized education plan (IEP) (Volkmar et al., 1993). In addition, several research studies have delineated Vineland profiles that are relatively specific to autism (Loveland and Kelley, 1991; Volkmar et al., 1987). This unique pattern consists of relative strengths in the areas of daily living and motor skills and significant deficits in the areas of socialization and, to a lesser extent, communication. Supplementary Vineland norms for autistic individuals are also now available (Carter et al., 1998).

Other instruments with subtests for assessing adaptive behaviors of very young children include the Brigance Inventory of Early Development (Brigance, 1978), the Early Learning Accomplishment Profiles (ELAP) (Glover et al., 1988), the Scales of Independent Behavior-Revised (Bruininks et al., 1996), the AAMD Adaptive Behavior Scales (Lambert et al., 1993) and the Learning Accomplishments Profile (LAP) (Sanford and Zelman, 1981). The Developmental Play Assessment Instrument (DAP) (Lifter et al., 1993) provides an evaluation of the quality of a child's toy play skills in relation to those of typically developing children, which can help to target the play level and actions that a child with autism needs to learn.

A primary consideration in selection of adaptive living goals should be the skills needed to promote age-appropriate independence in community living, so that a child can have access to the larger social community. For example, children who are not toilet trained are not likely to have access to classrooms with normally developing peers, and parents of children who present safety risks will be less likely to take them on community outings. Classrooms and home programs may begin with an early focus on independent daily living skills early in a child's intervention program, because progress in these areas is more easily achieved than in the more challenging domains that are diagnostic descriptors of autism (i.e., social, communication, and behavior). Thus, parents and teachers are pleased when their child makes tangible early progress, and they may be motivated to collaborate on more challenging tasks.

There are a number of published manuals that provide practical guidance on the design of instructional programs, along with detailed task analyses of various daily living and self-help skills. For example, *Steps to Independence* (Baker and Brightman, 1997) provides easy-to-follow guidelines for teaching skills such as shoe tying or hand washing. Behavioral intervention techniques can readily be used to teach adaptive skills (e.g., Ando, 1977; Azrin and Foxx, 1974; McGee et al., 1994), and self-care and other skills can be systematically taught (McClannahan et al., 1990), although it is critical that generalization of teaching be accomplished. Other

Good Sources

methods for teaching adaptive skills include peer tutoring for teaching community living skills (Blew et al., 1985). Additional resources for commonly encountered difficulties include books written for parents on eating disorders (Kedesdy and Budd, 1998) and sleep problems (Durand, 1998).

The books listed above, and similar resources, include suggestions for data collection during baseline planning, implementation and follow-up. The complexity of the data collection procedure will vary according to the challenge of the skills being taught (e.g., bladder control training usually requires very detailed records on successes and failures, while teaching a child to throw away their paper towels may be monitored with one probe). Ongoing assessment typically requires at least some baseline measurement, as well as periodic measures of skill performance during and after intervention. In order to assess the level of independence achieved for a given skill, it is necessary to evaluate the performance of the new skill in conditions of decreasing prompting.

INTERVENTION STUDIES

With the exception of research in communication and socialization, there are surprisingly few studies that directly evaluate the use of behavioral interventions to teach adaptive skills to young children with autism. However, there is a body of research on reinforcer potency that is directly relevant to efforts to use behavioral techniques for skill instruction with children with autism. Thus, constant versus varied reinforcement procedures were compared in a study of the learning patterns of three boys with autism, aged 6 to 8 years (Egel, 1981). Using a reversal design, it was shown that correct responding and on-task behavior during a receptive picture identification task increased using varied reinforcers. Satiation for food reinforcers was problematic in conditions in which constant reinforcers were used. Similar results were found in comparing sensory versus edible reinforcers; rewards having sensory properties were found to be less vulnerable to satiation (Rincover and Newsom, 1985). The importance of systematic reinforcer assessment has been demonstrated to improve learning and attention to task, and the use of highly potent rewards on learning tasks has also been shown to yield positive side-effects in terms of substantial drops in levels of maladaptive behaviors (Mason et al., 1989).

A Japanese study reported the first early application of operant conditioning procedures to the toilet training of five 6- to 9-year-old boys with profound mental retardation and "clear signs of autism" (Ando, 1977). Like other early behavioral interventions, aversive consequences (i.e., intense spankings) were prominent, and results of an evaluation using an ABAB reversal design showed inconsistent effectiveness. In contrast, a toilet-training manual written for parents of typical children (Azrin and Foxx, 1974) can be adapted relatively easily for use with children with autism (McGee et al., 1994) and may be more successful.

Peer tutoring was shown to be effective in teaching community living skills to two boys with autism, aged 5 and 8 years, who lived in a residential school (Blew et al., 1985). Single-subject, multiple baseline designs were used to evaluate the effectiveness of treatment components across intervention settings. Skills targeted included buying ice cream at a restaurant, checking out a book at the library, buying an item at the store, and crossing the street. Modeling by typical peers was not sufficient to produce acquisition, but both boys learned all target skills when the peers provided direct instruction.

Physical exercise has been found to decrease self-stimulatory behavior in children with autism, as well as to yield collateral changes in appropriate ball play, academic responding, on-task behavior, and ratings of general interest in school activities (Kern et al., 1982). With physician approval for each of three children (ranging in age from 4 to 7 years, plus three older children/adolescents), mildly strenuous jogging sessions were begun at about 5 minutes per day and gradually increased to 20 minutes per day. In a follow-up study with three children with autism, one of whom was age 7 (and two who were 9), it was shown that mild exercise (e.g., playing ball) had virtually no impact on self-stimulatory behavior (Kern et al., 1984), but positive benefits were replicated in conditions of vigorous physical exercise.

An assessment of the grooming of children and adolescents with autism may have some application for either skill assessment or for measuring the quality of care provided to children with autism. Quality of care was the central focus of a multiple baseline study of 12 children with autism, and the single-subject multiple baseline was nested within multiple baselines across residential settings (McClannahan et al., 1990). Thus, a grooming checklist (e.g., fingernails clean, hands washed, clothing unstained, etc.) was administered to children residing in one large residential placement, and major improvements were documented when these children were transitioned into community-based group homes that provided more individualized care. Further, when feedback on grooming details was regularly provided to group home teaching parents, the children's appearance improved to a level similar to that of children with autism who lived at home with their families. Applications to young children with autism would likely involve both skill building and assistance to parents in managing the responsibilities of caring for their children with autism. Appearance becomes a practical concern as more and more children with autism are gaining access to inclusion with typical peers, and attractiveness may influence their receipt of social bids.

When adaptive skills are broadly defined, there are a number of applications reported for young children with autism. Thus, a variety of approaches have been used to increase engagement both with adult-directed tasks and in general attending to the environment; these include delayed contingency management (Dunlap et al., 1987), self-management techniques (Callahan and Rademacher, 1998), and strategies for environmental arrangement (McGee et al., 1991). Inclusion and interaction with typically developing peers (Kohler et al., 1997) have been used as a medium for increasing engagement and play skills (Strain et al., 1994; Wolfberg and Schuler, 1993). Now that children with autism are beginning to gain access to regular preschool and elementary school settings, there has developed a need for teaching them to transition smoothly across educational activities (Venn et al., in press).

As discussed earlier, there have been demonstrations that young children with autism can be taught to increase the frequency and variety of their play skills. Such interventions are expedited by pivotal response training and by targeting the skills displayed by typical children at similar developmental levels (Lifter et al., 1993, Stahmer, 1995). Young children with autism have been taught peer imitation abilities in the course of Follow the Leader games (Carr and Darcy, 1990).

INTERVENTION PROGRAMS

Virtually all of the well-known programs for young children with autism provide instruction in adaptive daily living skills, which often form the basis for development of communication, social, and even motor skills. Several published program outcome evaluations have specifically examined progress in adaptive skills as measured on the Vineland. For example, 20 children with autism enrolled in the Douglass Developmental Disabilities Center showed better-than-average progress in all four domains assessed on the Vineland, but the most marked progress was in communication skills (Harris et al., 1995). Similarly, the Walden family program component was shown to yield developmental gains that were larger than those expected in typical development (i.e., greater than one month gain per month), and children's progress at home corresponded closely to the intervention priorities selected by parents (McGee et al., 1993).

The Vineland results were less robust for children treated in the Young Autism Project at the University of California at Los Angeles, although the children were described as "indistinguishable from average children in adaptive behavior" (McEachin et al., 1993). The nine children with best outcomes in the 1987 treatment outcome study (Lovaas, 1987) were reassessed at an average age of 11.5 years. Although their overall composite scores were within the normal range, five of the nine had marginal or clinically significant scores in one more domain. Results were also mixed in two systematic replications. The May Institute's home-based program reported that 31 percent of the children receiving intervention made at least one month gain in social age per month of intervention, and 12 of 13 showed progress on another measure of adaptive behavior (Anderson et al., 1987). A more recent systematic replication compared intensive and nonintensive interventions (Smith et al., 2000). A randomly assigned group of children with autism and pervasive developmental disorder–not otherwise specified (PDD-NOS) received intervention for approximately 25 hours per week for at least 1 year, while a similar group of children received 5 hours per week of parent training over a period of 3 to 9 months. Vineland results showed no significant differences between the two intervention groups. Chapter 12 presents more information on various model programs' approaches to intervention in the area of adaptive behavior.

Unless a specific focus on generalization of skills is included in the intervention program, it is possible for children with autistic spectrum disorders to learn skills in a highly context-dependent way. That is, even though a child is capable of some particular behavior, it occurs only in highly familiar and structured contexts. Thus, results of adaptive behavior assessments have been less robust in some cases (McEachin et al., 1993; Smith et al., 2000). However, inclusion of an explicit home-based program has been reported to be associated with progress on measures of adaptive behavior (Anderson et al., 1987).

FROM RESEARCH TO PRACTICE

Because there is a substantial literature about teaching adaptive skills to children with developmental disabilities, one question is how often and when strategies that are effective with other populations of young children are applicable to children with autism. Skills requiring specific adaptations peculiar to autism may benefit from direct investigation (e.g., severely restricted eating patterns, toileting rituals, etc.). A major adaptation that is often required is the improved assessment and selection of reinforcers so that the child with autism will be motivated to develop new adaptive skills (Mason et al., 1989). Questions of generalization are important but need to be considered for a particular behavior and child. For example, a child might learn a very structured tooth brushing routine that is tied to a specific kind of toothbrush—which may be very helpful even if not very generalizable. However, only using a particular kind of toilet would be much more problematic.

Overall, results are encouraging regarding the potential for teaching a range of adaptive behaviors to young children with autism. However, the variability of results in this area are of crucial importance in considering each individual child's preparation for independent functioning in everyday situations. Interpretations of positive findings on one measure cannot be used to make blanket declarations of "recovery" from autism.

There is substantial data, particularly with older children and adolescents, that behavioral interventions, particularly those with attention to generalization, can result in improved adaptive behavior in children with autism. Adaptive goals are a significant part of both home and school programs for young children. Although general measures of adaptive behavior may indicate increasing discrepancies from normal development with age, the potential to make practical changes in the lives of children with autistic spectrum disorders through teaching specific skills that have value in the community (e.g., toilet training, pedestrian safety) or for the child (e.g., dressing) is very clear, not only for their own sakes, but also because of the increased opportunities they offer. Teaching adaptive skills, with specific plans for generalization across settings, is an important educational objective for every young child with autism. This objective includes teaching behaviors that can be accomplished within a year and that are anticipated to affect a child's participation in education, the community, and family life.

At this time, the greatest challenge is one of translation from research to practice. Often teachers do not know what is available in the research literature. User-friendly manuals and training resources are needed to ensure the availability of effective instruction in adaptive skills for young children with autistic spectrum disorders to teachers and parents.

10

Problem Behaviors

Problem behaviors of children with autistic spectrum disorders—and other children—are among the most challenging and stressful issues faced by schools and parents in their efforts to provide appropriate educational programs. Problem behaviors such as property destruction, physical aggression, self-injury, and tantrums are major barriers to effective social and educational development (Horner et al., 2000; Riechle, 1990). Such behaviors put young children at risk for exclusion and isolation from social, educational, family, and community activities (Sprague and Rian, 1993). In addition, problem behaviors may place an onerous burden on families, particularly as children grow from preschool into school age (Bristol et al., 1993). Concerns about school behavior problems led to new standards and procedures for discipline, student suspension, and expulsion in the 1997 amendments to the Individuals with Disabilities Education Act (IDEA, 1997; Department of Education IDEA regulations, March, 1999). Specifically, the regulations include provisions for the use of functional behavioral assessments and positive behavioral interventions and support.

The definition of problem behaviors depends on whether the behaviors are considered from the perspective of a child with an autistic spectrum disorder or from the perspective of a parent or teacher. From a child's perspective, problem behaviors include the inability to understand demands of a classroom or a parent and to communicate his or her needs and wants, severe difficulty in initiating and maintaining social interactions and relationships, confusion about the effects and consequences of many of his or her behaviors, and engagement in restrictive and repetitive behaviors and interests that may limit the child's ability to learn and to fit in with peers. From a teacher's or parent's perspective, problem behaviors include lack of compliance with or disruption of classroom routines, tantrums, destruction of property, and aggression against self or others.

The research evidence reviewed suggests that educational interventions that do not address the development of positive and prosocial behaviors (the potential for problems from the child's perspective) will be unsuccessful in the long-term elimination of problem behaviors from others' perspectives. Chapters 5 through 9 discuss the essential elements (communication, social interaction, cognitive features, adaptive behaviors, and sensorimotor skills) needed for effective, appropriate educational programs for children with autistic spectrum disorders to address core problem behaviors. These elements are discussed in this chapter only as they are directly relevant, but they are essential in any consideration of problem behaviors.

Different literatures provide the empirical base for interventions for problem behaviors in young children with autistic spectrum disorders: data from comprehensive programs; single-subject design studies that address specific problem behaviors; psychopharmacological studies that assess the safety and efficacy of pharmacological interventions on both global and specific problem behaviors; the growing literature on the neurobiology of autism; and legal reviews of the 1997 IDEA provisions related to autism (Turnbull et al., 1999) and findings in due process and court cases involving children with autism (Mandlawitz, 1999).

Many studies evaluated were not designed specifically for this committee's interest in children with autistic spectrum disorders from birth to age 8. Some degree of latitude was taken in generalizing from findings in studies of older children and children with autistic spectrum disorders if the behaviors of interest and the behavioral principles involved would be expected to apply to children with autistic spectrum disorders in the birth to eight-year-old age group. The focus of this chapter is on the most commonly reported problem behaviors of young children with autistic spectrum disorders. As reported by Horner and colleagues (2000), this focus represents only a selected subset of a large literature that primarily involves treatment of severe, dangerous, chronic cases of behavior problems, mostly in older children. An extensive review of medical studies is beyond the charge of the committee, but selected results are included here as relevant.

NATURE AND PERSISTENCE OF BEHAVIOR PROBLEMS

Most behavior problems displayed by young children with autistic spectrum disorders are "normal" behaviors in that they may be observed, albeit at lower frequency, in typically developing children. However, in autistic spectrum disorders, the intensity, frequency, duration, or persistence of the behaviors distinguish them from similar behaviors of normally developing young children. For example, several studies have shown that self-injurious and stereotyped behaviors occur in normal infants and then decrease, although they do not necessarily disappear, as locomotion develops in these children during the first and second years of life (Thelen, 1979; Werry et al., 1983). Body-rocking occurred in 19 percent and head-banging in 5 percent of one sample of typical children ages 3 to 6 years (Sallustro and Atwell, 1978). Similar levels of body-rocking have also been reported in normal college students (Berkson et al., 1999; Rafaeli-Mor et al., 1999).

These repetitive movements and potentially self-injurious behaviors are presumed to serve some function in normal development (Berkson and Tupa, 2000). Berkson and Tupa (2000) found that about 5 percent of toddlers with developmental disabilities (including autistic spectrum disorders) engaged in head-banging, about the same percentage as reported for typically developing children. The incidence of head-banging with actual injuries in the group with developmental disabilities is presumably greater: between 1.3 and 3.3 percent, depending on the type of measurement. This rate is similar to the prevalence rates reported for older, non-institutionalized populations of children and adults with developmental disabilities (Rojahn, 1986; Griffin et al., 1987).

Understanding what causes these problem behaviors to emerge during the early childhood and preschool years, what maintains them, and what evokes their moment-to-moment expression holds promise of treatments to prevent them from becoming permanent and abnormal (Berkson and Tupa, 2000). Once moderate to severe problem behaviors become an established part of a child's repertoire, unlike children with typical development, children with autistic spectrum disorders or other disabilities do not usually outgrow them. Without appropriate intervention, these behaviors persist and worsen (Schroeder et al., 1986).

With increasing research into the neurobiology and genetics of autism, the organicity of some aspects of behavior in autism is becoming clearer. For example, Lewis (1996) has attempted to explicate some of the underlying neurobiology of repetitive or stereotyped behaviors. Other researchers (Symons et al., 1999) have demonstrated that the locus of some types of self-injurious behavior might show different genetic patterns. Thompson and his colleagues (Thompson et al., 1995) argue that self-injurious behaviors have consequences other than social changes. For example, some self injurious behaviors involve the release of neurochemical transmitters and modulators that subsequently bind to specific brain receptors. By using sophisticated methods that study form, location, and intensity of self-injury, these researchers conclude that some people may learn to self-injure in body locations that produce the greatest neuro-chemical release and receptor binding (Symons and Thompson, 1997; Thompson et al., 1995). Schroeder and colleagues (Schroeder et al., 1995) reviewed animal studies of neonatal dopamine depletion relevant to the prevention of self-injurious behavior and recently used an animal model to demonstrate primary prevention of self-injurious behavior using oper-ant conditioning (Tessel et al., 1995).

Epidemiological studies indicate that a substantial minority of all young children, with or without developmental disorders, exhibit prob-lem behaviors at some time that might benefit from intervention (McDougal and Hiralall, 1998; Emerson, 1995). Young children with poor social skills or limited communication, including children with autistic spectrum disorders, are especially at risk for such problems (Borthwick-Duffy, 1996; Koegel et al., 1992). An analysis of five reviews of interven-tion approaches for the general population of individuals with develop-mental disabilities, conducted between 1976 and 2000, found that the target behaviors most often addressed in intervention studies were ag-gression, destruction of property, disruption of activities, self-injury, ste-reotypic behavior, and inappropriate verbal behavior (Horner et al., 2000). Horner and colleagues' review of applied behavior analysis studies that were published since 1990 and restricted to children with autism between birth and age 8 found that the behavior problems most frequently ad-dressed were tantrums, including crying and shouting (six studies); ag-gression (four studies); stereotypic behavior (two studies); and self-injury (one study).

PREVENTIVE INTERVENTIONS

Appropriate Individualized Educational Plans

No single intervention has been shown to deal effectively with prob-lem behaviors for all children with autism. However, there is an increas-ing consensus among developmental, psychosocial, applied behavior, and legal experts that prevention of such problems should be a primary focus, particularly during the early childhood and preschool years (Berkson and Tupa, 2000; Schroeder at al., 1986; Dunlap and Fox, 1999; Schopler et al., 1995). There is also a growing consensus that the most effective form of prevention of problem behaviors is the provision and implementation of an appropriate individualized education plan (IEP) based on proven in-terventions that have some scientific evidence supporting their value. The New York State Department of Health panel that developed *The Clini-cal Practice Guideline for Autism/Pervasive Developmental Disorders* (New York State Department of Health, 1999) went further: "The use of an ineffective assessment or intervention method [is] a type of indirect harm if its use supplants an effective assessment or intervention method that the child might have otherwise received."

The 1999 U.S. Department of Education Regulations for the 1997 Amendments to the Individuals with Disabilities Education Act (IDEA) provides for scientifically supported interventions (see, e.g., 20 U.S.C., 1400©(4)). The IDEA further requires that schools must confirm, before any changes of placement due to a behavioral problem can be considered, that the IEP and placement were appropriate and that special education services, supplementary aids and services, and behavior intervention strategies were provided consistent with the IEP and placement (34 C.F.R., 300.523, 1999; Turnbull et al., 1999). In short, before assessing deficiencies in a child who is misbehaving, it is critical to assess the adequacy of the intervention program the child is receiving. IDEA requires that interventions must show demonstrable benefits to be continued. A number of different approaches to interventions for problem behaviors meet the IDEA criteria for scientific support and benefit to individual children.

Comprehensive Treatment Programs

Various comprehensive treatment programs encompass a number of different philosophical and theoretical positions, ranging from strict operant discrimination learning (Lovaas, 1987) to broader applied behavior analysis programs (Harris et al., 1991; Fenske et al., 1985; Kohler et al., 1996), and those that highlight incidental learning (McGee et al., 1999) to more developmentally oriented programs (Schopler et al., 1995; Rogers and Lewis, 1989; Greenspan and Wieder, 1997). Comprehensive programs generally require 25 or more hours of active student engagement per week for 2 or more years and attempt to change the clinical course of an autistic spectrum disorder, including prevention of or reduction in problem behaviors. Reviews of eight model comprehensive early intervention programs (Dawson and Osterling, 1997; Harris, 1998; Rogers, 1998), taken together, identified several critical elements common to many programs that addressed problem behaviors (a more extensive review of program elements is provided in Chapter 12):

- curriculum content that emphasized direct instruction in basic skill domains and abilities: attending to elements of the environment that are essential for learning, especially to social stimuli; imitating others; comprehending and using language; playing appropriately with toys; and interacting socially with others;
- highly supportive teaching environments and generalization strategies;
- predictability and routine;
- a functional approach to problem behaviors;

- plans for transition from preschool classroom;
- family involvement;
- identification of and intervention with children with autistic spectrum disorders as early as possible;
- working with young children in small teacher-to-child ratios, often one to one in the early stages; and
- active engagement of the child from 20-40 hours per week

Programs that do not include the above features should be reevaluated for suitability before discussing the "suitability" of the disruptive student.

Applied Behavior Analysis

Forty years of single-subject-design research testifies to the efficacy of time-limited, focused applied behavior analysis methods in reducing or eliminating specific problem behaviors and in teaching new skills to children and adults with autism or other developmental disorders. Initially, applied behavior analysis procedures were reactive, focusing on consequences of behaviors after they occurred, and interventions of this type continue to play an important role (see below). However, there has been increasing attention to intervention procedures that focus on what to do before or between bouts of problem behaviors (Carr et al., 1999a; Carr et al., 1994; Schroeder et al., 1986). Since the mid-1980s, applied behavior analysis prevention strategies have focused on antecedent conditions in the child or the environment that set the stage for or trigger the problem behaviors (Carr et al., 1999c); some of these are discussed below in the sections on positive behavioral interventions and supports and functional behavioral assessment.

Interventions that involve changing schedules, modifying curricula, rearranging the physical setting, and changing social groupings have been shown to decrease the likelihood of problem behaviors (Carr et al., 1998; Dunlap et al., 1991, 1993). This has been termed a "shift from viewing behavior support as a process by which individuals were changed to fit environments, to one in which environments are changed to fit the behavior patterns of people in the environments" (Horner et al., 2000:6). Many of these antecedent interventions have been implemented for years by some of the comprehensive, developmental programs described earlier (Mesibov et al., 2000). The broader interest in these antecedents now brings the methodological rigor of applied behavior analysis to directly test the causal relationship between these environmental changes and skill acquisition and reduction in problem behaviors.

Communication Training

The research evidence regarding the role that communication deficits play in the emergence, remediation, and maintenance of reduction in problem behaviors is particularly robust across researchers and methodologies (Carr et al., 1999b; Koegel et al., 1992; Schroeder et al., 1986; Wacker et al., 1998). Interventions that deal with receptive communication—for example, use of schedules, work systems, and task organization (Schopler et al., 1995) that assist students in understanding classroom routines and requirements as well as effective instruction in spontaneous, expressive communication (Schreibman et al., 2000; Wacker et al., 1996)—are needed to prevent problems and maintain reductions in those behaviors (see a more detailed discussion of functional behavioral analysis below).

AFTER THE FACT: TEACHING ALTERNATIVE BEHAVIORS

Consequence-Based Approaches

Most empirically based intervention approaches designed to reduce or eliminate specific, identified problem behaviors have an applied behavior analysis theoretical base. From this perspective, problem behavior is viewed as being composed of two environmental features and one behavior or set of behaviors that have a temporal relationship. Antecedents, the first feature, are events (e.g., mother tells child it is time to go to the store) or internal conditions (e.g., child feels pain or hunger) that occur before a problem behavior (e.g., running around the house instead of going to the door) occurs. Consequences are events that follow the behavior and that either increase the likelihood that the behavior (running) will be repeated (reinforcement, e.g., mother makes a game of chasing the child to get him into the car) or decrease the likelihood that the behavior will be repeated (e.g., mother shouts "No!" when the child runs away).

One approach rewards behaviors that are incompatible with the problem behavior: for example, rewarding a child for taking his mother's hand to go to the car so the child cannot engage in running away at the same time (differential reinforcement of alternative behavior). Another approach removes the consequences of the behavior that are thought to be reinforcing (extinction-based procedures). For example, when adult attention is thought to be a reinforcer for the child's running away from his mother, an extinction-based strategy would be for the mother to demonstrate no attention to the running, provided the child is safe. In the example above, for some children, the parent's shouted "No!" functions as a punisher and reduces running behavior. For others, the parent's attention is rewarding and increases the likelihood that the child will "play" the running away game.

Pivotal Response Training

Interventions that enable children to have some control over their environments, such as task preferences, choice-making, reinforcement selection, and self-monitoring, can all contribute to reductions in problem behaviors (Fisher et al., 1992; Koegel et al., 1987; Koegel et al., 1992; McGee and Daly, 1999; Newman et al., 1997). Teaching of pivotal skills, such as increasing motivation or self-management, can produce improvement in wide areas of functioning that might otherwise require hundreds or even thousands of discrete trials for the child to master individually (Koegel et al., 1999).

Functional Behavioral Assessment

Functional assessment is the process of identifying the variables that reliably predict and maintain problem behaviors (Horner and Carr, 1997). Although such an approach is implied in much of the research described above, a more formal approach to functional behavioral assessment has evolved in the literature and is required in certain cases of discipline under IDEA (see, for example 34 C.F.R., 300.520, 1999). The functional behavioral assessment process typically involves:

- identifying the problem behavior(s);
- developing hypotheses about the antecedents and consequences likely to trigger or support the problem behavior;
- testing the hypotheses; and
- designing an intervention, based on the conclusions of the assessment, in which antecedents or consequences are altered and the child's behavior is monitored.

Initial identification of the problem behavior and development of ideas of why it occurs often involve interviews with people in the child's classroom or family and direct observation of the behavior in its usual context. Testing hypotheses may occur through additional observation or, less frequently, through systematic functional analysis in which the environment is manipulated to test the hypotheses (Carr et al., 1994; Dunlap et al., 1993; Iwata et al., 1982; Repp and Horner, 1999). Such analyses are expected to lead to the identification and training of alternative, appropriate behaviors that can give the child the same "payoff" he or she received from the previous problem behavior. In several reviews, as many as 16 different motives for problem behavior were identified (Reiss and Havercamp, 1997; Carr et al., 1999c), and more may exist, including multiple functions for some behaviors. Prominent among these functions or motives for problem behaviors are a means of communicating needs and wants effectively; social attention; social avoidance; escape from difficult or boring tasks or other aversive situations; access to desirable tangible items and preferred activities; and generation of sensory reinforcement in the form of auditory, visual, tactile, olfactory, and gustatory stimulation.

For example, problem behaviors such as self-injury or destructive behavior often produce reliable changes in the child's environment. A child bites his hand and learns over time that the parent or teacher may approach and soothe the child, provide a favorite toy, or "rescue" the child from a difficult situation. For young children with autistic spectrum disorders, who often have little or no ability to communicate using conventional words or even gestures, hand-biting, tantrums, or other disruptive behaviors become effective ways for the child to convey a message. Wacker and colleagues (Wacker et al., 1998) trained parents, in their homes, to conduct functional analyses of the problem behaviors of their young children (between 1 and 6 years of age) with autism or other severe developmental disorders. Parents were then trained to use a functional communication system with their children, based on their own child's existing communication skills. Children learned from their parents verbal or nonverbal appropriate means (such as signing "please" to gain parent attention, "break" to get a brief break from tasks, or "help" to obtain parent assistance in completing a task) to obtain what they wanted. After treatment, aberrant behavior had decreased an average 87 percent across the range of children, and appropriate social behavior had increased an average 69 percent. The intervention took approximately 10 minutes per day. On a parent-rating measure of acceptability (from 1 = not acceptable to 7 = very acceptable), the average overall acceptability was 6.35.

Three findings on functional behavioral assessment emerge from 10 reviews of research from 1988 to 2000 on problem behaviors in persons with developmental disabilities including autistic spectrum disorders (Horner et al., 2000): (1) functional behavioral assessment results more frequently in the choice of positive rather than punishment procedures than do problem reduction strategies not starting from functional behavioral assessment; (2) interventions developed from functional behavioral assessment information are more likely to result in significant reductions in problem behaviors than those that do not systematically assess the function of the problem behavior; and (3) in some cases in which functional behavioral assessments were conducted, interventions were designed that were not consistent with or may even have been contraindicated by the assessment information (Scotti et al., 1996). Thus, additional training of how to implement results of a functional behavioral assessment in home and school interventions is often needed to link the assessments with interventions.

Positive Behavioral Interventions and Supports

IDEA requires that if a child's behavior impedes his or her learning or the learning of others, the IEP team must consider, if appropriate, strategies, including positive behavioral interventions, strategies, and supports to address that behavior (20 U.S.C., 1414 (d)(3)(B)(i), 1999; 34 C.F.R., 300.346(a)(2)(i), 1999. "Positive behavioral interventions and supports" describes an approach to deal with a child's impeding behavior that focuses on the remediation of deficient contexts (i.e., environmental conditions and behavioral repertoires) that are confirmed by functional behavioral assessment to be the source of the problem (Carr et al., 1999a). An expanded definition of this proactive rather than reactive process brings together four interrelated components that draw on aspects of many of the interventions described above. Positive behavioral interventions and supports include (Turnbull et al., 1999):

1. systems change (e.g., the process of considering, modifying, or substantially changing an agency's policies, procedures, practices, personnel, organization, environment, or funding);
2. environmental alterations (including building on a child's strengths and preferences, connecting the child with community supports, increasing the quality of the student's physical environment, making environmental alterations, such as changing when or for how long an activity occurs or introducing a schedule for the student, and making instructional accommodations for the student);
3. skill instruction, consisting of instruction for both the student and those who interact with him or her on appropriate academic, independent living, or other skills; teaching the student alternative behaviors and adaptive behaviors that reduce or ameliorate the impeding behaviors; and teaching skills to those involved with the student regarding communication with the student, development of social relationships, problem solving, and appropriate responses to the student's impeding behaviors; and
4. behavioral consequences (so that impeding behaviors are eliminated or minimized and appropriate behaviors are established and increased).

The expected outcomes from positive behavioral interventions and supports are increases in positive behavior, decreases in problem behavior, and improvements in life-style (Horner et al., 1990). This includes the expectation of systems change, including changes in the behaviors of others in the environment and broad environmental reorganization and restructuring. Many of these features are implemented as standard practice in the comprehensive or focused behavioral programs reviewed above and in Chapter 12. The concept of positive behavioral interventions and supports represents a theoretical, scientific, and legal attempt to bring all aspects of these successful, positive interventions to bear on resolving behavior problems in children with autism or other disorders.

A total of 366 outcomes of positive behavioral interventions and supports were examined in a detailed review of applied behavioral analysis studies of persons with autistic spectrum disorders (10%), mental retardation (about 50%), or combined diagnoses of retardation and autism, frequently accompanied by additional diagnoses (e.g., seizure disorder, brain damage; about 40%) (Carr et al., 1999a). These outcomes included 168 outcomes for children from birth to age 12; they addressed problems of aggression, self-injurious behavior, property destruction, tantrums, and combinations of problem behaviors. The success rate (90% or greater reduction in problem behavior from baseline levels) across pooled outcomes was generally within 5 points of 50 percent of individuals, regardless of the type of intervention. Good maintenance rates were observed for a substantial majority of outcomes (68.7%, 63.6%, and 71.4% for 1-5 months, 6-12 months, and 13-24 months, respectively). Males and females scored equivalent successes.

A similar review of a differently defined, overlapping data set (Horner et al., 2000) concluded that the available interventions are reasonably effective at reducing problem behaviors of persons with developmental disabilities, including autistic spectrum disorders. Reductions of 80 percent or greater were reported in one-half to two-thirds of the comparisons. Some reductions of 90 percent or greater were reported for individuals with all diagnostic labels and all classes of problem behaviors. The lowest success rate (23.5 percent) was for interventions that targeted sensory functions, compared with approximately 60 percent success rates for interventions based on functional behavioral assessments that identified other functions of problem behaviors (e.g., attention, escape, tangible, or multiple types).

A review of applied behavioral analysis interventions specifically for children with autistic spectrum disorders from birth to age 8 (Horner et al., 2000) addressed problems of tantrums, aggression, stereotypy, and self-injury. This targeted review found, for 37 comparisons, mean rates of reduction in problem behaviors of 85 percent (with a median reduction level of 93.2% and a mode of 100%). Fifty-nine percent of the comparisons recorded problem behavior reductions of 90 percent or greater, and 68 percent of the comparisons reported reductions of 80 percent or greater. The mean length of maintenance (assessed in 57% of studies; rates maintained within 15% of initial outcome levels) was 12 weeks, with the longest assessment occurring at one year after intervention (Koegel et al., 1998).

Though these are very positive findings, evaluating studies, and their results, requires cognizance of the prevailing scientific trend, adopted by many journal editors, that favors publication of studies that report successful, rather than unsuccessful, interventions. Thus, the results summarized above, represented as percentages of published comparisons, represent possible outcomes when these procedures are carefully implemented and progress monitored; they do not reflect the number of unsuccessful interventions, which are not reported. As described above, research concerning problem behaviors in individuals with developmental disabilities has generally been strong and plentiful. However, there are relatively few studies directly addressing issues for young children with autistic spectrum disorders. In many cases, interventions that were successful with other populations may be appropriate for young children with autistic spectrum disorders (Wolery and Garfinkle, 2000). Studies testing this assumption with appropriately described and diagnosed children are crucial before it can be accepted. Using the guidelines established by this committee, published research concerning positive behavior approaches to young children was relatively strong in measurement of generalizability and in internal and external validity (see Figures 1-1, 1-2, and 1-3 in Chapter 1). Limitations in the existing studies are not due to a generally poor quality of research, but to changes (and differences) in standards of reporting and research designs in applied behavior analysis and those of the more general, educational and clinical guidelines for treatment evaluation (see Chapter 1). These limitations in these studies were particularly apparent in the selection and description of subjects, random assignment to treatment conditions, and independence of evaluation. As for other areas, these limitations also related to differences in the contexts in which methods were developed. For behavioral interventions that addressed such targets as dangerous self-injury in institutionalized adolescents with profound mental retardation, random assignment, accurate diagnosis, and independence of evaluation may have been of less concern than developing an immediately implementable effective individualized program. However, in order to evaluate treatments for milder difficulties in young children with autistic spectrum disorders, provision of standard, descriptive information about subject selection, subject characteristics and other aspects of research design is crucial in determining what approaches will be most effective for which children.

With these caveats in mind, consistent findings across reviews of published studies indicate several conclusions about current positive behavioral interventions and supports:

- effectiveness in significantly reducing (and maintaining reduction of) problem behaviors in at least one-half, if not more, of all applied behavioral analysis studies of problem behaviors in children with autistic spectrum and related disorders;
- doubled effectiveness when functional behavioral assessments were used to determine what reliably predicted and maintained the behavior before undertaking the intervention, that is, what function that behavior served for the child;
- ability to be effectively carried out in community settings by the children's usual caregivers, although effective treatment data for the most difficult cases generally involved specialized personnel in less typical settings;
- minimal effectiveness (fewer than one-fourth of the cases) in reducing behavior problems that prior functional behavioral analysis indicated were maintained by sensory input; and
- increased problem behavior for a small percentage of outcomes studied (6-8%).

These conclusions are particularly important because such interventions must be considered, under IDEA, if a child's behavior impedes his or her learning or the learning of others.

OTHER INTERVENTIONS

IDEA contains what has been termed a "rebuttable presumption" (Turnbull et al., 1999) in favor of using positive behavioral interventions and supports in cases of "impeding behavior." This presumption (having legal weight) can be refuted by evidence to the contrary, but positive behavioral interventions and supports is the only intervention strategy specifically required for consideration by IDEA; other strategies may be considered. If positive behavioral interventions and supports is seen as a rebuttable assumption, it means that an IEP team can consider other intervention strategies only in comparison with positive behavioral interventions and supports and must have adequate cause for adopting a different strategy. Evidence for the efficacy of positive behavioral interventions and supports (presented above), although encouraging, also indicates that current positive behavioral interventions and supports strategies, as presently implemented, may be ineffective or only minimally effective for up to one-third of all problem behaviors and for up to three-quarters of those problem behaviors maintained by sensory input. In these cases, different or additional strategies may be required, after first considering positive behavioral interventions and supports.

Physically Intrusive or Physically Aversive Procedures

In an analysis of 102 interventions included in an overall review of positive behavioral interventions and supports (Carr et al., 1999a), about one-half were associated with the use of extinction (removing or preventing the occurrence of whatever has been found to reinforce and increase the problem behavior) and one-half with the use of seven different punishment procedures: verbal reprimand, forced compliance, response cost, overcorrection, timeout, brief restraint (physically interrupting the response and preventing its recurrence), and water mist (one case, considered highly intrusive and aversive). Although research indicates that reinforcement-based procedures are often not as effective in eliminating severe problem behaviors as quickly as are punishment-based procedures (Iwata et al., 1982), punishment-based procedures can also cause undesirable side effects, such as the child avoiding the punisher.

The increase in efficacy of positive interventions, when based on functional behavioral analysis, reduces the need for punishment-based procedures (Neef and Iwata, 1994). When a behavior is not maintained by social reinforcement, however, it may be difficult to treat effectively with reinforcement-based procedures only (Iwata et al., 1994). Suppression of competing problem behaviors may sometimes be needed before reinforcement of functional alternative behaviors can be effective (Pelios et al., 1999). In any case, there is agreement (New York State Department of Health, 1999) that physically intrusive measures (e.g., response interruption, holding, or physical redirection) should only be used after positive measures have failed and only as a temporary part of a broader intervention plan to teach appropriate behaviors. The use of physical aversives such as hitting, spanking, or slapping is not recommended.

Medications to Reduce Behavior Problems

Although a comprehensive review of medications and medical interventions is beyond the scope of this report, because of the widespread use of psychoactive medications, they are addressed briefly as they relate to problem behaviors in young children with autistic spectrum disorders. Psychoactive medications alter the chemical make-up of the central nervous system and affect mental functioning or behavior. Most were developed to treat a variety of psychiatric and neurological conditions other than autistic spectrum disorders; all may have benefits, side effects, and toxicity (Aman and Langworthy, 2000; Gordon, 2000; King, 2000; and McDougle et al., 2000). There are currently no medications that effectively treat the core symptoms of autism, but there are medications that can reduce problematic symptoms and some that play critical roles in severe, even life-threatening situations, such as self-injurious behavior.

Just as autism coexists with mental retardation, autistic spectrum disorders may coexist with treatable psychiatric and neurological disorders (Tuchman, 2000). Treatment of such diagnosed disorders will not cure autism, but can, in some cases, enable a child to remain in less restrictive community placements and enhance the child's ability to benefit from educational interventions (Cohen and Volkmar, 1997). Medications have been shown in some instances to enhance and to be enhanced by systematic, individualized behavioral intervention programs (Durand, 1982; Symons and Thompson, 1997).

More than 100 articles have been published on the use of psychoactive medications for autistic spectrum disorders. A more limited number of published reports include double-blind, placebo-controlled studies with young children with autism. Double-blind studies of haloperidol (Cohen et al., 1980; Campbell et al., 1982; Anderson et al., 1984,1989), naltrexone (Campbell et al., 1990; Bouvard et al., 1995; Kolmen et al., 1997; Willemsen-Swinkels et al., 1995, 1996), clonidine (Fankhauser et al., 1992; Jaselskis et al., 1992), and fenfluramine (Stern et al., 1990) included young children with autistic spectrum disorders, some as young as 2 years of age. In addition, newer medications, including selective serotonin uptake inhibitors, atypical neuroleptics, other antidepressants, and stimulant medications such as methylphenidate, have been studied, although most not yet in double-blind studies. A double-blind, placebo-controlled study of Risperidone™ was completed in adults (McDougle et al., 2000), and a study in children is presently under way in the National Institute of Mental Health Research Units for Pediatric Psychopharmacology (NIMH RUPPs).

The key findings from the published studies include:

- Haloperidol was effective in reducing aggression and agitation and had mixed results for improving learning with long-term users, but it carries significant risk of involuntary muscular movements (dyskinesias).
- Naltrexone-treated groups showed less irritability and hyperactivity than placebo groups on some measures, particularly global ratings, did not differ from placebo groups on others, and showed increases in particular problem behaviors in some instances.
- Clonidine-treated subjects showed improvements in hyperarousal but reported increased drowsiness, decreased activity, they showed increasing tolerance when used to treat attention deficit disorders.
- Risperidone shows promise in treating aggression and agitation with less concern about the development of dyskinesias than for the older neuroleptics.
- Open trials of serotonin selective uptake inhibitors have shown promise in treating stereotypic or perseverative behavior, possibly because of effects on anxiety.

- Stimulants may affect sleep and growth in developing children and, in some cases, may worsen autistic symptoms, especially self-stimulation behaviors.
- Secretin-treated children did not differ from placebo-treated children.
- Functional behavioral assessment to determine the function(s) of the problem behaviors increases the likelihood of choosing the correct medication and behavioral interventions.

Research is under way to predict responders and nonresponders to medication and to determine which children will benefit from behavioral treatment alone and what combinations of medication and behavioral treatment are most effective. Many parents also treat their children with nonprescription drugs and nutritional supplements. These agents have received even less study than prescription drugs, and their assessment is beyond the scope of this report. Several psychotropic medications have appeared to result in improvements for some patients but make others worse. Since medication is often instituted in a crisis, the possibility that it is actively contributing to deterioration is often not considered. Children's responses to medication must be monitored very carefully.

Children with autistic spectrum disorders are also at increased risk for certain medical conditions, notably seizure disorders. From one-fourth to one-third of people with autism are expected to develop seizure disorders sometime in their lifetime (Bristol et al., 1996; Kanner, 2000; Tuchman, 2000). School personnel need training in recognizing the symptoms of seizures and other medical problems and in monitoring the effects of medications over time. Although technically outside the scope of the educational program, it is important that educators and parents be informed of the importance of quality medical care and both the potential value and the possible problems of pharmacological intervention.

Except in unusual medical circumstances, medications are usually not considered first-line interventions for behavior problems in young children, but an exception, for example, would be behavioral manifestations of seizure disorder. Because young children are developing and learning, it is essential that both positive outcomes and unintended side effects of medications for behavioral problems are considered and that cognitive as well as behavioral effects are monitored if a decision is made to use medication. In addition to a functional behavioral analysis of the problem behavior, medication for behavioral intervention should be based on knowledge of medical pathology, psychosocial and environmental conditions, health status, current medications, history, previous intervention, and parental concerns and desires (New York State Department of Health, 1999).

A new generation of rational drug design will be based on emerging findings concerning the neurobiology of behaviors in autism. Future research offers the possibility of developing or refining medications based on the specific mechanisms that maintain problem behaviors in children with autism and related disorders. The new field of pharmacogenomics goes farther by hoping ultimately to match medications to genetic profiles for individual patients.

Other Interventions to Reduce Behavior Problems

Although there are some effective interventions to address sensory aspects of behavior problems, e.g., substituting appropriate sources of kinesthetic, visual, auditory, or olfactory stimulation for aberrant ones (Favell et al., 1982), there is a pressing need for more basic and applied research in this area. Interventions such as relaxation training (Groden et al., 1998) and physical exercise (Quill et al., 1989; Kern et al., 1984), appropriately adapted for young children, are also promising avenues for stress reduction and concomitant decreases in problem behaviors.

FROM RESEARCH TO PRACTICE

Problem behaviors such as property destruction, physical aggression, self-injury, stereotypy, and tantrums put young children at risk for exclusion from social, educational, family, and community activities. Serious behavior problems occur in a minority of young children with autistic spectrum disorders, but they are costly financially, socially, and academically to children, their families, and their classmates. The concept of problem behaviors in autism varies depending on whether the problem is defined in terms of the child's needs or the effect of the behavior on the home or classroom environment. Both research evidence and clinical judgment agree that the primary approach to problem behaviors in young children should be prevention by providing the child with the skills needed to effectively deal with the physical, academic, social, and sensory aspects of his family's school, preschool, early childhood, or community environment.

The foundation of prevention of problem behaviors is an appropriate and fully implemented IEP. Critical elements of effective, comprehensive educational programs and of focused, problem-specific applied behavior analysis programs, identified for young children with autistic spectrum disorders, need further independent replication, direct comparison of different treatment approaches, and clinical trials of methods that have proven effective in what Rogers (1998) notes as the clinical equivalent of "open trials." Broader implementation and evaluation of functional behavioral assessment and positive behavioral interventions and supports should lead to an expanded array of effective strategies for the majority of problem behaviors. More rigorous evaluation of existing medications and development of new medications based on burgeoning knowledge of the neuroscience of autism is likely to add new tools to the armamentarium.

IDEA requires benefits from interventions, presumes in favor of positive interventions, disallows those that do not produce benefits, and authorizes a wide range of beneficial interventions without preferring any particular ones. Although the interventions discussed in this chapter have shown evidence of accelerating the child's development and reducing behavior problems, none attains the strict research standards for replicated, randomly assigned, controlled, long-term comparison studies (Bristol et al., 1996).

Education is at heart an enterprise that must be informed by science, and it should stimulate hypotheses, case studies, and descriptive research to identify promising approaches for further rigorous study. As Greenspan (1999) points out, researchers, clinical practitioners, and consumers will need to work together to refine existing methods and develop new approaches. Joint efforts of federal, state, and local agencies will be needed to stimulate and fund longitudinal sites sharing common measures and a common database to address the daunting questions of which treatments are most effective for reducing behavior problems for which children. In the meantime, researchers, educators, and parents should not ignore testable, not yet fully assessed methods or measures that hold promise for reducing problem behaviors in children with autistic spectrum disorders. IDEA sets up perhaps the most practical and in some ways the most difficult challenge—that of generating a functional analysis of each child's behavior to fashion an individualized program that will enable the child to progress and to participate in the academic and social life of family, school, and community.

11

Instructional Strategies

This chapter provides a brief introduction to instructional strategies for young children with autistic spectrum disorders. In Chapter 12 we discuss ten representative comprehensive programs. Many instructional strategies summarized in Chapter 11 are used by most of those programs.

TYPES OF INSTRUCTIONAL STRATEGIES

Behavioral Strategies

Teaching New Behaviors

The continuum of behavioral teaching approaches has been carefully described (Anderson and Romanczyk, 1999; Prizant and Wetherby, 1998; Schreibman, 2000). Behavioral strategies take various approaches to the concepts of discrete trials, massed trials, naturalistic behavior, and peer mediation.

A discrete trial is defined as a set of acts that includes a stimulus or antecedent, a behavior, and a consequence. Differences in the delivery of a discrete trial (e.g., selecting different settings for the trials) mark different uses and styles of behavioral teaching.

Massed trials (see, e.g., Lovaas et al., 1981) are adult-directed (adult leads, child responds) teaching episodes in which a child responds to a teacher or to environmental instructions (antecedents). Consequences, or reinforcers, are not necessarily related to the child's activity or action. Each skill being taught is initially repeated several times in succession.

Naturalistic behavioral strategies are forms of discrete-trial teaching in which the child's own motives or behavior initiate the instruction and lead to a reinforcing event ("natural reinforcer"). These approaches are more child-centered than massed trial teaching, in that children's motivations, interests, favored activities, and choices figure strongly in the teaching. Two examples of naturalistic strategies are pivotal response training and incidental teaching.

Incidental teaching consists of a chain of prespecified child-tutor interactions. The interactions involve materials that are highly preferred by the child, prompting and shaping techniques embedded in natural contexts, and child-initiated ("natural") interactions. Incidental teaching has been demonstrated, with replication, to be an effective technique for increasing language learning in both typical children (Hart and Risley, 1975) and in children with autism (McGee et al., 1983, 1999).

In pivotal response training (Koegel et al., 1999), certain behaviors are seen as central to wide areas of functioning. Changing these pivotal behaviors is thought to change other associated behaviors without specifically targeting the associated behaviors. Pivotal response techniques include child choice, reinforcement, and correcting behaviors.

Peer-mediated strategies (e.g., Strain and Kohler, 1998) also demonstrate a naturalistic application of behavioral teaching. The typical peers of a child with an autistic spectrum disorder are instructed in a more adult-centered, mass-trial approach, while children with autistic spectrum disorders are taught by their peers in a more child-centered, naturalistic type of approach.

Decreasing or Altering Existing Behaviors

These strategies may include aversive approaches, functional analysis, differential reinforcement of other behaviors, extinction, antecedent manipulation, and combinations of these strategies (Dunlap et al., 1994. Aversive approaches involve administration of an aversive stimulus, or punisher, which, according to behavioral terminology, is an event to which a person responds by escaping or avoiding the stimulus. When an aversive stimulus is used as a consequence in the antecedent-behavior-consequence chain, the frequency of the behavior decreases over time. Mildly aversive approaches are commonly used with all children (e.g., saying "no"), but most strategies aimed at decreasing the frequency of unwanted behaviors currently emphasize the use of positive reinforcement strategies, which reward a child for performing more appropriate behaviors in place of the unwanted behaviors. In order to plan an effective intervention, one needs to know what current reinforcing consequences (both positive and negative reinforcers) are maintaining the unwanted behavior. This requires a functional analysis of behavior.

Def. A functional analysis of a behavior is an assessment procedure that yields an understanding of how the unwanted behavior functions for a child—what needs the child is addressing through the use of the behavior (what reinforcements are maintaining it). This evaluation involves interviews and observations to develop a hypothesis about the functions of the behavior and then controlled manipulations to test the hypotheses. Detailed procedures for performing a functional assessment of behavior are available to practitioners (O'Neill et al., 1990).

Def. The approach generally referred to as differential reinforcement of other behaviors, or differential reinforcement of incompatible behaviors, involves replacing the unwanted behavior with a more desirable behavior, built on the same reinforcing consequence that is currently supporting the unwanted behavior. This approach requires that the replacement behavior is just as powerful (quick, easy, efficient, and successful at gaining the reinforcement) as the unwanted behavior. For young children, the replacement behavior is very often a conventional social-communicative behavior ("functional communication").

Def. Extinction involves the removal of the consequence from an antecedent-behavior-consequence chain. It is often used in combination with a differential reinforcement approaches, so that the unwanted behavior is no longer followed by the reinforcing consequence (extinction), while the new, adaptive behavior, is followed by the reinforcing consequence. This results in an increase in the frequency of the adaptive behavior.

Def. In antecedent manipulation approaches, instead of manipulating the behavior-consequence part of the chain, the focus is on the antecedent-behavior links. In some functional analyses, a very specific antecedent can be identified, and this antecedent can be manipulated in such a way that the behavior is not performed (and therefore not reinforced). For example, if an analysis reveals that a child hits in response to an adult saying "Don't ___", the adult may change the antecedent instruction to "Would you please___". Use of prompts is a common way of performing antecedent manipulations.

Behavioral instruction of young children with autistic spectrum disorders often involves use of multiple interventions in an environment. One example might be the use of clearly marked visual cues (antecedent interventions) along with communication training to make requests and refusals (intervention by differential reinforcement of incompatible behaviors) (Watson et al., 1989).

Developmental Strategies for Building New Skills

In a developmental approach, the skills of a child with an autistic spectrum disorder are compared with the skills of a developmental sequence seen in typical children. Patterns of typical development for each skill area are established by the many early childhood assessment tools. The skills that a child demonstrates ("passes" on the assessment tools) indicate the child's current developmental level. As part of goal development for a child, failed or partially accomplished items then become the targets of teaching.

A developmental approach to teaching generally refers to a child-centered approach (child leads, adult follows) that uses materials and tasks that fit a child's developmental level in a particular area. Materials are provided to the child, and the child's behavior with the materials is scaffolded by the teacher along the lines of the targeted developmental skill. Children's behaviors and initiative with materials guide the adult, who may use modeling or demonstration, prompting, or hand-over-hand instruction. Children's preferences guide the selection of materials; adults provide support and encourage, but do not require, that materials are used and activities are carried out in the desired way. Rather than adult-supplied consequences for certain behaviors, internal, naturally occurring reinforcers are assumed to provide the motivation for learning. An example of an internal reinforcer is a sense of mastery and efficacy in functioning (e.g., pleasure in completing a puzzle).

Augmentative and Alternative Strategies

Augmentative and alternative strategies use assistive devices that provide a symbolic communication system other than speech (as described in Chapter 5). Examples are the use of visual systems like the Picture Exchange System, visual schedules, computerized communication systems, and manual language in place of verbal language. Although there are sometimes concerns voiced by parents and teachers that using an augmentative or alternative strategy may prevent a child with an autistic spectrum disorder from developing more conventional skills in that area (e.g. using manual signs might slow the acquisition of speech), there is no empirical evidence that demonstrates a negative result from using alternative strategies. Rather, there is some evidence that alternative strategies may assist development in some areas (Bondy and Frost, 1994).

Current practices in education of young children with autistic spectrum disorders generally support the tailored use of alternative and augmentative communication strategies, where appropriate, to facilitate participation in the educational environment by some children with autistic spectrum disorders. While some educational approaches gain maximal participation with carefully structured teaching and without much use of alternative or augmentative systems (e.g., the Walden preschool program), other approaches emphasize the use of strategies such as schedules or picture systems, along with many other methods to assist children with autism (e.g., the TEACCH program [Treatment and Education of

Autistic and Related Communication Handicapped Children]). In part, these results may be affected by how children are selected for the programs. There is no available empirical evidence that compares the gains made with and without such systems, but the best-documented approaches are uniform in their emphasis on maximizing child participation in educational experiences.

INDIVIDUAL VERSUS GROUP INSTRUCTION

Because young children with autistic spectrum disorders lack social and communicative skills necessary for attending to an adult and learning from distal instruction, it is generally assumed that initial skill development will be accomplished from individual instruction. Providing children with autistic spectrum disorders the language, social, and attentional behaviors needed to learn from an adult in a group situation is, in fact, a goal of early intervention for young children with autistic spectrum disorders.

Delivery of individual instruction episodes can take place in a variety of settings, including situations in which only a child and teacher are present (model of initial instruction at the University of California at Los Angeles program) and situations in which a child is in a typical group setting with a fairly large number of peers, but adults or peers join the child to deliver a discrete trial within the group situation. The various empirically supported models vary widely in the amount of time children are alone in a space with a teacher, compared with the amount of time they are in a group of peers, but these programs are quite similar in the use of individual teaching episodes to establish basic language, social, and cognitive skills.

Appropriate responding in a group situation is a specific part of the curriculum in empirically supported models. Carefully planned and implemented instruction is used to teach children to participate independently in typical classroom routines like hanging up a coat, sitting in a circle with a small group, moving from one center to another, getting materials, using them appropriately, putting them away, and lining up for outdoor time. Instruction in these group routines is usually delivered like other areas of instruction for children with autistic spectrum disorders: the initial teaching is provided with maximal individual instruction and support, and then adult instruction and prompting are gradually faded as the child learns to carry out the routine independently. Task analysis is often used to identify the specific skills involved in classroom routines and to develop teaching strategies.

Visual strategies, like the use of picture schedules and picture communication systems, visually structured independent work schedules, visual organization and cueing of the environment (names on chairs, coat hooks, and cubbies), are also used by many programs of both behavioral and developmental orientation to support children with autistic spectrum disorders in group situations. Group instruction provides an important environment for maintenance, generalization, and normalization of skills that may have first been taught individually.

THE USE OF PEERS AS INSTRUCTORS

Studies have demonstrated that interactions established between children with autism and adults do not easily generalize to peer partners. However, typical peers have been shown to be effective intervention agents for young children with autism. In these approaches, the peers are taught particular strategies for eliciting social, play, and communicative responses from a young child with autism. Most of these procedures have also been demonstrated to be effective when used in an inclusive setting, in which most of the children present are typically developing (Goldstein et al., 1992; Strain et al., 1977, 1979; Oke and Schreibman, 1990; McGee et al., 1992; Odom and Strain, 1986). However, it is important to note that, though these approaches are intended to be used in inclusive settings, they require planning and implementation by well-trained staff, as they would in any setting.

Variables found to be important in maintenance and generalization include characteristics of the peers, methods of prompting and reinforcing peers, fading reinforcers, ages of children, and characteristics of the setting, as well as the use of multiple peer trainers (Brady et al., 1987; Sainato et al., 1992). Self-monitoring systems for the peers have also been used successfully (Strain et al., 1994). These interventions have been found to be most powerful when delivered in inclusive preschools, but they have also been used successfully by parents and siblings in homes (Strain and Danko, 1995; Strain et al., 1994; parent training is discussed in detail in Chapter 3). These highly effective peer-mediation approaches are complex to deliver, requiring socially skilled typical peers and precise adult control in training peers, managing and fading reinforcement, and monitoring ongoing child interaction data. However, the approach is manualized and well described in many publications (Danko et al., 1998).

THE ROLES OF SELECTED DISCIPLINES

Provision of evaluation and treatment by occupational, physical, and speech and language therapists is mandated by the Individuals with Disabilities Education Act when speech and language and motor deficits are impeding a child's educational progress. The knowledge held by speech and language therapists and motor therapists is crucial for evaluating the needs of young children with autistic spectrum disorders and developing goals and objectives, as well as assessing progress. These therapists can have an important role in identifying appropriate goals and teaching techniques in their area of expertise. They can teach classroom staff and parents to use those techniques and to identify learning opportunities for the child in the classroom, community, and home. Speech/language and motor therapists are also carefully trained in specific treatment techniques in their individual areas.

The current role of psychologists and behavior specialists as interventionists in the education of young children with autistic spectrum disorders most often involves assessment, consultation, and development of intervention strategies. Psychologists and behavior specialists are often involved in providing functional analyses of problem behaviors; designing behavioral interventions; providing cognitive, adaptive, and social assessments; guiding the educational curriculum in these areas; and consulting with the rest of the educational team about educational strategies and interventions. Psychologists, social workers, and speech language therapists are sometimes involved in carrying out social skills groups, generally for older school age children. Psychologists and behavior specialists are often involved in parent training and support as well.

Whatever the discipline involved, justification for individual therapy as part of an educational program should be based on the use of particular intervention strategies in which the therapist is skilled. The research literature suggests that the greatest effects of any direct treatment for young children with autistic spectrum disorders lie in the generalization of learning achieved through working with classroom personnel and parents. There is little reason to believe that individual therapies carried out infrequently (e.g., once or twice a week) have a unique long-term value for young children, unless the techniques are taught to and used regularly by the child and the people who are with him or her in natural contexts. The value of one-on-one therapy lies in generalization, which must be planned and directly addressed. On the other hand, the assumption in all of the model programs is that skill development begins in individual instruction that may occur in the classroom or in individual treatment. Adequate amounts of individual instruction, whether by a teacher or parent or therapist, are crucial to early learning.

12

Comprehensive Programs

An overview of well-known model approaches to early autism intervention reveals a consensus across programs on the factors that result in program effectiveness. Similarities far outweigh differences in ten state-of-the-art programs that were selected for comparison. On the other hand, program differences suggest that there are viable alternatives on many program dimensions. Both differences and similarities among the programs are fundamental. Despite limitations of the outcome research available, it is likely that many children benefit substantially in the different programs reviewed. The national challenge is to close the gap between the quality of model programs and the reality of most publicly funded early educational programs.

This chapter begins with a description of the process by which the ten models were selected for review and a brief description of each program. The theoretical backgrounds of the various approaches are then considered, followed by an examination of points of convergence and divergence across the program models and consideration of the empirical underpinnings of each approach.

SELECTION AND OVERVIEW OF MODEL PROGRAMS

Representative model programs were selected for the purpose of illustrating key features related to program effectiveness; however, this is not an exhaustive review, and not all existing programs are described here.

Criteria for Selection of Programs

In order to select representative programs objectively, the committee established a set of criteria that relied on the availability of recently published program descriptions (Harris and Handleman, 1994; Handleman and Harris, 2000) and existing reviews of model programs for children with autistic spectrum disorders (Dawson and Osterling, 1997; Rogers, 1998). The committee also reviewed research and program descriptions in recent special issues on autistic spectrum disorders of professional journals, including *Infants and Young Children* (Neisworth and Bagnato, 1999), *School Psychology Review* (Harrison, 1999), and *The Journal of the Association for Persons with Severe Handicaps* (Brown and Bambara, 1999). Programs that had received federal funding for peer-reviewed grants by the National Institutes of Health and by the U.S. Department of Education were also included. Model programs that provided invited representation in the Autistic Spectrum Disorders Forum Workgroup of the National Early Childhood Technical Assistance Systems were also included.

A simple frequency count was conducted of the number of times each program was described in these sources. The programs selected were cited and described as program models between three and nine times in the designated resources. Excluded from the count were publications of isolated procedures rather than overall program descriptions. For example, references to an incidental teaching or discrete-trial procedure were not counted as a reference to a specific program model. However, references to a model by either title or investigator(s) were counted.

These criteria yielded a total of 12 programs, all in the United States. The committee sent an invitation to the director or developer of each, asking for program description materials and peer-reviewed data that they deemed best represented their model. Two of the programs did not respond, leaving ten programs for the committee's review.

Brief Overview of Programs

Most of the ten representative models selected began as research programs in which empirically demonstrated strategies for addressing specific problems were gradually packaged as components of overall clinical models. However, there have been different approaches to the development of these models.

All ten of the models individualize programming around the needs of particular children, and intervention regimens are designed to be implemented in a flexible manner. Essential differences in program design pertain to whether the curriculum is aimed at addressing some or all of a child's needs and whether the program staff provide direct service or serve as consultants to external providers. The following description of the ten programs (presented in alphabetical order), and the review that follows it, summarize the similarities and differences across programs.

Children's Unit at the State University of New York at Binghamton This program was designed in 1975 as an intensive, short-term program (approximately 3 years) for children with severe behavioral disorders. Consistent with the original purpose, the program operates from a deficit-oriented perspective that seeks to identify the factors most crucial in preventing a child from benefiting fully from services in the local community. The program primarily uses traditional applied behavior analysis techniques, although more naturalistic procedures may be implemented as children progress. An elaborate individualized goal selection curriculum has been developed, and there is an extensive computerized assessment and monitoring system (Romanczyk et al., 2000).

Denver Model at the University of Colorado Health Sciences Center This program originally opened in 1981 as the Playschool Model, which was a demonstration day treatment program. This developmentally oriented instructional approach is based on the premise that play is a primary vehicle for learning social, emotional, communicative, and cognitive skills during early childhood. The role of the adult and the purpose of play activities vary across learning objectives. The overarching curriculum goals are to increase cognitive levels, particularly in the area of symbolic functions; increase communication through gestures, signs, and words; and enhance social and emotional growth through interpersonal relationships with adults and peers. In 1998, the treatment unit was closed, and the intervention format was changed to the more natural contexts available in home and preschool environments with typical peers (Rogers et al., 2000).

Developmental Intervention Model at The George Washington University School of Medicine As in the Denver Model, this relationship-based approach is derived from a developmental orientation. There is a home component of intensive interactive floor-time work, in which an adult follows a child's lead in play and interaction, and children concurrently participate in individual therapies and early education programs. Intense floor time sessions at home are aimed at "pulling the child into a greater degree of pleasure." The curriculum is aimed at six developmental capacities: shared attention and regulation; engagement; affective reciprocity and communications through gestures; complex, pre-symbolic, shared social communication and problem-solving; symbolic and creative use of ideas; and logical and abstract use of ideas and thinking (Greenspan and Wieder, 1999).

Douglass Developmental Center at Rutgers University The center opened in 1972 to serve older children with autism; the preschool programs were added in 1987. Douglass now has a continuum of three programs that serve young children with autistic spectrum disorders, including an intensive home-based intervention, a small-group segregated preschool, and an integrated preschool. The curriculum is developmentally sequenced and uses applied behavior analysis techniques, beginning with discrete-trial formats and shifting across the continuum to more naturalistic procedures. Initial instruction is focused on teaching compliance, cognitive and communication skills, rudimentary social skills, and toilet training, as well as on the elimination of serious behavior problems. The small-group classroom emphasizes communication, cognitive skills, and self-help skills; social intervention begins in the form of interactive play with teachers. The emphasis in the integrated classroom is on communication, socialization, and pre-academic skills (Harris et al., 2000).

Individualized Support Program at the University of South Florida at Tampa A parent-training program developed in West Virginia served as the predecessor of this model, which started in its current form in 1987. The Individualized Support Program is implemented in children's homes and community settings during a relatively short period of intensive assistance and ongoing follow-up. The program is intended to be adjunctive to ongoing, daily, special educational services delivered in preschool and by other clinical providers. Specifically, it is oriented toward helping families gain the knowledge and skills needed to solve problems, as well as the competence and confidence needed to continue effective intervention and advocacy over the course of their children's educational history. Essential elements of the model include: development of functional communication skills, facilitation of the child's participation in socially inclusive environments, and multifaceted family support (Dunlap and Fox, 1999a, 1999b).

Learning Experiences, an Alternative Program for Preschoolers and their Parents (LEAP) Preschool at the University of Colorado School of Education LEAP opened in 1982 as a federally funded demonstration program and soon after incorporated into the Early Childhood Intervention Program at Western Psychiatric Institute and Clinic, University of Pittsburgh. In recent years, the original classrooms continue to operate in Pittsburgh, but new LEAP classrooms are now being developed in the Denver Public School System. LEAP includes both a preschool program and a behavioral skill training program for parents, as well as national outreach activities. LEAP was one of the first programs in the country to include children with autism with typical children, and the curriculum is well-known for its peer-mediated social skill interventions. An individualized curriculum targets goals in social, emotional, language, adaptive behavior, cognitive, and physical developmental areas. The curriculum blends a behavioral approach with developmentally appropriate practices (Strain and Cordisco, 1994; Strain and Hoyson, 2000).

Pivotal Response Model at the University of California at Santa Barbara Beginning in 1979, components of the current model were evaluated in applications with children of varied ages. In recent years, the primary focus has been on early intervention. Using a parent education approach, the ultimate goal of the Pivotal Response Model is to provide individuals with autism with the social and educational proficiency to participate in inclusive settings. In early stages, this model used a discrete-trial applied behavior analysis approach, but there has been a shift toward use of more naturalistic behavioral interventions. The overriding strategy is to aim at change in certain pivotal areas (e.g., responsiveness to multiple cues, motivation, self-management, and self-initiations). Intervention consists of in-clinic and one-on-one home teaching, and children concurrently participate in special education services in the schools. Specific curriculum goals are targeted in areas of communication, self-help, academic, social, and recreational skills (Koegel et al., 1998).

Treatment and Education of Autistic and Related Communication Handicapped Children (TEACCH) at the University of North Carolina School of Medicine at Chapel Hill This program was founded in 1972 as a statewide autism program that serves people with autistic spectrum disorders of all ages. Regional centers provide regular consultation and training to parents, schools, preschools, daycare centers, and other placements throughout the state. There is one demonstration classroom. TEACCH is based on a structured teaching approach, in which environments are organized with clear, concrete, visual information. Parents are cotherapists and taught strategies for working with their children. Programming is based on individualized assessments of a child's strengths, learning style, interests, and needs, so that the materials selected, the activities developed, the work system for the child, and the schedule for learning are tailored to this assessment information and to the needs of the family. TEACCH has developed a communication curriculum that makes use of behavioral procedures, with adjustments that incorporate more naturalistic procedures along with alternative communication strategies for nonverbal children (Watson et al., 1989; Marcus et al., 2000).

The University of California at Los Angeles (UCLA) Young Autism Project The development of this program was based on earlier research with older children and adolescents with autism; its applications to young children with autism began during the 1970s. The behavioral intervention curriculum is delivered in a one-to-one discrete-trial format, which is implemented by parents and trained therapists who work in a child's home. The treatment is focused primarily on developing language and early cognitive skills and decreasing excessive rituals, tantrums, and aggressive behaviors. The first year of intervention is aimed at teaching children to respond to basic requests, to imitate, to begin to play with toys, and to interact with their families. During the second year, the focus on teaching language continues; the most recent curriculum descriptions note a shift toward teaching emotion discriminations, pre-academic skills, and observational learning. For children who eventually enter inclusive settings, a paraprofessional assists with participation in regular preschool or kindergarten settings (Smith et al., 2000a).

Walden Early Childhood Programs at the Emory University School of Medicine The Walden program was developed in 1985 at the University of Massachusetts at Amherst, where the primary function was as a laboratory preschool to accommodate research in incidental teaching. Following relocation to Emory University in Atlanta, toddler and prekindergarten programs were added to complete an early intervention continuum. The classrooms include children with autism with a majority of typical peers. The incidental teaching approach is based on behavioral research, although there are developmental influences on goal selection. There is a toddler program with both center- and home-based components, and initial goals include establishment of sustained engagement, functional verbal language, responsiveness to adults, tolerance and participation with typical peers, and independence in daily living (e.g., toilet training). The preschool is aimed at language expansions and beginning peer interaction training. The prekindergarten emphasizes elaborated peer interactions, academic skills, and conventional school behaviors (McGee et al., 2000).

Organizational Structures

Irrespective of curriculum content, there are certain organizational similarities in the ten selected programs. For example, all are university-based programs. Four are housed within psychiatry departments (Denver, Developmental Intervention Model, TEACCH, Walden; also formerly LEAP), and four are affiliated with psychology departments (Children's Unit, Douglass, Pivotal Response Model, Young Autism Project; also formerly Walden). The Individualized Support Program is sponsored by a Department of Child and Family Studies, and LEAP is currently in a Department of Special Education.

Virtually all of these programs are or formerly were a component of a larger autism center. The Denver Model is operated within one of the

National Institutes of Health Autism Research Centers. Three of the programs are components of statewide autism centers (i.e., the Individualized Support Program in Florida, TEACCH in North Carolina, and Walden in Georgia), and two other preschools (Douglas Disabilities Developmental Center and the Children's Unit) are the early childhood components of programs that serve people with autism through adulthood. Three programs operate out of university-based clinics, although a significant portion of the interventions take place in homes and community settings (i.e., Developmental Intervention Model, Pivotal Response Training, and the Young Autism Project). The LEAP, TEACCH, and Denver programs are carried out primarily in public schools; all programs provide consultation or technical assistance to schools serving participating children, either concurrently or following early intervention.

Many of the selected programs were developed while funded with extramural research support. At least seven of the programs' directors have or have had funding from the U.S. Department of Education (Dunlap and Fox, the Koegels, Lovaas, McGee, Rogers, Schopler, and Strain). Five of these program directors have had research funding from the National Institutes of Health (Koegel, Lovaas, Rogers, Schopler, and Strain). In addition, virtually all have had state funding, either directly (e.g., Children's Unit, Douglass, TEACCH) or through child or school district tuitions.

Trends in the Development of the Programs

This review focuses on the most recently published practices of each model; it should be acknowledged that each of these programs has undergone considerable evolution over the years. Over the past two decades, the development of preschool programs for children with autistic spectrum disorders has influenced and been influenced by major shifts in intervention approaches (Dunlap and Robbins, 1991). Early behavioral interventions often targeted behavior reduction as a major goal, and some used aversive procedures. However, very few programs for young children currently report planned use of aversive stimuli as punishments. Another trend includes broadened conceptualizations of family involvement, which has expanded from simple participation in parent training to preparation for parental roles as collaborators, advocates, and recipients of family support. There has also been a shift toward instruction in more natural environments, and there has been a growing emphasis on inclusion of children with autism with typically developing peers. For example, virtually all model programs list inclusion among typical peers as a major emphasis of their program, either as a goal or as a strategy for promoting social learning (Handleman and Harris, 2000; Harris and Handleman, 1994). In the past few years, there has been an increased focus on identification and treatment of toddlers with autistic spectrum disorders, in contrast to previous models of early intervention that began when children were in preschool or elementary school.

THEORETICAL ORIENTATIONS OF PROGRAM MODELS

The ten program models described derive from either developmental or behavioral orientations, which influence goals, intervention procedures, and methods of evaluation. Thus, the Denver Model and the Developmental Intervention Model were conceptualized from a deductive framework, in which developmental theory was used to organize hypotheses regarding the fundamental nature of autistic spectrum disorders. Group design research has been aimed at seeking confirmatory evidence regarding deviations from normal development that need to be addressed in intervention. With the exception of TEACCH, which is eclectic with elements of both developmental and behavioral orientations, the other seven programs derive from the field of applied behavioral analysis. Behavioral interventions have been developed from a "bottom-up" approach in which procedures based on principles of learning are subjected to (largely single-subject) empirical tests, and techniques of demonstrated efficacy have then been assembled into program models (Anderson and Romanczyk, 1999).

Although these differing conceptual frameworks influence the intervention models in substantial ways, in practice, there is also considerable overlap between and across the various models. Within the behavioral approaches, a wide range of applications are used within and across programs, ranging from traditional discrete-trial training procedures to newer naturalistic approaches.

Developmental Approaches

The Denver Model recognizes the interplay among cognitive, communicative, and social and emotional development (Rogers and DiLalla, 1991). It was originally based on Piaget's (1966) experientially based theory of cognitive development, with additional influence from Mahler's conceptualization of interpersonal development via the attachment-separation-individuation process (Mahler et al., 1975). The underlying assumption was that, if intervention is directed at establishing strong, affectionate interpersonal relationships, then it may be possible to accomplish broad developmentally crucial improvements. From this perspective, it has been argued that the traditional behavioral approach of teaching specific behaviors is too narrow to have an impact on the fundamental nature of autistic spectrum disorders (Rogers et al., 1986). Although the Pivotal Response Model evolved from behavioral research, it arrived at a similar conclusion, that it is more efficacious to aim intervention at key autistic spectrum disorders deficits that will yield broad changes in collateral behaviors than to address individual behaviors in an isolated fashion (Koegel et al., 1999a).

The approach of the Developmental Intervention Model is based upon the assumption that a child's symptoms reflect unique biologically based processing difficulties that may involve affect, sensory modulation and processing, motor planing, and symbol formation (Greenspan and Wieder, 1997). Relationships and affective interactions may go awry secondarily, and intervention is aimed at helping a child try to work around the processing difficulties to reestablish affective contact.

Behavioral Approaches

By far, the bulk of autistic spectrum disorders intervention research has been conducted from the perspective of applied behavior analysis. An exhaustive review of 19,000 published journal articles revealed that there were 500 papers on applied behavior analysis and autistic spectrum disorders, and 90 of these were studies using single-subject designs to evaluate specific interventions for young children with autistic spectrum disorders (Palmieri et al., 1998). Rather than being tied to specific procedures, applied behavior analysis includes any method that changes behavior in systematic and measurable ways (Sulzer-Azaroff and Mayer, 1991). Historically, the behavioral approaches emphasized acquisition of discrete skills, and interventions were evaluated in terms of whether they produced observable and socially significant changes in children's behavior (Baer et al., 1968).

Traditional behavioral interventions impose structure in the form of distraction-free environments and presentation of opportunities-to-respond in discrete trials, and appropriate behavior is rewarded when it occurs. Technically sophisticated discrimination training procedures have been derived from years of research in applied behavior analysis. Lovaas' Young Autism Project, Harris and Handleman's Douglass Center, and Romanczyk's Children's Unit represent classic behavioral interventions, although all now use more naturalistic interventions as children's basic skills improve.

In an effort to improve the generalization of skills from teaching settings to daily use in the real world, comprehensive behavioral interventions have modified traditional applied behavior analysis techniques in a way that permits instruction in natural environments. The LEAP model was the first to recognize the importance of direct instruction in peer-related social behaviors, and that more natural instructional settings were required to accommodate the presence of typically developing classmates (Strain and Hoyson, 2000; Strain et al., 1985). Walden's incidental teaching approach incorporated the technical procedures generated by behavior analysis research into the environmental contexts in which social and communication behaviors typically occur for children without disabilities (McGee et al., 1997, 1999). Both the Individualized Support Program (Dunlap and Fox, 1999b) and the pivotal response model have emphasized the use of naturalistic procedures as a method to reduce stress on families.

btw dev. &
beh. approaches

Conceptual Differences and Practical Similarities

The conceptual differences between developmental and behavioral approaches to intervention are real, yet the gaps in practice appear to be narrowing. Developmental researchers may criticize behavioral approaches for failure to target the specific deficits associated with autistic spectrum disorders (Rogers et al., 1986), and it has been argued that this failure to select target skills within a meaningful developmental framework results in isolated skills that are difficult to transfer to other situations and skills (Rogers and Lewis, 1988). Behaviorists counter that the irregularity of skill development in children with autistic spectrum disorders decreases the relevance of careful adherence to normal developmental sequencing (Anderson and Romanczyk, 1999). However, developmental approaches to autistic spectrum disorders treatment have incorporated methods that recognize the needs of children with autistic spectrum disorders for high levels of structure, adult attention, and consistency. At the same time, behavioral interventions are increasingly being used to address complex social and communication goals in normal environmental settings.

CONVERGENCE AND VARIABILITY OF PROGRAM DIMENSIONS

Common elements among the early intervention models presented here include specific curriculum content, highly supportive teaching environments and generalization strategies, predictable routines, use of a functional approach to problem behaviors, carefully planned transitions across intervention settings, and active family involvement (Dawson and Osterling, 1997). Additional similarities include highly trained staff, adequate resources, and supervisory and review mechanisms (Anderson and Romanczyk, 1999). All ten model programs/approaches recognize the importance of individualizing interventions in a manner that meets the needs of each child and family. The similarities and range of variability of features across the models are summarized in Table 12-1 and discussed below.

TABLE 12-1   Features of Comprehensive Programs

Program	Mean Age at Entry (range), in Months	Hours Per Week	Usual Setting[a]	Primary Teaching Procedure
Children's Unit	40 (13 to 57)	27.5	School (S)	Discrete trial
Denver Community Based Approach	46 (24 to 60)	20	School (I), home, community	Playschool curriculum
Developmental Intervention Model	36 (22 to 48)	10-25	Home, clinic	Floor time therapy
Douglass	47 (32 to 74)	30-40	School (S and I), home	Discrete trial; naturalistic
Individualized Support Program	34 (29 to 44)	12	School (I), home, community	Positive behavior support
LEAP	43 (30 to 64)	25	School (I), home	Peer-mediated intervention; naturalistic
Pivotal Response Training	36 (24 to 47)	Varies	School (I), home, community, clinic	Pivotal response training
TEACCH	36 (24 and up)	25	School (S), clinic	Structured teaching
UCLA Young Autism Project	32 (30 to 46)	20-40	Home	Discrete-trial
Walden	30 (18 to 36)	36	School (I), home	Incidental teaching

[a](S) segregated classroom; (I) inclusive classroom

[handwritten margin note: start early = better LRB later]

Intervention Begins Early

All ten programs emphasize the importance of starting intervention when children are at the earliest possible ages. At least two retrospective studies have found less restrictive placement outcomes for children who began intervention at earlier rather than later ages (Fenske et al., 1985; Handleman and Harris, 2000). Several of the approaches were initially developed for elementary aged students and gradually applied to children at increasingly early ages (e.g., Douglass, Pivotal Response Training, TEACCH). Others were developed specifically for preschool-aged children (e.g., Denver, Individualized Support Program, LEAP). Although several programs (e.g., Developmental Intervention Model, Young Autism Project) have accepted children at ages younger than preschool, only the Walden toddler program was specifically designed to address the needs of toddlers with autistic spectrum disorders. Questions of how best to modify well-established approaches to fit the needs of very young children and their families are critical in future planning as children are identified at earlier ages.

Extension of services to children younger than preschool ages has sometimes been limited by funding mechanisms, which apply when children turn 3 years of age. In addition, a few approaches have established cutoffs for cognitive functioning that impose some limits on entry to intervention at the earliest ages. Despite policy and funding influences, all ten programs show recognition of the importance of early intervention by reporting outcome data on at least some children below the age of 3 years (see below).

Intervention Is Intensive in Hours

All of the comprehensive program models that are introduced to provide a child's major educational program report children participating in from 20 to 45 hours of intervention per week (see Table 12-1). The programs usually operate on a full-year basis, across several early childhood years. Lovaas (1987) provided the most direct evidence of the importance of intervention intensity in a comparison of 40 hours per week of traditional behavioral intervention compared with less than 10 hours per week of the same intervention. However, Sheinkopf and Siegel (1998) did not find a dose-response relationship between more than 20 hours of interventions and outcome, in part because children's skills at entry were such strong predictors of improvement. In addition, there is indirect evidence of the importance of intervention hours in a comparison of replications of the UCLA program, which have used fewer hours (18 to 25 hours per week) and obtained positive but more limited results (Smith, 1999; Smith et al., 2000a).

The Individualized Support Program and Pivotal Response Training Models offer relatively few hours of intervention per week; however, these approaches were designed to be provided in addition to other educational and therapeutic interventions. Similarly, the Developmental Intervention Model is implemented at widely varying numbers of hours per week (Greenspan and Wieder, 1997). However, the outcome evaluation of this approach included only children who had received at least 2 years of intervention (see below), which serves to illustrate that intensity encompasses duration as well as hours per week of participation. Hours reported for the TEACCH model were also few, but these are hours of technical assistance provided by TEACCH regarding individual children, and not the total number of hours of educational intervention received by each child. Usually, children identified with autism who receive TEACCH services begin full-day schooling, in a range of different placements and combinations of placements, at age 3 years.

Another source of variability in hours is how much emphasis each model places on intervention by families. For example, although the LEAP model has been cited as providing relatively low levels of hours intensity (Dawson and Osterling, 1997), a very active family program component easily expands the intervention to more than 25 hours per week (Strain and Cordisco, 1994). However, there is a range of family capability to provide intervention (Dunlap and Fox, 1999a), and although widely regarded as crucial, family intervention hours are difficult to quantify precisely.

Intervention intensity cannot be simply measured in terms of hours of enrollment or even attendance in an intervention program (Wolery and Garfinkle, 2000). In other words, hours of participation do not unilaterally translate to hours of time engaged in intervention. It has been argued that intensity is best thought of in the context of "large numbers of functional, developmentally relevant, and high-interest opportunities to respond actively" (Strain and Hoyson, 2000). Evidence from the general education and developmental literature support claims that intensity of education is associated with amount of progress (Ceci, 1991; Frasier and Morrison, 1998). While some level of dose-response relationship might be expected if the "active component" of the "dose" could be measured accurately, simplistic dose-response functions of intensity are not characteristic of typical child development. Rather, a more productive focus might be how variations in intensity are associated with day-to-day contexts (e.g., full school day compared with a 2-hour preschool program; full-year programming compared with a 9- or 10-month school year).

Families Are Actively Involved in Their Children's Intervention

All ten models explicitly acknowledge the importance of having parents play a central role in their children's intervention, although how parents are asked to participate differs across programs and approaches. Virtually all of the programs provide parents with at least the opportunity to be trained in specialized skills in teaching their children with autistic spectrum disorders.

However, there is a wide range of how many hours parents are asked to participate and whether or not that participation is optional or required. At least three of the programs (Developmental Intervention Model, Walden, and the Young Autism Project) require a parental commitment to deliver at least 10 hours of intervention per week in their homes or community settings. These programs provide parents with extensive instruction and supervision on the specialized skills needed to effectively teach their child with an autistic spectrum disorder. The Douglass and LEAP programs strongly recommend parent participation for 10 to 15 hours per week, but they do not require completion of the assignments to parents.

The format of parent participation varies considerably across programs, but all provide for some individual meetings with professionals at a clinic, center, or home. In some programs (Developmental Intervention Model, Young Autism Project), family intervention requires that parents set aside time to work intensively with their child in a one-on-one format. In others (Individualized Support Program, Pivotal Response Training, Walden), parental instruction is blended into normal daily home and community activities. The Denver Model, which is community-based, aims for a combination of intervention in both one-on-one and natural contexts (Rogers et al., 2000). An example of the range of formats offered is available from the Douglass Center, which offers a workshop on applied behavior analysis, formal clinics with therapist modeling and parent-demonstration of skills, preschool observational clinics, home visits twice a month, voluntary support groups, sibling groups, and four educational meetings per year (Harris et al., 2000). Other programs place emphasis on training advocacy skills (McGee et al., 1999), and a few offer psychological counseling or social work support services (Rogers and Lewis, 1988; Romanczyk et al., 2000). Parents' observation of children's school participation is another venue for parent education (Rogers and Lewis, 1988).

There is an increasing trend toward providing families with support to deal with the considerable emotional and logistical stresses of raising a child with an autistic spectrum disorder, so that intervention goes beyond parent training. For example, the Individualized Support Program was explicitly designed to accommodate the individualized needs of families (Dunlap and Fox, 1999b). The intervention begins with a family needs assessment to determine whether parents require information to increase their understanding of the disability, assistance in gaining access to services, skills for improving interactions with their child, or other family, social, or financial support. Families receive home visits for several hours per week, along with phone consultations as needed. Parents may also be accompanied on visits to physicians, other providers, or Individualized Educational Plan (IEP) meetings at their children's schools.

In sum, all of the model programs reviewed placed a high priority on parental involvement in the early education of their children with autistic spectrum disorders. In addition, the trend towards broadened parent supports reflects an appreciation of the challenges faced by these families.

Staff Are Highly Trained and Specialized in Autism

All ten programs are directed by at least one doctoral-level professional with a long-standing reputation in the treatment of autistic spectrum disorders. All the program developers have demonstrated academic productivity as evidenced by their status on a university faculty. The program developers have Ph.D.s in various fields (e.g., clinical psychology, developmental psychology, experimental psychology, special education, speech and hearing pathology); one has an M.D. In addition, virtually every program developer is assisted by either doctoral or master's-level personnel who have worked collaboratively with the program director for several years.

Professional staff members in the selected programs are broadly interdisciplinary, and staffing patterns vary according to local licensing and accreditation guidelines. The two certified school programs (Children's Unit and Douglass) have staff with the most traditional credentials, including certified teachers, speech and language pathologists, and an adaptive physical educator (Harris and Handleman, 1994; Romanczyk et al., 2000). The Children's Unit has a social worker, school psychologist, art and music therapists, and a consulting occupational therapist. The inclusion of typical children at LEAP and Walden requires that at least some teachers have degrees in regular or special early childhood education (McGee et al., 1994; Strain and Cordisco, 1994). Most of the programs also have an array of bachelor's level staff (who often have degrees in psychology). The Individualized Support Program and LEAP have employed a parent of a child with a disability to work directly with families, and LEAP also invites and trains parents to work as staff volunteers in their classrooms (Dunlap and Fox, 1999b; Strain and Cordisco, 1994).

The programs vary in terms of their use of specialized therapists and whether or not those therapists are part of the regular staff. In the programs with specialty therapists, there is variability in whether one-to-one direct therapy is provided. In most of the programs, there is an emphasis on the therapist's role as a consultant to the classroom staff, so that therapeutic suggestions can be blended into the regular daily intervention program.

In almost all of the programs, college students play key roles in their service delivery systems. One advantage of these programs' university affiliations is the relatively low-cost labor pools of students, who range from undergraduates to graduate students to post-doctoral fellows. In a number of programs, the bulk of the direct services are provided by supervised college students. In addition to obvious cost advantages, the reliance on student labor provides the opportunity to expand expertise in the autistic spectrum disorders to future professionals.

Elaborate training and supervisory systems have been developed to accommodate the training and supervision needs of the student personnel. For example, Children's Unit provides a 1-week initial orientation with lectures, observation, and a weekend "immersion" training session (Romanczyk et al., 2000). Student trainees must pass a written exam on program policies and procedures, and they are videotaped in interactions with children before and after training. Following initial training, there are weekly supervision and feedback sessions, as well as two objective performance reviews each year.

In the UCLA Young Autism Project, the primary therapists are undergraduates who have worked for a minimum of 6 months under supervision (McEachin et al., 1993). Supervisory staff must have a master's degree in psychology and 2 or more years of experience with the intervention program. This project, like many of the others, has packaged both manuals (Lovaas et al., 1981) and tapes (Lovaas and Leaf, 1981) to standardize personnel training. The Young Autism Project is also engaged in large-scale program replication activity. There have been published outcome reports on systematic (or partial) replications at the May Center in New England, (Anderson et al., 1987) and at UCLA with children with pervasive developmental delays–not otherwise specified (Smith et al., 2000b).

Standardization of the training protocols has permitted most of the programs to be replicated outside the administrative umbrella of the original site. Having developed replication formats early on in the process of building a statewide system, TEACCH has now been replicated internationally (in Denmark, France, Norway, Sweden, and Switzerland). TEACCH offers well-known teacher training workshops in North Carolina and at other locations around the country. A number of the programs were developed as model demonstration programs (Denver, Individualized Support Program, LEAP, and Walden) with support from the U.S. Department of Education, and these grants came with the requirement that the models be packaged and tested in replication sites.

In an evaluation of one of these model replications (Rogers et al., 1987), the Denver Model was disseminated to four public schools by using a standardized teacher training approach. Preservice training included a 6-hour introductory workshop, a 1-day visit to the new site to determine needs and resources, and a 40-hour training institute (which included 20 hours of didactic presentations, 8 hours of guided observation, and 12 hours of individual consultation on plans for implementing the model in the new site). Program implementation was monitored with videotaped samples, and formal feedback on teacher performance was provided to replication site staff at 6-week intervals across a period of 4 months. The trainers also conducted at least two 2-day follow-up visits to each replication site. Multidimensional program evaluation data (including surveys of trainee satisfaction, pre- and post-knowledge tests, a model implementation checklist that was completed with objective scoring of videotaped teacher performances, and measures of child change) documented the effectiveness of this comprehensive training model.

The model programs are being directed and implemented by teams of professionals who have had extensive training and experience in early autistic spectrum disorders intervention. It is unlikely that similar child outcomes can be achieved if expertise in autistic spectrum disorders is not readily available. However, the use of student personnel and replication demands have driven the preparation of training formats that could be effective in expanding the number of personnel qualified in education of young children with autistic spectrum disorders.

Ongoing Objective Assessment of a Child's Progress

Although the assessment measures varied, all ten programs reviewed have a mechanism for tracking the progress of individual children, and the systems for ongoing assessment permit timely adjustments in the child's intervention plan. As would be predicted by both the goals and associated methodological trends, the programs with a developmental orientation tend to rely on standardized assessment instruments, while the applied behavior analysis programs include a component for direct observation and measurement of specific target behaviors. However, the behavioral programs also collect standardized assessment data for purposes of program evaluation, and the developmental programs have means for ongoing tracking of child progress.

Specific issues pertaining to assessment are discussed in Chapter 2 of this report; this section emphasizes the unique methods of assessment that are used by the selected programs. However, as noted in Chapter 2, nearly all of the programs have collected data using the Childhood Autism Rating Scale (Schopler et al., 1988), the Vineland Scales of Adaptive Functioning (Sparrow et al., 1984), and one of several available.

The Developmental Intervention Model uses an instrument called the Functional Emotional Assessment Scale (FEAS), which is used to assess developmental levels of emotional, social, cognitive, and language functioning at the time of the initial evaluation and at each follow-up visit to the clinic (Greenspan and Wieder, 1997). Detailed therapist notes written at the time of each appointment are also viewed as a source of data that is used to monitor child progress.

The Denver Model uses an instrument called the Early Intervention Profile and Preschool Profile (Schafer and Moersch, 1981), which is completed by teachers. More objective measures of child progress were also obtained from systematic scoring of videotaped vignettes of a child in play interactions with teachers and parents (Rogers et al., 1986). The Play Observation Schedule was used to rate the developmental level of a child's play.

The traditional behavioral programs (Children's Unit, Douglass, Young Autism Project) tend to rely on trial-by-trial teacher-collected data, which is graphed daily and reviewed weekly or quarterly. Behavior analyses are conducted to provide information regarding the frequency, intensity, and duration of each target behavior, and more detailed functional analyses may be accomplished to determine the controlling antecedent or consequent events. The Children's Unit has one of the most elaborate data collection systems, in which a rotating videotaping schedule is scored for multiple behaviors and subsequently analyzed in a computerized database for the rate and pattern of specific behaviors (Romanczyk et al., 2000). A similar system is in place in the Walden programs, with the major exception being a relatively stronger emphasis on tracking ongoing language and social behavior in free-play activities, in contrast to tracking specific problem behaviors or skills during direct instruction (McGee et al., 1997).

For programs in which children are learning in the course of naturally occurring early childhood activities, it is difficult to obtain trial-by-trial data. The solution selected by most of these programs has been to obtain videotaped samples and score them according to operational definitions of various behaviors of relevance to the instructional curriculum. For example, the LEAP program obtains 20-minute videotaped probes of parent-child interactions, and tapes are scored and reduced in terms of the percentage of intervals the child is engaged in appropriate behavior. In addition, the LEAP program developed a detailed system for analyzing various components of peer interactions (Kohler et al., 1996).

The emphasis of the Pivotal Response Model on communication is reflected in the collection of unstructured videotaped language samples (Koegel et al., 1999a), which are analyzed according to Brown's pragmatics criteria (Miller, 1981). Videotapes of parent-child interactions are also obtained under standardized probe conditions and scored for levels of child initiations. In addition, community functioning data is collected by this and other models, including information from report cards and school files regarding school placement, academic achievement, social circles, living situation, and extracurricular activities.

The Individualized Support Program obtains systematic videotaped probes an average of once or twice per week. The tapes allow tracking of child functioning under conditions in which staff maintains consistent demands and reinforcers. Unique to this model is the family-guided developmental and ecological assessment format, along with systematic tracking of the person-centered planning accomplishments related to the person-centered planning process. As in the more traditional behavioral programs, functional assessments are conducted to develop a plan for reducing significant problem behaviors. In keeping with its community-based emphasis, this approach uses interview and direct observation forms that are more likely to be used in non-research settings than the strict analogue assessment conditions that are described in the research literature (Carr et al., 1994; O'Neill et al., 1997).

To summarize, ongoing assessment of children's progress is viewed as a hallmark of each of the model programs, although the methods of measurement logically vary with the curriculum emphasis. Virtually all of the model programs assess cognitive functioning, while relatively few directly assess the effects of intervention on a child's everyday social functioning.

Curricula Provide Systematic, Planful Teaching

Each of the program models has a custom-designed curriculum, a term used broadly here to refer to the environment, staffing, materials, and teaching interactions. Several of the programs have commercially packaged portions of their curriculum, including the Children's Unit (Romanczyk et al., 1998), the Developmental, Individual Difference, Relationship-Based Model (DIR; Greenspan and Wieder, 1998), TEACCH (Schopler, 1995; Schopler et al., 1980, 1983; Watson et al., 1989), and the Young Autism Project (Lovaas et al., 1981). The other models have unpublished program manuals for use in staff training and program replication activities.

Some of the programs make use of other commercially packaged curriculum materials. For example, LEAP uses the *Creative Curriculum* (Dodge and Colker, 1988) to organize activities of interest to typical children as well as children with autistic spectrum disorders, although these materials are only one component of the overall LEAP curricula (Hoyson et al., 1984).

There are many shared features in these varied model curricula. These points of convergence, as well as some interesting points of divergence, are discussed in the rest of this section.

Highly Supportive Physical, Temporal, and Staffing Environments

As described above, the model programs are implemented in a wide range of environments, including classrooms, homes, clinics, and community settings. The programs also vary on dimensions of environmental stimulation, with traditional behavioral programs generally conducted in distraction-free settings and more naturalistic procedures being implemented in more "everyday" environments. However, even in the most natural environments, it is common that the curriculum specifies certain environmental arrangements. For example, the early Denver classroom was described as being "choreographed" in a manner that reflected precise planning and coordination of physical space, equipment, materials, activities, staff roles, and timing (Rogers and Lewis, 1988).

Consistent across programs is the existence of predictable daily routines, which are organized according to written schedules of activities. The center-based programs tend to vary activities from one-to-one to small group to large group, with goals addressed in the most compatible format (e.g., new language can be difficult to teach in a large group situation). For center-based programs, the class size varies from 6 (Denver) to 18 (Walden prekindergarten), although there is variability across children's ages. Class size also varies, depending on the ratio of children with special needs to total number of children (e.g., the Walden preschool program has 18 children, but only 6 have autism).

Perhaps more relevant than the number of children with autistic spectrum disorders is the adult:child ratio, which all of the programs keep high in order to ensure that each child's individualized needs can be met. Across the ten programs, the adult-child staffing ratios range from 1:1 to 1:8, depending on the program format, class size, and children's developmental and chronological age. The Developmental Intervention Model and the Young Autism Project remain nearly exclusively 1:1 throughout the intervention period, including the use of a one-on-one "shadow" if a child is eventually included in a regular early childhood center. Other programs offer staffing of approximately 1:3, although each of these provides for some 1:1 sessions in the course of each child's day. A number of programs (e.g., Children's Unit, Douglass, Walden) systematically and intentionally fade the adult:child ratios across time in intervention, in order to prepare children to function independently in future sites.

Focus on Communication Goals and Other Developmental Areas

All ten programs explicitly address the communication irregularities associated with autistic spectrum disorders, although there is some variability in the specific target objectives and in the strategies for promoting communication. The programs also target other developmental domains, including engagement, social, play, cognitive and academic skills, self-help, behavioral challenges, and motor skills. The distribution of treatment time devoted to teaching skills in different developmental areas varies across programs, and the programs also vary on the sequencing in which the developmental domains are addressed across treatment years. The developmental areas addressed are discussed below.

Communication It is not possible to directly compare verbal abilities of the children across programs because of differing ages and other potential differences in child populations, but reported data suggest that for many of the model programs, the predictions that only 50 percent of children with autism will develop functional speech (Lord and Paul, 1997) are far exceeded. For example, the Denver Model reported that 73 percent of their preschool graduates were verbal at exit (Rogers and DiLalla, 1991), and Walden reported that 82 percent of children who began intervention as toddlers were functionally verbal by the time they entered preschool (McGee et al., 1999).

Most of the programs reported teaching speech as well as alternative means of communication. Children in several programs (i.e., Denver, Douglass, and TEACCH) were taught speech, sign language, and use of the Picture Exchange Communication Systems (PECS; Bondy and Frost, 1994). All the programs that teach alternative forms of communication maintain a vigorous effort (either simultaneous or sequential) at teaching language development as well. Only Walden formally avows a verbal-only approach to language instruction (McGee et al., 1994, 1999). The Developmental Intervention Model stands alone in focusing on nonverbal communication and interactions rather than teaching verbal language (Greenspan and Wieder, 1997). The Individualized Support Program (and most of the behavioral programs) places a heavy emphasis on development of communication skills that are functional equivalents of problem behaviors (Dunlap and Fox, 1996).

As a rule, the programs that emphasize a naturalistic approach to language intervention focus on conversational language. Thus, both the Douglass (Taylor and Harris, 1995) and the Pivotal Response Model (Koegel et al., 1999a) programs have reported procedures for teaching how to ask questions (e.g., "What's that?" "Where is it?" "Whose is it?" "What's happening?"). LEAP and Walden also emphasize the importance of directly teaching verbal interactions with typical peers (McGee et al., 1992; Odom and Strain, 1984).

Engagement Although the terminology in which it is discussed and achieved varies, from the outset of intervention, all of the ten programs either explicitly or implicitly teach engagement. Engagement is defined as sustained attention to an activity or person. The traditional behavioral programs emphasize compliance with one-step directions (e.g., "Sit down," "Stand up") as a first step of intervention, with a goal of preparing the child to follow teaching instructions (Lovaas et al., 1981). In the

Developmental Intervention Model, a child is encouraged to initiate purposeful behavior, and the therapist follows the child's lead to extend
engagement (Greenspan and Wieder, 1997). At Walden, an engineered
environment provides high-preference toys, which are dispensed by
teachers in a systematic manner to ensure that children's engagement
levels are maintained at least 80 percent of the time (McGee and Daly,
1999). The Pivotal Response Training approach uses a variety of procedures (e.g., interspersing previously learned tasks among newer and more
challenging tasks, reinforcing attempts to respond) to keep children's
motivational levels high (Koegel and Koegel, 1986; Koegel et al., 1988).

Social Interactions Virtually every program lists social interactions as an
intervention priority, although the programs differ as to whether the con-
centration is on interactions with adults (i.e., Developmental Intervention
Model, Young Autism Project) or on interactions with peers (i.e., LEAP,
Walden). Because the Individualized Support Program is a family support model, this approach emphasizes social interactions with parents
and siblings (Fox et al., 1997).

Because all of the programs have an overriding goal of promoting
children's long-term independent functioning in the community, all recognize inclusion of children with autistic spectrum disorders in classes
with typical children as a desired long-term outcome. The major differences center around whether the program takes a "readiness" position,
which assumes that certain prerequisite skills are needed for a children
with autistic spectrum disorders to benefit from inclusion (e.g., the
Children's Unit and TEACCH [Marcus et al., 2000; Romanczyk et al.,
2000]), or a position that early social skills are most feasibly developed
when children are included with typical children from the outset in intervention (Strain et al., 2001). The Developmental Intervention Model and
the Young Autism Project tend to include successful children with autism
with typical peers near the end of their early intervention period
(Greenspan and Wieder, 1997; Smith et al., 2000a). Douglass now provides a continuum of settings, across which children move from one-to-
one, to small-group segregated classes, to an integrated class that includes
a majority of typical peers (Harris et al., 2000). One reason the original
Denver center-based treatment program closed was in recognition of the
importance of including children with autism with their typical peers,
which is now done through technical assistance in preschool settings
(Rogers, 1998).

A number of models maintain an a priori position that favors inclusion from the outset, based on various arguments for inclusion (Strain et
al., in press). Both LEAP and Walden have developed their curricula with
a major emphasis on promoting normal social learning opportunities from
the earliest possible moment, when all young children are learning how

to interact socially. The Pivotal Response Model takes the position that inclusion is most easily accomplished when children are in preschool because this is the period when academic demands are lowest (Koegel et al., 1999a). Although the Individualized Support Program is philosophically committed to inclusive education, the reality of very limited inclusion options for children with autistic spectrum disorders leads to a pragmatic approach of providing intervention in the most natural settings available.

Play Play skills are closely related to both social and communication domains, and the ten models vary considerably in how play is addressed. Thus, play is a major emphasis of the Denver approach (Rogers and Lewis, 1988). Teaching in the course of play activities is also intrinsic to the models that primarily use incidental teaching or other naturalistic instructional procedures (i.e., Individualized Support Program, LEAP, and Walden), and inclusive programs are most likely to target creative or interactive play with peers (McGee et al., 1992; Odom and Strain, 1984). In fact, most programs target goals related to recreation (e.g., Pivotal Response Training [Koegel et al., 1999a]) and leisure skills (e.g., Children's Unit [Romanczyk et al., 2000]), which, for young children, involve toy play. A review of published curriculum materials and program descriptions suggests that basic functional play skills (such as stacking rings and putting pegs in a pegboard) are routine goals at the Children's Unit, Douglass, TEACCH, and the Young Autism Project.

Cognitive and Academic Skills Virtually all of the programs teach cognitive skills, although the distribution of treatment time to this area varies considerably. Cognitive growth is a major emphasis of the Denver, Douglass, TEACCH, and Young Autism Project models. Although cognitive abilities tend not to be a major curriculum priority in programs that focus on peer interaction skills (i.e., LEAP, Pivotal Response Model, and Walden), skills such as mathematics, reading, and writing are taught because academic preparation may help secure a child's placement in a regular kindergarten classroom (Koegel et al., 1999a).

Self-Help The behavioral programs use an array of procedures of demonstrated efficacy in teaching self-help skills. The developmental programs tend to place less emphasis on self-help skills, probably because self-help skills are not viewed as core autism deficits. Although there are relatively few published studies on self-help skills that are specific to young children with autism, virtually all of the selected model programs were found to track the development of independent daily living skills.

Behavioral Challenges To a growing extent, strategies for promoting engagement have become nearly synonymous with methods of preventing challenging behaviors (McGee and Daly, 1999), because the behavioral challenges presented by young children with autistic spectrum disorders are usually not of a severity to warrant more intrusive intervention procedures (see Chapter 10). However, the Young Autism Project acknowledged use of aversive procedures with children participating in a 1987 outcome study. In a recent replication, aversives were discontinued after the first few subjects (Smith, 2000b). In another replication of the Lovaas (1987) outcome study, there was speculation on the possibility that the absence of aversives could have accounted for less positive child outcomes (Anderson et al., 1987).

At least five approaches (i.e., Denver, Individualized Support Program, LEAP, Pivotal Response Model, and Walden) rely exclusively on positive procedures for preventing challenging behaviors or for building incompatible appropriate behaviors. Because the Individualized Support Program model is a more short-term, problem resolution approach (Dunlap and Fox, 1999a), a comprehensive positive behavior support strategy has been developed to accomplish demonstrable improvements in relatively short time-frames (see Chapter 10).

Motor Skills The Developmental Intervention Model places a major emphasis on motor skills, including motor planning and sequencing. Most of the programs teach age-appropriate gross and fine motor skills. The UCLA program encourages gestural and vocal imitation. The Denver Model emphasizes motor imitation and motor planning.

Carefully Planned, Research-Based, Teaching Procedures Include Plans for Generalization and Maintenance of Skills

The ten representative programs use a range of research-based teaching procedures. The behavioral programs use procedures based on principles of learning, but the format of instruction falls along a continuum of discrete-trial procedures to incidental teaching. At the ends of the continuum, the Young Autism Project has historically used discrete-trial procedures nearly exclusively (Lovaas et al., 1981), while Walden provides all instruction using an incidental teaching approach (McGee et al., 2000). The other five behavioral programs use a mixture of discrete-trial and naturalistic teaching procedures, although the Individualized Support Program (Dunlap and Fox, 1999a), LEAP (Strain and Cordisco, 1994), and the Pivotal Response Model (Koegel et al., 1999a) models use predominately natural context procedures, and the Children's Unit most commonly uses a highly structured discrete-trial approach (Romanczyk et al.,

2000). The Douglass Center's treatment continuum moves children from discrete-trial instruction to eventual placement in a classroom that uses mostly natural contexts teaching formats (Harris et al., 2000).

The trend toward use of naturalistic teaching procedures began as an attempt to improve generalization of skills to use in everyday life. Procedural comparisons of discrete-trial instruction and incidental teaching have indicated that, given comparable reinforcement procedures, acquisition occurs at approximately the same pace for both of the procedures (McGee et al., 1985). However, generalization or transfer of skills from the teaching setting to unprompted use in new settings or with new people is enhanced when skills have been learned through incidental teaching. Incidental teaching is a systematic protocol of instruction derived from principles of behavior analysis, and haphazard or unplanned instruction of any type is unlikely to produce acquisition in children with autism (McGee et al., 1999).

A method called structured teaching is used at TEACCH (Marcus et al., 2000). Structured teaching shares features common to discrete-trial instructional procedures but also emphasizes instructional formats derived from the developmental literature and psycholinguistics, as well as some incidental teaching (Watson et al., 1989). The focus is on environmental structure, visual schedules, routines, organizational strategies (e.g., working from left to right), and visual work systems that help a child achieve independence in various skills. With respect to reinforcement, the TEACCH model works from the idea that task performance and task completion will be motivating for children if they understand a task that is at an appropriate developmental level (e.g., supporting the development of emerging skills) and that builds on individual interests. The TEACCH structured teaching approach focuses on helping parents and teachers adapt the environment while helping children to develop skills.

The two developmental programs use somewhat different approaches, although both are delivered during play interactions between adults and children. The technical foundation for the Denver Model and the Developmental Intervention Model differ significantly from the behavioral approaches, yet each involves teaching in natural contexts. Meaningful differences, however, tend to center on the role of reinforcement in the instructional process. The use of discrimination training techniques is most common in both discrete-trial and incidental teaching procedures.

Individualized Intervention Plans Are Needed to Adjust for the Wide Range of Children's Strengths and Needs

All ten programs give explicit attention to the importance of individualizing treatment; their methods vary. In general, the procedural approaches tend to be entirely custom-designed for each child, while the "programs" provide for individual adjustments within an overall packaged curriculum.

Transitions from Preschool to School Are Planned and Supported

Most of the selected programs report specific preparation for children's transition from intensive intervention into school programs. For example, Douglass reports a process that occurs across the child's last 9 months prior to program exit. Transition preparation begins with staff visits to future schools to assess the match of child with placement and to determine specific skills the child will need to function successfully in the next environment (Handleman and Harris, 2000). Receiving teachers are invited to visit Douglass to get an understanding of the child's intervention history, and follow-up consultation is offered to receiving classrooms. In some cases, children make transitions gradually, with either partial-day placements or accompaniment by familiar staff.

Nearly all of the programs report placement outcomes, although it is recognized that a child's progress is not the sole determining factor in placement decisions. The range of children going to typical classrooms following intervention differs widely across the programs, with program evaluation data reporting a range from 15 percent of children treated at the Children's Unit (Romanczyk et al., 2000) to 79 percent of the children from Walden (McGee et al., 2000). It should be noted that children at the Children's Unit were selected on the basis of severity of problem behaviors. Programs that exclude or do not encourage children with autism and other severe difficulties have tended to have more uniform positive outcomes.

The political climate and local policies are also factors that influence placement outcomes. For example, 35 percent of the first 20 children treated in the Denver Model went to nonspecialized schools or daycare centers with normally functioning peers (Rogers et al., 1986); however, today, those numbers would be higher, because Colorado now has a statewide policy of including the vast majority of children with disabilities in regular settings. The Walden program was able to replicate placement outcomes achieved in Massachusetts, an area in which inclusion was well accepted and promoted, when the program relocated to Georgia, where inclusion of children with autistic spectrum disorders was rare. However, the policies of the program itself also play a role. Walden, for example, recommends inclusion for nearly all children with autistic spectrum disorders, irrespective of level of functioning, due to a program policy emphasizing that all children with autistic spectrum disorders have social needs that require exposure to normal social behavior.

INTERVENTION STUDIES

There is a need for well-controlled clinical outcome research on these and other models of service delivery. The available research strongly suggests that a substantial subset of children with autistic spectrum disorders are able to make marked progress during the period that they receive intensive early intervention, and nearly all children with autistic spectrum disorders appear to show some benefit. However, the research to date is not at a level of experimental sophistication that permits unequivocal statements on the efficacy of a given approach, nor do the data support claims of "recovery" from autistic spectrum disorders as a function of early intervention. There is no outcome study published in a peer-reviewed journal that supports comparative statements of the superiority of one model or approach over another. Rather, with a few exceptions, much of the current outcome information is in the form of program evaluation data or measures of children's progress when comparisons are made before and after intervention without control groups or blinded assessments of outcome. Although many children have participated in the ten model programs, outcome data is generally based on small samples, and the small sample size has also prohibited analysis of the role of individual differences within children in the effectiveness of different models.

The components of the ten program models discussed above are empirically grounded. Researchers working with each of them have published numerous peer-reviewed findings specific to the procedures developed in their programs, although the level of standards for intervention studies varies considerably across journals. In some cases, the programs originated as applied laboratories in which to develop and test intervention procedures, so research about the effects of specific procedures was the natural output. As reviewed in other sections of this report, this cumulative body of procedural research serves as evidence that early educational interventions do enable young children with autistic spectrum disorders to acquire a variety of skills.

However, the quality and quantity of research that evaluates the overall efficacy of these models has lagged behind the procedural research. The paucity of outcome data may be due to the fact that early education programs for children with autistic spectrum disorders are relatively new. The ethical and logistical complexity of conducting clinical outcome research with young children is also a major contributing factor.

Examples of the outcome data generated by the ten selected models to date are presented in this section; the models are covered in alphabetical order. The studies discussed were published in peer-reviewed journals; these journals vary widely in the experimental rigor of their review process. In several cases, published data were provided to augment program description information rather than as results of experimental tests.

Children's Unit

Although this program regularly collects a comprehensive set of both observational and standardized measures of child progress, outcomes have been reported primarily in non-peer-reviewed book chapters (Romanczyk et al., 1994, 2000). There have also been a number of controlled evaluations of the computer data systems, staff training efforts, and clinical procedures (Romanczyk, 1984; Taylor et al., 1994; Taylor and Romanczyk, 1994), but these are beyond the scope of the model outcome data considered here.

Denver Model

There are at least four peer-reviewed outcome reports on the Denver Model, including the evaluation of a comprehensive training model described above (Rogers and DiLalla, 1991; Rogers et al., 1986; Rogers and Lewis, 1988; Rogers et al., 1987). An evaluation of the progress of 49 children treated in the Denver Playschool Model reported better than predicted gains in all developmental areas assessed by the Early Intervention Developmental Profile and Preschool Profile (Schafer and Moersch, 1981), with the exception of self-help skills. The developmental assessment was based on ratings by classroom teachers obtained early and late in treatment (Rogers and DiLalla, 1991). In addition, impressive language gains were demonstrated on standardized language assessments (one of five commonly used instruments) conducted by the children's speech and language pathologists.

An earlier assessment of the progress of the first 31 children treated in this model revealed small but statistically significant improvements in symbolic and social and communicative play skills, as rated on an objective observational system by blind observers (Rogers and Lewis, 1988). Moreover, there were indications that the intervention had impacted the severity of autism, as measured in the Childhood Autism Rating Scale (CARS).

Douglass Developmental Center

There have been four peer-reviewed publications of data on the Douglass Center (Handleman and Harris, 2000; Harris et al., 1990, 1991, 1995). These studies include documentation of progress as measured on the Stanford-Binet (Thorndike et al., 1986), the Preschool Language Scale (Zimmerman et al., 1979), and the Vineland (Sparrow et al., 1984).

The most recent report is on 27 children who entered intervention between the ages of 31 and 65 months (Handleman and Harris, 2000). After 4-6 years following termination of intervention, the children's placements were analyzed in relation to their entry data to determine whether reliable predictors of treatment outcome could be identified. Both IQ scores and age of entry into treatment were found to be predictors of long-term placement. Of 11 children who entered intervention before the age of 48 months, pre- to posttreatment IQ score gains averaged 26 points, and all but one child were in regular placements (seven with support and three without support). For those who entered intervention at or older than 48 months, the average IQ score gain was only 13 points, and only one child was in a regular class placement at follow-up.

Developmental Intervention Model

Greenspan and Wieder (1997) provide a detailed review of the case records of 200 children who had participated in the Developmental Intervention Model for 2 or more years. Based on clinical notes and scores on the Functional Emotional Assessment Scale, 58 percent had "good to outstanding" outcomes, 25 percent had "medium" outcomes, and 17 percent had "low" outcomes. Overall, this pattern of outcomes was better than that of a comparison group of children who entered treatment with the Developmental Intervention Model following treatment with traditional behavioral services. However, there was a major confounding element in use of a comparison group: their parents had been dissatisfied with their previous intervention. Ratings were also not blind to intervention status. A more in-depth examination of 20 of the highest functioning children detailed marked gains on the Vineland (Sparrow et al., 1984) and CARS (Schopler et al., 1988). Somewhat inconsistent with the outcomes reported by others, expressive language scores were reported to be above those for receptive language, and self-care skills were lower than communication and socialization abilities.

Individualized Support Program

The Individualized Support Program model has reported single-subject data on the first six participating children (Dunlap and Fox, 1999a). Although this report was in a peer-reviewed journal, only one of the children's interventions was evaluated with an experimental design. Positive pre-post changes were reported on the Autism Behavior Checklist (Krug et al., 1980), and proportional change index scores (Wolery, 1983) were computed for pre-post scores on the Battelle Developmental Inventory (Newborg et al., 1984).

LEAP

The LEAP program's effect on children's cognitive growth (Hoyson et al., 1984) and social interaction development (Strain, 1987) was compared with that of a comparison group treated at another autism treatment program, with results documenting more positive developmental progress by children in the experimental program. More recently, a summary of case reports of the long-term progress of the first six children in the LEAP program is now available (Strain and Hoyson, 2000), but without comparisons or controls. The children ranged in age from 30 to 53 months at the onset of treatment, and they scored in the moderate to severe range of autism on the CARS (Schopler et al., 1988). By the time of program exit, and continuing until the children were 10 years old, the CARS scores for these children fell beneath the cutoff for autism. Large decreases in noncompliance were demonstrated in videotaped samples of parent-child interactions, both at program exit and when the children were 10 years old. There were also clinically significant increases in the amount of time the children spent engaged in positive peer interactions, both at program exit and at age 10. Five of the six children spent their school careers in regular education placements.

Pivotal Response Model

The Pivotal Response Model has reported long-term follow-up on a total of ten children (Koegel et al., 1999b). The first six children had similar language ages at entry, but they differed in their levels of initiating interactions. At the time of follow-up, it was found that higher initiation levels at entry predicted less restrictive school placements, higher adaptive and language test scores, and more appropriate parent-child interactions. The next four children, who displayed low levels of initiation at the time of entry into intervention, were provided with specific training on how to independently initiate interactions. At follow-up, three of the four children trained in self-initiations had placements in regular education settings, as well as impressive outcomes on measures of language pragmatics, adaptive behavior measured by the Vineland (Sparrow et al., 1984), and lower levels of autistic behaviors reflected on the CARS (Schopler et al., 1988). As a group, the 10 children treated with Pivotal Response Training had very good outcomes, but the absence of experimental design leaves it unclear whether these improvements can be attributed directly to the program's intervention; this is a difficulty that holds true for almost all of the data reported for the ten model programs.

TEACCH

Program evaluation information on the TEACCH model has included consumer satisfaction data from parents, trainees, and replication sites (Mesibov, 1997), as well as objective assessment of parent teaching skills

(Marcus et al., 1978) and child progress (Schopler et al., 1982). There have been a number of studies describing progress in follow-up samples of young children who received services at TEACCH (Venter et al., 1992), and substantial IQ score gains have been commonly reported for nonverbal children who were diagnosed at early ages (Lord and Schopler, 1989). However, these studies are not direct evaluations of treatment outcomes.

Most recently, a 10-hour home-based TEACCH program training teachers to serve young children with autism was compared with a discrete-trial classroom without the home-based program (Ozonoff and Cathcart, 1998). The focus of intervention in both programs was cognitive, academic, and prevocational skills. Following 4 months of intervention, the group served in the TEACCH home-based program showed more improvement than the comparison group on imitation, on fine and gross motor skills, and on tests of nonverbal conceptual skills.

UCLA Young Autism Project

Although the UCLA program has generated the most rigorously controlled early intervention research published to date, there has been considerable controversy due to various methodological and interpretational limitations (Gresham and MacMillan, 1997). In the original report (Lovaas, 1987), 38 children with autism were divided into two treatment groups: half of the children received intervention for at least 40 hours per week for 2 or more years, and the other half received the same intervention for less than 10 hours per week. There was a second comparison group who received treatment outside of the UCLA program. Nine of the 19 children who received intensive intervention showed IQ gains of at least 20 points. Gains were far less for children in both of the comparison groups.

The Young Autism Project has also reported the longest follow-up tracking of children with autism who have received intensive early intervention (McEachin et al., 1993). By age 13, eight of the nine high-outcome children from the Lovaas (1987) study continued to have high IQ scores, and they were functioning unsupported in regular education classrooms. In contrast, only one child who received less intensive intervention had a "best outcome."

Several peer-reviewed evaluations have been conducted of replications of the Young Autism Project (Anderson et al., 1987; Birnbrauer and Leach, 1993; Sheinkopf and Siegel, 1998; Smith et al., 2000b). The replication results have been generally positive but mixed. With fewer hours of intervention, some of the replication programs were able to achieve similarly high IQ sore gains; results were more variable on other measures. For example, the most recent replication (Smith et al., 2000b), which served both children with autism and children with pervasive developmental delay–not otherwise specified, yielded improvements in IQ scores, but, there were no significant changes in the children's diagnoses or their adaptive or problem behaviors (Smith et al., 2000b).

Most critiques of the outcome research generated by the Young Autism Project do not deny impressive child outcomes (Mesibov, 1993; Mundy, 1993); the debate centers on methodological issues related to subject selection and assessment measures (see Chapter 15). One of the most controversial issues surrounding the program pertains to descriptions of the best-outcome children in the 1987 study as "recovered" or "normal functioning," especially in light of the paucity of measures of social or communicative functioning (McEachin et al., 1993).

Walden Toddler Program

Pre-post data on the preschool and overall Walden programs have been reported in non-peer-reviewed book chapters (McGee et al., 1994, 2000), and an evaluation of the family program is described by McGee and colleagues (McGee et al., 1993). Therefore, only the outcome data published on the toddler program is considered here. A total of 28 children with autism began intervention at an average age of 30 months, and those who participated in the program for at least 6 months were included (McGee et al., 1999). Pre-post comparisons without other experimental controls provide the majority of data. Videotaped observations of each child's ongoing behavior were obtained daily across the first 10 days and last 10 days of enrollment in the toddler center. Results showed that although only 36 percent of the children were verbal at program entry, 82 percent of the children were verbalizing meaningful words by the time that they exited the toddler program to enter preschool. In addition, by the time of program exit, 71 percent of the children showed increases in the amount of time that they spent in close proximity to other children, with only one child showing levels of peer proximity that were outside the ranges displayed by typical children.

Summary of Intervention Studies

As a group, these studies show that intensive early intervention for children with autistic spectrum disorders makes a clinically significant difference for many children. The most systematic evaluation data are associated with intensive intervention approaches. However, each of the studies has methodological weaknesses, and most of the reports were descriptive rather than evaluations with controlled experimental research designs. There are virtually no data on the relative merit of one model over another, either overall or as related to individual differences in children; there is very limited information about interventions for children under 30-36 months of age. There is overlap in the levels of intensity with which the models are implemented, and the measures of outcome differ widely across interventions.

In addition, as summarized in Figures 1-1,1-2, and 1-3 (in Chapter 1), studies that addressed general aspects of interventions consistently had methodological limitations that were often even more common than in studies about interventions for narrower target areas (see Kasari, 2000). These limitations in part reflect the tremendous scope required in carrying out research concerning comprehensive intervention programs. On the whole, issues related to internal and external validity were addressed only minimally in about 80 percent of the published studies, with measurement of generalization outside the original setting occurring only minimally in 70 percent of the research reports. Given the difficulty and the cost in time and money of such studies, it seems most useful to consider alternative methods to addresses these concerns.

The models presented positive and remarkably similar findings, which included better-than-expected gains in IQ scores, language, autistic symptoms, future school placements, and several measures of social behavior. Although possible changes in diagnosis are implied, these have not been systematically documented or supported with independent observations or reports. Considered as a group, these peer-reviewed outcome studies suggested positive change in the language, social, or cognitive outcomes of children with autistic spectrum disorders who received intensive early intervention beginning at young ages. However, only three of the studies (plus one follow-up) had comparison group data, and only one of the studies (Smith et al., 2000b) practiced random assignment of children to conditions, and this procedure was complex. Pre-post assessment measures reflected positive outcomes for the majority of children receiving intervention, and most children showed some progress. However, there was almost no information on the contribution of the other interventions and therapies in which the children participated.

In sum, it appears that a majority of children participating in comprehensive behavioral interventions made significant progress in at least some developmental domains, although methodological limitations preclude definitive attributions of that progress to specific intervention procedures.

III
Policy, Legal, and
Research Context

13

Public Policy and Legal Issues

When parents discover they have a child with an autistic spectrum disorder, they naturally seek professional help. Some find help from private practitioners. Others find public programs that provide assistance. In many cases, even private programs are supported by public policies established decades ago at the federal level and at the state level, when families who had children with disabilities joined hands with professionals and political leaders to create policy that would bring aid to parents who had children with special needs.

Public or social policies are the rules and standards by which scarce public resources are allocated to almost unlimited needs (Gallagher, 1994). Written social policies should provide the answer to four major questions:

1. Who shall receive the resources or services? (eligibility)
2. Who shall deliver the services? (provider)
3. What is the nature of the services? (scope)
4. What are the conditions under which the services will be delivered? (environments and procedures)

If the answers to these four questions are presented with clarity and precision, the problems of legal interpretation are reduced. However, the last three questions represent substantial policy issues for children with autistic spectrum disorders. The phrases "scarce resources" and "almost unlimited needs" guarantee a continuing struggle to obtain those needed resources by those concerned with the well being of children with autistic spectrum disorders and their families.

Federal policy for children with special needs emerged in two forms: legislation passed by Congress and a series of decisions by the courts. Some states and local communities had previously established services and policies for children with special needs, but these policies were limited and widely scattered. Congress decided that a federal mandate was necessary to provide a more unified set of services and to keep parents from frantically running from community to community, and state to state, in search of needed assistance for their children. This chapter reviews briefly the key legislation and court decisions that currently form public policy with regard to children with autism and then comments on the adequacy of services and resources.

LEGISLATION

IDEA Regulations

The first key federal legislation relevant to children with autistic spectrum disorders was the Education of All Handicapped Children Act (P.L. 94-142) in 1975. This legislation has been amended many times since and now carries the title of Individuals with Disability Education Act (IDEA) (P.L. 105-17). However, legislation can only set the rules; it cannot guarantee that they will be carried out or followed faithfully. The citizens' recourse, when they think the law is not being faithfully administered, is to turn to the courts for help. By the end of 1999, almost 150 cases seeking more appropriate educational programs for children with autistic spectrum disorders were in the hearing rooms of the courts (Mandlawitz, 1999). So, clearly, there are serious policy issues still unsettled in this special area.

Children with autism are specifically included in the IDEA legislation (U.S.C. 1401(3)(A)):

The term 'child with a disability' means a child:
i. with mental retardation, hearing impairments (including deafness) speech or language impairments, visual impairments (including blindness), serious emotional disturbance (hereinafter referred to as 'emotional disturbance') orthopedic impairments, *autism*, traumatic brain injury, other health impairments or specific learning disabilities and
ii. who, by reason thereof, needs special education and related services.

The regulations (34 C.F.R. 300.7 © (1)) further define autism:
Autism means a developmental disability significantly affecting verbal and nonverbal communication and social interaction, generally evident before age three that adversely affects a child's educational performance. Other characteristics often associated with autism are engagement in repetitive activities and stereotyped movements, resistance to environ-

mental change or change in daily routines, and unusual responses to sensory experiences.

There is no question of the intent of Congress to include children with autism in this legislation. However, there are two questions that must be answered before a child qualifies for services under IDEA: Does the child have a qualifying disability? Does the child need special education due to the disability?

The diagnosis "with autism" clearly answers the first question, and it is rare that a child with autism does not need special education services as well as a number of related services also approved under this law. Therefore, children with autism, including all autistic spectrum disorders, are a full-fledged subgroup entitled to all the provisions of this comprehensive legislation.

In addition to special educational services, children with autism can take advantage of the provisions in IDEA that deal with "related services." These services include speech-language pathology and audiology services, psychological services, physical and occupational therapy, recreation (including therapeutic recreation), early identification and assessment of disabilities, counseling services, including rehabilitation counseling, orientation and mobility services, medical services for diagnostic or evaluation purposes, school health services, social work services in school, and parent counseling and training.

Six major principles, extending back to the original legislation, have formed the basis of legal rights of children with special needs under the IDEA (Kirk et al., 2000):

1. Zero reject. All children with disabilities must be provided a free and appropriate public education (FAPE). This means local school systems do not have the option to decide whether or not to provide needed services. For children with autistic spectrum disorders, this means that no such child, regardless of degree of impairment or manifestation of difficult behavior, can be denied educational services.

2. Nondiscriminatory evaluation. Each student must receive a full individual examination before being placed in a special education program, with tests appropriate to the child's cultural and linguistic background. For children with autistic spectrum disorders this means an appropriate evaluation that is carried out by personnel with experience in the use of the appropriate tests and protocols for children with these disorders.

3. Individualized Education Program. One of the unique aspects of this law was the requirement for an individualized education plan (IEP).

A team of people are required to establish an IEP, and the law notes that this team should consist of at least one general education teacher, the special education teacher, a representative of the school district qualified to provide or supervise specially designed instruction, an individual who can interpret the instructional implications of evaluation results, the student (if appropriate), and other individuals who have knowledge or special expertise (20 U.S.C, 1414 (d) (1) (B)). An IEP must be written for every student with a disability who is receiving special education. The IEP must describe the child's current performance and goals for the school year, the particular special education services to be delivered, and the procedures by which outcomes are evaluated. For children with autistic spectrum disorders, this is an important provision, because it requires the schools to develop a program, carried out by personnel who are skilled in working with children with these disorders, that fits the needs of each particular child and does not just routinely place a child in a program that already exists for other children with special needs. A child with autistic spectrum disorders should have the IEP team assembled in the school district, and it is their responsibility to chart strengths and needs of the child and family, as well as goals of the individual program, the means for carrying it out, and the means for determining if the plan is successful.

A companion bill for infants and toddlers with disabilities (P.L. 99-457) had a similar provision to the IEP for an Individual Family Service Plan (IFSP). Providing services to address the needs of children under age 3 years with disabilities is a responsibility of states. How this responsibility is assigned varies from state to state, but it may fall to education or health or social service agencies. As local educational authorities are obligated to provide appropriate educational programs for children with disabilities who are 3 years and older, so states and local communities are obligated to provide appropriate services for children under age 3 years. However, as for older children, the gap between the intent of the law and its implementation is often large. The number of lawsuits brought by parents are one indication of dissatisfaction with the planning process. Similar to an IEP, an IFSP multidisciplinary team should be assembled that specifies the strengths and needs of children and their families, goals of the individualized program, how these goals will be addressed, and ways to measure the effectiveness of the plan. The appropriateness of an IFSP should be determined by the extent to which it meets the needs of children with autistic spectrum disorders and their families.

4. Least Restrictive Environment. As much as possible, children with disabilities must be educated with children without disabilities. The educational philosophy is to move children with special needs as close to the normal setting (regular classroom) as feasible. For a child with an autistic spectrum disorder, this means that there is an expectation that the child

should be interacting on a regular basis with children without autism, if at all possible, and within a regular classroom, with reverse mainstreaming or in other supervised settings. When recommending another placement, a school must explain in writing why a child is *not* being placed in a regular classroom.

The appropriateness of the placement has received much attention for children with autism. Some general ways that the courts have used to settle such placement issues is to pose the following questions (Richmond Community Schools 301DELR 208 ([SEA IN 1999]):

a. What are the educational benefits to the student in the general education classroom, with supplementary aids and services, as compared with the educational benefits of a special education classroom?

b. What will be the nonacademic or personal benefits to the student in interactions with peers who do not have disabilities?

c. What would be the effect of the presence of the student on the teacher and other students in the general education classroom?

d. What would be the relative costs for providing necessary supplementary aids and services to the student in the general education classroom?

5. Due Process. Due process is a set of legal procedures to ensure the fairness of educational decisions and the accountability of both professionals and parents in making those decisions. For a child with an autistic spectrum disorder, this means that the parents can call a hearing when they do not agree with the school's plans for their child, they can obtain an individual evaluation from a qualified examiner outside the school system, and they can take other actions to ensure that both family and child have channels through which to voice their interests and concerns.

6. Parental Participation. Parents are to be included in the development of the IEP, and they have the right to access their child's educational records. For a child with an autistic spectrum disorder, this means that parents can obtain the test results and educational evaluations of their child and can participate as an equal in the development of the IEP.

This IDEA law is an entitlement, meaning that all citizens with disabilities have access to its provisions. Other relevant laws, such as the Americans with Disabilities Act (P.L. 101-336) and Section 504 of the Rehabilitation Act (29 U.S.C., Sec. 794) are designed as protection against discrimination or unfair treatment because of a disability. They come into play when discrimination can be documented. A substantial number of due process hearings and court cases have resulted from the concerns of some parents of children with autistic spectrum disorders that the legal rights of their child and family have not been observed.

Role of the Courts

For the past few decades the courts have been one of the protectors of the rights of children with disabilities and their families. Beginning with the PARC case (*Pennsylvania Association for Retarded Children v. Commonwealth of Pennsylvania, 1972*), the courts have tended to side with the rights of the child to a free and appropriate education. But just what does "appropriate" mean in this context? This term has been the basis of many of the legal issues raised by parents and advocates. Parents often believe that the local education authority (LEA) is assuming less responsibility than it should in providing special services for children with autistic spectrum disorders. The schools, faced with high costs for some of the recommended treatments for their students with autism, have tried to find a way of providing services that, while appropriate, will not overburden their budgets. These two understandable positions create the fertile ground for many legal disputes.

One of the key judicial decisions in recent times was made in what is widely known as the Rowley case (*Board of Education of the Hendrick Hudson School District v. Rowley*, 458 U.S. 176, 1982). In that decision, the court rejected the request of a girl with deafness for a classroom interpreter, reasoning that the school had already provided amplification devices for the girl and she seemed to be performing at an appropriate level in school. Therefore, there was no compelling evidence that she was being harmed through the services being provided by the school.

The Supreme Court held in the Rowley case that the purpose of IDEA was to provide appropriate, not optimal, special education, and, to that end, courts may not substitute their notion of sound educational policy for those of the school authorities. A subsequent case (*Polk v. Central Susquehanna Intermediate Unit 16*, 853 F.2nd 171, 180-184 (3rd Cir. 1988)) made it clear that such services must be more than *de minimus*: "While appropriate does not mean 'the best possible education that a school could provide if given access to unlimited funds,' it does require the state to provide personalized instruction with sufficient support services to permit the handicapped child to benefit educationally."

So where is the line to be drawn between optimal and meaningful services? While the Supreme Court clearly meant the school systems to have the predominant role in deciding what "appropriate treatment" should be, if a school system appears to be less than diligent in making such plans, or violates procedures of due process, or if expert testimony suggests that the schools are doing less than necessary, then decisions may be rendered against the schools (Mandlawitz, 1999).

One of the more common issues is to determine whether the states and schools, through their control of the development of the legally required IFSP and IEP, are respectively providing only the treatments or personnel that they have available, rather than the treatment that the child needs. Courts have been well aware that the presumed equality of parents in the process of developing an IEP often is not observed, and that some schools have tried to present their version of an IEP plan whether or not the parents really agreed.

Intensity of treatment has become a major source of contention in the courts for cases of children with autism. Many parents, convinced of the benefits of applied behavioral analysis techniques and of Lovaas-type therapies (Lovaas, 1987), have sued the school systems so that their child could receive the intense treatments (25-40 hours a week) that such therapies require. Hearing officers and the courts have determined that the degree of intensity should depend on the needs of an individual child. In many of these cases, the schools have countered with a suggestion of fewer hours of therapy and more in-class activities. The setting for the treatment program has become another issue, since IDEA stresses that the services should be provided in the least restrictive environment, while many parents wish to have home-based service provided.

ADEQUACY OF SERVICES AND RESOURCES

At the present time, IDEA serves as the basic education legislation that provides support for children with disabilities, which clearly includes children with autistic spectrum disorders. Some advocates have proposed special legislation dealing only with children with autism, but two objections have been raised. First, there is substantial doubt that legislation dealing with such a small segment of the populace would receive favorable treatment. It took many years, with the entire disability community behind it, to reach the current level of support for IDEA. Second, there is little reason to believe that the language in IDEA is the source of the problem. It is a "disability neutral" piece of legislation, and it appears that it is the way the current law is being *implemented* that raises questions about services for children with autistic spectrum disorders, not the provisions of the law itself. Another law would likely have the same problems of implementation as IDEA.

The 1997 amendments to IDEA (P.L. 105-17) did include some specific references to children with autism, including provisions for outcome-based education, greater access to the general curriculum, clarification of discipline provisions, and creation of a rebuttable presumption in favor of functional behavioral assessment and positive behavioral interventions and supports. This addition of special sections and amendments to the base legislation to deal with the special problems of children with autism is an appropriate strategy to follow in the future.

Parents and advocates for children with autistic spectrum disorders sometimes question whether the general facilities made available for children with disabilities really fit the needs of children with these disorders. If a school psychologist with no experience or background in examining children with autism is called into the IEP hearings, can his or her contribution be considered of professional quality in developing a plan for this child? Similarly, are teachers trained in general special education techniques, but with no additional preparation regarding children with autistic spectrum disorders, really ready to accept the instructional responsibilities for those children? It is possible that even a well designed special education program for a school district could still fall short of adequately providing for the special needs of children with autistic spectrum disorders. It seems clear that the treatment costs for children with autism— sometimes amounting to $40,000 to $60,000 a year—lie at the heart of many of the disputes between parents and school systems, with the schools trying to reduce their financial obligations while still providing appropriate services to the child and family. A number of states have attempted to bring a variety of resources together to deal with the fiscal problems created by the recommended intensive treatments for children with autism and their families. Several states (e.g., Wisconsin, Vermont) have used Medicaid reimbursement as a primary source of funds, while other states (North Carolina, Connecticut) use a combination of funds (developmental disabilities, Part C of IDEA, private insurance, etc.). Some systematic strategy and pattern of funding clearly seems to be called for (Hurth et al., 2000).

Many disputes arise because of the uncertainties of the various parties about what is appropriate and available in individual circumstances. It would be useful for all concerned to have an updated summary of current case law on cases with children with autistic spectrum disorders, accessible on the Internet or from other sources, so that schools and parents can understand the various options available to them that are consistent with FAPE. Policies are always evolving as new knowledge and problems are introduced into the environment. The professional community that wishes to stand with the parents and the needs of their children should not be placed in an antagonistic posture to them by rules and regulations that hinder rather than help the positive relationship between school and family.

In addition, levels of information about autistic spectrum disorders vary greatly within the professional communities that make funding and policy recommendations and decisions, including state task forces in peer education and review panels in federal agencies. It is therefore crucial that persons knowledgeable in the range of needs and interventions associated with autistic spectrum disorders be included in or consulted by these communities.

14

Personnel Preparation

NEED FOR A SUPPORT INFRASTRUCTURE

The nature of autistic spectrum disorders and other disabilities that frequently accompany them has significant implications for approaches to education and intervention at school, in the home, and in the community. As might be expected in a field with different philosophies and instructional strategies, there is also diversity in the approaches to personnel preparation. Approaches vary from preservice university models in a traditional special education program to mentoring in a major treatment center, where instruction is provided by psychologists, psychiatrists, special educators, speech and language pathologists, and others.

Fundamental questions include: Who should receive special instruction? Who should provide special instruction? What should the content of the program be? Where should this instruction take place? Approaches that emphasize specific "packages" may be particularly efficient, but they may understate the immediate and long-term needs of individual students with autistic spectrum disorders for behavior support and for instruction across areas. However, it is encouraging that there are models of personnel preparation programs in place within state systems and some universities, and, as indicated in the previous chapters, a wealth of knowledge about educational interventions in autistic spectrum disorders from which to draw. The challenge for states and communities and the children and families they are serving is to choose and implement effective approaches for personnel preparation, beyond a single training effort, to provide a continuum of services across time.

Teachers must be familiar with theory and research concerning best practices for children with autistic spectrum disorders, including methods of applied behavior analysis, naturalistic learning, incidental teaching, assistive technology, socialization, communication, inclusion, adaptation of the environment, language interventions, assessment, and the effective use of data collection systems. Specific problems in generalization and maintenance of behaviors also affect the need for training in methods of teaching children with autistic spectrum disorders. The wide range of IQ scores and verbal skills associated with autistic spectrum disorders, from profound mental retardation and severe language impairments to superior intelligence, make the need for training of personnel even greater. To enable teachers to adequately work with parents and with other professionals to set appropriate goals, teachers need familiarity with the course of autism and the range of possible outcomes.

Effective programming for children with autism and their families requires that the direct service provider (e.g., special education teacher, regular education teacher, early childhood teacher, speech and language pathologist) be a part of a support system team, not an isolated individual, that is struggling with complex neurological, sociological, educational, and behavioral problems. What is needed is a support infrastructure that can provide the direct service provider with the needed assistance (Gallagher and Clifford, 2000). Just as a physician in medicine is surrounded by an infrastructure of specialists, laboratories, medical schools, support personnel, and pharmaceutical research, a program for children with autistic spectrum disorders should have the various elements of infrastructure noted in Box 14.1. As shown in the box, there is a need for personnel preparation to produce qualified teachers and support staff and to provide technical assistance to answer problems faced by local practitioners, as well as to generate research, enhance communication, and support demonstration projects. As discussed earlier in the report, prevalence estimates of autistic spectrum disorders reflect continuing increases in the number of children who need services. The Twentieth Annual Report to Congress from the Department of Education's Office of Special Education (OSEP) (1999:III-I) announced, "There is a serious shortage of special education teachers."

Finding certified teachers in special education has always been an uphill struggle. If there is a shortage in general special education, that shortage is even more serious in the growing field of autistic spectrum disorders. Without an accurate data system in and across states, no one knows how many specialists are being trained, how many training programs are operational, or the professional disciplines that are involved. Of concern is not only the preparation of special education teachers or early interventionists, but also that of school psychologists, speech pathologists, behavior analysts, occupational and physical therapists, and

BOX 14-1
Elements of a Support Infrastructure

Personnel Preparation	There is need for continuous flow of qualified personnel. To that end, there needs to be a series of training programs and experiences directed at preservice and inservice needs.
Technical Assistance	Many professionals and programs run into situations related to autism that cause them to seek additional professional help. Programs of technical assistance are designed to provide consultation and short-term training to meet the needs of the requester.
Applied Research and Program Evaluation	There is a strong need to be reflective about our own performance as part of a strategy of continuous improvement. Public calls for accountability stress the importance of developing the proper tools and measuring instruments and personnel to conduct effective program evaluation.
Communication	It is important to establish a communications network sothat there is continuous contact with other professionals who are working on the same or similar problems. It is a way of keeping up with the latest knowledge and practices.
Demonstration	One of the strategies that has been often used to improve program quality is to identify outstanding programs, establish them as demonstration centers, and then urge other professionals to observe and e mulate what is happening in those centers or programs that could be transferred to their own program.
Data Systems	There are many important policy questions that cannot be answered without an organized data system. Questions such as, "How many children with autism are there?" or "How many teachers are needed?" can only be addressed if one has a data system to compile the demographics of the individuals or programs.
Comprehensive Planning	One of the key aspects of an infrastructure is the ability to do comprehensive statewide planning and to be able to allocate resources over time and in a systematic manner to more easily reach the goals of the program.

SOURCE: Gallagher and Clifford (2000).

other professionals who fill important roles in the treatment programs of children with autistic spectrum disorders.

Special education statistics on the number of children with autism that are being served are available (OSEP, 1999), but it is not clear how accurate they are, given that school systems vary in the degree to which their classification systems have reflected the broadening of diagnostic criteria for autistic spectrum disorders in the last ten years. Without comprehensive planning and estimates, it will not be possible to allocate the proper amounts of personnel and fiscal resources. Personnel preparation has become an increasingly well-publicized issue as the number of children identified with autistic spectrum disorders has increased and their special needs have become more evident. Despite the widespread acceptance of the importance of an infrastructure to support the service delivery system, however, there has been relatively little written on the task of personnel preparation for providing interventions for children with autistic spectrum disorders. This chapter identifies the major trends in personnel preparation in this field and the special challenges they present to the professional communities involved.

KINDS OF PERSONNEL

Special education teachers and early interventionists come to working with children with autistic spectrum disorders from diverse backgrounds. These backgrounds may provide strong instruction in some aspects of development and education relevant to autistic spectrum disorders and little or no instruction in other aspects. Thus, many qualified special education and early intervention teachers have little experience or knowledge about the specific communication problems, limited social skills, and unusual behaviors of children with autistic spectrum disorders. Even if they had received solid training in general special education or special early intervention, they may also have had little or no instruction about such important strategies as applied behavior analysis, the use of physical structure and visual systems in teaching, or appropriate use of alternative or complementary methods of communication, such as sign language or picture systems.

As described earlier in Chapters 11 and 12, there is no one ideal curriculum for children with autistic spectrum disorders. Because these children have diverse needs and learn best in diverse contexts, most of the well-established comprehensive intervention programs discussed in Chapters 11 and 12 use many different curricula to design highly individualized programs for students (Anderson and Romanczyk, 1999; Strain and Hoyson, 2000). The need to address many different goals requires that teachers be familiar with alternative sets of curricula and various methods of implementing them. This requirement is strengthened by the fact that many of the early intervention programs place great emphasis on a child's engagement in learning and social activities as key elements predicting progress. A teacher of a child with autistic spectrum disorders is responsible for identifying the child's needs, using appropriate curricula to address those needs, selecting appropriate methods to teach that curricula, and ensuring engagement in these activities despite the child's limited social awareness. A teacher cannot acquire the skills to do this from academic classes or didactic presentations alone. In addition to an infrastructure and ongoing team to help in this process, opportunities to learn from and work with models of working classrooms and effective teachers are crucial for the new teacher of children with autistic spectrum disorders.

The importance of the increasing use of inclusion as an educational strategy makes some form of instruction for general educators or childcare workers also important. Such special instruction may take a form different from that of preparation of special education teachers, who might be expected to encounter a larger number of different children with autistic spectrum disorders in their careers. Issues such as the quick availability of support teams to provide in-service training and workshops for general educators are most relevant for this population. Availability of consultation about specific children is also critical.

One of the potential resources for providing special services for children with autism is the paraprofessional. Pickett (1996) has reported that there are 280,000 paraeducators who work in special education settings. Given the personnel shortages that seem likely to continue into the future, some attempt to include paraeducators within educational intervention programs for children with autism seems highly desirable (French, 1997; Skelton, 1997). Key issues are how these paraprofessionals are to be prepared and what roles they are to play in educational programs. OSEP has provided funds to the National Resource Center for Paraprofessionals at the City University of New York to develop guidelines for paraeducator roles and responsibilities, as well as to develop model standards for their training and supervision. Such standards could be helpful as a guide for training paraprofessionals and for alerting other professionals to their important supervisory responsibilities for such personnel.

One systematic use of paraprofessionals can be seen in the Young Autism Project at UCLA. This program uses a behavioral intervention curriculum that is designed to be delivered in a one-to-one, discrete trial format implemented by parents and trained college student therapists working in a child's home. Brief training is provided to the student therapists before they begin, and ongoing supervision is an integral part of the treatment structure. This strategy includes programming that differs from most early interventions in being both home-based and very intensive. Thus, children receive extensive treatment in situations where it would have been extremely difficult to develop similar programs if fully qualified teachers had provided equivalent services.

The burden of recruiting, organizing, and maintaining a cadre of student therapists requires commensurate management skills and sometimes requires time and personal funds from parents. Many families find it difficult to achieve their goals in terms of intensity of treatment because of the complexities of dealing with student-therapist schedules and attrition (Smith et al., 2000). How to maintain an existing pool of paraprofessionals and how to better integrate the transmission to them of training and knowledge, and how to maintain the balance between stability that should be available in school and center-based systems and the flexibility possible in some home-based and integrated programs are important questions.

PROVIDERS OF PERSONNEL PREPARATION

Significant questions include: Who are the professionals who can be counted upon to provide assistance? Where are such professionals prepared, and who is doing the preparation? As for curriculum and intervention strategies, there are diverse opinions.

One controversy is whether to train specialists for children with autistic spectrum disorders (these specialists may come from a range of backgrounds and are generalists across disciplines within this specialty), or to consider autistic spectrum disorders a unique topic within discipline-specific training (e.g., training of speech and language pathologists or psychologists). Models of both approaches are available: the TEACCH program is an example of the generalist model (Marcus et al., 2000), and the Denver Model (Rogers et al., 2000) is an example of building on separate, but integrated, interdisciplinary approaches (see Chapter 12). Similarly, advocacy groups such as the Autism Society of America and state parents' and educational programs provide broad-based educational opportunities, while professional organizations (e.g., American Speech and Hearing Association) provide information that is more targeted to particular professions. The two models should be considered complementary.

CONTENT OF PERSONNEL PREPARATION PROGRAMS

The content of training programs reflects the diversity of approaches in the field of autism. There is little research comparing the relative effectiveness of personnel preparation models. Some programs have a specific philosophy and approach (e.g., UCLA, LEAP, TEACCH; see Chapter 12); others present more eclectic points of view. Some programs have extensive databases of specific activities (see McClannahan and

Krantz, 2000). The challenge for each program is how to provide differentiated curricula that are adapted to the social, cognitive, and communication needs of children with autistic spectrum disorders. Specific areas addressed by programs include patterns of development in autistic spectrum disorders, theories of underlying deficits and strengths, general and specific strategies of intervention, classroom-based approaches to communication and social development, and methods of evaluating effectiveness.

Teachers learn according to the same principles as their students. Multiple exposures, opportunities to practice, and active involvement in learning are all important aspects of learning in teachers, as well as in children. Many states and community organizations have invested substantial funds in teacher preparation, predominantly through workshops and large-audience lectures by well-known speakers. While such presentations can be inspiring, they do not substitute for training and ongoing supervision and consultation.

There are a number of creative models for the preparation of personnel who provide interventions for children with autistic spectrum disorders. These models have been implemented primarily at a state level (see Hurth et al., 2000). These models can be defined in terms of three stages of training, each related to a different level of experience with autistic spectrum disorders. The first level is initial training, which occurs preservice or in the first few weeks of school and assumes that the trainees have minimal knowledge or experience working with children with autistic spectrum disorders and their families (McClannahan and Krantz, 2000; Smith et al., 2000). The TEACCH program in North Carolina (Marcus et al., 2000) and the Denver program (Rogers et al., 2000), for example, have weeklong preservice workshops that are open to the public. This training usually has a strong hands-on component but also includes lectures and workshops. Across the comprehensive programs reviewed in Chapter 12, the range of time devoted to initial training was from a full-time week of lectures and teaching in a model classroom to didactic sessions held several times a week through the first four to six weeks of school.

A second level of personnel preparation consists of ongoing training and mentorship, usually in the first year of teaching. A lead teacher or supervisor who is available full-time to the staff often provides this training. The primary responsibility of this person, who typically does not have her or his own classroom, is the ongoing training and support of teaching staff in the programs for children with autistic spectrum disorders and also staff in regular classrooms where these children are included. Such a person is part of almost all the well-established programs (see, e.g., Powers, 1994; McGee et al., 1999). The lead teacher usually has general special education credentials and substantial experience in autism beyond university courses. Several programs use systematic checklists with which teachers are rated to provide feedback to both teachers and supervisors about target areas to address (McGee et al., 1999). In addition, many programs involve consultation, dissemination of their own models, and workshops and conferences. The workshops and conferences are not sufficient, by themselves, to train personnel; they are one component of ongoing, individualized, hands-on inservice training (Marcus et al., 2000; McGee et al., 1999).

Many of the comprehensive programs reviewed in this and other documents recruit undergraduate university students to work in classrooms and provide practice for graduate students (Harris and Handleman, 1994). Practicum sites provide extremely valuable opportunities for students to work with children with autistic spectrum disorders. Often this training is highly organized within a program that focuses on autistic spectrum disorders, but it also may have relations to the general special education curriculum. This integration is a critical goal as an investment in future teachers and other special education personnel.

A third stage of personnel preparation includes the major effort to provide technical assistance to existing programs through numerous state and federal agencies (Hurth et al., 2000). The Indiana Resource Center for Autism publishes an annual directory of autism training and technical assistance programs. The most recent edition reports over 30 programs in 22 states. The center provides technical assistance aimed at helping communities, organizations, and families acquire the knowledge and skills to support children and adults in early intervention, school, community, and work settings. Although much more work is needed, a number of successful programs and efforts to provide personnel support are in place in different states (see Hurth et al., 2000).

Research concerning change in educational and other opportunities suggests that administrative attitudes and support are critical for improving schools. Finding ways of building on the knowledge of teachers as they acquire experience with children with autism and finding ways of keeping skilled personnel within the field are critically important. Providing knowledge about autistic spectrum disorders to special education and regular education administrators, as well as specialized providers with major roles in early intervention (e.g., speech and language pathologists), will be critical in effecting proactive change.

RESOURCES

One of the clear needs in the field of autism is to increase the number of well-prepared professionals to work with children and their families. State and federal agencies have traditionally been the source of funds that can be used by institutions of higher learning, clinics, and other training centers to increase the supply of qualified persons. Increasingly, the demand for these programs has come from local communities and parent and other advocacy organizations. While the National Institutes of Health have supported a variety of research projects related to both children and adults with autism, the major federal agency for personnel preparation has been the Department of Education's Office of Special Education Programs. In 1999, the agency supported personnel preparation programs in eight universities that were preparing master's degree personnel in special education and in speech-language pathology with an emphasis on autism. Other OSEP funds went to technical assistance operations at the state and local levels. The agency also funds a major technical assistance program, the National Early Childhood Technical Assistance System, which has produced a series of widely distributed publications, such as an annotated bibliography on autistic spectrum disorders, a list of national contacts and other references on autism in early childhood, and a list of OSEP-funded early childhood projects and materials on autistic spectrum disorders. This last publication reports on a variety of print products, such as a social skills training program for the classroom, parent training modules, and suggestions for developing individualized supports for young children with autism and their families.

OSEP provides support for various demonstration projects designed to illustrate best practices in the area of autism, including Alaska's autism intensive early intervention project at The University of Alaska at Anchorage, a model for early treatment of toddlers at Emory University, and a school-based preschool program for children with autism at University of Washington. In addition, a major effort to replicate the Lovaas (1987) intervention program includes 13 centers in the United States and 4 in foreign countries; the United States sites are funded by the National Institute of Mental Health.

Outreach projects are designed to disseminate proven practices and to encourage their replication beyond the original program. An example of such outreach is a project at the University of South Florida, Delivering Individualized Support for Young Children with Autism, which assists state systems in implementing a program of comprehensive and effective support for young children with autism and their families.

The Council for Exceptional Children (2000) has been a leader in the development of standards for many different fields of special education. The council currently does not differentiate specific standards for educating children with autism; it combines standards for the category of autism with those for children with mental retardation and other developmental disabilities. The council is considering developing a separate certificate for special areas such as autism to recognize teachers who have participated in specific personnel preparation within this field.

The developers of educational strategies for children with autistic spectrum disorders have a responsibility to describe their procedures with enough clarity that others can replicate their approaches. Of all the interventions available, except for those discussed in Chapters 11 and 12, few interventions for these children are manualized at this time. Thus, much information is by word of mouth or informal communications. Providing treatment manuals, instructions, and procedures in print, videotape, and audiotape media will assist personnel preparation activities for improving the education of young children with autistic spectrum disorders.

15

Methodological Issues in Research on Educational Interventions

Research on educational interventions for young children with autism should inform consumers, policy makers, and scientists about practices that produce positive outcomes for children and families. Ultimately, such research should be able to demonstrate that there is a causal relationship between an educational intervention and immediate or long-term changes that occur in development, behavior, social relationships, and normative life circumstances. A primary goal of early intervention research is to determine the types of practices that are most effective for children with specific characteristics (Guralnick, 1997).

If young children with autistic spectrum disorders were homogeneous in intelligence, behavior, and family circumstances, and if researchers and educators could apply a uniform amount of treatment in nearly identical settings and life circumstances, then a standard, randomized-group, clinical-trial research design could be employed to provide unequivocal answers to questions about treatments and outcomes. However, the characteristics of young children with autistic spectrum disorders and their life circumstances are exceedingly heterogeneous in nature. This heterogeneity creates substantial problems when scientists attempt to use standard research methodology to address questions about the effectiveness of educational treatments for young children with autistic spectrum disorders.

In this chapter we examine a range of issues related to research designs and methodologies. We begin by discussing the different research literatures that could inform early intervention research but which currently are relatively independent. We then consider a range of methodological issues pertaining to research involving children with autistic spectrum disorders, including information useful for describing samples; the benefits and practical problems of using randomized, clinical trial research design and the movement toward treatment comparison and aptitude-by-treatment interactions; the relative benefits and limitations of single-subject research methodology; assessing fidelity of treatment; potential use of current methodologies for modeling developmental growth of children and factors affecting growth; and group size.

SEPARATE LITERATURES

There are several distinct, substantial, and independent bodies of research addressing issues concerning young children with autistic spectrum disorders. One basic body of literature describes and attempts to explain the neurological (Minshew et al., 1997), behavioral (Sigman and Ruskin, 1999), and developmental (Wetherby and Prutting, 1984) characteristics of children with autistic spectrum disorders. A second body of research has addressed issues related to diagnosis, particularly early diagnosis, of autism (Lord, 1997) and the related issue of prevalence (Fombonne, 1999). A third body of literature has examined the effects of comprehensive treatment programs on the immediate and long-term outcomes for young children with autistic spectrum disorders and their families (e.g., Harris et al., 1991; McEachin et al., 1993; Rogers and DiLalla, 1991; Strain and Hoyson, 2000). A fourth body of research has addressed individual instructional or intervention approaches that focus on specific aspects of a child's behavior, such as social skills (McConnell, 1999), language and communication (Goldstein, 1999), or problem behavior (Horner et al., 2000). These four bodies of literature have different primary purposes (and research questions), conceptual and theoretical frames of reference, and research methodologies. However, these research literatures all have the potential of informing the design, content, and evaluation of intervention procedures.

Similarly, funding for autism intervention and educational research has also come from a number of federal institutes with separate, but overlapping missions. These include the Office of Special Education Programs (OSEP) in the U.S. Department of Education and the National Institute of Child Health and Human Development (NICHD), National Institute of Mental Health (NIMH), National Institute of Neurological Disorders and Stroke (NINDS) and National Institute on Deafness and Other Communication Disorders (NIDCD), in the U.S. Department of Health and Human Services. More recently, parent-initiated, nonprofit agencies such as Autism Society of America Foundation, Cure Autism Now (CAN), and the National Alliance for Autism Research (NAAR) have had an increasing role in supporting and instigating research.

Although several of these literatures appear to be internally well integrated, there is remarkably little integration across literatures. For example, the information from the literature describing characteristics of children with autistic spectrum disorders is often not linked to treatment programs. Likewise, the developmental literature, which is descriptive in nature, has only rarely been integrated into individual intervention practice research, which tends to be behaviorally oriented (see Lifter et al., 1993 for a notable exception). Similarly, research that emphasizes the relationships among behaviors in response to treatment has been much more rare than descriptive studies of development in multiple domains (Wolery and Garfinkle, 2000).

Integration of the collective body of knowledge represented in these four literatures is important and could inform practice. It would be productive for leaders from these four research traditions to communicate regularly around the common issue of educational interventions for young children with autistic spectrum disorders. This communication could foster the research integration that appears to be missing from the literature. Communication could be enhanced by a series of meetings that bring together researchers and agencies who sponsor research, focusing on the task of reporting implications for designing programs for young children with autistic spectrum disorders.

EARLY SCREENING AND DIAGNOSIS

One assumption in early intervention research is that treatment should begin as soon as possible. However, to accomplish this, children must be identified. Early diagnosis has important implications for treatment, since different interventions would be appropriate for very young children (e.g., 15 months of age) than for children of 2 or 3 years old.

There is a difference between screening and diagnosis. Screening, as understood in the United States, may mean two things. One is a process carried out by a primary care provider to decide whether a referral for more services is warranted: for example, a pediatrician, told by parents that their 18-month old child has poor eye contact and has stopped speaking within the last month, must decide whether and where to refer the child for further assessment. A second type of screening is a public health process by which health care providers routinely assess for risk for autistic spectrum disorders in children whose parents have not necessarily raised concerns.

Diagnosis is a much more comprehensive process carried out by a specialized team of professionals. For autistic spectrum disorders, diagnosis involves not only identifying the disorder and any other developmental and behavioral disorders associated with it, but also helping parents to understand the meaning of the diagnostic terms and what the parents can do to help their children. (Issues relating to diagnosis are discussed in detail in Chapter 2.)

In the early 1990s, the Checklist for Autism in Toddlers (CHAT) was developed as a creative, theoretically based attempt at a public health screening instrument (Baron-Cohen et al., 1992). With follow-up, however, it appeared that the sensitivity of the CHAT in identifying autism in nonreferred children was far too low to be considered an appropriate screening tool (Baird et al., 2000). Nevertheless, the instrument has made a significant contribution as a first step in this area. The techniques described in the CHAT may also be helpful in providing a primary health care professional with some behaviors on which to focus during screening (e.g., eye contact, pretending). Pilot data from a modification of this instrument, the M-CHAT, are in press.

Other screening tools, such as the Pervasive Developmental Disorders Screening Test (PDDST; Siegel, 1998) and the Screening Tool for Autism in Two Year Olds (STAT, Stone, 1998), are used to determine whether further diagnostic assessments are merited after a concern has arisen. Each of these instruments has promise: an initial empirical evaluation of the STAT has just been published (Stone et al., 2000); an evaluation of the PDDST is not yet available. The Autism Screening Questionnaire (ASQ; Berument et al., 1999) was developed for screening research participants 4 years of age and older. It has not yet been tested with younger children or with families who have not already received a diagnosis of autistic spectrum disorder. Chapter 2 provides more information about screening, as do the interdisciplinary practice parameter guidelines described by Filipek and colleagues (2000). An adequate screening instrument is not currently available either for public health screening or for a brief assessment when a concern arises. Addressing this need is a high priority for researchers. It involves determining how specifically the features of autistic spectrum disorders can be defined in toddlers and contrasting the benefits of this approach with more general identification of risk status.

Research in diagnosis is at a quite different stage. Well-standardized and documented diagnostic instruments have been available for years. These include the Childhood Autism Rating Scale (CARS; Schopler et al., 1988), the Autism Diagnostic Interview-Revised (ADI-R; Lord et al., 1993), and the Autism Diagnostic Observation Schedule (ADOS; Lord et al., 2000). Although there are many ways that these instruments could be improved, their ability to document autism in a reliable and standardized way has been demonstrated. There are also numerous other instruments, including the Autism Behavior Checklist (Krug et al., 1980) and the Gilliam Autism Rating Scale (Gilliam, 1995), about which there are more questions regarding the degree to which their scores reflect accurate diagnosis.

Difficulties also remain for the most well-standardized instruments. While the CARS has been repeatedly shown to produce autism categorizations much like diagnoses, the items on the scale no longer reflect current diagnostic criteria. The ADI-R and the ADOS produce operational categories that fit with current conceptualizations of autism, but they require training and are intended to be used by experienced clinicians. The ADI-R is also quite lengthy, taking about 2 hours to administer. Standardization samples for both instruments are small, though replications of their diagnostic categorizations have been good (Yirmiya et al., 1994; Tanguay, 1998). Neither provides adequate discrimination between autism and other autistic spectrum disorders, though the ADOS makes a first attempt to do so. Thus, these instruments are important in providing standards for research, but their contributions to educational practice will require training of specialists (both in and outside educational systems) and perhaps modification of the instruments.

DESCRIPTION OF PARTICIPANTS IN STUDIES

To interpret the results of early intervention research and to conduct some of the sophisticated analyses described below, it is important to understand the characteristics of the participants in the studies. As mentioned above, heterogeneity in child characteristics is nearly as much a defining feature of autistic spectrum disorders as are the DSM-IV criteria. Children with the same diagnosis of autistic spectrum disorders, gender, chronological age, and IQ score may well have a range of other different characteristics (e.g., problem behaviors, communication skills, play skills) and may respond differently to intervention treatments. In most research on comprehensive intervention programs using group designs, a limited amount of information is provided about the children participating in the study. Individual intervention practices research often uses a single-subject design; anecdotal descriptions of participants' behaviors are sometimes provided in addition to demographic information, but such descriptions do not follow a standard format. These limitations are reflected in the small proportion of studies that meet the highest standards for research in internal or external validity, as shown in Figures 1-1 and 1-2 (in Chapter 1), and the greater but still variable proportion that meet the second level of criteria in these areas.

Vaguely described samples pose a problem for both group and single-subject designs. One problem is related to internal validity of the study (i.e., the degree to which a researcher can rule out alternative hypotheses that account for treatment outcomes [Campbell and Stanley, 1963]). Unless specific information about participants is provided, it is impossible to know to whom the results of the study apply. For group design research, there are additional problems. When random assignment to treatment groups occurs, the assumption is that the groups will be equivalent. However, with a relatively small sample size, which is the case for most studies of intervention effectiveness, it is essential for the researcher to confirm that participants in different groups are equivalent on major variables that might affect outcome. If participants are vaguely described, then there is limited information about the equivalence of comparison groups.

The recruitment, selection, and attrition of participants are also important issues. Standards and expectations for reporting how potential research participants were identified and persuaded to participate, how they were selected from the pool of potential participants, and how many participants completed the study have been very different within different disciplines (e.g., experimental psychology and epidemiology) and different perspectives (e.g., developmental and behavioral). With increasing attempts to integrate perspectives (see Filipek et al., 2000) to produce practical guidelines or meta-analyses, this information becomes crucial. For example, it is much more difficult to interpret results of a meta-analysis of success rates when a potentially large number of participants proposed for the research may have not been selected because they were deemed likely to be poor responders to an intervention, and another significant proportion of participants may not have completed their course of treatment. If samples are to be combined, and if interpretations are going to span fields, then there will be a need for more information about these processes.

Researchers are often interested in the interactions between child or family characteristics and treatment, sometimes referred to as aptitude-by-treatment interactions. Such analyses allow researchers to determine if the intervention was more effective for participants with certain characteristics. For example, one type of comprehensive treatment program might produce more positive outcomes for children who communicate verbally than for children who are nonverbal. The analysis requires that a reliable measure of the child characteristic or "aptitude" variable be collected. Vague participant descriptions could preclude the possibility of such analyses.

General, nonstandard participant descriptions also affect the external validity of studies (i.e., the degree to which the findings of a study can be generalized to other individuals not in the study [Campbell and Stanley, 1963]). To interpret for whom an individual intervention procedure or comprehensive intervention program might be effective, one has to have a clear understanding of who participated in the study. Both single-subject and group studies build their evidence for external validity on study replications. To compare the findings of different studies, researchers must be able to determine that children with similar characteristics participated in the study.

In many studies of children with autistic spectrum disorders, descriptions of the families' characteristics are either limited or absent. Family and community characteristics represent potential risk and opportunity variables (Gabarino and Ganzel, 2000); yet, there has been very limited research on the effects of such family and community variables on outcomes for children with autistic spectrum disorders (Wolery and Garfinkle, 2000). For example, it is possible that a young child with autism who lives in a single-parent family and low-income neighborhood will respond differently to treatment than a child with autism from a two-parent family living in a middle-class neighborhood. In order to investigate the effect of family and community characteristics on treatment outcomes, it is necessary to provide descriptive information about families of children who participate in intervention research.

In order to further knowledge of the effects of interventions, it is critical that researchers develop and use standard procedures for describing the characteristics of participants in their studies and of their families. In addition to the information that is routinely provided (e.g., standardized diagnosis, chronological age, gender, IQ), standard information should include measures of adaptive behavior, communication, social skills, school placement, and race. Also, information about the family should include number of parents living in the family, parents' education levels, and socioeconomic status. Although some recent studies have begun providing such information, this has not been the norm for the field.

METHODOLOGICAL ISSUES

To examine effectiveness of comprehensive early intervention programs and individual intervention practices for children with autistic spectrum disorders, standards must be established for determining the causal relationship between the treatment procedures and the identified outcomes. The various experimental methodologies employed reflect the different literatures noted earlier. Studies documenting the effects of comprehensive treatment programs have employed experimental group designs, while those documenting individual practices have primarily employed single-subject designs, often replicated across several subjects.

Randomized Clinical Trials

The most rigorous approach for experimental group research design is the randomized clinical trial. In this design, study participants are randomly assigned, if possible by someone not associated with the program or knowledgeable about the participants' characteristics, to a treatment group that receives the educational intervention or to a comparison group that receives no educational intervention or a different form of intervention (Kasari, 2000). Measurement of potential treatment effects (e.g., developmental assessments, family measures) occurs before the educational intervention begins and again at the end of the intervention; the measurement is blind to which group a participant has been assigned to. Assuming that the groups are equivalent on the pretest measures, differences at the end of the intervention are attributed to the treatment. As noted above, the purpose of random assignment is to control for or reduce the likelihood that confounding variables (e.g., very determined parents requesting a particular treatment) would account for differences in outcomes for the treatment and contrast groups.

Reviews of the literature to date (Rogers, 1998) and individual papers prepared for this committee (Kasari, 2000; Wolery and Garfinkle, 2000) show that the randomized clinical trial model has only rarely been used to determine treatment outcomes (see Jocelyn et al.[1998] and Smith et al. [2000] for exceptions). Other studies have attempted to address the research question of treatment effectiveness by employing quasi-experimental designs (Cook and Campbell, 1979) in which nonrandomized control or contrast groups are used as a basis for gauging treatment effects (Fenske et al., 1985). Another approach has been to use single group designs in which the changes in children's development while they are in the program are compared with children's rates of development before they entered the program, or to the rate of development of typically developing children (Harris et al., 1991; Hoyson et al., 1984). These designs, while providing some information about treatment outcomes, may not control for important confounding variables, such as subject selection and nonspecific or placebo effects (see Campbell and Stanley's [1963] classic paper on group experimental methodology).

For programs providing treatment to young children with autistic spectrum disorders and their families, random assignment is often a difficult procedure. By its very nature, it requires that some children and families be assigned to an alternative treatment condition. Unless two treatments of equal potential value can be compared, such assignment creates the ethical issue of not providing the most promising treatment to children who might benefit. An argument is sometimes made (as it often is in medical treatment studies) that until a treatment is supported by a randomized clinical trial, the evidence for effectiveness of the treatment does not exist. In addition, when children are randomly assigned to two different treatment conditions, a researcher still must closely assess the experiences of the child and family, because families may seek and obtain services for their children outside of the treatment study. Ideally, children and families could be assigned to equally attractive alternative treatments, so that the research question changes from one of single treatment effectiveness to treatment comparison. However, this approach would require the availability of two different and equally strong programs, usually within the same geographic area, and the willingness of the programs and parents to participate. This situation does not often occur.

Another issue related to random assignment is the heterogeneity of the population of children with autistic spectrum disorders. Most treatment studies, because of the prevalence of autistic spectrum disorders and the expense and labor intensity of treatment, will have small sample sizes. Random assignment within a relatively small, heterogeneous sample does not ensure equivalent groups, so a researcher may match children on relevant characteristics (e.g., IQ score, age) and then select from the matched sets to randomly assign children to control and treatment groups. As noted above, such stratification of the sample of participants requires a thorough description of the participants as well as confidence that the variable(s) on which children are matched are of greatest significance.

An issue related to the size and heterogeneity of groups in the randomized clinical trail approach is statistical power (Cohen, 1988). Groups have to be large enough to detect a significant difference in treatment outcomes when it occurs. The smaller the size of the group, the larger the difference in treatment outcomes has to be in order to show a statistically significant effect. Also, variability on pretest measures, as may occur with heterogeneous samples, sometimes obscures treatment differences if the sample size is not sufficiently large. Because the number of children with autistic spectrum disorders enrolled in particular treatment programs often is not large, sample size and within-group variability are challenges to the use of randomized clinical control methodology for determining the effectiveness of educational interventions for those children.

Single-Subject Designs

In contrast to group experimental designs, single-subject design methodology uses a smaller number of subjects and establishes the causal relationship between treatment and outcomes by a series of intrasubject or intersubject replications of treatment effects (Kazdin, 1982). The two most frequently used methods are the withdrawal-of-treatment design and the multiple baseline design.

In the withdrawal of treatment design, a baseline level of performance (e.g., frequency of stereotypic behavior or social interactions) is established over a series of sessions, and a treatment is applied in a second phase of the study. When reliable changes in the outcome variable occur, the treatment is withdrawn in the third phase of the study, and concomitant changes in the outcome variable are examined. Often, the treatment is reinstated in a fourth phase of the study, with changes in the outcome variable expected. Changes in the outcome variable (e.g., increases in desired behavior or decreases in undesirable behavior) that reliably occur when the treatment is implemented and withdrawn indicate a functional (i.e., causal) relationship between the treatment and outcome variables (Barlow and Hersen, 1984). This design is usually replicated with at least two or three participants.

In a multiple baseline design, three (or more) participants may be involved. Data are collected for all participants in an initial baseline phase, and then the treatment is begun with one participant while the others remain in the baseline phase of the study. When changes occur for the first participant, the treatment is introduced for the second participant, and when changes occur for the second participant, the treatment is introduced for the third participant. Variations on this design include multiple baselines across behaviors of single individuals and multiple baselines across settings. Again, the researcher infers a functional relationship when changes reliably occur only after the treatment is implemented across (usually three) participants, settings, or behaviors.

Single-subject designs differ from group designs in three ways. First, changes in the outcome variables are measured frequently (e.g., daily, weekly) rather than at the beginning and end of the treatment. The second is that visual analysis of differences in trends in the data (e.g., increases in social interaction or decreases in stereotypic behavior) is usually used to determine the effectiveness of treatment, rather than statistical analyses between groups. Third, unlike group designs, in which the treatments often represent a range of theoretical perspectives, treatments evaluated through single-subject designs tend to follow an applied behavior analysis theoretical orientation (Kazdin, 1982).

There are methodological problems and limitations when single-subject designs are applied to studying children with autistic spectrum disorders. The most obvious is that only a small number of children are involved in any single study, so the applicability of findings of a single study to other children is limited. Single-subject designs build their external validity on systematic replications across studies (Tawney and Gast, 1983). One set of current standards stipulates (Lonigan et al., 1998) that nine replications of studies with good experimental designs and treatment comparisons should be required for effectiveness of an intervention to be "well-established," while three replications of studies with the acceptable methodological characteristics are necessary for an intervention to be identified as "probably efficacious." These are arbitrary, though useful, designations.

The issue of inter- and intrasubject variability also exists for this methodology. Single-subject designs require that some level of stability in the participants' performance be reached before another phase is implemented, and variability in participants' behavior, as occurs for children with autistic spectrum disorders, may obscure comparisons across phases.

As noted above, the characteristics of the participants must be described explicitly in single-subject methodology, and variability in the characteristics of children with autistic spectrum disorders could result in children with very different characteristics participating in the same study. Such variability could contribute to the limitations of the external validity of a study.

Two key issues in single-subject methodology relate to generalization and maintenance of treatment effects. In this context, generalization refers to the occurrence of desired treatment outcomes outside of the treatment settings and with individuals who were not involved in the treatment. Maintenance refers to the continued performance of the behaviors or skills acquired in treatment after the treatment has ended. Reviews of the literature suggest that evidence for generalization and maintenance data is weak for some single-subject treatments or has not routinely been assessed (Horner et al., 2000; McConnell, 1999). It should be emphasized that the issues of maintenance and generalization are not unique to single-subject research. Group design studies of comprehensive intervention programs have not often used measures of generalization and maintenance; the notable exceptions are the studies that have examined long-term follow-up of participants in comprehensive treatment programs (e.g., Harris and Handleman, 2000; McEachin et al., 1993; Strain and Hoyson, 2000). As shown in Figure 1-3 (in Chapter 1), generalization to natural settings was studied in about 30 percent of reported research concerning social and communication interventions, and not at all in the research reviewed in other areas. Some measurement of generalization and/or maintenance was addressed in an additional 10 to 40 percent of studies, with the greatest frequency in positive behavioral and communication interventions, but there is still much room for improvement. For research on early interventions for young children with autistic spectrum disorders, assessment of generalization and maintenance should be a standard feature of single-subject and group design studies. Particularly in autism, generalization to new contexts cannot be assumed, though it is the goal of most interventions.

Developmental and Nonspecific Effects

Two other related methodological issues affect both single-subject and pre-post group designs: the effects of development on maturation and the nonspecific, positive effects of participating in an intervention (even if no specific treatment is offered, as in placebo effects). Nonspecific treatment effects may also occur in single-subject designs. Both of these issues are relevant, to different degrees, to many studies in autistic spectrum disorders conducted from a range of theoretical perspectives. For many behaviors, most children with autistic spectrum disorders show gradual improvement, whether or not they receive intervention. For example, some children with autism learn to talk without direct language intervention; many learn to sit, dress themselves, and sort and match items without highly specific interventions. In addition, there are carryover effects of one intervention to another (e.g., teaching appropriate play often decreases repetitious behavior and may increase eye contact). This carryover is a positive factor that is extremely important for children. However, it limits interpretation of designs, such as multiple baselines, that assume that behaviors are independent, and designs such as pre-post testing, which assume that all improvements are due to the treatment specified (and not to carryover from other phenomena, such as a change in parents' behavior).

For children and their families, there are also strong effects of being in a program and feeling that they are receiving treatment, even when there is no "active ingredient" of the intervention. These effects have been repeatedly documented in education, medicine, and psychology in comparisons of open trials with randomized clinical trials; they are also relevant to single-subject designs in which the intervenor is also the principal data collector. "Blindness" to which children and families receive which treatments, and to the characteristics of participants, in at least some of the assessments—even in single-subject designs—would considerably improve the interpretability of results.

On the whole, developmental and nonspecific or placebo effects are positive factors for children and families. They attest to the positive trajectory of many behaviors and the power of hope and perceived purpose. However, recognizing the potential contributions of these factors is crucial in interpreting the results of specific interventions. There are methodological features of research designs that can be applied to control for maturation and nonspecific effects. For example, a randomized group design using a contrast intervention as a control for a treatment of interest and a single-subject design in which the baseline has a form of treatment being provided can be applied to enhance the interpretation of such effects.

Replications and Measures of Treatment Effects

For single-subject and group experimental designs, the issues of replication of studies and measurement of treatment outcomes are important. Research on comprehensive intervention programs and individual intervention approaches tends to be conducted and replicated by individuals who developed the approaches. Evidence for the effectiveness of these approaches is strengthened when researchers who are independent of the developers replicate findings of effectiveness. This form of replication has generally not occurred in the research on comprehensive treatment programs. For individual intervention techniques, interventions addressing language and communication skills (see Goldstein, 1999) and problem behaviors (see Horner et al., 2000) are the most often replicated by different investigators.

Independent measurement or verification of treatment outcome is another important issue. The potential effect of experimenter bias exists when outcome assessments are conducted by individuals who know about the nature of the research study, the treatment groups to which children are assigned, and the phases of studies in which children are participating. For most group and single-subject design research, outcome data are collected by project staff; this may introduce a potential confounding effect. This confounding effect may be countered by having blind or naive assessors collect pre- and post-outcome data for group designs and daily performance data for single-subject designs. Also, for single-subject designs, the assessment of socially important outcomes of interventions by individuals outside of the project, called "social validity" (Schwartz and Baer, 1991; Wolf, 1978), provides some control of potential bias by observers, raters, and testers.

Interaction Between Treatment and
Child or Family Characteristics

In experimental group designs, the average or mean performances of children on outcome measures and standard deviations are generally reported for each group. The standard deviation describes the variation of outcome scores around the mean. In group-design studies, children make different amounts of progress, with some possibly scoring much higher and some scoring much lower than the mean. Analyses of group means does not provide information about which children benefited the most or least from treatment.

To obtain more specific knowledge about the characteristics of children that are associated with performance, researchers analyze aptitude-by-treatment interactions or ATIs. For example, an examination of different language training curricula for preschool children with disabilities (not specifically autism) did not find a main effect for treatment (i.e., both treatments appeared to be equally effective) (Cole et al., 1991). However, when they analyzed the interaction of treatment by aptitude, they found that children who were higher performers on pretest measures benefited more from a didactic language training approach, and children who were lower performers at pretest benefited more from a responsive curriculum approach to language training.

This type of aptitude-by-treatment-interaction analysis has the potential for providing valuable information about the characteristics of children with autistic spectrum disorders that are associated with outcomes for comprehensive treatment programs, but these analyses have rarely been conducted. Studying interactions between child or family features and treatment requires a sample size large enough to generate sufficient power to detect a difference. For example, in one study, children diagnosed as having autism or pervasive developmental disorder were randomly assigned to an intensive intervention program based upon the UCLA Young Autism Project model or a parent training model. Although it appeared that children with pervasive developmental disorder scored consistently higher than children with autism on some measures, there were no significant differences between groups (Smith et al., 2000). The authors attributed the failure to find significant difference to the small sample size (6-7 in each subgroup in each experimental condition). In another example, Harris and Handleman (2000) examined class placements of children with autism 4-6 years after they had left a comprehensive early intervention program. In an aptitude-by-treatment-interaction type analysis, they found that children who entered their program at an earlier age (mean = 46 months) and had relatively higher IQ scores at intake (mean = 78 months) were significantly more likely to be in regular class placements, and children with relatively lower IQ scores at intake who entered the program later (54 months) were more likely to be placed in special education classes. Even with a relatively small number of participants (28), the robustness of this finding provided information about characteristics of the children who were likely to benefit most from the program.

Fidelity of Treatment

In addition to assessing outcome measures, it is important for researchers examining the effects of educational interventions to verify that the treatment was delivered. Measurement of the delivery of an individual intervention practice or comprehensive intervention program has been called fidelity of treatment, treatment implementation, and procedural reliability (Billingsley et al., 1980; Hall and Louchs, 1977). Here we use the term *treatment fidelity*.

Treatment fidelity requires that researchers operationally define their intervention or the components of their comprehensive program well enough so that they or others can assess the degree to which procedures have been carried out. Such assessment takes different forms (e.g., direct observations with discrete behavioral categories, checklists, etc.). For example, staff of the LEAP preschool program (see Chapter 12) have developed a set of fidelity-of-treatment protocols that assess whether eight components of the program are being implemented: positive behavioral guidance, interactions with families, teaching strategies, interactions with children, classroom organization and planning, teaching communication skills, IEPs and measuring progress, and promoting social interaction (LEAP Preschool and Outreach Project, 1999). These protocols could be used in a research capacity to document the level of implementation of the comprehensive program. Also, as Strain (2000) indicated, they were used in the LEAP program to provide feedback to staff on their level of implementation in order to maintain treatment fidelity. Some researchers use hours of service provided as a measure of the intensiveness of intervention (Smith et al., 2000). Although it provides important information, hours of service is not an adequate measure of treatment fidelity, because it does not describe the procedures used during the service hours. Assessment of treatment fidelity has a long history in general education (see Leinhardt, 1980) and has been proposed as a standard for high quality intervention research in early intervention for children with disabilities (LeLaurin and Wolery, 1992). However, one review of early intervention programs for children with autism (Wolery and Garfinkle, 2000) found that only 4 out of 15 programs provided any evidence of implementation of program components. In future research on educational intervention for young children with autistic spectrum disorders and their families, measurement of the fidelity of treatment should be a standard feature of the program of research and publication of findings.

Modeling Growth and Intervention Effects

In most experimental group studies, as noted above, the developmental growth of children with autistic spectrum disorders is measured through the collection of pretest and posttest outcome measures, followed by analyses of differences between groups. More sophisticated procedures for examining the growth and development of children are available (Dunst and Trivette, 1994), but they have not been used in analyses of intervention outcomes for young children with autistic spectrum disorders. Growth curve analysis (Burchinal and Appelbaum, 1991) and the related techniques of hierarchical linear regression modeling (Bryk and Raudenbush, 1987) and structural equation modeling (Willet and Sayer, 1994) have been used to model the growth of groups of children for whom longitudinal data are available. These techniques may also be used to examine patterns of growth for children with different types of characteristics or children involved in different types of treatment conditions or programs (e.g., Burchinal, 1999; Burchinal, Bailey and Synder, 1994; Hatton et al., 1997). Natural history studies of development in children with autistic spectrum disorders are critical using these methods to provide both theoretically based insight and empirical "baselines."

The advantage of growth curve analysis and related regression models is that they allow researchers to control for nested variables (e.g., children participating in the same intervention but in different classrooms), nonrandom missing data (i.e., an assessment that occurred at the wrong time or that is missing), and extreme scores of students (Burchinal et al., 1994). Also, hierarchical linear regression modeling and structural equation modeling allow researchers to determine the relationships of variables, in addition to assignment to an early intervention and contrast group conditions, that are associated with development of children (e.g., family characteristics, degree of implementation of the program).

One difficulty in using these techniques in studies of children with autistic spectrum disorders is that many of these techniques require large sample sizes, but most studies of young children with autistic spectrum disorders have small numbers. Nevertheless, to the extent possible, researchers of educational intervention programs for young children with autistic spectrum disorders should consider adopting these or similar models for analyzing variables affecting children's development and learning. This may require that program developers include sufficient sample sizes in their programs over several years; multiple data points per participant are also required.

Group Size and Experimental Group Design

A clear problem mentioned at several points in the preceding discussion is that methodological tools available to researchers, such as studies of individual differences in response to treatments and sophisticated regression-based techniques, such as hierarchical linear regression modeling, are limited by the number of children with autistic spectrum disorders in intervention programs and the number of data points collected. Implementing an early intervention program for children and families is a labor-intensive and expensive endeavor. Because of the expense, length of treatment, and heterogeneous nature of autistic spectrum disorders, the number of young children in an individual treatment program is usually small. As noted, one solution for program developers is to collect data for multiple cohorts, building their numbers across years. However, this approach requires multiple years of funding and long-term commitments from investigators.

One solution of the sample size problem is the development of a multi-site study of treatment effectiveness. Such a study could be based on a treatment comparison model and could perhaps (because of its potential magnitude) be funded by multiple coordinating agencies (e.g., National Institute of Child Health and Human Development, Office of Special Education Programs, National Institute of Mental Health, Center for Disease Control, National Institute on Deafness and Other Communication Disorders, National Institute of Neurological Disorders and Stroke). There is a precedent for federal funding for large initiatives such as this in other areas (e.g., Fast Track project for aggressive children, Infant Health and Development Project, National Institute for Child Health and Human Development Child Care Study). The current coordination of the biomedical grants in autism funded by the National Institute for Child Health and Human Development and the National Institute on Deafness and Other Communication Disorders in the Collaborative Program for Excellence in Autism (CPEA), and efforts to coordinate genetics studies funded by many different agencies, may represent models for such a project.

Qualitative Research

We have not reviewed qualitative or ethnographic research studies. Although such studies may add to the knowledge about program features and outcomes for young children with autistic spectrum disorders (Schwartz et al., 1998), the research literature is quite small and does not contain systematic examinations of programwide effects for young children and families. Qualitative and ethnographic research does hold promise for uncovering important features in educational interventions programs that affect the development of young children with autistic spectrum disorders and their families.

FROM RESEARCH TO PRACTICE

There is an active research literature on the developmental characteristics, diagnostic criteria, comprehensive treatment programs, and individual intervention strategies for young children with autistic spectrum disorders. The literature provides a tentative but important basis on which to design intervention strategies and decisions about treatment options for individual children. However, there are concerns about methodological issues. Considering these concerns, funding agencies and professional journals should require minimal standards in design and description of intervention research studies. These studies should include the following information: participants' chronological age, developmental assessment data (including verbal and nonverbal levels of performance), standardized diagnoses, gender, race, family characteristics, socioeconomic status, and relevant health or other biological impairments.

In addition, fidelity of treatment documentation must operationally define the intervention in sufficient detail so that an external group could replicate it as well as assess the degree of implementation. Independent, objective assessment of expected outcomes should be conducted at regular intervals, and immediate and long-term assessment of effects on children and families should include measures of generalization and maintenance.

Future research on intervention programs for young children with autistic spectrum disorders should address the following methodological issues: application of standardized procedures for describing participants in intervention studies, including children's diagnoses, chronological age, developmental and behavioral information, family information, gender, sociometric status, race, and pertinent health or biological information; the association between fidelity of treatment information and treatment outcomes; the association between participants' characteristics and treatment outcomes (e.g., aptitude-by-treatment interactions); the development of early identification procedures and their relationship to early access to services; and identification of program features (i.e., "active ingredients" of intervention programs) that relate most directly to child and family outcomes. The impact on growth for young children with autistic spectrum disorders may be measured by techniques such as growth curve analysis, hierarchical linear modeling, and/or structural equation modeling to model the longitudinal growth and treatment.

Addressing these methodological issues will require larger sample sizes, longitudinal follow-ups of participants, and interdisciplinary collaboration. To enable such needed research, initiatives should be funded jointly by federal agencies responsible for research, development, and services for young children with autistic spectrum disorders (including the Office of Special Education Programs, the Office of Educational Research and Improvement, the National Institute of Child Health and Human Development, the National Institute of Mental Health, the National Institute of Neurological Disorders and Stroke, and the National Institute on Deafness and Other Communication Disorders). These initiatives should include a task force that meets regularly to design and provide a synthesis of the diagnostic, developmental, behavioral, and treatment research that would inform the design and implementation of early educational treatment for young children with autistic spectrum disorders; consideration of the feasibility of a national, cross-site, longitudinal investigation of early intervention treatments for young children with autistic spectrum disorders and their families; and development of specific measurement tools for early diagnosis of children with autistic spectrum disorders and treatment outcomes (e.g., social functioning, spontaneous communication and language, peer relationships, and competence in natural settings). Agencies funding competitive research initiatives should include personnel with sufficient research and experiential background to judge the scientific and practical merits of proposals.

16

Conclusions and Recommendations

This chapter summarizes the committee's conclusions about the state of the science in early intervention for children with autistic spectrum disorders and its recommendations for future intervention strategies, programs, policy, and research. The chapter is organized around seven key areas pertaining to educational interventions for young children with autistic spectrum disorders: how the disorders are diagnosed and assessed and how prevalent they are; the effect on and role of families; appropriate goals for educational services; characteristics of effective interventions and educational programs; public policy approaches to ensuring access to appropriate education; the preparation of educational personnel; and needs for future research.

DIAGNOSIS, ASSESSMENT, AND PREVALENCE

Conclusions

Autism is a developmental disorder of neurobiologic origin that is defined on the basis of behavioral and developmental features. Autism is best characterized as a spectrum of disorders that vary in severity of symptoms, age of onset, and association with other disorders (e.g., mental retardation, specific language delay, epilepsy). The manifestations of autism vary considerably across children and within an individual child over time. There is no single behavior that is always typical of autism and no behavior that would automatically exclude an individual child from a diagnosis of autism, even though there are strong and consistent commonalities, especially relative to social deficits.

The large constellation of behaviors that define autistic spectrum disorders—generally representing deficits in social interaction, verbal and nonverbal communication, and restricted patterns of interest or behaviors—are clearly and reliably identifiable in very young children to experienced clinicians and educators. However, distinctions among classical autism and atypical autism, pervasive developmental disorder-not otherwise specified (PDD-NOS), and Asperger's disorder can be arbitrary and are often associated with the presence or severity of handicaps, such as mental retardation and severe language impairment.

Identifying narrow categories within autism is necessary for some research purposes; however, the clinical or educational benefit to subclassifying autistic spectrum disorders purely by diagnosis is debated. In contrast, individual differences in language development, verbal and nonverbal communication, sensory or motor skills, adaptive behavior, and cognitive abilities have significant effects on behavioral presentation and outcome, and, consequently, have specific implications for educational goals and strategies. Thus, the most important considerations in programming have to do with the strengths and weaknesses of the individual child, the age at diagnosis, and early intervention.

With adequate time and training, the diagnosis of autistic spectrum disorders can be made reliably in 2-year-olds by professionals experienced in the diagnostic assessment of young children with autistic spectrum disorders. Many families report becoming concerned about their children's behavior and expressing this concern, usually to health professionals, even before this time. Research is under way to develop reliable methods of identification for even younger ages. Children with autistic spectrum disorders, like children with vision or hearing problems, require early identification and diagnosis to equip them with the skills (e.g., imitation, communication) to benefit from educational services, with some evidence that earlier initiation of specific services for autistic spectrum disorders is associated with greater response to treatment. Thus, well meaning attempts not to label children with formal diagnoses can deprive children of specialized services. There are clear reasons for early identification of children, even as young as two years of age, within the autism spectrum.

Epidemiological studies and service-based reports indicate that the prevalence of autistic spectrum disorders has increased in the last 10 years, in part due to better identification and broader categorization by educators, physicians, and other professionals. There is little doubt that more children are being identified as requiring specific educational interventions for autistic spectrum disorders. This has implications for the provision of services at many levels. Analysis of data from the Office of

Special Education Programs, gathered for school-age children since the autism category was recognized in 1991, would support investigation of whether the dramatic increases in the numbers of children served with autistic spectrum disorders are offset by commensurate decreases in other categories in which children with autistic spectrum disorders might have previously been misclassified or whether these dramatic increases have come about for other reasons.

Although children with autistic spectrum disorders share some characteristics with children who have other developmental disorders and may benefit from many of the same educational techniques, they offer unique challenges to families, teachers, and others who work with them. Their deficits in nonverbal and verbal communication require intense effort and skill even in the teaching of basic information. The unique difficulties in social interaction (e.g., in joint attention) may require more individual guidance than for other children in order to attract and sustain their children's attention. Moreover, ordinary social exchanges between peers do not usually occur without deliberate planning and ongoing structuring by the adults in the child's environment. The absence of typical friendships and peer relationships affects children's motivation systems and the meaning of experiences. Appropriate social interactions may be some of the most difficult and important lessons a child with autistic spectrum disorders will learn.

In addition, the frequency of behavior problems, such as tantrums and self-stimulatory and aggressive behavior, is high. The need for systematic selection of rewards for many children with autistic spectrum disorders, whose motivation or interests can be limited, requires creativity and continued effort from teachers and parents to maximize the child's potential. Although general principles of learning and behavior analysis apply to autistic spectrum disorders, familiarity with the specific nature of the disorder should contribute to analysis of the contexts (e.g., communicative and social) of behaviors for individual children and result in more effective programming. For example, conducting a functional assessment that considers contexts, and then replacing problem behaviors with more appropriate ways to communicate can be an effective method for reducing problem behaviors.

Recommendations

1-1   Because of their shared continuities and their unique social difficulties, children with any autistic spectrum disorder (autistic disorder, Asperger's disorder, atypical autism, PDD-NOS, childhood disintegrative disorder), regardless of level of severity or function, should be eligible for special educational services within the category of *autistic spectrum disorders*, as opposed to other terminology used by school systems, such as other health impaired, social emotionally maladjusted, significantly developmentally delayed, or neurologically impaired.

1-2   Identification of autistic spectrum disorders should include a formal multidisciplinary evaluation of social behavior, language and nonverbal communication, adaptive behavior, motor skills, atypical behaviors, and cognitive status by a team of professionals experienced with autistic spectrum disorders. An essential part of this evaluation is the systematic gathering of information from parents on their observations and concerns. If the school system cannot carry out such an assessment, the local education authority should fund the assessment through external sources. Early diagnosis should be emphasized. Because of variability in early development, younger children with autistic spectrum disorders should receive a follow-up diagnostic and educational assessment within one to two years of initial evaluation.

1-3   Professional organizations, with the support of the National Institutes of Health (NIH) and the Department of Education's Office of Special Education Programs (OSEP), should disseminate information concerning the nature and range of autistic spectrum disorders in young children to all professionals who have contact with children, particularly those who work with infants, toddlers, and preschool children. This information should include the variable presentations and patterns of behavior seen in autistic spectrum disorders from toddlers to school age children. Members of "child find" teams within the early intervention systems, as well as primary care providers, should be trained in identifying the "red flags of autistic spectrum disorders" and the importance and means of early referral for comprehensive diagnostic evaluation. Advocacy groups and relevant federal agencies, as well as professional organizations, should use effective media resources, including the Internet, to provide information concerning the range of behaviors in autistic spectrum disorders.

ROLE OF FAMILIES

Conclusions

Having a child with an autistic spectrum disorder is a challenge for any family. Involvement of families in the education of young children with autistic spectrum disorders can occur at multiple levels, including advocacy, parents as participating partners in and agents of education or behavior change, and family-centered consideration of the needs and strengths of the family as a unit. Nearly all empirically supported treatments reviewed by the committee included a parent component, and most research programs used a parent-training approach. More information is needed about the benefits of a family-centered orientation or combined family-centered and formalized parent training in helping parents.

It is well established that parents can learn and successfully apply skills to changing the behavior of their children with autistic spectrum disorders, though little is known about the effects of cultural differences, such as race, ethnicity, and social class, nor about the interactions among family factors, child characteristics, and features of educational intervention. For most families, having a child with an autistic spectrum disorder creates added stress. Parents' use of effective teaching methods can have a significant effect on that stress, as can support from within the family and the community. Parents need access to balanced information about autistic spectrum disorders and the range of appropriate services and technologies in order to carry out their responsibilities. They also need timely information about assessments, educational plans, and the available resources for their children. This information needs to be conveyed to them in a meaningful way that gives them time to prepare to fulfill their roles and responsibilities.

In the last ten years the widespread availability of the Internet and media attention to autistic spectrum disorders have increased parents' knowledge but often conveyed perspectives that were not balanced nor well-supported scientifically. Of crucial importance is the question of how to make information available to parents and to ensure their active role in advocacy for their children's education.

Recommendations

2-1   Parents' concerns and perspectives should actively help to shape educational planning. Specifically:

   a.   In order for a family to be effective members of the Individualized Education Plan (IEP) team that plans a child's education, the local school system should provide to the parents, at the beginning of the assessment process, written information concerning the nature of autistic spectrum disorders and eligibility categories, the range of alternatives within best practices in early education of autistic spectrum disorders, sources of funding and support (e.g., a support guide and bibliography), and their child's rights.
   b.   Prior to the IEP meeting, the local school system should provide to each family the written results of their child's assess-

ment, and a contact person to explain the findings if they wish, and should indicate that they will have the opportunity to present their concerns. Early during the IEP meeting, parents should be given an opportunity to voice their questions, concerns, and perspectives about their child's development and educational programming.

2-2   As part of local educational programs and intervention programs for children from birth to age 3, families of children with autistic spectrum disorders should be provided the opportunity to learn techniques for teaching their child new skills and reducing problem behaviors. These opportunities should include not only didactic sessions, but also ongoing consultation in which individualized problem-solving, including in-home observations or training, occur for a family, as needed, to support improvements at home as well as at school.

2-3   Families that are experiencing stress in raising their children with an autistic spectrum disorder should be provided with mental health support services. Under Part C of the Individuals with Disabilities Education Act (IDEA), which addresses family support and service coordination, including private service providers, services should be extended to include families of children at least up to age 8 years.

GOALS FOR EDUCATIONAL SERVICES

Conclusions

At the root of questions about the most appropriate educational interventions lie differences in assumptions about what is possible and what is important to give students with autistic spectrum disorders through education. The appropriate goals for educational services are the same as those for other children: personal independence and social responsibility. These goals imply continuous progress in social and cognitive abilities, verbal and nonverbal communication skills, adaptive skills, amelioration of behavioral difficulties, and generalization of abilities across multiple environments. In some cases, reports have suggested that particular treatments can foster permanent "recovery". However, as with other developmental disabilities, the core deficits of autistic spectrum disorders have generally been found to persist, to some degree, in most individuals.

Research concerning outcomes can be characterized by whether the goal of intervention is broadly defined (e.g., "recovery" or "best outcome") or more specifically defined (e.g., increasing vocabulary or peer-directed social behavior); whether the design involves reporting results in terms of group or individual changes; and whether the goals are short term (i.e., to be achieved in a few weeks or months) or longer term (i.e., over years). A large body of single-subject research has demonstrated substantial progress in individual responses to specific intervention techniques in relatively short periods of times (e.g., several months) in many specific areas, including gains in social skills, language acquisition, nonverbal communication, and reductions in challenging behaviors. Studies over longer periods of time have documented joint attention, symbolic play, early language skills, and imitation as core deficits and hallmarks of the disorder that are predictive of longer term outcome in the domains of language, adaptive behaviors, and academic skills.

Many treatment studies report postintervention placement as an outcome measure. While successful participation in regular classrooms is an important goal for some children with autistic spectrum disorders, the usefulness of placement in regular education classes as an outcome measure is limited, because placement may be related to many variables other than the characteristics of the child (e.g., prevailing trends in inclusion, availability of other services). The most commonly reported outcome measure in group treatment studies of children with autistic spectrum disorders has been changes in IQ scores, which also have many limitations.

Studies have reported substantial changes in large numbers of children in intervention studies and longitudinal studies in which children received a variety of interventions. Even in the treatment studies that have shown the strongest gains, children's outcomes are variable, with some children making substantial progress and others showing very slow gains. The needs and strengths of young children with autistic spectrum disorders are very heterogeneous. Although there is evidence that many interventions lead to improvements and that some children shift in specific diagnosis along the autism spectrum during the preschool years, there does not appear to be a simple relationship between any particular intervention and "recovery" from autistic spectrum disorders. Thus, while substantial evidence exists that treatments can reach short-term specific goals in many areas, gaps remain in addressing larger questions of the relationships between particular techniques, child characteristics, and outcomes.

Recommendations

The IEP and Individual Family Service Plan (IFSP) should be the vehicles for planning and implementing educational objectives.

3-1   Appropriate educational objectives for children with autistic spec-
        trum disorders should be observable, measurable behaviors and
        skills. These objectives should be able to be accomplished within
        1 year and expected to affect a child's participation in education,
        the community, and family life. They should include the devel-
        opment of:

        a. Social skills to enhance participation in family, school, and
        community activities (e.g., imitation, social initiations and re-
        sponse to adults and peers, parallel and interactive play with
        peers and siblings);
        b. Expressive verbal language, receptive language, and non-
        verbal communication skills;
        c. A functional symbolic communication system;
        d. Increased engagement and flexibility in developmentally
        appropriate tasks and play, including the ability to attend to the
        environment and respond to an appropriate motivational system;
        e. Fine and gross motor skills used for age appropriate func-
        tional activities, as needed;
        f. Cognitive skills, including symbolic play and basic con-
        cepts, as well as academic skills;
        g. Replacement of problem behaviors with more conven-
        tional and appropriate behaviors; and
        h. Independent organizational skills and other behaviors that
        underlie success in regular education classrooms (e.g., complet-
        ing a task independently, following instructions in a group, ask-
        ing for help).

3-2   Ongoing measurement of educational objectives must be docu-
        mented in order to determine whether a child is benefiting from a
        particular intervention. Every child's response to the educational
        program should be assessed after a short period of time. Progress
        should be monitored frequently and objectives adjusted accord-
        ingly.

CHARACTERISTICS OF EFFECTIVE INTERVENTIONS

Conclusions

In general, there is consistent agreement across comprehensive intervention programs about a number of features, though practical and, sometimes, ethical considerations have made well-controlled studies with random assignment very difficult to conduct without direct evaluation.
Characteristics of the most appropriate intervention for a given child must

be tied to that child's and family's needs. However, without direct evaluation, it is difficult to know which features are of greatest importance in a program. Across primarily preschool programs, there is a very strong consensus that the following features are critical:

- entry into intervention programs as soon as an autism spectrum diagnosis is seriously considered;
- active engagement in intensive instructional programming for a minimum of the equivalent of a full school day, 5 days (at least 25 hours) a week, with full year programming varied according to the child's choronological age and developmental level;
- repeated, planned teaching opportunities generally organized around relatively brief periods of time for the youngest children (e.g., 15-20 minute intervals), including sufficient amounts of adult attention in one-to-one and very small group instruction to meet individualized goals;
- inclusion of a family component, including parent training;
- low student/teacher ratios (no more than two young children with autistic spectrum disorders per adult in the classroom); and
- mechanisms for ongoing program evaluation and assessments of individual children's progress, with results translated into adjustments in programming.

Curricula across different programs differ in a number of ways. They include the ways in which goals are prioritized, affecting the relative time spent on verbal and nonverbal communication, social activities, behavioral, academic, motor, and other domains. Strategies from various programs represent a range of techniques, including discrete trials, incidental teaching, structured teaching, "floor time", and individualized modifications of the environment, including schedules. Some programs adopt a unilateral use of one set of procedures, and others use a combination of approaches. Programs also differ in the relative amount of time spent in homes, centers, or schools, when children are considered ready for inclusion into regular classrooms, how the role of peers as intervention agents is supported, and in the use of distraction-free or natural environments. Programs also differ in the credentials that are required of direct support and supervisory staff and the formal and informal roles of collateral staff, such as speech language pathologists and occupational therapists.

Overall, many of the programs are more similar than different in terms of levels of organization, staffing, ongoing monitoring, and the use of certain techniques, such as discrete trials, incidental learning, and structured teaching. However, there are real differences in philosophy and practice that provide a range of alternatives for parents and school systems considering various approaches. The key to any child's educational program lies in the objectives specified in the IEP and the ways they are addressed. Much more important than the name of the program attended is how the environment and educational strategies allow implementation of the goals for a child and family. Thus, effective services will and should vary considerably across individual children, depending on a child's age, cognitive and language levels, behavioral needs, and family priorities.

Recommendations

The committee's recommendations for effective treatment are made on the basis of empirical findings, information from selected representative programs, and findings in the general education and developmental literature. In particular, it is well established that children with autism spend much less time in focused and socially directed activity when in unstructured situations than do other children. Therefore, it becomes crucial to specify time engaged in social and focused activity as part of a program for children with autistic spectrum disorders.

4-1   Based on a set of individualized, specialized objectives and plans that are systematically implemented, educational services should begin as soon as a child is suspected of having an autistic spectrum disorder. Taking into account the needs and strengths of an individual child and family, the child's schedule and educational environment, in and out of the classroom, should be adapted as needed in order to implement the IEP. Educational services should include a minimum of 25 hours a week, 12 months a year, in which the child is engaged in systematically planned, developmentally appropriate educational activity aimed toward identified objectives. Where this activity takes place and the content of the activity should be determined on an individual basis, depending on characteristics of both the child and the family.

4-2   A child must receive sufficient individualized attention on a daily basis so that individual objectives can be effectively implemented; individualized attention should include individual therapies, developmentally appropriate small group instruction, and direct one-to-one contact with teaching staff.

4-3   Assessment of a child's progress in meeting objectives should be used on an ongoing basis to further refine the IEP. Lack of objectively documentable progress over a 3 month period should be taken to indicate a need to increase intensity by lowering student/teacher ratios, increasing programming time, reformulating curricula, or providing additional training and consultation.

4-4   To the extent that it leads to the specified educational goals (e.g., peer interaction skills, independent participation in regular education), children should receive specialized instruction in settings in which ongoing interactions occur with typically developing children.

4-5   Six kinds of interventions should have priority:

   a.   Functional, spontaneous communication should be the primary focus of early education. For very young children, programming should be based on the assumption that most children can learn to speak. Effective teaching techniques for both verbal language and alternative modes of functional communication, drawn from the empirical and theoretical literature, should be vigorously applied across settings.
   b.   Social instruction should be delivered throughout the day in various settings, using specific activities and interventions planned to meet age-appropriate, individualized social goals (e.g., with very young children, response to maternal imitation; with preschool children, cooperative activities with peers).
   c.   The teaching of play skills should focus on play with peers, with additional instruction in appropriate use of toys and other materials.
   d.   Other instruction aimed at goals for cognitive development should also be carried out in the context in which the skills are expected to be used, with generalization and maintenance in natural contexts as important as the acquisition of new skills. Because new skills have to be learned before they can be generalized, the documentation of rates of acquisition is an important first step. Methods of introduction of new skills may differ from teaching strategies to support generalization and maintenance.
   e.   Intervention strategies that address problem behaviors should incorporate information about the contexts in which the behaviors occur; positive, proactive approaches; and the range of techniques that have empirical support (e.g., functional assessment, functional communication training, reinforcement of alternative behaviors).
   f.   Functional academic skills should be taught when appropriate to the skills and needs of a child.

PUBLIC POLICIES

Conclusions

The Individuals with Disabilities Education Act (IDEA) contains the necessary provisions for ensuring rights to appropriate education for children with autistic spectrum disorders. However, the implementation and specification of these services are variable. Early intervention for young children with autistic spectrum disorders is expensive, and most local schools need financial help from the state and federal programs to provide appropriate services.

The large number of court cases is a symptom of the tension between families and school systems. Case law has yielded an inconsistent pattern of findings that vary according to the characteristics of the individual cases. The number of challenges to decision-making for programming within school systems reflects parents' concerns about the adequacy of knowledge and the expertise of school systems in determining their children's education and implementing appropriate techniques.

The treatment of autistic spectrum disorders often involves many disciplines and agencies. This confuses lines of financial and intellectual responsibility and complicates assessment and educational planning. When communication between families and school systems goes awry, it can directly affect children's programming and the energy and financial resources that are put into education rather than litigation. Support systems are not generally adequate in undergirding local service delivery programs and maximizing the usefulness of different disciplines and agencies, and transitions between service delivery agencies are often problematic.

A number of states have successful models for providing services to children with autism, and mechanisms are becoming increasingly efficient and flexible in some states. In most cases, existing agencies at state and federal levels can develop appropriate programs without restructuring—with the possible addition of special task forces or committees designed to deal with issues particular to children with autistic spectrum disorders.

Recommendations

The committee recommends that a variety of steps be taken to ensure that policies are effectively carried out at the state and local levels.

5-1   At the federal level, the National Institutes of Health's Autism Coordinating Committee and the Federal Interagency Coordinating Council should jointly appoint a clinical research oversight task force of professionals knowledgeable in the field of autistic spectrum disorders, to review and periodically report on basic and applied research programs to the parent agencies and to track program implementation through the State Interagency Coordinating Councils or relevant state agencies. Administrative support for these efforts should be provided by the appropriate department of the Secretary's office.

5-2   States should have regional resource and training centers with expertise in autistic spectrum disorders to provide training and technical support to local schools. States should also have a mechanism to evaluate the adequacy of current support systems to local schools and recommend ways for improvement. One such mechanism could be an autistic spectrum disorders support systems task force that would examine the relevant provisions for personnel preparation, technical assistance, and demonstration of exemplary programs and would make recommendations as to what would be needed to bring a state's support systems into alignment with quality education for children with autistic spectrum disorders. States should monitor coordination among and transitions between service delivery systems and should develop ways to facilitate these processes.

5-3   Families should have access to consultation and legal knowledge such as provided by an ombudsman who is independent of the school system and who could be a standard part of Individualized Educational Plan planning and meetings. The ombudsman should be knowledgeable about autistic spectrum disorders and about relevant law and court decisions. The ombudsman's role should include attending IEP meetings, interpreting the school system's communications about a child to parents, and proposing, at the parents' request, alternatives to those presented by the school system. Professional and advocacy groups should work together to provide this service, with the Governor's Council for Developmental Disabilities or the Autistic Spectrum Disorders Support Systems Task Force responsible for ensuring funding for training and support of this service.

5-4   State and federal agencies should consider ways to work with and support professional and advocacy groups to provide up-to-date, practical, scientifically valid information to parents and practitioners.

5-5   States should have clearly defined minimum standards for personnel in educational settings for children with autistic spectrum disorders. For example, at a minimum, teachers should have some special preparation (e.g., preservice course work, equivalent inservice training, workshops, and supervised practice in research-based practices in autistic spectrum disorders) and should have well-trained, experienced support personnel available to provide ongoing training and additional consultation.

5-6   States should develop a systematic strategy to fund the interventions that are necessary for children with autistic spectrum disorders in local schools, so that this cost is not borne primarily by the parents or local school systems. State education departments should develop interagency collaborations to pool support for local systems. A state fund for intensive intervention, or more systematic use of Medicaid waivers or other patterns of funding currently in place in some states, should be considered. Families should not be expected to fund or provide the majority of educational programming for their children.

5-7   An updated, accurate summary of case law, consultation services, and mediation mechanisms in autistic spectrum disorders should be made accessible by the Office of Special Education Programs so that schools and parents can understand the options available to them when conflicts arise.

5-8   Since levels of information about autistic spectrum disorders vary greatly within the groups and agencies that make funding and policy decisions about autistic spectrum disorders, including state task forces in education and review panels in federal agencies, it is crucial that persons knowledgeable in the range of needs and interventions associated with autistic spectrum disorders be included in those decision-making activities.

PERSONNEL PREPARATION

Conclusions

The nature of autistic spectrum disorders and other disabilities that frequently accompany them has significant implications for approaches to education and intervention at school, in the home, and in the community. Approaches that emphasize the use of specific "packages" of materials and methods associated with comprehensive intervention programs may understate the multiple immediate and long-term needs of children for behavior support and for instruction across areas.

Teachers are faced with a huge task. They must be familiar with theory and research concerning best practices for children with autistic spectrum disorders, including methods of applied behavior analysis, naturalistic learning, assistive technology, socialization, communication, inclusion, adaptation of the environment, language interventions, assessment, and the effective use of data collection systems. Specific problems in generalization and maintenance of behaviors also affect the need for training in methods of teaching children with autistic spectrum disorders. The wide range of IQ scores and verbal skills associated with autistic spectrum disorders, from profound mental retardation and severe language impairments to superior intelligence, intensify the need for personnel training. To enable teachers to adequately work with parents and with other professionals to set appropriate goals, teachers need familiarity with the course of autistic spectrum disorders and the range of possible outcomes.

Teachers learn according to the same principles as their students. Multiple exposures, opportunities to practice, and active involvement in learning are all important aspects of learning for teachers, as well as students. Many states and community organizations have invested substantial funds in teacher preparation through workshops and large-audience lectures by well-known speakers. While such presentations can stimulate enthusiasm, they do not substitute for ongoing consultation and hands-on opportunities to observe and practice skills working with children with autistic spectrum disorders.

Personnel preparation remains one of the weakest elements of effective programming for children with autistic spectrum disorders and their families. Ways of building on the knowledge of teachers as they acquire experience with children with autistic spectrum disorders, and ways of keeping skilled personnel within the field, are critical. This is particularly true given recent trends for dependence on relatively inexperienced assistants for in-home programs. Providing knowledge about autistic spectrum disorders to special education and regular education administrators, as well as to specialized providers with major roles in early intervention (e.g., speech language pathologists) will be critical in effecting change that is proactive. Findings concerning change in educational and other opportunities suggest that administrative attitudes and support are critical in improving schools.

Recommendations

The committee recommends that relevant state and federal agencies institute an agenda for upgrading personnel preparation for those who work with, and are responsible for, children with autistic spectrum disorders and their families. These efforts should be part of a larger effort to coordinate and collaborate with the already established infrastructure of special education, regional resource centers, technical assistance programs, personnel preparation, communication sharing, and other relevant aspects of the existing infrastructure. Professionals aware of the special nature of these children are already carrying out many of these recommendations in a limited fashion. The committee urges agencies to provide the personnel preparation resources needed for intensified efforts to build a viable support structure for educating children with autistic spectrum disorders.

6-1   The Office of Special Education Programs should establish a 5-year plan to provide priority funds for preservice and inservice preparation for teachers, paraprofessionals, and other personnel providing services for children with autistic spectrum disorders, including children under age 3 years.

6-2   The need for a team approach involving many professions should be addressed by personnel preparation and practicum work within multidisciplined organizations and teams.

6-3   A special emphasis should be placed on training of trainers. There is a short supply of expertise and experience in the field of education for children with autistic spectrum disorders, and special attention should be paid to rapidly increase the capabilities of the trainers, who may have experience in special education or related fields, but not in the special skills and practices for children with autistic spectrum disorders.

6-4   The existing support systems that provide short-term training (e.g., technical assistance systems, resource centers, etc.) should include people with special expertise in autistic spectrum disorders on their staff.

6-5   The content of the curriculum for children with autistic spectrum disorders should be based on sound research. A continuing program should be established from such agencies as the National Institute of Mental Health and the National Institute of Child Health and Human Development to translate their research into usable information for practitioners. Work on family research is particularly relevant.

NEEDED RESEARCH

Conclusions

There are several distinct and substantial bodies of research relevant to young children with autistic spectrum disorders. One body identifies neurological, behavioral, and developmental characteristics. Another body of research addresses diagnostic practices and related issues of prevalence. Another has examined the effects of comprehensive early treatment programs on the immediate and long-term outcomes of children and their families. These treatment studies tended to use some form of group experimental design. An additional body of research has addressed individual instructional or intervention approaches, with many studies in this literature using single-subject experimental methodology. Altogether, a large research base exists, but with relatively little integration across bodies of literature. Highly knowledgeable researchers in one area of autistic spectrum disorders may have minimal information from other perspectives, even about studies with direct bearing on their findings.

Most researchers have not used randomized group comparison designs because of the practical and ethical difficulties in randomly assigning children and families to treatment groups. In addition, there have been significant controversies over the type of control or contrast group to use and the conditions necessary for demonstrating effectiveness. Although a number of comprehensive programs have provided data on their effectiveness, and, in some cases, claims have been made that certain treatments are superior to others, there have been virtually no comparisons of different comprehensive interventions of equal intensity.

Across several of the bodies of literature, the children and families who have participated in studies are often inadequately described. Standardized diagnoses, descriptions of ethnicity, the social class, and associated features of the children (such as mental retardation and language level) are often not specified. Fidelity of treatment implementation has not been consistently assessed. Generalization, particularly across settings, and maintenance of treatment effects are not always measured. Though there is little evidence concerning the effectiveness of discipline-specific therapies, there is substantial research supporting the effectiveness of many specific therapeutic techniques.

Recommendations

7-1   Funding agencies and professional journals should require minimium standards in design and description of intervention projects. All intervention studies should provide the following information:

a. Adequate information concerning the children and families who participated, and who chose not to participate or withdrew from participation, including chronological age, developmental assessment data (including verbal and nonverbal IQ levels), standardized diagnoses, gender, race, family characteristics, socioeconomic status, and relevant health or other biological impairments;

b. description of the intervention in sufficient detail so that an external group could replicate it; detailed documentation is crucial especially if no treatment manual is available;

c. fidelity of treatment and degree of implementation;

d. specific objective measures of expected outcomes, assessed at regular intervals; and

e. measures of outcome that are independent of the intervention, in terms of both the evaluators and the measures, and include broad immediate and long-term effects on children and families, particularly generalization and maintenance effects.

7-2   Funders and performers of research should recognize that valuable information can be provided by a variety of approaches to research in intervention, including group experimental and single-subject designs.

7-3   In order to help educators and consumers make informed decisions about appropriate methods of intervention for particular children, federal agencies involved in autistic spectrum disorders initiatives (including the Office of Special Education Programs, the Office of Educational Research and Improvement, the National Institute of Child Health and Human Development, the National Institute of Mental Health, the National Institute of Neurological Disorders and Stroke, and the National Institute on Deafness and Other Communication Disorders) and nonprofit agencies with similar national missions (such as Autism Society of America Foundation, Cure Autism Now, and National Alliance for Autism Research) should form a research task force and specifically allocate federal responsibilites for recruiting and funding a comprehensive program of research related to intervention and treatment. This program should include:

a. development of more specific, precise measures of important areas of outcome, such as social functioning, peer relationships, spontaneous communication and language, and the acquisition of competence in natural contexts (e.g., classroom, home);

b. definition of appropriate educational skills and sequences in social and cognitive development, informed by normal developmental literature;

c. measurement of the effects of the interactions between family variables (e.g., family structure, family supports, socioeconomic status), child factors (such as degree of language impairment), and responses to educational interventions (including family-centered, parent training, and other approaches) on outcomes.

d. longitudinal treatment studies, where feasible, built on a clinical model with randomly assigned samples of sufficient size to assess the effectiveness of differing modes of treatment.

7-4   Treatment studies should recognize the common components of many comprehensive programs (e.g., standardized curriculum, family training, presence of typically developing peers) and should target and measure, longitudinally when feasible, "active ingredients" and mediating variables that influence the effects of intervention (e.g., communication and interaction opportunities for engagement, levels of interaction and initiation, specific teaching techniques, proportion of time in close proximity of peers). The concomitant development of innovative treatments building on these "active ingredients" should be supported.

7-5   In response to amendments in IDEA to make education more outcome oriented, a federal initiative should solicit and fund studies in the following areas, not easily supported under the current review system:

a. the development of instruments for measurement of diagnosis and critical aspects of development, particularly tools for early screening of autistic spectrum disorders and for measurement of response to interventions;

b. the development and application of sophisticated statistical methods of analysis of change and growth, particularly multivariate designs and those applicable to small samples; and

c. the development and dissemination of novel research designs that combine individual and group approaches in ways that minimize biases and maximize the power of small samples.

7-6   Competitively funded initiatives in early education in autistic spectrum disorders should require plans and contain sufficient funding for short- and long-term assessment of child outcomes and measures of program efficacy.

References

NOTE: Papers prepared for the committee are marked with an asterisk (*) and are available from the Board on Behavioral, Cognitive, and Sensory Sciences at the National Research Council.

CHAPTER 1

American Psychological Association
  2000   *Criteria for Treatment Guidelines*. Washington, DC: Template Implementation Work Group of the Board of Professional Affairs, Board of Scientific Affairs and Committee for the Advancement of Professional Psychology, American Psychological Association.
Baranek, G.T.
  *1999 Efficacy of Sensory and Motor Interventions for Children with Autism. Paper presented at the First Workshop of the Committee on Educational Interventions for Children with Autism, National Research Council, December 13-14, 1999. University of North Carolina-Chapel Hill School of Medicine.
Barlow, D.H.
  1996   Health care policy, psychotherapy research, and the future of psychotherapy. *American Psychologist* 51(10):1050-1058.
Chambless, D.L., and S.D. Hollon
  1998   Defining empirically supported therapies. *Journal of Consulting and Clinical Psychology* 66(1):7-18.
Dawson, G., and J. Osterling
  1997   Early intervention in autism: Effectiveness and common elements of current approaches. Pp. 307-326 in *The Effectiveness of Early Intervention: Second Generation Research*, M.J. Guralnick, ed. Baltimore, MD: Paul H. Brookes Publishing.

Filipek, P.A., P.J. Accardo, S. Ashwal, G.T. Baranek, E.H. Cook, Jr., and G. Dawson
   2000   Practice parameter: Screening and diagnosis of autism. *Neurology* 55(4):468-479.
Goldstein, H.
   *1999   Communication Intervention for Children with Autism: A Review of Treatment
         Efficacy. Paper presented at the First Workshop of the Committee on Educa-
         tional Interventions for Children with Autism, National Research Council, De-
         cember 13-14, 1999. Department of Communication Sciences, Florida State Uni-
         versity.
Horner, R.H., E.G. Carr, P.S. Strain, A.W. Todd, and H.K. Reed
   *2000   Problem Behavior Interventions for Young Children with Autism: A Research
         Synthesis. Paper presented at the Second Workshop of the Committee on Educa-
         tional Interventions for Children with Autism, National Research Council, April
         12, 2000. Department of Special Education, University of Oregon.
Howlin, P.
   1998   Practitioner review: Psychological and educational treatments of autism. *Journal
         of Child Psychology and Psychiatry and Allied Disciplines* 39(3):307-322.
Hurth, J., K. Whaley, D. Kates, and E. Shaw
   *2000   Enhancing Services for Young Children with Autism Spectrum Disorder (ASD)
         and Their Families: Infrastructure, Training, and Collaborative Funding. Paper
         presented at the Second Workshop of the Committee on Educational Interven-
         tions for Children with Autism, National Research Council, April 12, 2000.
Kasari, C.
   *2000   Assessing Change in Early Intervention Programs for Children with Autism.
         Paper presented at the Second Workshop of the Committee on Educational Inter-
         ventions for Children with Autism, National Research Council, April 12, 2000.
         Graduate School of Education and Information Studies, University of California
         at Los Angeles.
Lonigan, C.J., J.C. Elbert, and S.B. Johnson
   1998   Empirically supported psychosocial interventions for children: An overview.
         Journal of Clinical Child Psychology 27(2):138-145.
Mandlawitz, M.
   *1999   The Impact of the Legal System on Educational Programming for Young Chil-
         dren with Autism Spectrum Disorder. Paper presented at the First Workshop of
         the Committee on Educational Interventions for Children with Autism, National
         Research Council, December 13-14, 1999.
McConnell, S.R.
   *1999   Interventions to Facilitate Social Interaction for Young Children With Autism:
         Review of Available Research and Recommendations for Future Research. Paper
         presented at the First Workshop of the Committee on Educational Interventions
         for Children with Autism, National Research Council, December 13-14, 1999.
         Department of Educational Psychology, University of Minnesota.
New York State Department of Health
   1999   *Clinical Practice Guideline: The Guideline Technical Report. Autism/Pervasive Devel-
         opmental Disorders, Assessment and Intervention for Young Children (0-3 Years).* Al-
         bany, NY: New York State Department of Health, Early Intervention Program.
Rogers, S.J.
   1998   Empirically supported comprehensive treatments for young children with au-
         tism. *Journal of Clinical Child Psychology* 27(2):168-179.
Rumsey J.M., B. Vitiello, J. Cooper, and D. Hirtz
   2000   Special issue: Treatments for people with autism and other pervasive develop-
         mental disorders: Research perspectives - Editorial preface. *Journal of Autism and
         Developmental Disorders* 30(5):369-371.

CHAPTER 2

Aman, M., and N.N. Singh
    1986   *Manual for the Aberrant Behavior Checklist.* East Aurora, NY: Slosson Educational
            Publications.
Arvidsson, T, B. Danielsson, P. Forsberg, C. Gillberg, M. Johansson, and G. Kjellgren
    1997   Autism in 3-6-year-old children in a suburb of Goeteborg, Sweden. *Autism*
            1(2):163-173.
Baird, G., T. Charman, S. Baron-Cohen, A. Cox, J. Sweetenham, S. Wheelwright, and A.
Drew
    2000   A screening instrument for autism at 18 months of age: A 6-year follow-up study.
            Journal of the American Academy Child Adolescent Psychiatry 39(6):694-702.
Baron-Cohen, S., J. Allen, and C. Gillberg
    1992   Can autism be detected at 18 months? The needle, the haystack, and the CHAT.
            British Journal of Psychiatry 161:839-843.
Baron-Cohen, S., A. Cox, G. Baird, J. Swettenham, N. Nightingale, K. Morgan, A. Drew, and
T. Charman
    1996   Psychological markers in the detection of autism in infancy in a large population.
            British Journal of Psychiatry 168:158-163.
Berument, S.K., M. Rutter, C. Lord, A. Pickles, and A. Bailey
    1999   Autism screening questionnaire: Diagnostic validity. *British Journal of Psychiatry*
            175:444-451.
California Department of Developmental Services
    2000   Changes in the Population of Persons with Autism and Pervasive Developmental
            Disorders in California's Developmental Service System: 1987 through 1998.
            Available: http://www.dds.cahwnet.gov/Autism/main/incidencrptfinal.pdf
            [Accessed May 2, 2001].
Centers for Disease Control and Prevention
    2000   *Prevalence of Autism in Brick Township, New Jersey, 1998: Community Report.* At-
            lanta GA: Department of Health and Human Services.
Charman, T., J. Swettenham, S. Baron-Cohen, A. Cox, G. Baird, and A. Drew
    1997   Infants with autism: An investigation of empathy, pretend play, joint attention,
            and imitation. *Developmental Psychology* 33:781-789.
    1998   An experimental investigation of social-cognitive abilities in infants with autism:
            Clinical implications. *Infant Mental Health Journal* 19:260-275.
Cox, A., K. Klein, T. Charman, G. Baird, S. Baron-Cohen, J. Swettenham, A. Drew, S. Wheel-
wright, and N. Nightengale
    1999   The early diagnosis of autism spectrum disorders: Use of the Autism Diagnostic
            Interview-Revised at 20 months and 42 months of age. *Journal of Child Psychology
            and Psychiatry* 40:705-718.
Deykin, E.Y., and B. MacMahon
    1979   The incidence of seizures among children with autistic symptoms. *American Jour-
            nal of Psychiatry* 136(10):1310-1312.
Dykens, E.M., and F.R. Volkmar
    1997   Medical conditions associated with autism. Pp. 388-410 in *Handbook of Autism and
            Pervasive Developmental Disorders*, D.J. Cohen and F.R. Volkmar. New York: John
            Wiley and Sons.
Fay, W.H.
    1973   On the echolalia of the blind and of the autistic child. *Journal of Speech and Hear-
            ing Disorders* 38(4):478-489.
Filipek, P.A., P.J. Accardo, S. Ashwal, G.T. Baranek, E.H. Cook, Jr., and G. Dawson
    2000   Practice parameter: Screening and diagnosis of autism. *Neurology* 55(4):468-479.

Fombonne, E.
*1999   Epidemiological Findings on Autism and Related Developmental Disorders. Pa-
         per presented at the First Workshop of the Committee on Educational Interven-
         tions for Children with Autism, National Research Council, December 13-14, 1999.
Garnett, M.S., and A.J. Attwood
1998   The Australian scale for Asperger's syndrome. In *Asperger's Syndrome: A Guide
         for Parents and Professionals*, T. Attwood, ed. London: Jessica Kingsley Publishers.
Hobbs, N.
1975   *Issues in the Classification of Children*. San Francisco: Jossey-Bass.
Hughes, C.
1996   Brief report: Planning problems in autism at the level of motor control. *Journal of
         Autism and Developmental Disorders* 26(1):99-107.
Jones, V., and M. Prior
1985   Motor imitation abilities and neurological signs in autistic children. *Journal of
         Autism and Developmental Disorders* 15(1):37-46.
Kadesjoe, B., C. Gillberg, B. Hagberg, C. Gillberg, and B. Hagberg
1999   Autism and Asperger syndrome in seven-year-old children: A total population
         study. *Journal of Autism and Developmental Disorders* 29(4):327-331.
Kanner, L.
1943   Autistic disturbances of affective contact. *Nervous Child* 2:217-250.
Klin, A.
1993   Auditory brainstem responses in autism: Brainstem dysfunction or peripheral
         hearing loss? *Journal of Autism and Developmental Disorders* 23(1):15-35.
Krug, D.A., J. Arick, and P. Almond
1980   Behavior checklist for identifying severely handicapped individuals with high
         levels of autistic behavior. *Journal of Child Psychology and Psychiatry* 21(3):221-229.
Lord, C.
1995   Follow-up of two-year-olds referred for possible autism. *Journal of Child Psychol-
         ogy and Psychiatry* 36:1365-1382.
1997   Diagnostic instruments in autism spectrum disorders. Pp. 460-483 in *Handbook of
         Autism and Pervasive Developmental Disorders*, D.J. Cohen and F.R. Volkmar, eds.
         New York: John Wiley and Sons, Inc.
Lord, C., and E. Schopler
1989   Stability of assessment results of autistic and non-autistic language-impaired chil-
         dren from preschool years to early school age. *Journal of Child Psychology and
         Psychiatry* 30(4):575-590.
Lord, C., and R. Paul
1997   Language and communication in autism. Pp. 195-225 in *Handbook of Autism and
         Pervasive Developmental Disorders*, D.J. Cohen and F.R. Volkmar, eds. New York:
         John Wiley and Sons, Inc.
Lord, C., M. Rutter, and A. Le Couteur
1994   Autism Diagnostic Interview—Revised: A revised version of a diagnostic inter-
         view for caregivers of individuals with possible pervasive developmental disor-
         ders. *Journal of Autism and Developmental Disorders* 24(5):659-685.
Lord, C., S. Risi, L. Lambrecht, E.H. Cook, B.L. Leventhal, P.C. DiLavore, A. Pickles, and M.
Rutter
2000   The autism diagnostic observation schedule-generic: A standard measure of so-
         cial and communication deficits associated with the spectrum of autism. *Journal
         of Autism and Developmental Disorders* 30(3):205-233.
Prizant, B.M., and J.F. Duchan
1981   The functions of immediate echolalia in autistic children. *Journal of Speech and
         Hearing Disorders* 46(3):241-249.

Prizant, B.M., and A.L. Schuller
   1997   Facilitating communication: Theoretical foundations. Pp. 289-300 in *Handbook of Autism and Pervasive Developmental Disorders*, D.J. Cohen and F.R. Volkmar, eds. New York: John Wiley and Sons.
Ricks, D.M., and L. Wing
   1975   Language, communication, and the use of symbols in normal and autistic children. *Journal of Autism and Child Schizophrenia* 5(3):191-221.
Robins, D., D. Fein, M. Barton, and M. Liss
   1999   *The Autism Screening Project: How Early Can Autism Be Detected?* Paper presented at the American Psychological Association Meeting, Boston.
Schopler, E., R.J. Reichler, R.F. DeVellis, and K. Daly
   1980   Toward objective classification of childhood autism: Childhood Autism Rating Scale (CARS). *Journal of Autism and Developmental Disorders* 10(1):91-103.
Siegel, B., C. Pliner, J. Eschler, and G.R. Elliott
   1988   How children with autism are diagnosed: Difficulties in identification of children with multiple developmental delays. *Journal of Developmental Behavioral Pediatrics* 9(4):199-204.
Siegel, B., J. Vukicevic, G.R. Elliott, and H.C. Kraemer
   1990   The use of signal detection theory to assess DSM IIIR criteria for autisitic disorder. *Journal of the American Academy of Child and Adolescent Psychiatry* 28(4):542-548.
Sparrow, S.
   1997   Developmentally based assessments. Pp. 411-447 in *Handbook of Autism and Pervasive Developmental Disorders*, D.J. Cohen and F.R. Volkmar, eds. New York: John Wiley and Sons, Inc.
Stone, W.L., E.B. Lee, L. Ashford, J. Brissie, S.L. Hepburn, E.E. Coonrod, and B. Weiss
   1999   Can autism be diagnosed accurately in children under three years? *Journal of Child Psychology and Psychiatry* 40:219-226.
Stone, W.L., E.E. Coonrod, and O.Y. Ousley
   2000   Brief report: Screening tool for autism in two-year-olds (STAT): Development and preliminary data. *Journal of Autism and Developmental Disorders* 30(6):607-612.
Tager-Flusberg, H., S. Calkins, T. Nolin, T. Baumberger, M. Anderson, and A. Chadwick-Dias
   1990   A longitudinal study of language acquisition in autistic and Down syndrome children. *Journal of Autism and Developmental Disorders* 20(1):1-21.
Volkmar, F.R., and D.S. Nelson
   1990   Seizure disorders in autism. *Journal of the American Academy of Child Adolescent Psychiatry* 29(1):127-129.
Volkmar, F.R., A. Klin, and D.J. Cohen
   1997   Diagnosis and classification of autism and related conditions: Consensus and issues. Pp. 5-40 in *Handbook of Autism and Pervasive Developmental Disorders*, D.J. Cohen and F.R. Volkmar, eds. New York: John Wiley and Sons, Inc.
Volkmar, F.R., E. Cook, J. Pomeroy, G. Realmuto, and P. Tanguay
   1999   Practice parameters for the assessment and treatment of children and adolescents with autism and pervasive developmental disorders. *Journal of the American Academy of Child and Adolescent Psychiatry* 38(12):32S-54S.
Wetherby, A.M., D.G. Yonclas, and A.A. Bryan
   1989   Communicative profiles of preschool children with handicaps: Implications for early identification. *Journal of Speech and Hearing Disorders* 54(2):148-158.

CHAPTER 3

Bailey, A., S. Palferman, L. Heavey, and A. Le Couteur
  1998   Autism: The phenotype in relatives. *Journal of Autism and Developmental Disorders* 28:369-392.
Baker, B.L.
  1989   *Parent Training and Developmental Disabilities.* Washington DC: American Association on Mental Retardation.
Bettelheim, B.
  1974   *A Home for the Heart.* New York: Alfred A. Knopf.
Bristol, M.M.
  1987   Mothers of children with autism or communication disorders: Successful adaptation and the double ABCX model. *Journal of Autism and Developmental Disorders* 17:469-486.
Bristol, M.M., and E. Schopler
  1983   Stress and coping in families of autistic adolescents. In *Autism in Adolescents and Adults,* E. Schopler and G.B. Mesibov, eds. New York: Plenum Press.
Bristol, M.M., J.J. Gallagher, and E. Schopler
  1988   Mothers and fathers of young developmentally disabled and non disabled boys: Adaptation and spousal support. *Developmental Psychology* 24:441-451.
Bristol, M.M., J.J. Gallagher, and K.D. Holt
  1993   Maternal depressive symptoms in autism: Response to psychoeducational intervention. *Rehabilitation Psychology* 38:3-9.
Celiberti, D.A., and S.L. Harris
  1993   The effects of a play skills intervention for siblings of children with autism. *Behavior Therapy* 24:573-599.
DeMyer, M.K., and P. Goldberg
  1983   Family needs of the autistic adolescent. In *Autism in Adolescents and Adults,* E. Schopler and G.B. Mesibov, eds. New York: Plenum Press.
Dunst, C.J.
  1999   Placing parent education in conceptual and empirical context. *Topics in Early Childhood Special Education* 19:141-147.
Fong, P.
  1991   Cognitive appraisal in high and low stress mothers of adolescents with autism. *Journal of Consulting and Clinical Psychology* 59:471-474.
Gallagher, J.J.
  1991   The family as a focus for intervention. In *Handbook of Early Childhood Interventions,* S. Meisels and J. Shonkoff, eds. Cambridge MA: Cambridge University Press.
  1992   The role of values and facts in policy development for infants and toddlers with disabilities and their families. *Journal of Early Intervention* 16:1-10.
Gill, M.J., and S.L. Harris
  1991   Hardiness and social support as predictors of psychological discomfort in mothers of children with autism. *Journal of Autism and Developmental Disorders* 21:407-416.
Glasberg, B.
  2000   The development of siblings understanding of autism spectrum disorders. *Journal of Autism and Developmental Disorders* 30:143-156.
Hanson, M.J., E.W. Lynch, and K.I. Wayman.
  1990   Honoring the cultural diversity of families when gathering data. *Topics in Early Childhood Special Education,* 10(1):112-131.

Harris, S.L.
  1983   *Families of the Developmentally Disabled: A Guide to Behavioral Intervention.*
          Elmsford, NY: Pergamon Press.
  1986   Parents as teachers: A four to seven year follow-up of parents of children with
          autism. *Child and Family Behavior Therapy* 8:39-47.
  1994   Treatment of family problems in autism. Pp. 161-175 in *Behavioral Issues in Au-
          tism*, E. Schopler and G..B. Mesibov, eds. New York: Plenum Press.
  1996   Serving families of children with developmental disabilities: Reaching diverse
          populations. *Special Services in the Schools* 12:79-86.
Heller, T., R. Markwardt, L. Rowitz, and B. Farber
  1994   Adaptation of Hispanic families to a member with mental retardation. *American
          Journal on Mental Retardation* 99:289-300.
Koegel, R.L., A. Bimbela, and L. Schreibman
  1996   Collateral effects of parent training on family interactions. *Journal of Autism and
          Developmental Disorders* 26:347-359.
Koegel, R.L., L. Schreibman, J. Johnson, R.E. O'Neill, and G. Dunlap
  1984   Collateral effects of parent training in families of autistic children. In *Parent
          Training: Foundations of Research and Practice,* R.F. Dangel and R.A. Polster, eds.
          New York: Guilford Press.
Koegel, R.L., L. Schreibman, L M. Loos, H. Dirlich-Wilhelm, G. Dunlap, F.R. Robbins, and
A.J. Plienis
  1992   Consistent stress predictors in mothers of children with autism. *Journal of Autism
          and Developmental Disorders* 22:205-216.
Kolko, D.J.
  1984   Parents as behavior therapists for their autistic child. In *The Effects of Autism on
          the Family,* E. Schopler and G.B. Mesibov, eds. New York: Plenum Press.
Konidaris, J.A.
  1997   A sibling's perspective on autism. Pp. 1021-1031 in *Handbook of Autism and Perva-
          sive Developmental Disorders, 2nd edition*, D. Cohen and F. Volkmar (eds.). John
          Wiley and Sons: New York.
Konstantareas, M.M., S. Homatidis, and C.M.S. Plowright
  1992   Assessing resources and stress in parents of severely dysfunctional children
          through the Clarke modification of Holroyd's questionnaire on resources and
          stress. *Journal of Autism and Developmental Disorders* 22:217-234.
Lobato, D.
  1990   *Brothers, Sisters and Special Needs.* Baltimore, MD: Paul H. Brookes Publishing.
Lovaas, O.I.
  1987   Behavioral treatment and normal educational and intellectual functioning in
          young autistic children. *Journal of Consulting and Clinical Psychology* 55:3-9.
Lovaas, O.I., R. Koegel, J.Q. Simmons, and J.S. Long
  1973   Some generalization and follow-up measures on autistic children in behavior
          therapy. *Journal of Applied Behavior Analysis* 6:131-166.
McHale, S.M., and V.S. Harris
  1992   Children's experiences with disabled and nondisabled siblings: Links with per-
          sonal adjustment and relationship evaluations. In *Children's Sibling Relationships.
          Developmental and Clinical Issues,* F. Boer and J. Dunn, eds. Hillsdale, NJ: Erlbaum
          Associates.
Milgram, N.A., and M. Atzil
  1988   Parenting stress in raising autistic children. *Journal of Autism and Developmental
          Disorders* 18:415-424.

Ozonoff, S., and K. Cathcart
  1998   Effectiveness of a home program intervention for young children with autism. *Journal of Autism and Developmental Disorders* 28:25-32.
Prieto-Bayard, M., and B.L. Baker
  1986   Parent training for Spanish-speaking families with a retarded child. *Journal of Community Psychology* 14:134-143.
Rodrigue, J.R., S.B. Morgan, and G.R. Geffken
  1990   Families of autistic children: Psychosocial functioning of mothers. *Journal of Clinical Child Psychology* 19:371-379.
  1992   Psychosocial adaptation of fathers of children with autism, Down syndrome, and normal development. *Journal of Autism and Developmental Disorders* 22, 249-263.
Rodrigue, J.R., G.R. Geffken, and S.B. Morgan
  1993   Perceived competence and behavioral adjustment of siblings of children with autism. *Journal of Autism and Developmental Disorders* 23:665-674.
Schopler, E., and R.J. Reichler
  1971   Parents as cotherapists in the treatment of psychotic children. *Journal of Autism and Childhood Schizophrenia* 1:87-102.
Seligman, M., and R.B. Darling
  1997   *Ordinary Families, Special Children, 2nd ed.* New York: Guilford Press.
Shapiro, J., and D. Simonsen
  1994   Educational/support group for Latino families of children with Down syndrome. *Mental Retardation* 32:403-415.
Smith, M.J., and A. Ryan
  1987   Chinese-American families of children with developmental disabilities: An exploratory study of reactions to service providers. *Mental Retardation* 25:345-350.
Stahl, A.
  1991   Beliefs of Jewish-Oriental mothers regarding children who are mentally retarded. *Education and Training in Mental Retardation* 26:361-369.
Szatmari, P., M.B. Jones, L. Zwaigenbaum, and J.E. MacLean
  1998   Genetics of autism: Overview and new directions. *Journal of Autism and Developmental Disorders* 28:351-368.
Wolery, M., and A.N. Garfinkle
  *2000   Measures in Intervention Research with Young Children Who Have Autism. Paper presented at the Second Workshop of the Committee on Educational Interventions for Children with Autism, National Research Council, April 12, 2000.

CHAPTER 4

Cook, E.H., J.E. Kieffer, D.A. Charak, and B.L. Leventhal
  1993   Case study: Autistic disorder and post-traumatic stress disorder. *Journal of the American Academy of Child and Adolescent Psychiatry* 32(6):1292-1294.
Hanson, M., and S. Odom
  1999   "Can I play with you?" Peer culture in inclusive preschool programs. *Journal for the Association of Persons with Severe Handicaps* 24(2):69-84.
Handleman, J.S., and S. Harris
  2000   *Preschool Education Programs for Children with Autism (2nd ed.).* Austin, TX: Pro-Ed.
Kasari, C.
  *2000   Assessing Change in Early Intervention Programs for Children with Autism. Paper presented at the Second Workshop of the Committee on Educational Interventions for Children with Autism, National Research Council, April 12, 2000. Graduate School of Education and Information Studies, University of California at Los Angeles.

Kavale, K.A., and S.R. Forness
   1999   *Efficacy of Special Education and Related Services.* Washington, DC: American Association on Mental Retardation.
Kern, L., R.L. Koegel, and G. Dunlap
   1984   The influence of vigorous versus mild exercise on autistic stereotyped behaviors. *Journal of Autism and Developmental Disorders* 14:57–67.
Klin, A.
   1992   Listening preferences in regard to speech in four children with developmental disabilities. *Journal of Child Psychology and Psychiatry and Allied Disciplines* 33:763-769.
Koegel, L., R.L. Koegel, J. Harrower, and C. Carter
   1999   Pivotal response intervention I: Overview of approach. *Journal of the Association for Persons with Severe Handicaps* 24:174-185.
Lovaas, O.I.
   1987   Behavioral treatment and normal educational and intellectual functioning in young autistic children. *Journal of Consulting and Clinical Psychology* 55:3-9.
National Research Council
   1997   *Educating One and All: Students with Disabilities and Standards-Based Reform.* Committee on Goals 2000 and the Inclusion of Students with Disabilities, L.M. McDonnell, M.J. McLaughlin, and P. Morison, eds. Commission on Behavioral and Social Sciences and Education. Washington, DC: National Academy Press.
Pierce, K., and L. Schreibman
   1997   Multiple peer use of pivotal response training to increase social behaviors of classmates with autism: Results from trained and untrained peers. *Journal of Applied Behavior Analysis* 30:157-160.
Prizant, B.M., and E. Rubin
   1999   Contemporary issues in interventions for autism spectrum disorders: A commentary. *Journal of the Association for Persons with Severe Handicaps* 24:199-208.
Rogers, S.J., and B.F. Pennington
   1991   A theoretical approach to the deficits in infantile autism. *Development and Psychopathology* 3:137-162.
Sigman, M., E. Ruskin, S. Arbeile, R. Corona, C. Dissanayake, M. Espinosa, N. Kim, A. Lopez, and C. Zierhut
   1999   Continuity and change in the social competence of children with autism, Down syndrome, and developmental delays. *Monographs of the Society for Research in Child Development* 64:1-114.
Stone, W.L., O.Y. Ousley, and C. Littleford
   1997   Motor imitation in young children with autism: What's the object? *Journal of Abnormal Child Psychology* 25:475-485.
Szatmari, P., G. Bartolucci, R.S. Bremner, S. Bond, and S. Rich
   1989   A follow-up study of high functioning autistic children. *Journal of Autism and Developmental Disorders* 19:213-226.
Watson, L., C. Lord, B. Schaffer, and E. Schopler
   1989   *Teaching Spontaneous Communication to Autistic and Developmentally Handicapped Children.* New York, NY: Irvington Publishers.

CHAPTER 5

American Psychiatric Association
   1980   *Diagnostic and Statistical Manual of Mental Disorders* (Third edition). Washington, DC: American Psychiatric Association.

1987   *Diagnostic and Statistical Manual of Mental Disorders* (Third edition revised). Washington, DC: American Psychiatric Association.

1994   *Diagnostic and Statistical Manual of Mental Disorders* (Fourth edition). Washington, DC: American Psychiatric Association.

American Speech-Language-Hearing Association

1989   Competencies for speech-language pathologists providing services in augmentative communication. *American Speech-Language-Hearing Association* 31:107-110.

Anderson, S., and R. Romanczyk

1999   Early intervention for young children with autism: Continuum-based behavioral models. *Journal of the Association for Persons with Severe Handicaps* 24:162-173.

Baltaxe, C.

1977   Pragmatic deficits in the language of autistic adolescents. *Journal of Pediatric Psychology* 2:176-180.

Baltaxe, C., and J. Simmons

1975   Language in childhood psychosis: A review. *Journal of Speech and Hearing Disorders* 40:439-458.

Barrera, R.D., and B. Sulzer-Azaroff

1983   An alternating treatment comparison of oral and total communication training programs with echolalic autistic children. *Journal of Applied Behavior Analysis* 16:379-394.

Barrera, R.D., D. Lobatos-Barrera, and B. Sulzer-Azaroff

1980   A simultaneous treatment comparison of three expressive language training programs with a mute autistic child. *Journal of Autism and Developmental Disorders* 10:21-37.

Beukelman, D., and P. Mirenda

1998   *Augmentative and Alternative Communication: Management of Severe Communication Disorders in Children and Adults (Second edition)*. Baltimore, MD: Paul H. Brookes Publishing.

Biklen, D.

1993   *Communication Unbound*. New York: Teacher's College Press.

Bondy, A., and L. Frost

1994   The picture exchange communication system. *Focus on Autistic Behavior* 9:1-19.

Bristol, M.M.

1984   Family resources and successful adaptation to autistic children. In *The Effects Of Autism On The Family*, E. Schopler and G.B. Mesibov, eds. New York: Plenum Press.

Brown, L., M.B. Branston, S. Hamre-Nietupski, L. Pumpian, N. Certo, and L. Gruenewald

1979   A strategy for developing chronological age-appropriate and functional curricular content for severely handicapped adolescents and young adults. *Journal of Special Education* 13:81-90.

Bryson, S.

1996   Brief report: Epidemiology of autism. *Journal of Autism and Developmental Disorders* 26:165-167.

Buffington, D., P. Krantz, L. McClannahan, and C. Poulson

1998   Procedures for teaching appropriate gestural communication skills to children with autism. *Journal of Autism and Developmental Disorders* 28:535-545.

Cafiero, J.M.

1995   Teaching Parents of Children with Autism Picture: Communication Symbols as a Natural Language to Decrease Levels of Family Stress. Unpublished doctoral dissertation: University of Toledo.

2000   *A Parent Guide to Picture Language for their Non-Speaking Children*. Rockville, MD: CCA Publications.

Calculator, S., D. Fabry, S. Glennon, B.M. Prizant, and A. Schubert
  1995   *Technical Report on Standards of Practice for Facilitated Communication.* Rockville,
          MD: American Speech-Language-Hearing Association.
Carr, E.G., and P.A. Dores
  1981   Patterns of language acquisition following simultaneous communication with
          autistic children. *Analysis and Intervention in Developmental Disabilities* 1:347-361.
Carr, E.G., and V.M. Durand
  1985   Reducing behavior problems through functional communication training. *Jour-
          nal of Applied Behavior Analysis* 18:111-126.
Charlop, M.H., L. Schreibman, and M.G. Thibodeau
  1985   Increasing spontaneous verbal responding in autistic children using a time delay
          procedure. *Journal of Applied Behavior Analysis* 18:155-166.
Charlop, M.H., and J.E. Trasowech
  1991   Increasing children's daily spontaneous speech. *Journal of Applied Behavioral
          Analysis* 24:747-761.
Chen, S.H.A., and V. Bernard-Opitz
  1993   Comparison of personal and computerized instruction for children with autism.
          Mental Retardation 31:368-376.
Dawson, G., and A. Adams
  1984   Imitation and social responsiveness in autistic children. *Journal of Abnormal Child
          Psychology* 12:209-226.
Dawson, G., and J. Osterling
  1997   Early intervention in autism. Pp. 307-326 in *The Effectiveness of Early Intervention,*
          M. Guralnick, ed. Baltimore, MD: Paul H. Brookes Publishing.
Dawson, G., D. Hill, A. Spencer, L. Galpert, and L. Watson
  1990   Affective exchanges between young autistic children and their mothers. *Journal
          of Abnormal Child Psychology* 18:335-345.
Dexter, M.
  1998   The Effects of Aided Language Stimulation Upon Verbal Output and Augmenta-
          tive Communication During Storybook Reading for Children with Pervasive De-
          velopmental Disabilities. Unpublished doctoral dissertation, The Johns Hopkins
          University, Baltimore, MD.
Elder, P., and C. Goossens
  1994   *Engineering Training Environments for Interactive Augmentative Communication:
          Strategies for Adolescents and Adults Who Are Moderately/Severely Developmentally
          Delayed.* Birmingham, AL: Southeast Augmentative Communication Conference
          Publications.
Frost, L., and A. Bondy
  1994   *PECS: The Picture Exchange Communication System Training Manual.* Cherry Hill,
          NJ: Pyramid Educational Consultants.
Garfin, D., and C. Lord
  1986   Communication as a social problem in autism. Pp. 237-261 in *Social Behavior in
          Autism,* E. Schopler and G. Mesibov, eds. New York: Plenum Press.
Garrison-Harrell, L., D. Kamps, and T. Kravits
  1997   The effects of peer networks on social-communicative behaviors for students with
          autism. *Focus on Autism and Other Developmental Disabilities* 12:241-254.
Goldstein, H.
  *1999   Communication Intervention for Children with Autism: A Review of Treatment
          Efficacy. Paper presented at the First Workshop of the Committee on Educa-
          tional Interventions for Children with Autism, National Research Council, De-
          cember 13-14, 1999. Department of Communication Sciences, Florida State Uni-
          versity.

Goossens, C., S. Crain, and P. Elder
1995   *Engineering the Preschool Environment for Interactive, Symbolic Communication.* Birmingham, AL: Southeast Augmentative Communication Conference Publications.

Greenspan, S.I., and S. Wieder
1997   Developmental patterns and outcomes in infants and children with disorders in relating and communicating: A chart review of 200 cases of children with autistic spectrum diagnoses. *Journal of Developmental and Learning Disorders* 1:87-141.

Gresham, F., and D. MacMillan
1997   Autistic recovery? An analysis and critique of the empirical evidence on the early intervention project. *Behavior Disorders* 22:185-201.

Hall, L., L. McClannahan, and P. Krantz
1995   Promoting independence in integrated classrooms by teaching aides to use activity schedules and decreased prompts. *Education and Training in Mental Retardation and Developmental Disabilities* 34:208-217.

Hart, B.
1985   Naturalistic language training strategies. Pp. 63-88 in *Teaching Functional Language*, S. Warren and A. Rogers-Warren, eds. Baltimore, MD: University Park Press.

Heimann, M., K.E. Nelson, T. Tjus, and C. Gillberg
1995   Increasing reading and communication skills in children with autism through an interactive multimedia computer program. *Journal of Autism and Developmental Disorders* 25:459-480.

Hodgdon, L.
1995   Visual Strategies for Improving Communication. Troy, MI: QuirkRoberts Publishing.

Horner, R.H., E.G. Carr, P.S. Strain, A.W. Todd, and H.K. Reed
*2000   Problem Behavior Interventions for Young Children with Autism: A Research Synthesis. Paper presented at the Second Workshop of the Committee on Educational Interventions for Children with Autism, National Research Council, April 12, 2000. Department of Special Education, University of Oregon.

Horner, R.H., G. Dunlap, R. Koegel, E. Carr, W. Sailor, J. Anderson, R. Albin, and R. O'Neill
1990   Toward a technology of "nonaversive" behavioral support. *Journal of the Association for Persons with Severe Handicaps* 15:125-147.

Hwang, B., and C. Hughes
2000   Increasing early social-communicative skills of preverbal children with autism through social interactive training. *Journal of the Association for Persons with Severe Handicaps* 25:18-28.

Kaiser, A.
1993   Functional language. Pp. 347-379 in *Instruction of Students with Severe Disabilities*, M. Snell, ed. New York: Macmillan Publishing Company.

Kaiser, A.P., P.J. Yoder, and A. Keetz
1992   Evaluating milieu teaching. Pp. 9-47 in *Causes and Effects in Communication and Language Intervention*, S.F. Warren and J. Reichle, eds. Baltimore, MD: Paul H. Brookes Publishing.

Kasari, C., M. Sigman, P. Mundy, and N. Yirmiya
1990   Affective sharing in the context of joint attention. *Journal of Autism and Developmental Disorders* 20:87-100.

Klinger, L., and G. Dawson
1992   Facilitating early social and communicative development in children with autism. Pp. 157-186 in *Causes and Effects in Communication and Language Intervention*, S.F. Warren and J. Reichle, eds. Baltimore, MD: Paul H. Brookes Publishing.

Koegel, L.
  1995   Communication and language intervention. Pp. 17-32 in *Teaching Children with Autism*, R. Koegel and L. Koegel, eds. Baltimore, MD: Paul H. Brookes Publishing.
Koegel, R., M.C. O'Dell, and L.K. Koegel
  1987   A natural language paradigm for teaching nonverbal autistic children. *Journal of Autism and Developmental Disorders* 17:187-199.
Koegel, R., L. Koegel, and A. Surratt
  1992   Language intervention and disruptive behavior in preschool children with autism. *Journal of Autism and Developmental Disorders* 22:141-153.
Koegel, L., R. Koegel, Y. Shoshan, and E. McNerney
  1999   Pivotal response intervention II: Preliminary long-term outcome data. *Journal of the Association for Persons with Severe Handicaps* 24:186-198.
Koegel, R., S. Camarata, L. Koegel, A. Ben-Tall, and A. Smith
  1998   Increasing speech intelligibility in children with autism. *Journal of Autism and Developmental Disorders* 28:241-251.
Krantz, P., and L. McClannahan
  1998   Social interaction skills for children with autism: A script fading procedure for beginning readers. *Journal of Applied Behavior Analysis* 31:191-202.
Krantz, P.J., S. Zalewski, L. Hall, E. Fenski, and L. McClannahan
  1981   Teaching complex language to autistic children. *Analysis and Intervention in Developmental Disabilities* 1:259-297.
Lahey, M.
  1988   *Language Disorders and Language Development*. New York: MacMillan Publishing.
LaPointe, L., and R. Katz
  1998   Neurogenic disorders of speech. Pp. 434-447 in *Human Communication Disorders*, G. Shames, E. Wiig, and W. Secord, eds. Boston: Allyn and Bacon.
Layton, T.
  1988   Language training with autistic children using four different modes of presentation. *Journal of Communication Disorders* 21:333-350.
Lewy, A.L., and G. Dawson
  1992   Social stimulation and joint attention in young autistic children. *Journal of Abnormal Child Psychology* 20(6):555-566.
Light, J., B. Roberts, R. DiMarco, and N. Greiner
  1998   Augmentative and alternative communication to support receptive and expressive communication for people with autism. *Journal of Communication Disorders* 31:153-180.
Lord, C., and R. Paul
  1997   Language and communication in autism. Pp. 195-225 in *Handbook of Autism and Pervasive Developmental Disorders*, D. Cohen and F. Volkmar, eds. New York: John Wiley and Sons.
Lovaas, O.I.
  1977   *The Autistic Child: Language Development Through Behavior Modification*. New York: Irvington Press.
  1981   *Teaching Developmentally Disabled Children: The "Me" Book*. Baltimore, MD: University Park Press.
Loveland, K., and S.H. Landry
  1986   Joint attention and language in autism and developmental language delay. *Journal of Autism and Developmental Disorders* 16:335-349.
Marcus, L., E. Schopler, and C. Lord
  2000   TEACCH services for preschool children. In *Preschool Education Programs for Children with Autism*, J.S. Handleman and S.L. Harris, eds. Austin, TX: Pro-Ed.

McArthur, D., and L.B. Adamson
   1996   Joint attention in preverbal children: Autism and developmental language disorders. *Journal of Autism and Developmental Disorders* 26:481-496.
McEachin, J.J., T. Smith, and O.I. Lovaas
   1993   Long-term outcome for children with autism who received early intensive behavioral treatment. *American Journal on Mental Retardation* 97:359-372.
McGee, G.G., P.J. Krantz, and L.E. McClannahan
   1985   The facilitative effects of incidental teaching on preposition use by autistic children. *Journal of Applied Behavior Analysis* 18:17-31.
McGee, G., M. Morrier, and T. Daly
   1999   An incidental teaching approach to early intervention for toddlers with autism. *Journal of the Association for Persons with Severe Handicaps* 24:133-146.
McHale, S., R. Simeonsson, L. Marcus, and J. Olley
   1980   The social and symbolic quality of autistic children's communication. *Journal of Autism and Developmental Disorders* 10:299-310.
McIlvane, W.J., R.W. Bass, J.M. O'Brien, B.J. Gerovac, and L.T. Stoddard
   1984   Spoken and signed naming of foods after receptive exclusion training in severe retardation. *Applied Research in Mentally Retarded* 5:1-28.
Mirenda, P.
   1997   Functional communication training and augmentative communication: A research review. *Augmentative and Alternative Communication* 13:207-225.
Mirenda, P., and J. Santogrossi
   1985   A prompt-free strategy to teach pictorial communication system use. *Augmentative and Alternative Communication* 1:143-150.
Mirenda, P., T. MacGregor, and S. Keough
   In press   Teaching communication skills for behaviour support in the context of family life. In *Families and Positive Behavioral Support: Addressing the Challenge of Problem Behaviors in Family Contexts*, J. Lucyshyn, G. Dunlap, and R. Albin, eds. Baltimore, MD: Paul H. Brookes Publishing.
Mundy, P., M. Sigman, and C. Kasari
   1990   A longitudinal study of joint attention and language development in autistic children. *Journal of Autism and Developmental Disorders* 20:115-128.
Mundy, P., M. Sigman, J. Ungerer, and T. Sherman
   1987   Nonverbal communication and play correlates of language development in autistic children. *Journal of Autism and Developmental Disorders* 17:349-364.
Parsons, C., and D. LaSorte
   1993   The effect of computers with synthesized speech and no speech on the spontaneous communication of children with autism. *Australian Journal of Human Communication Disorders* 21:12-31.
Peterson, S., A. Bondy, Y. Vincent, and C. Finnegan
   1995   Effects of altering communicative input for students with autism and no speech: Two case studies. *Augmentative and Alternative Communication* 11:93-100.
Pierce, K., and L. Schreibman
   1994   Teaching daily living skills to children with autism in unsupervised settings through pictorial self-management. *Journal of Applied Behavior Analysis* 27:471-482.
   1995   Increasing complex social behaviors in children with autism: Effects of peer-implemented pivotal response training. *Journal of Applied Behavior Analysis* 28(3):285-295.

Prizant, B.M., and P.J. Rydell
    1993   Assessment and intervention considerations for unconventional verbal behavior.
            In *Communicative Alternatives to Challenging Behavior: Integrating Functional As-
            sessment and Intervention Strategies,* J. Reichle and D. Wacker, eds. Baltimore, MD:
            Paul H. Brookes Publishing.
Prizant, B., and A.Wetherby
    1998   Understanding the continuum of discrete-trial traditional behavioral to social-
            pragmatic developmental approaches in communication enhancement for young
            children with autism/PDD. *Seminars in Speech and Language* 19:329-353.
Prizant, B.M., and E. Rubin
    1999   Contemporary issues in interventions for autism spectrum disorders: A com-
            mentary. *Journal of the Association for Persons with Severe Handicaps* 24:199-208.
Prizant, B.M., A.L. Schuler, A.M. Wetherby, and P. Rydell
    1997   Enhancing language and communication: Language approaches. Pp. 572-605 in
            Handbook of Autism and Pervasive Developmental Disorders (2nd Edition), D. Cohen
            and F.R. Volkmar, eds. New York: John Wiley and Sons.
Quill, K.
    1997   Instructional considerations for young children with autism: The rationale for
            visually cued instruction. *Journal of Autism and Developmental Disorders* 27:697-
            714.
Rogers, S.J.
    1996   Early intervention in autism. *Journal of Autism and Developmental Disorders* 26:243-
            246.
Rogers, S.J., and H. Lewis
    1989   An effective day treatment model for young children with pervasive develop-
            mental disorders. *Journal of the American Academy of Child and Adolescent Psychia-
            try* 28:207-214.
Rogers, S.J., and D. DiLalla
    1991   A comparative study of a developmentally based preschool curriculum on young
            children with autism and young children with other disorders of behavior and
            development. *Topics in Early Childhood Special Education* 11:29-48.
Romski, M., and R. Sevcik
    1996   *Breaking the Speech Barrier: Language Development Through Augmented Means.* Bal-
            timore, MD: Paul H. Brookes Publishing.
Schepis, M., D. Reid, M. Behrman, and K. Sutton
    1998   Increasing communicative interactions of young children with autism using a
            voice output communication aid and naturalistic teaching. *Journal of Applied Be-
            havior Analysis* 31:561-578.
Schopler, E., M. Lansing, and L. Waters
    1983   *Individualized Assessment and Treatment for Autistic and Developmentally Disabled
            Children: Vol. 3. Teaching Activities for Autistic Children.* Austin, TX: Pro-Ed.
Schuler, A.L., B.M. Prizant, and A.M. Wetherby
    1997   Enhancing language and communication: Prelanguage approaches. Pp. 539-571
            in *Handbook of Autism and Pervasive Developmental Disorders (2nd Edition),* D. Cohen
            and F. Volkmar, eds. New York: John Wiley.
Schwartz, I., A. Garfinkle, and J. Bauer
    1998   The Picture Exchange Communication System: Communicative outcomes for
            young children with disabilities. *Topics in Early Childhood Special Education* 18:144-
            159.
Seal, B., and J. Bonvillian
    1997   Sign language and motor functioning in students with autistic disorder. *Journal
            of Autism and Developmental Disorders* 27:437-466.

Shane, H., ed.
  1994   *Facilitated Communication: The Clinical and Social Phenomenon.* San Diego, CA: Singular Publishing Group.
Sheinkopf, S.J., and B. Siegel
  1998   Home-based behavioral treatment of young children with autism. *Journal of Autism and Developmental Disorders* 28(1):15-23.
Shonkoff, J., P. Hauser-Cram, M. Krauss, and C. Upshur
  1988   Early intervention efficacy research: What have we learned and where do we go from here? *Topics in Early Childhood Special Education* 8:81-93.
  1992   Development of infants with disabilities and their families—Implications for theory and service delivery. *Monographs of the Society for Research in Child Development* 57(6):Serial Number 230.
Sigman, M., and J. Ungerer
  1984   Cognitive and language skills in autistic, mentally retarded and normal children. *Developmental Psychology* 20:293-302.
Sigman, M., and E. Ruskin
  1999   Continuity and change in the social competence of children with autism, Down syndrome, and developmental delays. *Monographs of the Society for Research in Child Development* 64(1):v-114.
Stahmer, A.C.
  1995   Teaching symbolic play skills to children with autism using pivotal response training. *Journal of Autism and Developmental Disorders* 25(2):123-142.
Steibel, C.
  1999   Promoting augmentative and alternative communication in daily routines: A parent problem-solving intervention. *Journal of Positive Behavior Interventions* 1:159-169.
Stone, W.L., and L.M. Caro-Martinez
  1990   Naturalistic observations of spontaneous communication in autistic children. *Journal of Autism and Developmental Disorders* 20:437-453.
Stone, W., O. Ousley, P. Yoder, K. Hogan, and S. Hepburn
  1997   Nonverbal communication in 2- and 3-year old children with autism. *Journal of Autism and Developmental Disorders* 27:677-696.
Tager-Flusberg, H.
  1996   Brief report: Current theory and research on language and communication in autism. *Journal of Autism and Developmental Disorders* 26:169-178.
Thorp, D.M., and L. Schreibman
  1995   Effects of sociodramatic play training on children with autism. *Journal of Autism and Developmental Disorders* 25(3):265-282.
Venter, A., C. Lord, and E. Schopler
  1992   A follow-up study of high-functioning autistic children. *Journal of Child Psychology and Psychiatry* 33:489-507.
Watson, L., C. Lord, B. Schaffer, and E. Schopler
  1989   *Teaching Spontaneous Communication to Autistic and Developmentally Handicapped Children.* New York, NY: Irvington Publishers.
Wetherby, A., and C. Prutting
  1984   Profiles of communicative and cognitive-social abilities in autistic children. *Journal of Speech and Hearing Research* 27:364-377.
Wetherby, A., and B. Prizant
  1999   Enhancing language and communication development in autism: Assessment and intervention guidelines. Pp. 141-174 in *Autism: Identification, Education, and Treatment,* D. Berkell Zager, ed. Mahwah, NJ: Lawrence Erlbaum Associates.

Wetherby, A., D. Yonclas, and A. Bryan
   1989   Communicative profiles of handicapped preschool children: Implications for
           early identification. *Journal of Speech and Hearing Disorders* 54:148-158.
Wetherby, A.M., A. Schuler, and B. Prizant
   1997   Enhancing language and communication: Theoretical foundations. Pp. 513-538
           in *Handbook of Autism and Pervasive Developmental Disorders, 2nd Edition,* D. Cohen
           and F. Volkmar, eds. New York: John Wiley and Sons.
Wetherby, A., B. Prizant, and T. Hutchinson
   1998   Communicative, social-affective, and symbolic profiles of young children with
           autism and pervasive developmental disorder. *American Journal of Speech-Lan-
           guage Pathology* 7:79-91.
Wetherby, A., B. Prizant, and A. Schuler
   2000   Understanding the nature of the communication and language impairments. Pp.
           109-141 in *Autism Spectrum Disorders: A Transactional Developmental Perspective,*
           A. Wetherby and B. Prizant, eds. Baltimore, MD: Paul H. Brookes Publishing.
Wing, L., J. Gould, R.R. Yeates, and L.M. Brierley
   1977   Symbolic play in severely mentally retarded and in autistic children. *Journal of
           Child Psychology and Psychiatry* 18:167-178.
Yoder, P.J., and T.L. Layton
   1988   Speech following sign language training in autistic children with minimal verbal
           language. *Journal of Autism and Developmental Disorders* 18:217-230.

CHAPTER 6

Anderson, S.R., and R.G. Romanczyk
   1999   Early intervention for young children with autism: Continuum-based behavioral
           models. *Journal of the Association for People with Special Handicaps* 24(3):162-173.
Ayres, A.J., and L.S. Tickle
   1980   Hyper-responsivity to touch and vestibular stimuli as a predictor of positive re-
           sponse to sensory integration procedures by autistic children. *American Journal of
           Occupational Therapy* 34:375-381.
Baron-Cohen, S., H.A. Ring, S. Wheelwright, E.T. Bullmore, M.J. Brammer, A. Simmons,
and S.C.R. Williams
   1999   Social intelligence in the normal and autistic brain: An fMRI study. *European
           Journal of Neuroscience* 11:1891-1898.
Bartak, L., and M. Rutter
   1973   Special educational treatment of autistic children: A comparative study: I. Design
           of study and characteristics of units. *Journal of Child Psychology and Psychiatry and
           Allied Disciplines* 14(3):161-179.
Bergman, P., and S.K. Escalona
   1949   Unusual sensitivities in very young children. *Psychoanalytic Study of the Child*
           333-352.
Bernal, M.E., and W.H. Miller
   1971   Electrodermal and cardiac responses of schizophrenic children to sensory stimuli.
           Psychophysiology 7:155-168.
Bowlby, J.
   1969   *Attachment and Loss: Volume I, Attachment.* New York: Basic Books.
Brady, M.P., R.E. Shores, M.A. McEvoy, D. Ellis, and J.J. Fox
   1987   Increasing social interactions of severely handicapped autistic children. *Journal of
           Autism and Developmental Disorders* 17(3):375-390.

Bricker, D.
   1993   *AEPS: Measurement for Birth to Three Years.* Baltimore, MD: Paul H. Brookes
         Publishing.
Bruininks, R., R. Woodcock, R. Weatherman, and B. Hill
   1996   *Scales of Independent Behavior - Revised (SIB-R).* Chicago, IL: Riverside Publishing
         Co.
Capps, L., M. Sigman, and P. Mundy
   1994   Attachment security in children with autism. *Development and Psychopathology*
         6:249-261.
Charman, T., J. Swettenham, S. Baron-Cohen, A. Cox, G. Baird, and A. Drew
   1998   An experimental investigation of social-cognitive abilities in infants with autism:
         Clinical implications. *Infant Mental Health Journal* 19(2):260-275.
Cipani, E., and F. Spooner
   1994   *Curricular and Instructional Approaches for Persons with Severe Disabilities.* Boston:
         Allyn and Bacon.
Corona, R., C. Dissanayake, S. Arbelle, P. Wellington, and M. Sigman
   1998   Is affect aversive to young children with autism? Behavioral and cardiac re-
         sponses to experimenter distress. *Child Development* 69(6):1494-1502.
Danko, C.D., J. Lawry, and P.S. Strain
   1998   Social Skills Intervention Manual Packet. Unpublished. St. Peters Child Develop-
         ment Center, Pittsburgh, PA.
Dawson, G., and A. Lewy
   1989   Arousal, attention, and the socioemotional impairments of individuals with au-
         tism. Pp. 49-74 in *Autism: Nature, Diagnosis, and Treatment*, G. Dawson, ed. New
         York: Guilford Press.
Dawson, G., and L. Galpert
   1990   Mothers' use of imitative play for facilitating social responsiveness and toy play
         in young autistic children. *Development and Psychopathology* 2:151-162.
Dawson, G., L.G. Klinger, H. Panagiotides, A. Lewy, and P. Castellos
   1995   Subgroups of autistic children based on social behavior display distinct patterns
         of brain activity. *Journal of Abnormal Child Psychology* 23(5):569-583.
Dawson, G., A.N. Meltzoff, J. Osterling, J. Rinaldi, and E. Brown
   1998   Children with autism fail to orient to naturally occurring social stimuli. *Journal of
         Autism and Developmental Disorders* 28(6):479-485.
DeMyer, M.K., G.D. Alpern, S. Barton, W.E. DeMyer, D.W. Churchill, J.N. Hingtgen, C.Q.
Bryson, W. Pontius, and C. Kimberlin
   1972   Imitation in autistic, early schizophrenic, and nonpsychotic subnormal children.
         Journal of Autism and Childhood Schizophrenia 2(3):264-287.
DesLauriers, A.M., and C.F. Carlson
   1969   *Your Child Is Asleep: Early Infantile Autism.* Homewood, IL: Dorsey Press.
Fewell, R.R.
   1994   *Play Assessment Scale.* Unpublished, University of Hawaii-Manoa: Honolulu, HI.
Goldstein, H., L. Kaczmarek, R. Pennington, and K. Shafer
   1992   Peer-mediated intervention: Attending to, commenting on, and acknowledging
         the behavior of preschoolers with autism. *Journal of Applied Behaviour Analysis*
         25:289-305.
Goldstein, H., S. Wickstrom, M. Hoyson, B. Jamieson, and S.L. Odom
   1988   Effects of sociodramatic play training on social and communicative interaction.
         Education and Treatment of Children 11:97-117.
Gowen, J.W., N. Johnson-Martin, B.D. Goldman, and B. Hussey
   1992   Object play and exploration in children with and without disabilities: A longitu-
         dinal study. *American Journal on Mental Retardation* 97(1):21-38.

Gray, C., and J. Garand
  1993   Social stories: Improving responses of students with autism with accurate social information. *Focus on Autistic Behavior* 8:1-10.
Greenspan, S.I., B. Kalmanson, R. Shahmoon-Shanok, S. Wieder, G. Gordon-Williamson, and M. Anzalone
  1997   *Assessing and Treating Infants and Young Children with Severe Difficulties in Relating and Communicating.* Washington, DC: Zero to Three.
Hoyson, M., B. Jamieson, and P.S. Strain
  1984   Individualized group instruction of normally developing and autistic-like children: The LEAP curriculum model. *Journal of the Division of Early Childhood* 8:157-172.
Hutt, C., and S.J. Hutt
  1964   Arousal and childhood autism. *Nature* 204:908-909.
James, A.L., and R.J. Barry
  1980   Respiratory and vascular responses to simple visual stimuli in autistics, retardates, and normals. *Psychophysiology* 17:541-547.
Kanner, L.
  1943   Autistic disturbances of affective contact. *Nervous Child* 2:217-250.
Kasari, C., and M. Sigman
  1997   Linking parental perceptions to interactions in young children with autism. *Journal of Autism and Developmental Disorders* 27(1):39-58.
Kasari C., M. Sigman, P. Mundy, and N. Yermiya
  1990   Affective sharing in the context of joint attention interactions of normal, autistic, and mentally retarded children. *Journal of Autism and Developmental Disorders* 20(1):87-100.
Koegel, L.K., R.L. Koegel, J.K. Harrower, and C.M. Carter
  1999   Pivotal response intervention 1: Overview of approach. *Journal of the Association for People with Special Handicaps* 24(3):174-185.
Kohler, F.W., P.S. Strain, M. Hoyson, and B. Jamieson
  1997   Merging naturalistic teaching and peer-based strategies to address the IEP objectives of preschoolers with autism: An examination of structural and child behavior outcomes. *Focus on Autism and Other Developmental Disabilities* 12(4):196-206.
Krantz, P.J., and L.E. McClannahan
  1993   Teaching children with autism to initiate to peers: Effects of a script-fading procedure. *Journal of Applied Behavior Analysis* 26:121-132.
  1998   Social interaction skills for children with autism: A script-fading procedure for beginning readers. *Journal of Applied Behavior Analysis* 31:191-202.
LeMay, D.W., P.M. Griffin, and A.R. Sanford
  1983   *Learning Accomplishment Profile.* Winston-Salem, NC: Kaplan Press.
Libby, S., S. Powell, D. Messer, and R. Jordan
  1998   Spontaneous play in children with autism: A reappraisal. *Journal of Autism and Developmental Disorders* 28(6):487-497.
Lifter, K., B. Sulzer-Azaroff, S.R. Anderson, J.T. Coyle, and G.E. Cowdery
  1993   Teaching play activities to preschool children with disabilities: The importance of developmental considerations. *Journal of Early Intervention* 17(2):139-159.
Lord, C., and J.M. Hopkins
  1986   The social behavior of autistic children with younger and same-age nonhandicapped peers. *Journal of Autism and Developmental Disorders* 16(3):249-262.

Lord, C., and E. Schopler
  1989   Stability of assessment results of autistic and non-autistic language-impaired chil-
          dren from preschool years to early school age. *Journal of Child Psychology and
          Psychiatry* 30(4):575-590.
Lord, C., and A. Pickles
  1996   Language level and nonverbal social communicative behaviors in autistic and
          language delayed children. *Journal of the American Academy of Child and Adolescent
          Psychiatry* 35(11):1542-1550.
Lotter, V.
  1978   Follow-up studies. Pp. 475-495 in *Autism: A Reappraisal of Concepts and Treatment*,
          M. Rutter and E. Schopler, eds. New York: Plenum Press.
Lovaas, I.O.
  1987   Behavioral treatment and normal educational and intellectual functioning in
          young autistic children. *Journal of Consulting and Clinical Psychology* 55(1):3-9.
Lovaas, I.O., G. Freitag, V.J. Gold, and I.C. Kassorla
  1965   Experimental studies in child schizophrenia: Analysis of self-destructive behav-
          ior. *Journal of Experimental Child Psychology* 2:67-84.
Mahler, M.
  1952   On child psychosis and schizophrenia: autistic and symbiotic infantile psychoses.
          Psychoanalytic Study of the Child 7: 286-306.
McClannahan, L.E., and P.J. Krantz
  1994   The Princeton Child Development Institute. In *Preschool Education Programs for
          Children with Autism*, S.L. Harris and J.S. Handleman, eds. Austin, TX: Pro-Ed.
McConnell, S.R.
  *1999   Interventions to Facilitate Social Interaction for Young Children With Autism:
          Review of Available Research and Recommendations for Future Research. Paper
          presented at the First Workshop of the Committee on Educational Interventions
          for Children with Autism, National Research Council, December 13-14, 1999.
          Department of Educational Psychology, University of Minnesota.
McGee, G.G., M.J. Morrier, and T. Daly
  1999   An incidental teaching approach to early intervention for toddlers with autism.
          Journal of the Association for Persons with Severe Handicaps 24(3):133-146.
McGee, G.G., M.C. Almeida, B. Sulzer-Azaroff, and R.S. Feldman
  1992   Promoting Reciprocal Interactions Via Peer Incidental Teaching. *Journal of Ap-
          plied Behavior Analysis* 25(1):117-126.
Miller, L.J., J. Reisman, D.N. McIntosh, and J. Simon
  2000   An ecological model of sensory modulation: Performance of children with frag-
          ile X syndrome, autism, attention deficit disorder with hyperactivity and sensory
          modulation dysfunction. In *The Nature Of Sensory Integration With Diverse Popula-
          tions*, S. Smity-Roley, E. Imperatore-Blanche, and R.C. Schaaf, eds. San Antonio,
          TX: Therapy Skill Builders.
Mundy, P., M. Sigman, and C. Kasari
  1990   A longitudinal study of joint attention and language development in autistic chil-
          dren. *Journal of Autism and Developmental Disorders* 20:115-128.
Mundy, P., M. Sigman, J. Ungerer, and T. Sherman
  1987   Nonverbal communication and play correlates of language development in autis-
          tic children. *Journal of Autism and Developmental Disorders* 17(3):349-364.
Munson, L.J., and S.L. Odom
  1996   Review of rating scales that measure parent-infant interaction. *Topics in Early
          Childhood Special Education* 16:1-25.

Nadel, J., and A. Peze
   1993   What makes immediate imitation communicative in toddlers and autistic chil-
           dren? Pp. 139-156 in *New Perspectives In Early Communication Development*, J.
           Nadel and L. Camaioni, eds. London: Routledge.
Newborg, J., J.R. Stock, L. Wnek, J. Guidubaldi, and J. Svinicki
   1984   *Battelle Developmental Inventory Examiner's Manual.* Allen, TX: DLM Teaching
           Resources.
Norris, C., and J. Dattilo
   1999   Evaluating effects of a social story intervention on a young girl with autism.
           Focus on Autism and Other Developmental Disabilities 14(3):180-186.
Odom, S.L., and P.S. Strain
   1986   A comparison of peer-initiation and teacher-antecedent interventions for promot-
           ing reciprocal social interaction of autistic preschoolers. *Journal of Applied Behav-
           ior Analysis* 19(1):59-71.
Odom, S.L., and I. Ogawa
   1992   Direct observation of young children's social interaction with peers: A review of
           methodology. *Behavioral Assessment* 14:443-464.
Odom, S.L., and L.J. Munson
   1996   Assessing social performance. Pp. 399-434 in *Assessing Infants and Preschoolers
           with Special Needs*, M. McLean, D. Bailey, and M. Wolery, eds. Baltimore, MD:
           Paul H. Brookes Publishing.
Oke, N.J., and L. Schreibman
   1990   Training social initiations to a high-functioning autistic child: Assessment of a
           collateral behavior change and generalization in a case study. *Journal of Autism
           and Developmental Disabilities* 20(4):479-497.
Peterson, N.L., and J.G. Haralick
   1977   Integration of handicapped and nonhandicapped preschoolers: An analysis of
           play behavior and social interaction. *Education and Training of the Mentally Re-
           tarded* 12(3):235-245.
Piaget, J.
   1962   *Play, Dreams, and Imitation in Childhood.* New York: Norton.
Prizant, B.M., and A.M. Wetherby
   1998   Understanding the continuum of discrete-trial traditional behavioral to social-
           pragmatic developmental approaches in communication enhancement for young
           children with autism/pdd. *Seminars in Speech and Language* 19(4):329-353.
Rimland, B.
   1964   *Infantile Autism.* New York: Appleton-Century-Crofts.
Rogers, S.J.
   2000   *The Denver Model Treatment Manual.* Denver, CO: JFK Partners.
Rogers, S.J., and H. Lewis
   1989   An effective day treatment model for young children with pervasive develop-
           mental disorders. *Journal of the American Academy of Child and Adolescent Psychia-
           try* 28:207-214.
Rogers, S.J., H.C. Lewis, and K. Reis
   1987   An effective procedure for training early special education teams to implement a
           model program. *Journal of the Division of Early Childhood* 11(2):180-188.
Rogers, S.J., S. Ozonoff, and C. Maslin-Cole
   1991   A comparative study of attachment behavior in young children with autism or
           other psychiatric disorders. *Journal of the American Academy of Child and Adoles-
           cent Psychiatry* 30(3):483-488.

1993   Developmental aspects of attachment behavior in young children with pervasive
        developmental disorders. *Journal of the American Academy of Child and Adolescent
        Psychiatry* 32(6):1274-1282.
Rogers, S.J., J. Herbison, H. Lewis, J. Pantone, and K. Reis
1986   An approach for enhancing the symbolic, communicative, and interpersonal func-
        tioning of young children with autism and severe emotional handicaps. *Journal of
        the Division of Early Childhood* 10:135-148.
Rogers, S.J., T. Hall, D. Osaki, J. Reaven, and J. Herbison
2000   The Denver model: A comprehensive, integrated educational approach to young
        children with autism and their families. Pp. 95-133 in *Preschool Education Pro-
        grams for Children with Autism (2nd ed.)*, J.S. Handleman and S.L. Harris, eds.
        Austin, TX: Pro-Ed.
Rogers, S.J., C.M. Donovan, D.B. D'Eugenio, S.L. Brown, E.W. Lynch, M.S. Moersch, and
D.S. Schafer
1979   Early intervention developmental profile: Volume 2. In *Developmental Program-
        ming for Infants and Young Children*, D.S. Schafer and M.S. Moersch, eds. Ann
        Arbor, MI: University of Michigan Press.
Sainato, D.M., H. Goldstein, and P.S. Strain
1992   Effects of self-evaluation on preschool children's use of social interaction strate-
        gies with their classmates with autism. *Journal of Applied Behaviour Analysis*
        25:127-141.
Schopler, E., G.B. Mesibov, and K.A. Hearsey
1995   Structured teaching in the TEACCH system. Pp. 243-268 in *Learning and Cogni-
        tion in Autism*, E. Schopler and G.B. Mesibov, eds. New York: Plenum Press.
Shapiro, T., M. Sherman, G. Calamari, and D. Koch
1987   Attachment in autism and other developmental disorders. *Journal of the American
        Academy of Child and Adolescent Psychiatry* 26(4):480-484.
Sheinkopf, S.J., and B. Siegel
1998   Home based behavioral treatment of young autistic children. *Journal of Autism
        and Developmental Disorders* 28(1):15-24.
Sigman, M., and E. Ruskin
1999   Continuity and change in the social competence of children with autism, Down
        syndrome, and developmental delays. *Monographs of the Society for Research In
        Child Development* 64(1):1-113.
Smith, T., A.D Groen, and J.W. Wynn
2000   A randomized trial of intensive early intervention for children with pervasive
        developmental disorder. *American Journal on Mental Retardation* 5(4):269-285.
Sparrow, S.S., D.A. Balla, and D. Cicchetti
1984   *Vineland Adaptive Behavior Scales*. Circle Pines, MN: American Guidance Service.
Stahmer, A.C.
1995   Teaching symbolic play skills to children with autism using pivotal response
        training. *Journal of Autism and Developmental Disorders* 25(2):123-142.
Stone, W.L., O.Y. Ousley, and C.D. Littleford
1997   Motor imitation in young children with autism: What's the object? *Journal of
        Abnormal Child Psychology* 25(6):475-485.
Stone, W.L., K.L. Lemanek, P.T. Fishel, M.C. Fernandez, and W.A. Altemeier
1990   Play and imitation skills in the diagnosis of young autistic children. *Pediatrics*
        86:267-272.
Strain, P.S.
1983   Identification of social skill curriculum targets for severely handicapped children
        in mainstreamed preschools. *Applied Research in Mental Retardation* 4:369-382.

Strain, P.S., and C.D. Danko
  1995   Caregivers' encouragement of positive interaction between preschoolers with au-
          tism and their siblings. *Journal of Emotional and Behavioral Disorders* 3(1):2-12.
Strain, P.S., R.E. Shores, and M.A. Timm
  1977   Effects of peer social initiations on the behavior of withdrawn preschool children.
          Journal of Applied Behavior Analysis 10(2):289-298.
Strain, P.S., M.M. Kerr, and E.U. Ragland
  1979   Effects of peer-mediated social initiations and prompting/reinforcement proce-
          dures on the social behavior of autistic children. *Journal of Autism and Develop-
          mental Disorders* 9(1):41-54.
Strain, P.S., F.W. Kohler, and H. Goldstein
  1996   Learning experiences . . . An alternative program: Peer-mediated interventions
          for young children with autism. Pp. 573-586 in *Psychosocial Treatments for Child
          and Adolescent Disorders*, E. Hibbs and P. Jensen, eds. Washington, DC: American
          Psychological Association.
Strain, P.S., F.W. Kohler, K. Storey, and C.D. Danko
  1994   Teaching preschoolers with autism to self-monitor their social interactions: An
          analysis of results in home and school settings. *Journal of Emotional and Behavioral
          Disorders* 2(2):78-88.
Tanguay, P.E., J. Robertson, and A. Derrick
  1998   A dimensional classification of autism spectrum disorder by social communica-
          tion domains. *Journal of the American Academy of Child and Adolescent Psychiatry*
          37(3):271-277.
Thorp, D.M., A.C. Stahmer, and L. Schreibman
  1995   Effects of sociodramatic play training on children with autism. *Journal of Autism
          and Developmental Disorders* 25(3):265-282.
Tinbergen, E.A., and N. Tinbergen
  1972   *Early Childhood Autism: An Ethological Approach*. Berlin: Paul Parey.
Venter, A., C. Lord, and E. Schopler
  1992   A follow-up study of high-functioning autistic children. *Journal of Child Psychol-
          ogy and Psychiatry* 33:489-507.
Vygotsky, L.S.
  2000   Play and its role in the mental development of the child. In *Play: Its Role in
          Development and Evolution*, J. Bruner, A. Jolly, and S. Sylva, eds. New York: Basic
          Books.
Watson, L., C. Lord, B. Schaffer, and E. Schopler
  1989   *Teaching Spontaneous Communication to Autistic and Developmentally Handicapped
          Children*. New York, NY: Irvington Publishers.
Wehner, E., E. Griffith, and S.J. Rogers
  1998   *Attachment findings in autism*. Personal Communication.
Wetherby, A.M., and B.M. Prizant
  1993   *Communication and Symbolic Behavior Scales*. Riverside Publishing.
Wetherby, A.M., and C.A. Prutting
  1984   Profiles of communicative and cognitive-social abilities in autistic children. *Jour-
          nal of Speech and Hearing Research* 27:364-377.
Wing, L., and J. Gould
  1979   Severe impairments of social interaction and associated abnormalities in chil-
          dren: Epidemiology and classification. *Journal of Autism and Developmental Disor-
          ders* 9:11-29.

CHAPTER 7

Bagley, C., and V. McGeein
  1989   The taxonomy and course of childhood autism. *Perceptual and Motor Skills* 69(3, Pt 2):1264-1266
Baron-Cohen, S.
  1991   The development of a theory of mind in autism: Deviance and delay? *Psychiatric Clinics of North America* 14(1):33-51.
Brown, R.A., and Z.S. Pace
  1969   Treatment of extreme negativism and autistic behavior in a 6 year old boy. *Exceptional Child* 36(2):115-122.
Chen, S.H.A., and V. Bernard-Optiz
  1993   Comparison of personal and computer-assisted instruction for children with autism. *Mental Retardation* 31(6):368-376.
Clark, P., and M. Rutter
  1977   Compliance and resistance in autistic children. *Journal of Autism and Childhood Schizophrenia* 7(1):33-48.
DeMyer, M.K., J.N. Hingtgen, and R.K. Jackson
  1981   Infantile autism reviewed: A decade of research. *Schizophrenia Bulletin* 7(3):388-451.
Fein, D., M. Humes, et al.
  1984   The question of left hemisphere dysfunction in infantile autism. *Psychological Bulletin* 95(2):258-281.
Fombonne, E.
  1997   *Epidemiology of Autism and Related Conditions. Autism and Pervasive Developmental Disorders.* F.R. Volkmar. Cambridge, England: Cambridge University Press.
Frith, U.
  1970   Studies in pattern detection in normal and autistic children. I: Immediate recall of auditory sequences. *Journal of Abnormal Psychology* 76(3):413-420.
  1972   Cognitive mechanisms in autism: Experiments with color and tone sequence production. *Journal of Autism and Childhood Schizophrenia* 2(2):160-73.
  1996   Cognitive explanations of autism. *Acta Pediatrica Supplement* 416:63-68.
Frith, U., J. Morton, and A.M. Leslie
  1991   The cognitive basis of a biological disorder: Autism. *Trends in Neurosciences* 14(10):433-438.
Frith, U., F. Happe, and F. Siddons
  1994   Autism and theory of mind in everyday life. *Social Development* 3(2):108-124.
Gillies, S.
  1965   Some abilities of psychotic children and subnormal children. *Journal of Mental Deficiency Research* 9(1):89-101.
Green, L., D. Fein, S. Joy, and L. Waterhouse
  1995   Cognitive functioning in autism: An overview. Pp. 13-31 in *Learning And Cognition In Autism. Current Issues In Autism*, E. Schopler and G Mesibov, eds. New York: Plenum Press.
Griffith, E.M, B.F. Pennington, E.A. Wehner, and S.J. Rogers
  1999   Executive functions in young children with autism. *Child Development* 70(4): 817-832.
Hadwin, J., S. Baron-Cohen, P. Howlin, and K. Hill
  1997   Does teaching theory of mind have an effect on the ability to develop conversation in children with autism? *Journal of Autism and Developmental Disorders* 27(5):519-537.

Happe, F.G.
   1994   Annotation: current psychological theories of autism: The "theory of mind" account and rival theories. *Journal of Child Psychology and Psychiatry* 35(2):215-229.
Happe, F.G.
   1995   The role of age and verbal ability in the theory of mind task performance of subjects with autism. *Child Development* 66(3):843-855.
Heaton, R.K.
   1981   *Wisconsin Card Sorting Manual.* Odessa, FL: Psychological Assessment Resources.
Heimann, M., K.E. Nelson, T. Tjus, and C. Gillberg
   1995   Increasing reading and communication skills in children with autism through an interactive multimedia program. *Journal of Autism and Developmental Disorders* 25(5):459-480.
Hermelin, B., and N. O'Connor
   1970   *Psychological Experiments with Autistic Children.* New York: Pergamon.
Hermelin, B., and U. Frith
   1971   Psychological studies of childhood autism: Can autistic children make sense of what they see and hear? *Journal of Special Education Summary* 5(2):107-117.
   1991   Psychological studies of childhood autism: Can autistic children make sense of what they see and hear? *Focus on Autistic Behavior* 6(1):6-13.
Howlin, P.
   1997   Outcome in autism and related conditions. In *Autism and Pervasive Developmental Disorders*, F.R.Volkmar, ed. Cambridge, England: Cambridge University Press.
Jarrold, C., D.W. Butler, E.M. Cottington, and F. Jimenez
   2000   Linking theory of mind and central coherence bias in autism and in the general population. *Developmental Psychology* 36(1):126-138.
Kamps, D.M., D. Walker, J. Maher, and D. Rotholz
   1992   Academic and environmental effects of small group arrangements in classrooms for students with autism and other developmental disabilities. *Journal of Autism and Developmental Disorders* 22(2):277-293.
Kamps, D.M., E.P. Dugan, B.R. Leonard, and P.M. Daoust
   1994a   Enhanced small group instruction using choral responding and student interaction for children with autism and developmental disabilities. *American Journal on Mental Retardation* 99(1): 60-73
Kamps, D.M., B.M. Barbetta, B.R. Leonard, and P.M. Daoust
   1994b   Classwide peer tutoring: An integration strategy to improve reading skills and promote peer interactions among students with autism and general education peers. *Journal of Applied Behavior Analysis* 27(1):49-61.
Kamps, D.M., B. Leonard, J. Potucek, and L. Garrison-Harrell
   1995   Cooperative learning groups in reading: An integration strategy for students with autism and general classroom peers. *Behavioral Disorders* 21(1):89-109.
Kamps, D., D. Walker, P. Locke, J. Delquardi, and R.V. Hall
   1990   A comparison of instructional arrangements for children with autism served in a public school setting. *Education and Treatment of Children* 13(3):197-215.
Kamps, D.M., B.R. Leonard, E.P. Dugan, B. Boland, and C.R. Greenwood
   1991   The use of ecobehavioral assessment to identify naturally occurring effective procedures in classrooms serving students with autism and other developmental disabilities. *Journal of Behavioral Education* 1(4):367-397.
Kanner, L.
   1943   Autistic disturbances of affective contact. *Nervous Child* 2:217-250.

Kasari, C., M. Sigman, and N. Yirmaya
  1993 Focused and social attention of autistic children in interactions with familiar and unfamiliar adults: A comparison of autistic, mentally retarded, and normal children. *Development and Psychopathology* 5(3):403-414.
Klin, A., and B.A. Shepard
  1994 Psychological assessment of autistic children. *Child and Adolescent Psychiatry Clinics of North America* 3:131-148.
Klin, A., F.R. Volkmar, and S.S. Sparrow
  1992 Autistic social dysfunction: Some limitations of the theory of mind hypothesis. *Journal of Child Psychology and Psychiatry* 33(5):861-876.
Klin, A., F.R. Volkmar, S. Sparrow, D.V. Cicchetti, and B.P. Rourke
  1995 Validity and neuropsychological characterization of Asperger syndrome: Convergence with nonverbal learning disabilities syndrome. *Journal of Child Psychology and Psychiatry* 36(7):1127-1140.
Koegel, L.K., R.L. Koegel, and A. Smith
  1997 Variables related to differences in standardized test outcomes for children with autism. *Journal of Autism and Developmental Disorders* 27(3):233-243.
Koegel, L.K., R.L. Koegel, Y. Shoshan, and E. McNerney
  1999 Pivotal response intervention II: Preliminary long-term outcome data. *Journal of the Association for Persons with Severe Handicaps* 24(3):186-198.
Koegel, R.L., and A. Rincover
  1974 Treatment of psychotic children in a classroom environment: I. Learning in a large group. *Journal of Applied Behavior Analysis* 7(1):45-59.
Leslie, A.M.
  1987 Pretense and representation: The origins of "theory of mind." *Psychological Review* 94(4): 412-426.
  1992 Pretense, autism, and the theory-of-mind module. *Current Directions in Psychological Science* 1(1):18-21.
Leslie, A.M., and U. Frith
  1987 Metarepresentation and autism: How not to lose one's marbles. *Cognition* 27(3): 291-294.
Lockyer, L., and M. Rutter
  1970 A five- to fifteen-year follow-up study of infantile psychosis. IV: Patterns of cognitive ability. *British Journal of Social Clinical Psychology* 9(2):152-163.
Lord, C., and E. Schopler
  1989a The role of age at assessment, developmental level, and test in the stability of intelligence scores in young autistic children. *Journal of Autism and Developmental Disorders* 19(4):483-499.
  1989b Stability of assessment results of autistic and non-autistic language-impaired children from preschool years to early school age. *Journal of Child Psychology and Psychiatry* 30(4):575-590.
Lord, C., M.L. Rutter, and A. LeCouteur
  1994 Autism Diagnostic Interview—Revised: A revised version of a diagnostic interview for caregivers of individuals with possible pervasive developmental disorders. *Journal of Autism and Developmental Disorders* 24(5):659-685.
Losche, G.
  1990 Sensorimotor and action development in autistic children from infancy to early childhood. *Journal of Childhood Psychology and Psychiatry* 31(5):749-761.
Lovaas, O.I.
  1993 The development of a treatment-research project for developmentally disabled and autistic children. *Journal of Applied Behavioral Analysis* 26(4):617-630.

Maltz, A.
    1981   Comparison of cognitive deficits among autistic and retarded children on the Arthur Adaptation of the Leiter International Performance Scales. *Journal of Autism and Developmental Disorders* 11(4):413-426.
McDonald, M.A., P. Mundy, C. Kasari, and M. Sigman
    1989   Psychometric scatter in retarded, autistic preschoolers as measured by the Cattell. *Journal of Child Psychology and Psychiatry* 30(4):599-604.
McEvoy, R.E., S.J. Rogers, and B.F. Pennington
    1993   Executive function and social communication deficits in young autistic children. *Journal of Child Psychology and Psychiatry and Allied Disciplines* 34(4):563-578.
McGee, G.G., P.J. Krantz, and L.E. McClannahan
    1986   An extension of incidental teaching procedures to reading instruction for autistic children. *Journal of Applied Behavior Analysis* 19(2):147-157.
Mervis, C.B., and B.F. Robinson
    1999   Methodological issues in cross-syndrome comparisons: matching procedures, sensitivity (Se), and specificity (Sp). *Monographs of the Society for Research in Child Development* 64(1):115-130.
Minshew, N.J., G. Goldstein, L.R. Muenz, and J.B. Payton
    1992   Neuropsychological functioning in nonmentally retarded autistic individuals. *Journal of Clinical Experimental Neuropsychology* 14(5):749-761.
Mullen, E.
    1995   *Mullen Scales of Early Learning.* Circle Pines, MN: American Guidance Service, Inc.
Nordin, V., and C. Gillberg
    1996   Autism spectrum disorders in children with physical or mental disability or both. II: Screening aspects. *Developmental Medicine in Child Neurology* 38(4):314-324.
Otah, M.
    1987   Cognitive disorders of infantile autism: A study of employing the WISC, spatial relationship conceptualization, and gesture imitations. *Journal of Autism and Developmental Disorders* 17(1):45-62.
Ozonoff, S., and J.N. Miller
    1995   Teaching theory of mind: A new approach to social skills training for individuals with autism. *Journal of Autism and Developmental Disorders* 25(4):415-433.
Ozonoff, S., B.F. Pennington, et al.
    1991   Executive function deficits in high-functioning autistic individuals: Relationship to theory of mind. *Journal of Child and Psychological Psychiatry* 32(7):1081-1105.
Piaget, J.
    1952   *The Origins of Intelligence in Children.* New York: Norton.
Pring, L., B. Hermelin, and L. Heavey
    1995   Savants, segments, art and autism. *Journal of Child Psychology and Psychiatry* 36(6):1065-1076.
Prior, M., and S. Ozonoff
    1998   *Psychological Factors in Autism.* Pg. 64-108 in *Autism and Pervasive Developmental Disorders*, F.R. Volkmar, eds. Cambridge, England: Cambridge University Press.
Prior, M., D. Perry, and C. Gajzago
    1975   Kanner's syndrome or early-onset psychosis: A taxonomic analysis of 142 cases. *Journal of Autism and Childhood Schizophrenia* 5(1):71-80.
Raven, J.
    1989   The Raven Progressive Matrices: A review of national norming studies and ethnic and socioeconomic variation within the United States. *Journal of Educational Measurement* 26(1):1-16.

Rincover, A., and R.L. Koegel
  1977   Classroom treatment of autistic children: II. Individualized instruction in a group. *Journal of Abnormal Child Psychology* 5(2):113-126.
Riquet, C.B., N.D. Taylor, et al.
  1981   Symbolic play in autistic, Down's, and normal children of equivalent mental age. *Journal of Autism and Developmental Disorders* 11:439-448.
Rogers, S.J.
  1998   Empirically supported comprehensive treatments for young children with autism. *Journal of Clinical Child Psychology* 27(2):168-179.
Rogers, S.J., and B.F. Pennington
  1991   A theoretical approach to the deficits in infantile autism. *Development and Psychopathology* 3:137-162.
Rutter, M.
  1983   Cognitive deficits in the pathogenesis of autism. *Journal of Child Psychology and Psychiatry* 24(4):513-531.
Schreibman, L., and O.I. Lovaas
  1973   Overselective response to social stimuli by autistic children. *Journal of Abnormal Child Psychology* 1:152-168.
Shah, A., and U. Frith
  1993   Why do autistic individuals show superior performance on the block design task? *Journal of Child Psychology and Psychiatry* 34(8):1351-1364.
Sheinkopf, S.J., and B. Siegel
  1998   Home-based behavioral treatment of young children with autism. *Journal of Autism and Developmental Disorders* 28(1):15-23.
Sigman, M., C. Dissanayake, S. Arbelle, and E. Ruskin
  1997   Cognition and emotion in children and adolescents with autism. Pg. 248-265 in *Handbook of Autism and Pervasive Developmental Disorders*, D.J. Cohen and F.R. Volkmar, eds. New York: John Wiley and Sons.
Sigman, M., P. Mundy, T. Sherman, and J.A. Ungerer
  1986   Social interactions of autistic, mentally retarded and normal children and their caregivers. *Journal of Child Psychology and Psychiatry* 27(5):647-655.
Sigman, M., and J.A.Ungerer
  1984a   Attachment behaviors in autistic children. *Journal of Autism and Developmental Disorders* 14(3):231-244.
  1984b   Cognitive and language skills in autistic, mentally retarded, and normal children. *Journal of Developmental Psychology* 20:293-302.
Simon, H.
  1975   The functional equivalence of problem solving skills. *Cognitive Psychology* 7:268-288.
Smith, I.M., and S.E. Bryson
  1994   Imitation and action in autism: A critical review. *Psychological Bulletin* 116(2):259-273.
Smith, T., A.D Groen, and J.W. Wynn
  2000   A randomized trial of intensive early intervention for children with pervasive developmental disorder. *American Journal on Mental Retardation* 5(4):269-285.
Sparrow, S.
  1997   Developmentally based assessments. Pp. 411-447 in *Handbook of Autism and Pervasive Developmental Disorders*, D.J. Cohen and F.R. Volkmar, eds. New York: John Wiley and Sons, Inc.
Tager-Flusberg, H.
  1981   Sentence comprehension in autistic children. *Applied Psycholinguistics* 2:5-24.

Thorndike, R., E. Hagen, et al.
    1986   *Stanford-Binet Intelligence Scale, 4th Ed.* Chicago, IL: Riverside Publishing Company.

Treffert, D.
    1989   *Extraordinary People.* New York: Bantam.

Tymchuk, A.J., J.Q. Simmons, and S. Neafsey
    1977   Intellectual characteristics of adolescent childhood psychotics with high verbal ability. *Journal of Mental Deficiency Research* 21(2):133-138.

Venter, A., C. Lord, and E. Schopler
    1992   A follow-up study of high-functioning autistic children. *Journal of Child Psychology and Psychology and Allied Disciplines* 33(3):489-507.

Wing, L., and J. Gould
    1979   Severe impairments of social interaction and associated abnormalities. *Journal of Autism and Developmental Disorders* 9(1):11-29.

Wing, L., J. Gould, S.R. Yeates, and L.M. Brierly
    1977   Symbolic play in severely mentally retarded and in autistic children. *Journal of Child Psychology and Psychiatry* 18(2):167-178.

Wolf, E.G., C. Wenar, and B.A. Ruttenberg
    1972   A comparison of personality variables in autistic and mentally retarded children. *Journal of Autism Childhood Schizophrenia* 2(1):92-108.

CHAPTER 8

Adams, L.
    1998   Oral-motor and motor-speech characteristics of children with autism. *Focus on Autism and Other Developmental Disabilities* 13:108-112.

Adrien, J.L., E. Ornitz, C. Barthelemy, D. Sauvage, and G. Lelord
    1987   The presence or absence of certain behaviors associated with infantile autism in severely retarded autistic and nonautistic retarded children and very young normal children. *Journal of Autism and Developmental Disorders* 17:407-416.

Adrien, J.L., A. Perrot, D. Sauvage, I. Leddet, C. Larmande, L. Hameury, and C. Barthelemy
    1992   Early symptoms in autism from family home movies: Evaluation and comparison between 1st and 2nd year of life using I.B.S.E. scale. *Acta Paedopsychiatrica* 55:71-75.

Adrien, J.L., P. Lenoir, J. Martineau, A. Perrot, L. Hameury, C. Larmande, and D. Sauvage
    1993   Blind ratings of early symptoms of autism based upon family home movies. *Journal of the American Academy of Child and Adolescent Psychiatry* 32:617-626.

Ayres, J.
    1972   Improving academic scores through sensory integration. *Journal of Learning Disabilities* 5:338-343.

Ayres, A.J., and L.S. Tickle
    1980   Hyper-responsivity to touch and vestibular stimuli as a predictor of positive response to sensory integration procedures by autistic children. *American Journal of Occupational Therapy* 34:375-381.

Baranek, G.T.
   *1999a   Efficacy of Sensory and Motor Interventions for Children with Autism. Paper presented at the First Workshop of the Committee on Educational Interventions for Children with Autism, National Research Council, December 13-14, 1999. University of North Carolina-Chapel Hill School of Medicine.
   1999b Autism during infancy: A retrospective video analysis of sensory-motor and social behaviors at 9-12 months of age. *Journal of Autism and Developmental Disorders* 29:213-224.

Baranek, G.T., L.G. Foster, and G. Berkson
    1997   Tactile defensiveness and stereotyped behaviors. *American Journal of Occupational Therapy* 51:91-95.

Best, L., and R. Miln
    1997   *Auditory Integration Training in Autism.* Research and Development Directorate, Wessex Institute for Health Research and Development. Bristol, UK: University of Bristol.

Bettison, S.
    1996   The long-term effects of auditory training on children with autism. *Journal of Autism and Developmental Disorders* 26:361-74.

Case-Smith, J., and T. Bryan
    1999   The effects of occupational therapy with sensory integration emphasis on pre-school-age children with autism. *American Journal of Occupational Therapy* 53:489-497.

Cohen, D.J., and W.T. Johnson
    1977   Cardiovascular correlates of attention in normal and psychiatrically disturbed children: Blood pressure, peripheral blood flow, and peripheral vascular resistance. *Archives of General Psychiatry* 34:561-567.

Corona, R., C. Dissanayake, S. Arbelle, P. Wellington, and M. Sigman
    1998   Is affect aversive to young children with autism? Behavioral and cardiac responses to experimenter distress. *Child Development* 69(6):1494-1502.

Cox, A., K. Klein, T. Charman, G. Baird, S. Baron-Cohen, J. Swettenham, A. Drew, S. Wheelwright, and N. Nightengale
    1999   The early diagnosis of autism spectrum disorders: Use of the Autism Diagnostic Interview- Revised at 20 months and 42 months of age. *Journal of Child Psychology and Psychiatry* 40:705-718.

Dahlgren, S.O., and C. Gillberg
    1989   Symptoms in the first two years of life: A preliminary population study of infantile autism. *European Archives of Psychiatry and Neurological Sciences* 238:169-174.

Dawson, G., and A. Lewy
    1989   Arousal, attention, and the socioemotional impairments of individuals with autism. Pp. 49-74 in *Autism: Nature, Diagnosis, and Treatment*, G. Dawson, ed. New York: Guilford Press.

Dawson, G., and R. Watling
    2000   Interventions to facilitate auditory, visual, and motor integration in autism: A review of the evidence. *Journal of Autism and Developmental Disorders* 30(5):415-421.

DeMyer, M.K., S. Barton, and J.A. Norton
    1972   A comparison of adaptive, verbal, and motor profiles of psychotic and non-psychotic subnormal children. *Journal of Autism and Childhood Schizophrenia* 2:359-377.

Eaves, L.C., H.H. Ho, and D.M. Eaves
    1994   Subtypes of autism by cluster analysis. *Journal of Autism and Developmental Disorders* 24:3-22.

Ermer, J., and W. Dunn
    1998   The sensory profile: A discriminant analysis of children with and without disabilities. *American Journal of Occupational Therapy* 52:283-290.

Gepner, B., D. Mestre, G. Masson, and S. de Schonen
    1995   Postural effects of motion vision in young autistic children. *Neuroreport* 6:1211-1214.

Ghaziuddin, M., E. Butler, L. Tsai, and N. Ghaziuddin
 1994 Is clumsiness a marker for Asperger syndrome? *Journal of Intellectual Disability Research* 38:519-527.
Gillberg, C., M. Johansson, S. Steffenburg, and O. Berlin
 1997 Auditory integration training in children with autism. Brief report of an open pilot study. *Autism* 1:97-100.
Gillberg, C., S. Ehlers, H. Schaumann, G. Jakobson, S.O. Dahlgren, R. Lindbolm, A. Bagenhold, T. Tjus, and E. Blidner
 1990 Autism under age 3 years: A clinical study of 28 cases referred for autistic symptoms in infancy. *Journal of Child Psychology and Psychiatry* 31:921-934.
Goldstein, H.
 *1999 Communication Intervention for Children with Autism: A Review of Treatment Efficacy. Paper presented at the First Workshop of the Committee on Educational Interventions for Children with Autism, National Research Council, December 13-14, 1999. Department of Communication Sciences, Florida State University.
Gravel, J.S.
 1994 Auditory integrative training: Placing the burden of proof. *American Journal of Speech-Language Pathology* 3:25-29.
Greenspan, S., and S. Wieder
 1997 Developmental patterns and outcomes in infants and children with disorders in relating and communicating: A chart review of 200 cases of children with autistic spectrum diagnoses. *Journal of Developmental and Learning Disorders* 1:87-141.
Hoshino, Y., H. Kumashiro, Y. Yashima, R. Tachibana, M. Watanabe, and H. Furukawa
 1982 Early symptoms of autistic children and its diagnostic significance. *Folia Psychiatrica et Neurologica Japonica* 36:367-374.
Hughes, C., and J. Russel
 1993 Autistic children's difficulty with mental disengagement from an object: Its implications for theories of autism. *Developmental Psychology* 29:498-510.
Hutt, C., S. Hutt, D. Lee, and C. Ounsted
 1964 Arousal and childhood autism. *Nature* 204:909-919.
James, A.L., and R.J. Barry
 1980 Respiratory and vascular responses to simple visual stimuli in autistics, retardates and normals. *Psychophysiology* 17(6):541-547.
 1984 Cardiovascular and electrodermal responses to simple stimuli in autistic, retarded and normal children. *International Journal of Psychophysiology* 1:179-193.
Johnson, M.H., F. Siddons, U. Frith, and J. Morton
 1992 Can autism be predicted on the basis of infant screening tests? *Developmental Medicine and Child Neurology* 34:316-320.
Jones, V., and M. Prior
 1985 Motor imitation abilities and neurological signs in autistic children. *Journal of Autism and Developmental Disorders* 15:37-46.
Kaplan, M., D.P. Carmody, and A. Gaydos
 1996 Postural orientation modifications in autism in response to ambient lenses. *Child Psychiatry and Human Development* 27(2):81-91.
Kaplan, M., S.M. Edelson, and J.-A.L. Seip
 1998 Behavioral changes in autistic individuals as a result of wearing ambient transitional prism lenses. *Child Psychiatry and Human Development* 29(1):65-76.
Kershner, J.R., R.L. Cummings, K.A. Clarke, A.J. Hadfield, and B.A. Kershner
 1990 Two year evaluation of the Tomatis listening training program with learning disabled children. *Learning Disability Quarterly* 13:43-53.

Kientz, M.A., and W. Dunn
  1997   A comparison of the performance of children with and without autism on the Sensory Profile. *American Journal of Occupational Therapy* 51:530-537.
Kinsbourne, M.
  1987   Cerebral-brainstem relations in infantile autism. Pp 107-125 in *Neurobiological Issues in Autism*, E. Schopler, and G. Mesibov, eds. New York: Plenum Press.
Klin, A., F.R. Volkmar, and S.S. Sparrow
  1992   Autistic social dysfunction: Some limitations of the theory of mind hypothesis. *Journal of Child Psychology and Psychiatry* 3(3):861-876.
Kohen-Raz, R., F.R. Volkmar, and D.J. Cohen
  1992   Postural control in children with autism. *Journal of Autism and Developmental Disorders* 22:419-432.
Kootz, J.P., and D.J. Cohen
  1981   Modulation of sensory intake in autistic children: Cardiovascular and behavioral indices. *Journal of the American Academy of Child and Adolescent Psychiatry* 20:692-701.
Kootz, J.P., B. Marinelli, and D.J. Cohen
  1982   Modulation of response to environmental stimulation in autistic children. *Journal of Autism and Developmental Disorders* 12:185-193.
Le Couteur, A., M. Rutter, C. Lord, P. Rios, S. Robertson, M. Holdgrafer, and J. McLennan
  1989   Autism diagnostic interview: A standardized investigator-based instrument. *Journal of Autism and Developmental Disorders* 19:363-387.
Lord, C.
  1995   Follow-up of two-year-olds referred for possible autism. *Journal of Child Psychology and Psychiatry* 36:1365-1382.
Lord, C., M. Rutter, and A. Le Couteur
  1994   Autism Diagnostic Interview—Revised: A revised version of a diagnostic interview for caregivers of individuals with possible pervasive developmental disorders. *Journal of Autism and Developmental Disorders* 24:659-685.
Mars, A.E., J.E. Mauk, and P. Dowrick
  1998   Symptoms of pervasive developmental disorders as observed in prediagnostic home videos of infants and toddlers. *Journal of Pediatrics* 132:500-504.
Martos Perez, J., and M. Fortea Sevilla
  1993   Psychological assessment of adolescents and adults with autism. *Journal of Autism and Developmental Disorders* 23:653-664.
Masterton, B.A., and G.B. Biederman
  1983   Proprioceptive versus visual control in autistic children. *Journal of Autism and Developmental Disorders* 13:141-152.
Minshew, N.J., G. Goldstein, and D.J. Siegel
  1997   Neuropsychologic functioning in autism: Profile of a complex information processing disorder. *Journal of the International Neuropsychological Society* 3:303-316.
Ohta, M., Y. Nagai, H. Hara, and M. Sasaki
  1987   Parental perception of behavioral symptoms in Japanese autistic children. *Journal of Autism and Developmental Disorders* 17:549-563.
Osterling, J., and G. Dawson
  1999   Early Identification of 1-Year-Olds with Autism Versus Mental Retardation Based on Home Videotapes of First Birthday Parties. Proceedings of the Society for Research in Child Development, Albuquerque, NM.
Porges, S.W.
  1998   Love and the evolution of the autonomic nervous system: The Polyvagal theory of intimacy. *Psychoneuroendocrinolgy* 23:837-861.

Rapin, I.
   1996a Historical data. Pp. 58-97 in *Preschool Children with Inadequate Communication: Developmental Language Disorder, Autism, Low IQ*, I. Rapin, ed. London, England: MacKeith Press.
   1996b Neurological examination. Pp. 98-122 in *Preschool Children with Inadequate Communication: Developmental Language Disorder, Autism, Low IQ*, I. Rapin, ed. London, England: MacKeith Press.

Richdale, A.L., and M.R. Prior
   1992   Urinary cortisol circadian rhythm in a group of high-functioning children with autism. *Journal of Autism and Developmental Disorders* 22:433-447.

Rimland, B.
   1964   *Infantile Autism: The Syndrome and its Implications for a Neural Theory of Behavior.* New York: Appleton Century Crofts.

Rimland, B., and S.M. Edelson
   1995   Brief report: A pilot study of auditory integration training in autism. *Journal of Autism and Developmental Disorders* 25:61-70.

Rogers S.J.
   1998   Empirically supported comprehensive treatments for young children with autism. *Journal of Clinical Child Psychology* 27:168-179.

Rogers, S.J., L. Bennetto, R. McEvoy, and B.F. Pennington
   1996   Imitation and pantomime in high-functioning adolescents with autism spectrum disorders. *Child Development* 67:2060-2073.

Seal, B.C., and J.D. Bonvillian
   1997   Sign language and motor functioning in students with autistic disorder. *Journal of Autism and Developmental Disorders* 27:437-466.

Smith, I., and S. Bryson
   1998   Gesture imitation in autism I: Nonsymbolic postures and sequences. *Cognitive Neuropsychology* 15:747-770.

Stone, W.L., and K.L. Hogan
   1993   A structured parent interview for identifying young children with autism. *Journal of Autism and Developmental Disorders* 23:639-652.

Stone, W.L., O.Y. Ousley, and C.D. Littleford
   1997   Motor imitation in young children with autism: What's the object? *Journal of Abnormal Child Psychology* 25:475-485.

Stone, W.L., K.L. Lemanek, P.T. Fishel, M.C. Fernandez, and W.A. Altemeier
   1990   Play and imitation skills in the diagnosis of autism in young children. *Pediatrics* 86:267-272.

Stone, W.L., O.Y. Ousley, S.L. Hepburn, K.L. Hogan, and C.S. Brown
   1999   Patterns of adaptive behavior in very young children with autism. *American Journal of Mental Retardation* 104:187-199.

Volkmar, F.R., D.J. Cohen, and R. Paul
   1986   An evaluation of DSM-III criteria for infantile autism. *Journal of the American Academy of Child Psychiatry* 25:190-197.

Werner, E., G. Dawson, J. Osterling, and J. Dinno
   2000   Recognition of autism spectrum disorders before 1 year of age: A retrospective study based on home videotapes. *Journal of Autism and Developmental Disorders* 30:157-162.

Wing, L., and J. Gould
   1979   Severe impairments of social interaction and associated abnormalities in children: Epidemiology and classification. *Journal of Autism and Developmental Disorders* 9:11-29.

Zentall, S.S., and T.R. Zentall
  1983   Optimal stimulation: A model of disordered activity and performance in normal
          and deviant children. *Psychological Bulletin* 94:446-171.

CHAPTER 9

Ando, H.
  1977   Training autistic children to urinate in the toilet through operant conditioning
          techniques. *Journal of Autism and Childhood Schizophrenia* 7:151-163.
Anderson, S.R., D.L. Avery, E.K. DiPietro, G.L. Edwards, and W.P. Christian
  1987   Intensive home-based early intervention with autistic children. *Education and
          Treatment of Children* 10:352-366.
Azrin, N.H., and R.M. Foxx
  1971   A rapid method of toilet training the institutionalized retarded. *Journal of Applied
          Behavior Analysis* 4:89-99.
  1974   *Toilet Training in Less Than a Day.* New York: Pocket Books.
Azrin, N.H., C. Bugle, and F. O'Brien
  1971   Behavioral engineering: Two apparatuses for toilet training retarded children.
          Journal of Applied Behavior Analysis 4:249-253.
Baker, B.L., and A.J Brightman
  1997   *Steps to Independence: Teaching Everyday Skills to Children with Special Needs, 3rd
          Edition.* Baltimore, MD: Paul H. Brookes Publishing.
Blew, P., I.S. Schwartz, and S.C. Luce
  1985   Teaching functional community skills to autistic children using nonhandicapped
          peer tutors. *Journal of Applied Behavior Analysis* 18:337-342.
Blount, R.L., R.S. Drabman, N. Wilson, and D. Stewart
  1982   Reducing severe diurnal bruxism in two profoundly retarded females. *Journal of
          Applied Behavior Analysis* 15:565-571.
Brigance, A.H.
  1978   *Brigance Inventory of Early Development.* Woburn, MA: Curriculum Associates.
Bruininks, R., R. Woodcock, R. Weatherman, and B. Hill
  1996   *Scales of Independent Behavior - Revised (SIB-R).* Chicago, IL: Riverside Publishing
          Co.
Burack, J.A., and F.R. Volkmar
  1992   Development of low- and high-functioning autistic children. *Journal of Child Psy-
          chology and Psychiatry* 33:607-616.
Burd, L., W. Fisher, J. Kerbeshian, B. Vesely, B. Durgin, and P. Reep
  1988   A comparison of breastfeeding rates among children with pervasive develop-
          mental disorder, and controls. *Developmental and Behavioral Pediatrics* 9:247-251.
Callahan, K., and J.A. Rademacher
  1998   Using self-management strategies to increase the on-task behavior of a student
          with autism. *Journal of Positive Behavioral Interventions* 1:117-122.
Carr, E.G., and M. Darcy
  1990   Setting generality of peer modeling in children with autism. *Journal of Autism and
          Developmental Disorders* 20:45-59.
Carr, E.G., and M.V. Durand
  1985   Reducing behavior problems through functional communication training. *Jour-
          nal of Applied Behavior Analysis* 18:111-126.
Carter, A.S., J.E. Gillham, S.S. Sparrow, and F.R. Volkmar
  1996   Adaptive behavior in autism. *Mental Retardation* 5:945-960.

Carter, A.S., F.R. Volkmar, S.S. Sparrow, J. Wang, C. Lord, G. Dawson, E. Fombonne, K. Loveland, G. Mesibov, and E. Schopler
    1998   The Vineland Adaptive Behavior Scales: Supplementary norms for individuals with autism. *Journal of Autism and Developmental Disorders* 28:287-302.
Dahlgren, S.O., and C. Gillberg
    1989   Symptoms in the first two years of life: A preliminary population study of infantile autism. *European Archives of Psychiatry and Neurological Sciences* 238(3):169-174.
Dalrymple N.J., and L.A. Ruble
    1992   Toilet training and behavior of people with autism: Parent views. *Journal of Autism and Developmental Disorders* 22:265-275.
Dunlap, G., R.L. Koegel, J. Johnson, and R.E. O'Neill
    1987   Maintaining performance of autistic clients in community settings with delayed contingencies. *Journal of Applied Behavior Analysis* 20:185-191.
Durand, M.
    1998   *Sleep Better: A Guide to Improving Sleep for Children with Special Needs.* Baltimore, MD: Paul H. Brookes Publishing.
Egel, A.L.
    1981   Reinforcer variation: Implications for motivating developmentally disabled children. *Journal of Applied Behavior Analysis* 14:345-350.
Epstein, L.H., L. Parker, J.F. McCoy, and G.G McGee
    1976   Descriptive analysis of eating regulation in obese and non-obese children. *Journal of Applied Behavior Analysis* 9:407-415.
Foxx, R.M., and N. Azrin
    1973   *Toilet Training the Retarded: A Rapid Program for Day and Nighttime Independent Toileting.* Champaign, Illinois: Research Press.
Glover, M.E., J.L. Priminger, and A.R. Sanford
    1988   *Early Learning Accomplishments Profile.* Winston-Salem, NC: Kaplan Press.
Gruber, B., R. Reeser, and D.H. Reid
    1979   Providing a less restrictive environment for profoundly retarded persons by teaching independent walking skills. *Journal of Applied Behavior Analysis* 12:285-297.
Hansen, G.D.
    1979   Enuresis control through fading, escape, and avoidance training. *Journal of Applied Behavior Analysis* 12:303-307.
Haring, T.G.
    1985   Teaching between-class generalization of toy play behavior to handicapped children. *Journal of Applied Behavior Analysis* 18:127-139.
Haring, T.G., and C.H. Kennedy
    1988   Units of analysis in task-analytic research. *Journal of Applied Behavior Analysis* 21:207-215.
Haring, T.G., C.H. Kennedy, M.J. Adams, and V. Pitts-Conway
    1987   Teaching generalization of purchasing skills across community settings to autistic youth using videotape modeling. *Journal of Applied Behavior Analysis* 20:89-96.
Harris, S.L., and J.S. Handleman
    1994   *Preschool Education Programs for Children with Autism.* Austin, TX: Pro-Ed.
Harris, S.L., J.S. Handleman, J. Belchic, and B. Glasberg
    1995   The Vineland Adaptive Behavior Scales for young children with autism. *Special Services in the Schools* 10(1):45-52.
Hering, E., R. Epstein, S. Elroy, D.R. Iancu, and N. Zelnik
    1999   Sleep patterns in autistic children. *Journal of Autism and Developmental Disorders* 29:143-147.

Horner, R.D., and I. Keilitz
  1975   Training mentally retarded adolescents to brush their teeth. *Journal of Applied Behavior Analysis* 8:301-309.
Jacobson, J.W., and L.J. Ackerman
  1990   Differences in adaptive functioning among people with autism or mental retardation. *Journal of Autism and Developmental Disabilities* 20:205-219.
Kedesdy, J.H., and K.S. Budd
  1998   *Childhood Feeding Disorders: Biobehavioral Assessment and Intervention.* Baltimore, MD: Paul H. Brookes Publishing.
Kern, L., R.L. Koegel, and G. Dunlap
  1984   The influence of vigorous versus mild exercise on autistic stereotyped behaviors. *Journal of Autism and Developmental Disorders* 14:57-67.
Kern, L., R.L. Koegel, K. Dyer, P.A. Blew, and L.R. Fenton
  1982   The effects of physical exercise on self-stimulation and appropriate responding in autistic children. *Journal of Autism and Developmental Disorders* 12:399-419.
Kohlenberg, R.J.
  1970   The punishment of persistent vomiting: A case study. *Journal of Applied Behavior Analysis* 3:241-245.
Kohler, F.W., P.S. Strain, M. Hoyson, and B. Jamieson
  1997   Combining incidental teaching and peer-mediation with young children with autism. *Focus on Autism and Other Developmental Disorders* 12:196-206.
Lambert, N., K. Nihara, and H. Leland
  1993   *AAMR Adaptive Behavior Scale - School (2nd Ed.).* Austin, TX: Pro-Ed.
Lifter, K., B. Sulzer-Azaroff, S. Anderson, and G. Edwards-Cowdery
  1993   Teaching play activities to preschool children with disabilities: The importance of developmental considerations. *Journal of Early Intervention*: 17:1-21.
Lovaas, I.O.
  1987   Behavioral treatment and normal educational and intellectual functioning in young autistic children. *Journal of Consulting and Clinical Psychology* 55(1):3-9.
Loveland, K.A., and M.L. Kelley
  1991   Development of adaptive behavior in preschoolers with Autism or Down Syndrome. *American Journal on Mental Retardation* 96:13-20.
Lowe, M.L., and A.J. Cuvo
  1976   Teaching coin summation to the mentally retarded. *Journal of Applied Behavior Analysis* 9:483-489.
Luyben, P.D., D.M. Funk, J.K Morgan, K.A. Clark, and D.W. Delulio
  1986   Team sports for the retarded: Training a side-of-the-foot soccer pass using a maximum-to-minimum prompt reduction strategy. *Journal of Applied Behavior Analysis* 19:431-436.
Mace, F.C., and D. Knight
  1986   Functional analysis and treatment of severe pica. *Journal of Applied Behavior Analysis* 19:411-416.
Macht, J.
  1971   Operant measurement of subjective visual acuity in nonverbal children. *Journal of Applied Behavior Analysis* 4:23-26.
Mahoney, J., R.K. Van Wagenen, and L. Meyerson
  1971   Toilet training of normal and retarded children. *Journal of Applied Behavior Analysis* 4:173-181.
Mason, S.A., G.G. McGee, V. Farmer-Dougan, and T.R. Risley
  1989   A practical strategy for reinforcer assessment. *Journal of Applied Behavior Analysis* 22: 171-179.

McClannahan, L.E., G.G. McGee, G.S. MacDuff, and P.J. Krantz
1990   Assessing and improving child care: A personal appearance index for children with autism. *Journal of Applied Behavior Analysis* 23:469-482.
McEachin, J.J., T. Smith, and O.I. Lovaas
1993   Long-term outcome for children with autism who received early intensive behavioral treatment. *American Journal on Mental Retardation* 97:359-372.
McGee, G.G., T. Daly, S.G. Izeman, L. Man, and T.R. Risley
1991   Use of classroom materials to promote preschool engagement. *Teaching Exceptional Children* 23:44-47.
McGee, G.G., T. Daly, and H.A. Jacobs
1994   The Walden Preschool. Pp. 127-162 in *Preschool Education Programs for Children with Autism*, S.L. Harris and J.S. Handleman, eds. Austin, TX: Pro-Ed.
McGee, G.G., R.S. Feldman, and M.J. Morrier
1997   Benchmarks of social treatment for children with autism. *Journal of Autism and Developmental Disorders* 27:353-364.
McGee, G.G., H.A. Jacobs, and M.C. Regnier
1993   Preparation of families for incidental teaching and advocacy for their children with autism. *OSERS News in Print* 5:9-13.
McGee, G.G., P.J. Krantz, and L.E. McClannahan
1986   An extension of incidental teaching to reading instruction for autistic children. *Journal of Applied Behavior Analysis* 19:147-157.
McGee, G.G., M.J. Morrier, and T. Daly
1999   An incidental teaching approach to early intervention for toddlers with autism. *Journal of the Association for Persons with Severe Handicaps* 24:133-146.
Miller, M.A., A.J. Cuvo, and L.S. Borakove
1977   Teaching naming of coin values—comprehension before production versus production alone. *Journal of Applied Behavior Analysis* 10:735-736.
Neef, A.N., B.A. Iwata, and T.J. Page
1978   Public transportation training: In vivo versus classroom instruction. *Journal of Applied Behavior Analysis* 11:331-334.
Newsom, C.D., and K.M. Simon
1977   A simultaneous discrimination procedure for the measurement of vision in nonverbal children. *Journal of Applied Behavior Analysis* 10:633-644.
Nutter, D., and D.H. Reid
1978   Teaching retarded women a clothing selection skill using community norms. *Journal of Applied Behavior Analysis* 11:475-487.
O'Brien, F., C. Bugle, and N.H. Azrin
1972   Training and maintaining a retarded child's proper eating. *Journal of Applied Behavior Analysis* 5:67-72.
O'Brien, S., L.V. Ross, and E.R. Christophersen
1986   Primary encopresis: Evaluation and treatment. *Journal of Applied Behavior Analysis* 19:137-145.
O'Moore, M.
1978   Living with autism. *The Irish Journal of Psychology* 4(1):33-52.
Page, T.J., B.A. Iwata, and N.A. Neef
1976   Teaching pedestrian skills to retarded persons: Generalization from the classroom to the natural environment. *Journal of Applied Behavior Analysis* 9:433-444.
Rast, J., J.M. Johnston, C. Drum, and J. Conrin
1981   The relation of food quantity to rumination behavior. *Journal of Applied Behavior Analysis* 14:121-130.

Richdale, A.L., and M.R. Prior
  1995   The sleep/wake rhythm in children with autism. *European Child and Adolescent Psychiatry* 4:175-186.
Rincover, A., and C.D. Newsom
  1985   The relative motivational properties of sensory and edible reinforcers in teaching autistic children. *Journal of Applied Behavior Analysis* 18:237-248.
Riordan, M.M., B.A. Iwata, J.W. Finney, M.K. Wohl, and A.E. Stanley
  1984   Behavioral assessment and treatment of chronic food refusal in handicapped children. *Journal of Applied Behavior Analysis* 17:327-341.
Sajwaj, T., J. Libet, and S. Agras
  1974   Lemon juice therapy: The control of life-threatening rumination in a six-month-old infant. *Journal of Applied Behavior Analysis* 7:557-563.
Sanford, A.R., and J.G. Zelman
  1981   *Learning Accomplishments Profile.* Winston-Salem, NC: Kaplan Press.
Singh, N.N., P.J. Manning, and M.J. Angell
  1982   Effects of an oral hygiene punishment procedure on chronic rumination and collateral behaviors in monozygous twins. *Journal of Applied Behavior Analysis* 15:309-314.
Smith, T., A.D Groen, and J.W. Wynn
  2000   A randomized trial of intensive early intervention for children with pervasive developmental disorder. *American Journal on Mental Retardation* 5(4):269-285.
Sparrow, S.
  1997   Developmentally based assessments. Pp. 411-447 in *Handbook of Autism and Pervasive Developmental Disorders*, D.J. Cohen and F.R. Volkmar, eds. New York: John Wiley and Sons, Inc.
Sparrow, S., D. Balla, and D. Cicchetti
  1984   *Vineland Adaptive Behavior Scales.* Circle Pines, MN: American Guidance Service.
Sprague, J.R., and R.H. Horner
  1984   The effects of single instance, multiple instance, and general case training on generalized vending machine use by moderately and severely handicapped students. *Journal of Applied Behavior Analysis* 17:273-278.
Stahmer, A.
  1995   Teaching symbolic play skills to children with autism using Pivotal Response Training. *Journal of Autism and Developmental Disorders* 25:123-141.
Strain, P.S., C. Danko, and F.W. Kohler
  1994   Activity engagement and social interaction development in young children with autism: An examination of "free" intervention effects. *Journal of Emotional and Behavioral Disorders* 2:15-29.
Thompson, T., T. Hackenberg, D. Cerutti, D.T. Baker, et. al
  1994   Opioid antagonist effects on self-injury in adults with mental retardation: Response form and location as determinants of medication effects. *American Journal on Mental Retardation* 99(1):85-102.
Trace, M.S., A.J. Cuvo, and J.L. Criswell
  1977   Teaching coin equivalence to the mentally retarded. *Journal of Applied Behavior Analysis* 10:85-92.
van den Pol, R.A., B.A. Iwata, M.T. Ivancic, T.J. Page, N.A. Neef, and F.P. Whitley
  1981   Teaching the handicapped to eat in public places: Acquisition, generalization, and maintenance of restaurant skills. *Journal of Applied Behavior Analysis* 14:61-69.
VanMeter, L., D. Fein, R. Morris, L. Waterhouse, and D. Allen
  1997   Delay versus deviance in autistic social behavior. *Journal of Autism and Developmental Disorders* 27:557-569.

Venn, M.L., M. Wolery, A. Morris, L.D. DeCesare, and Cuffs
in   Use of progressive time delay to teach in-class transitions to preschoolers with
press autism. *Journal of Autism and Developmental Disorders.*

Volkmar, F.R., A. Carter, S.S. Sparrow, and D.V. Cicchetti
1993 Quantifying social development in autism. *Journal of the American Academy of Child and Adolescent Psychiatry* 32:627-632.

Volkmar, F.R., S.S. Sparrow, D. Goudreau, D.V. Cicchetti, R. Paul, and D.J. Cohen
1987 Social deficits in autism: An operational approach using the Vineland Adaptive Behavior Scales. *Journal of the American Academy of Child and Adolescent Psychiatry* 26:156-161.

Wilson, P.G., D.H. Reid, J.F. Phillips, and L.D. Burgio
1984 Normalization of institutional mealtimes for profoundly retarded persons: Effects and noneffects of teaching family-style dining. *Journal of Applied Behavior Analysis* 17:189-201.

Wolf, M.M., T.R. Risley, and H.L. Mees
1964 Application of operant conditioning procedures to the behavior problems of an autistic child. *Behavior Research and Therapy* 1:305-312.

Wolfberg, P.J., and A.L. Schuler
1993 Integrated play groups: A model for promoting the social and cognitive dimensions of play with children with autism. *Journal of Autism and Developmental Disorders* 23:467-489.

Woolcock, J.E., and L.A. Alferink
1982 An operant tracking procedure in the auditory assessment of profoundly retarded individuals. *Journal of Applied Behavior Analysis* 15:303-307.

Zlutnick, S., W.J. Mayville, and S. Moffat
1975 Modification of seizure disorders: The interruption of behavioral chains. *Journal of Applied Behavior Analysis* 8:1-12.

CHAPTER 10

Aman, M.G., and K.S. Langworthy
2000 Pharmacotherapy for hyperactivity in children with autism and other pervasive developmental disorders. *Journal of Autism and Developmental Disorders* 30(5):451-459.

Anderson, L.T., M. Campbell, D.M. Grega, R. Perry, A.M. Small, and W.H. Green
1984 Haloperidol in the treatment of infantile autism: Effects on learning and behavioral symptoms. *American Journal of Psychiatry* 141(10):1195-1202.

Anderson, L.T., M. Campbell, P. Adams, A.M. Small, R. Perry, and J. Shell
1989 The effects of haloperidol on discrimination learning and behavioral symptoms in autistic children. *Journal of Autism and Developmental Disorders* 19(2):227-239.

Berkson G., and M. Tupa
2000 Early development of stereotyped and self-injurious behaviors. *Journal of Early Intervention* 23(1):1-19.

Berkson, G., N. Rafaeli-Mor, and S. Tarnovsky
1999 Body-rocking and other habits of college students and persons with mental retardation. *American Journal on Mental Retardation* 104(2):107-116.

Borthwick-Duffy, S.A.
1996 Evaluation and quality of life: Special considerations for persons with mental retardation. Pp. 105-120 in *Quality of Life: Volume I Conceptualization and Measurement*, R.L. Schalock and G.N. Siperstein, eds. Washington, DC: American Association on Mental Retardation.

Bouvard, M.P., M. Leboyer, J.M. Launay, and C. Recasens
  1995   Low dose naltrexone effects on plasma chemistries and clinical symptoms in au-
         tism: A double blind, placebo controlled study. *Psychiatry Research* 58(3):191-
         201.
Bristol, M.M., J.J. Gallagher, and K.D. Holt
  1993   Maternal depressive symptoms in autism: Response to psychoeducational inter-
         vention. *Rehabilitation Psychology* 38:3-9.
Bristol, M.M., D.J. Cohen, E.J. Costello, M. Denckla, T.J. Eckberg, R. Kallen, H.C. Draemer,
C. Lord, R. Maurer, W.J. McIlvane, N. Minshew, M. Sigman, and M.A. Spence
  1996   State of science in autism: Report to the National Institutes of Health. *Journal of
         Autism and Developmental Disorders* 26:121-154.
Campbell, M., et al.
  1982   The effects of haloperidol on learning and behavior in autistic children. *Journal of
         Autism and Developmental Disorders* 12(2):167-175.
Campbell, M., L.T. Anderson, A.M. Small, J.J. Locascio, N.S. Lynch, and M.C. Choroco
  1990   Naltrexone in autistic children: A double blind and placebo controlled study.
         Psychopharmacology Bulletin 26(1):130-135.
Carr, E.G., L. Levin, G. McConnachie, J.I. Carlson, D.C. Kemp, and C.E. Smith
  1994   *Communication Based Intervention for Problem Behavior: A User's Guide for Producing
         Positive Change.* Baltimore, MD: Paul H. Brookes Publishing.
Carr, E.G., J.I. Carlson, N.A. Langdon, D. Magito-McLaughlin, and S.C. Yarbrough
  1998   Two perspectives on antecedent control. In *Antecedent Control: Innovative Ap-
         proaches To Behavioral Support*, J.K. Luiselli and J. Cameron (eds.). Baltimore, MD:
         Paul H. Brookes Publishing.
Carr, E.G., R.H. Horner, A.P. Turnbull, J.G. Marquis, D. Magito-McLaughlin, M.L. McAtee,
C.E. Smith, K.A. Anderson-Ryan, M.B. Ruef, and A. Doolabh
  1999a *Positive Behavior Support for People with Developmental Disabilities.* Washington,
         DC: American Association on Mental Retardation Monograph Series.
Carr, E.G., N.A. Langdon, and S. Yarbrough
  1999b Hypothesis-based intervention for severe problem behavior. In A.C. Repp and
         R.H. Horner, eds. *Functional Analysis of Problem Behavior: From Effective Assess-
         ment to Effective Support.* Belmont, CA: Wadsworth Publishing.
Carr, E.G., L. Levin, G. McConnachie, J.I. Carlson, D.C. Kemp, C.E. Smith, and D.M.
McLaughlin
  1999c Comprehensive multisituational intervention for problem behavior in the com-
         munity: Long-term maintenance and social validation. *Journal of Positive Behavior
         Interventions* 1:5-25.
Cohen, D.J., and F.R. Volkmar
  1997   *Handbook of Autism and Pervasive Developmental Disorders* (2nd ed.). New York,
         NY: John Wiley and Sons, Inc.
Cohen, I.L., M. Campbell, D. Posner, A.M. Small, D. Triebel, and L.T. Anderson
  1980   Behavioral effects of haloperidol in young autistic children: A double-blind and
         placebo-controlled study. *Psychopharmocology Bulletin* 26:130-135.
Dawson, G., and J. Osterling
  1997   Early intervention in autism: Effectiveness and common elements of current
         approaches. Pp. 307-326 in *The Effectiveness of Early Intervention: Second Generation
         Research*, M.J. Guralnick, ed. Baltimore, MD: Paul H. Brookes Publishing.
Dunlap, G., and L. Fox
  1999   A demonstration of behavioral support for young children with autism. *Journal
         of Positive Behavior Intervention* 1:77-87.

Dunlap G., L. Kern-Dunlap, C. Lee; S. Clarke, and F.R. Robbins
1991   Functional assessment, curricular revision, and severe behavior problems. *Journal of Applied Behavior Analysis* 24(2):387-397.
Dunlap, G., L. Kern, M. dePerczel, S. Clarke, D. Wilson, K.E. Childs, R. White, R., and G.D. Falk
1993   Functional analysis of classroom variables for students with emotional and behavioral challenges. *Behavioral Disorders* 18:275-291.
Durand, M.V.
1982   A behavioral/pharmacological intervention for the treatment of severe self-injurious behavior. *Journal of Autism and Developmental Disorders* 12(3):243-251.
Emerson, E.
1995   *Challenging Behaviour: Analysis and Intervention in People with Learning Difficulties.* New York: Cambridge University Press.
Fankhauser, M.P., V.C. Karumanchi, M.L. German, A. Yates, and S.D. Karumanchi
1992   A double-blind, placebo-controlled study of the efficacy of transdermal clonidine in autism. *Journal of Clinical Psychiatry* 53(3):77-82.
Favell, J.E., J.F. McGimsey, and R.M. Schell
1982   Treatment of self-injury by providing alternate sensory activities. *Analysis and Intervention in Developmental Disabilities* 2(1):83-104.
Fenske, E.C., S. Zalenski, P.J. Krantz, and L.E. McClannahan
1985   Age at intervention and treatment outcome for autistic children in a comprehensive intervention program. *Analysis and Intervention in Developmental Disabilities* 5(1-2):49-58.
Fisher, W., C.C. Piazza, L.G. Bowman, L.P. Hagopian, J.C. Owens, and I. Slevin
1992   A comparison of two approaches for identifying reinforcers for persons with severe and profound disabilities. *Journal of Applied Behavior Analysis* 25:491-498.
Gordon, C.T.
2000   Commentary: Considerations on the pharmacological treatment of compulsions and stereotypies with serotonin reuptake inhibitors in pervasive developmental disorders. *Journal of Autism and Developmental Disorders* 30(5):437-438.
Greenspan, S.I.
1999   Improving Interventions for Children with Disorders of Relating and Communicating: Two Cultures Working Together. Unpublished paper submitted to the Committee on Educational Interventions for Children with Autism, National Academy of Sciences, Washington, DC.
Greenspan, S.I., and S. Wieder
1997   Developmental patterns and outcomes in infants and children with disorders in relating and communicating: A chart review of 200 cases of children with autistic spectrum diagnoses. *The Journal of Developmental and Learning Disorders* 1:87-141.
Griffin, J.C., R.W. Ricketts, D.E. Williams, B.J. Locke, B.K. Altmeyer, and M.T. Stark
1987   A community survey of self-injurious behavior among developmentally disabled children and adolescents. *Hospital and Community Psychiatry* 38(9):959-963.
Groden, J., J. Cautela, and G. Groden
1998   *Relaxation Techniques for People with Special Needs: Breaking the Barriers.* Waterloo: Research Press.
Harris, S.L.
1998   Behavioural and educational approaches to the pervasive developmental disorders. Pp. 195-208 in *Autism and Pervasive Developmental Disorders*, F. Volkmar, ed. New York: Cambridge University Press.
Harris, S.L., J.S. Handleman, R. Gordon, B. Kristoff, and F. Fuentes
1991   Changes in cognitive and language functioning of preschool children with autism. *Journal of Autism and Developmental Disabilities* 21:281-290.

Horner, R.H., and E.G. Carr
  1997   Behavioral support for students with severe disabilities: Functional assessment and comprehensive intervention. *Journal of Special Education* 31:84-104.
Horner, R.H., E.G. Carr, P.S. Strain, A.W. Todd, and H.K. Reed
  *2000   Problem Behavior Interventions for Young Children with Autism: A Research Synthesis. Paper presented at the Second Workshop of the Committee on Educational Interventions for Children with Autism, National Research Council, April 12, 2000. Department of Special Education, University of Oregon.
Horner, R.H., G. Dunlap, R. Koegel, E. Carr, W. Sailor, J. Anderson, R. Albin, and R. O'Neill
  1990   Toward a technology of "nonaversive" behavioral support. *Journal of the Association for Persons with Severe Handicaps* 15:125-147.
Iwata, B.A., M.F. Dorsey, K.J. Slifer, K.E. Bauman, and G.S. Richman
  1982   Toward a functional analysis of self-injury. *Analysis and Intervention in Developmental Disabilities* 2:3-20.
Iwata, B.A., B.A. Duncan, J.R. Zarcone, D.C. Lerman, and B.A. Shore
  1994   A sequential, test-control methodology for conducting functional analyses of self-injurious behavior. *Behavior Modification* 18(3):289-306.
Jaselskis, C.A., E.H. Cook, and K.E. Fletcher
  1992   Clonidine treatment of hyperactive and impulsive children with autistic disorder. *Journal of Clinical Psychopharmacology* 12(5):322-327.
Kanner, A.M.
  2000   The treatment of seizure disorders and EEG abnormalities in children with autistic spectrum disorders: Are we getting ahead of ourselves? *Journal of Autism and Developmental Disorders* 30(5):491-495.
Kern, L., R.L. Koegel, and G. Dunlap
  1984   The influence of vigorous versus mild exericse on autistic stereotyped behaviors. *Journal of Autism and Developmental Disorders* 14(1):57–67.
King, B.H.
  2000   Pharmacological treatment of mood disturbances, aggression and self-injury in persons with pervasive developmental disorders. *Journal of Autism and Developmental Disorders* 30(5):439-445.
Koegel, L.K., R.L. Koegel, and A. Surratt
  1992   Language intervention and disruptive behavior in preschool children with autism. *Journal of Autism and Developmental Disorders* 22:141-153.
Koegel, L.K., D. Stiebel, and R.L. Koegel
  1998   Reducing aggression in children with autism toward infant and toddler siblings. *Journal of the Association for Persons with Severe Disabilities* 23:111-118.
Koegel, R.L., K. Dyer, and L.K. Bell
  1987   The influence of child-preferred activities on autistic children's social behavior. *Journal of Applied Behavior Analysis* 20(3):243-252.
Koegel, R.L., L.K. Koegel, and C.M. Carter
  1999   Pivotal teaching interactions for children with autism. *School Psychology Review* 28(4):576-594.
Kohler, F.W., P.S. Strain, and D.D. Shearer
  1996   Examining levels of social inclusion within an integrated preschool for children with autism. Pp. 305-332 in *Positive Behavioral Support: Including People With Difficult Behavior in the Community*, R.K. Koegel and L.K. Koegel, eds. Baltimore, MD: Paul H. Brookes Publishing Co.
Kolmen, B.K., H.M. Feldman, B.L. Handen, and J.E. Janosky
  1997   Naltrexone in young autistic children: Replication study and learning measures. *Journal of the American Academy of Child and Adolescent Psychiatry.* 36(11):1570-1578.

Lewis, M.H.
  1996   Brief report: Psychopharmacology of Autism Spectrum Disorders. *Journal of Autism and Developmental Disorders* 26(2):231-235.
Lovaas, I.O.
  1987   Behavioral treatment and normal educational and intellectual functioning in young autistic children. *Journal of Consulting and Clinical Psychology* 55(1):3-9.
Mandlawitz, M.
  *1999   The Impact of the Legal System on Educational Programming for Young Children with Autism Spectrum Disorder. Paper presented at the First Workshop of the Committee on Educational Interventions for Children with Autism, National Research Council, December 13-14, 1999.
McDougal, J., and A.S. Hiralall
  1998   Bridging Research into Practice to Intervene with Young Aggressive Students in the Public School Setting: Evaluation of the Behavior Consultation Team (BCT) Project. Unpublished paper presented at the Annual Convention of the National Association of School Psychologists, Orlando, FL, April 14-18.
McDougle, C.J., L.E. Kresch, and D.J. Posey
  2000   Repetitive thoughts and behavior in pervasive developmental disorders: Treatment with serotonin reuptake inhibitors. *Journal of Autism and Developmental Disorders* 30(5):427-435.
McGee, G.G, and T. Daly
  1999   Prevention of problem behaviors in preschool children. In *Functional Analysis of Problem Behavior: From Effective Assessment to Effective Support*, A.C. Repp, and R.H. Horner, eds. Belmont, CA: Wadsworth Publishing Co.
McGee, G.G., M.J. Morrier, and T. Daly
  1999   An incidental teaching approach to early intervention for toddlers with autism. *Journal of the Association for the Severely Handicapped* 24:133-146.
Mesibov, G.B, L.W. Adams, and E. Schopler
  2000   Autism: A brief history. *Psychoanalytic Inquiry* 20(5):637-647.
Neef, N.A., and B.A. Iwata
  1994   Current research on functional analysis methodologies: An introduction. *Journal of Applied Behavioral Analysis* 27:211-214.
Newman, B., L. Tuntigian, C.S. Ryan, and D.R. Reinecke
  1997   Self-management of a DRO procedure by three students with autism. *Behavioral Interventions* 12(3):149-156.
New York State Department of Health
  1999   *Clinical Practice Guideline: The Guideline Technical Report. Autism/Pervasive Developmental Disorders, Assessment and Intervention for Young Children (0-3 Years)*. Albany, NY: New York State Department of Health, Early Intervention Program.
Pelios, L., J. Morren, D. Tesch, and S. Axelrod
  1999   The impact of functional analysis methodology on treatment choice for self-injurious and aggressive behavior. *Journal of Applied Behavior Analysis* 32(2):185-195.
Quill, K., S. Gurry, and A. Larkin
  1989   Daily Life Therapy: A Japanese model for educating children with autism. *Journal of Autism and Developmental Disorders* 19(4):625-635.
Rafaeli-Mor, N., L. Foster, and G. Berkson
  1999   Self-reported body-rocking and other habits in college students. *American Journal of Mental Retardation* 104(1):1-10.
Reichle, J.
  1990   *National Working Conference on Positive Approaches to the Management of Excess Behavior: Final Report and Recommendations*. Minneapolis, MN: Institute on Community Integration, University of Minnesota

Reiss, S., and S.M. Havercamp
1997 Sensitivity theory and mental retardation: Why functional analysis is not enough. *American Journal on Mental Retardation* 101(6):553-566.

Repp, A., and R.H. Horner, eds.
1999 *Functional Analysis of Problem Behavior: From Effective Assessment To Effective Support*. Belmont, CA: Wadsworth Publishing.

Rogers, S.J.
1998 Empirically supported comprehensive treatments for young children with autism. *Journal of Clinical Child Psychology* 27:168-179.

Rogers, S.J., and H. Lewis
1989 An effective day treatment model for young children with pervasive developmental disorders. *Journal of the American Academy of Child and Adolescent Psychiatry* 28:207-214.

Rojahn, J.
1986 Self-injurious and stereotypic behavior of noninstitutionalized mentally retarded people: Prevalence and classification. *American Journal of Mental Deficiency* 91(3):268-276.

Sallustro, F., and C.W. Atwell
1978 Body rocking, head banging, and head rolling in normal children. *Journal of Pediatrics* 93(4):704-708.

Schopler, E., G.B. Mesibov, and K. Hearsey
1995 Structured teaching in the TEACCH system. Pp. 243-268 in *Learning and Cognition in Autism*, E. Schopler and G.B. Mesibov, eds. New York: Plenum Press.

Schreibman, L., C. Whalen, and A.C. Stahmer
2000 The use of video priming to reduce disruptive transition behavior in children with autism. *Journal of Positive Behavior Interventions* 2(1):3-11.

Schroeder, S.R., W.K. Bickel, and G. Richmond
1986 Primary and secondary prevention of self-injurious behaviors: A life-long problem. *Advances in Learning and Behavioral Disabilities* 5:63-85.

Schroeder, S.R., R.G. Hammock, J.A. Mulick, J. Rojahn, P. Walson, W. Fernald, P. Meinhold, and G. Saphare
1995 Clinical trials of D-sub-1 and D-sub-2 dopamine modulating drugs and self-injury in mental retardation and developmental disability. *Mental Retardation and Developmental Disabilities Research Reviews* 1(2):120-129.

Scotti, J.R., K.J. Ujcich, K.L. Wiegle, and C.M. Holland
1996 Interventions with challenging behavior of persons with developmental disabilities: A review of current research practices. *Journal of the Association for Persons with Severe Handicaps* 21(3):123-134.

Sprague, J.R., and V. Rian
1993 Support Systems for Students with Severe Problem in Indiana: A Descriptive Analysis of School Structure and Student Demographics. Unpublished manuscript. Bloomington, IN: Indiana University Institute for the Study of Developmental Disabilities.

Stern, L.M., M.K. Walker, M.G. Sawyer, and R.D. Oades
1990 A controlled crossover trial of fenfluramine in autism. *Journal of Child Psychology and Psychiatry and Allied Disciplines* 31(4):569-585.

Symons, F.J., and T. Thompson
1997 Self-injurious behaviour and body site preference. *Journal of Intellectual Disability Research* 41(6):456-468.

Symons, F.J., M.G. Butler, M.D. Sanders, I.D. Feurer, and T. Thompson
1999 Self injurious behavior and Prader-Willi syndrome: Behavioral forms and body locations. *American Journal of Mental Retardation* 104(3):260-269.

Tessel, R.E., S.R. Schroeder, C.J. Stodgell, and P.S. Loupe
  1995   Rodent models of mental retardation: Self-injury, aberrant behavior, and stress. *Mental Retardation and Developmental Disabilities Research Reviews* 1(2): 99-103.
Thelen, M.H.
  1979   Treatment of temper tantrum behavior by means of noncontingent positive attention. *Journal of Clinical Child Psychology* 8(2):140.
Thompson, T., F. Symons, D. Delaney, and C. England
  1995   Self-injurious behavior as endogenous neurochemical self-administration. *Mental Retardation and Developmental Disabilities Research Reviews* 1(2):137-148.
Tuchman, R.
  2000   Treatment of seizure disorders and EEG abnormalities of children with autism spectrum disorders. *Journal of Autism and Developmental Disorders* 30(5):485-489.
Turnbull, H.R., B.L. Wilcox, and M.J. Stowe
  *1999   A Brief Overview of Special Education Law with Focus on Autism. Paper presented at the First Workshop of the Committee on Educational Interventions for Children with Autism, National Research Council, December 13-14, 1999. Beach Center on Families and Disability, University of Kansas.
Wacker, D.P., W.K. Berg, J. Harding, and J. Asmus
  1996   Developing Long-Term Reciprocal Interactions Between Parents and Their Young Children with Problematic Behavior. Pp 51-80 in *Positive Behavioral Support: Including People with Difficult Behavior in the Community*, L.K. Koegel, R.L. Koegel, and G. Dunlap (eds.). Baltimore, MD: Paul H. Brookes Publishing Co.
Wacker, D.P, W.K. Berg, J.W. Harding, K.M. Derby, J.M. Asmus, and A. Healy
  1998   Evaluation and long-term treatment of aberrant behavior displayed by young children with disabilities. *Journal of Developmental and Behavioral Pediatrics* 19(4):260-266.
Werry, J.S., J. Carlielle, and J. Fitzpatrick
  1983   Rhythmic motor activities (stereotypies) in children under five: Etiology and prevalence. *Journal of the American Academy of Child Psychiatry* 22(4):329-336.
Willemsen-Swinkels, S.H.N., J.K. Buitelaar, F.G. Weijnen, and H. van Engeland
  1995   Placebo-controlled acute dosage naltrexone study in young autistic children. *Psychiatry Research* 58(3):203-215.
Willemsen-Swinkels, S.H.N., J.K. Buitelaar, and H. van Engeland
  1996   The effects of chronic naltrexone treatment in young autistic children: A double-blind placebo-controlled crossover study. *Biological Psychiatry* 39(12):1023-1031.
Wolery, M., and A.R. Garfinkle
  *2000   Measures in Intervention Research with Young Children Who Have Autism. Paper presented at the Second Meeting of the Committee on Educational Interventions for Children with Autism, National Research Council, April 12, 2000.

CHAPTER 11

Anderson, S.R., and R.G. Romanczyk
  1999   Early intervention for young children with autism: Continuum-based behavioral models. *Journal of the Association for the Severely Handicapped* 24:162-173.
Bondy, A.S., and L.A. Frost
  1994   The picture exchange communication system. *Focus on Autistic Behavior* 9:1-19.
Brady, M.P., R.E. Shores, M.A. McEvoy, D. Ellis, et al.
  1987   Increasing social interactions of severely handicapped autistic children. *Journal of Autism and Developmental Disorders* 17(3):375 390.

Danko, C.D., J. Lawry, and P.S. Strain
    1998   Social Skills Intervention Manual Packet. Unpublished. St. Peters Child Develop-
            ment Center, Pittsburgh, PA.
Dunlap, G., M. DePerczel, S. Clarke, D. Wilson, S. Wright, R. White, and A. Gomez
    1994   Choice making and proactive behavioral support for students with emotional
            and behavioral challenges. *Journal of the Association for Persons with Severe Dis-
            abilities* 20:248-258.
Goldstein, H., L. Kaczmarek, R. Pennington, and K. Shafer
    1992   Peer-mediated intervention: Attending to, commenting on, and acknowledging
            the behavior of preschoolers with autism. *Journal of Applied Behavior Analysis*
            25(2):289-305.
Hart, B., and T.R. Risley
    1975   Incidental teaching of language in the preschool. *Journal of Applied Behavior Analy-
            sis* 8(4):411-420.
Koegel, L.K., R.L. Koegel, J.K. Harrower, and C.M. Carter
    1999   Pivotal response intervention I: Overview of approach. *Journal of the Association
            for the Severely Handicapped* 24:174-185.
Lovaas, O.I., A.B. Ackerman, D. Alexander, P. Firestone, J. Perkins, and D. Young
    1981   *Teaching Developmentally Disabled Children: The ME Book.* Austin, TX: Pro-Ed.
McGee, G.G., M.J. Morrier, and T. Daly
    1999   An incidental teaching approach to early intervention for toddlers with autism.
            Journal of the Association for the Severely Handicapped 24:133-146.
McGee, G.G., P.J. Krantz, D. Mason, and L.E. McClannahan
    1983   A modified incidental-teaching procedure for autistic youth: Acquisition and
            generalization of receptive object labels. *Journal of Applied Behavior Analysis*
            16(3):329-338.
McGee, G.G., M.C. Almeida, B. Sulzer-Azaroff, and R.S. Feldman
    1992   Promoting reciprocal interactions via peer incidental teaching. *Journal of Applied
            Behavior Analysis* 25:117-126.
Odom, S.L., and P.S. Strain
    1986   A comparison of peer-initiation and teacher-antecedent interventions for promot-
            ing reciprocal social interaction of autistic preschoolers. *Journal of Applied Behav-
            ior Analysis* 19(1):59-71.
Oke, N.J., and L. Schreibman
    1990   Training social initiations to a high-functioning autistic child: Assessment of
            collateral behavior change and generalization in a case study. *Journal of Autism
            and Developmental Disorders* 20(4):479-497.
O'Neill, R.E., R.H. Horner, R.W. Albin, K. Storey, and J.R. Sprague
    1990   *Functional Analysis of Problem Behavior: A Practical Assessment Guide.*
            Sycamore, IL: Sycamore Publishing Company.
Prizant, B., and A.Wetherby
    1998   Understanding the continuum of discrete-trial traditional behavioral to social-
            pragmatic developmental approaches in communication enhancement for young
            children with autism/PDD. *Seminars in Speech and Language* 19:329-353.
Sainato, D.M., H. Goldstein, and P.S. Strain
    1992   Effects of self-evaluation on preschool children's use of social interaction strate-
            gies with their classmates with autism. *Journal of Applied Behaviour Analysis*
            25:127-141.
Schreibman, L.
    2000   Intensive behavioral/psychoeducational treatments for autism: Research needs
            and future directions. *Journal of Autism and Developmental Disorders* 30(5):373-
            378.

Strain, P.S., and C.D. Danko
   1995   Caregivers' encouragement of positive interaction between preschoolers with au-
           tism and their siblings. *Journal of Emotional and Behavioral Disorders* 3(1):2-12.
Strain, P.S., and F.W. Kohler
   1998   Peer-mediated social intervention for young children with autism. *Seminars in
           Speech and Language* 19:391-405.
Strain, P.S., R.E. Shores, and M.A. Timm
   1977   Effects of peer social initiations on the behavior of withdrawn preschool children.
           Journal of Applied Behavior Analysis 10(2):289-298.
Strain, P.S., M.M. Kerr, and E.U. Ragland
   1979   Effects of peer mediated social initiations and prompting/reinforcement proce-
           dures on the social behavior of autistic children. *Journal of Autism and Develop-
           mental Disorders* 9(1):41-54.
Strain, P.S., F.W. Kohler, K. Storey, and C.D. Danko
   1994   Teaching preschoolers with autism to self-monitor their social interactions: An
           analysis of results in home and school settings. *Journal of Emotional and Behavioral
           Disorders* 2(2):78-88.
Watson, L., C. Lord, B. Schaffer, and E. Schopler
   1989   *Teaching Spontaneous Communication to Autistic and Developmentally Handicapped
           Children.* New York: Irvington Press.

CHAPTER 12

Anderson, S.R., and R.G. Romanczyk
   1999   Early intervention for young children with autism: Continuum-based behavioral
           models. *Journal of the Association for the Severely Handicapped* 24:162-173.
Anderson, S.R., D.L. Avery, E.K. DiPietro, G.L. Edwards, and W.P. Christian
   1987   Intensive home-based early intervention with autistic children. *Education and
           Treatment of Children* 10:352-366.
Baer, D.M., M.M. Wolf, and T.R. Risley
   1968   Some current dimensions of applied behavior analysis. *Journal of Applied Behavior
           Analysis* 1:91-97.
Birnbrauer, J.S., and D.J. Leach
   1993   The Murdock Early Intervention Program after 2 years. *Behaviour Change* 10:63-
           74.
Bondy, A.S., and L.A. Frost
   1994   The picture exchange communication system. *Focus on Autistic Behavior* 9:1-19.
Brown, F., and L.M. Bambara
   1999   Special series on interventions for young children with autism. *The Journal of the
           Association for Persons with Severe Handicaps* 24(3).
Carr, E.G., L. Levin, G. McConnachie, J.I. Carlson, D.C. Kemp, and C.E. Smith
   1994   *Communication-Based Interventions for Problem Behavior: A User's Guide for Produc-
           ing Behavior Change.* Baltimore, MD: Paul H. Brookes Publishing..
Ceci, S.J.
   1991   How much does schooling influence general intelligence and its cognitive com-
           ponents? A reassessment of the evidence. *Development Psychology* 27:703-722.
Dawson, G., and J. Osterling
   1997   Early intervention in autism: Effectiveness and common elements of current
           approaches. Pp. 307-326 in *The Effectiveness of Early Intervention: Second Genera-
           tion Research*, M.J. Guralnick, ed. Baltimore, MD: Paul H. Brookes Publishing.
Dodge, D.T., and L.J. Colker
   1988   *The Creative Curriculum (3rd ed.).* Washington, DC: Teaching Strategies, Inc.

Dunlap, G., and L. Fox
  1996   Early intervention and serious problem behaviors: A comprehensive approach. Pp. 31-50 in *Positive Behavioral Support: Including People with Difficult Behavior in the Community*, L.K. Koegel, R.L. Koegel, and G. Dunlap, eds. Baltimore, MD: Paul H. Brookes Publishing.
  1999a A demonstration of behavioral support for young children with autism. *Journal of Positive Behavioral Interventions* 2:77-87.
  1999b Supporting families of young children with autism. *Infants and Young Children* 12:48-54.
Dunlap, G., and F.R. Robbins
  1991   Current perspectives in service delivery for young children with autism. *Comprehensive Mental Health Care* 1:177-194.
Fenske, E.C., S. Zalenski, P.J. Krantz, and L.E. McClannahan
  1985   Age at intervention and treatment outcome for autistic children in a comprehensive intervention program. *Analysis and Intervention in Developmental Disabilities* 5:49-58.
Fox, L., G. Dunlap, and L.A. Philbrick
  1997   Providing individual supports to young children with autism and their families. *Journal of Early Intervention* 21:1-14.
Frazier, J.A., and F.J. Morrison
  1998   The influence of extended-year schooling on growth of achievement and perceived competence in early elementary school. *Child Development* 69:495-517.
Greenspan, S.I., and S. Wieder
  1997   Developmental patterns and outcomes in infants and children with disorders in relating and communicating: A chart review of 200 cases of children with autistic spectrum diagnoses. *The Journal of Developmental and Learning Disorders* 1:87-141.
  1998   *The Child with Special Needs: Intellectual and Emotional Growth*. Reading, MA: Addison Wesley Longman.
  1999   A functional developmental approach to autism spectrum disorders. *The Association for Persons with Severe Handicaps* 24(3):147-161.
Gresham, F.M., and D.L. MacMillan
  1997   Autistic recovery? An analysis and critique of the empirical evidence on the Early Intervention Project. *Behavioral Disorders* 22:185-201.
Handleman, J.S., and S.L. Harris
  2000   *Preschool Education Programs for Children with Autism (2nd ed.)*. Austin, TX: Pro-Ed.
Harris, S.L., and J.S. Handleman, eds.
  1994   *Preschool Education Programs for Children with Autism*. Austin, TX: Pro-Ed.
Harris, S.L., J.S. Handleman, M.S. Arnold, and R.F. Gordon
  2000   The Douglass Developmental Disabilities Center: Two models of service delivery. Pp. 233-260 in *Preschool Education Programs for Children with Autism (2nd ed.)*, J.S. Handleman and S.L. Harris, eds. Austin, TX: Pro-Ed.
Harris, S.L., J.S. Handleman, J. Belchic, and B. Glasberg
  1995   The Vineland Adaptive Behavior Scales for young children with autism. *Special Services in the Schools* 10(1):45-52.
Harris, S.L., J.S. Handleman, B. Kristoff, L. Bass, and R. Gordon
  1990   Changes in language development among autistic and peer children in segregated and integrated preschool settings. *Journal of Autism and Developmental Disorders* 20:23-31.
Harris, S.L., J.S. Handleman, R. Gordon, B. Kristoff, and F. Fuentes
  1991   Changes in cognitive and language functioning of preschool children with autism. *Journal of Autism and Developmental Disabilities* 21:281-290.

Harrison, P.
1999   Special issue on assessment and treatment of children with autism in the schools. *School Psychology Review* 28:531-694.

Hoyson, M., B. Jamieson, and P.S. Strain
1984   Individualized group instruction of normally developing and autistic-like children: A description and evaluation of the LEAP curriculum model. *Journal of the Division of Early Childhood* 8:157-181.

Kasari, C.
*2000   Assessing Change in Early Intervention Programs for Children with Autism. Paper presented at the Second Workshop of the Committee on Educational Interventions for Children with Autism, National Research Council, April 12, 2000. Graduate School of Education and Information Studies, University of California at Los Angeles.

Koegel, L.K., and R.L. Koegel
1986   The effects of interspersed maintenance tasks on academic performance and motivation in a severe childhood stroke victim. *Journal of Applied Behavior Analysis* 19:425-430.

Koegel, L.K., S.M. Camarata, M. Valdez-Menchaca, and R.L. Koegel
1998   Setting generalization of question-asking by children with autism. *American Journal on Mental Retardation* 102:346-357.

Koegel, L.K., R.L. Koegel, J.K. Harrower, and C.M. Carter
1999a   Pivotal response intervention I: Overview of approach. *Journal of the Association for the Severely Handicapped* 24:174-185.

Koegel, L.K., R.L. Koegel, Y. Shoshan, and E. McNerney
1999b   Pivotal response intervention II: Preliminary long-term outcome data. *Journal of the Association for Persons with Severe Handicaps* 24:186-198.

Koegel, R.L., M.C. O'Dell, and G. Dunlap
1988   Producing speech use in nonverbal autistic children by reinforcing attempts. *Journal of Autism and Developmental Disorders* 18:525-538.

Kohler, F.W., P.S. Strain, and D.D. Shearer
1996   Examining levels of social inclusion within an integrated preschool for children with autism. Pp. 305-332 in *Positive Behavioral Support: Including People With Difficult Behavior in the Community*, R.K. Koegel and L.K. Koegel, eds. Baltimore, MD: Paul H. Brookes Publishing Co.

Krug, D.A., J.R. Arick, and P.J. Almond
1980   *Autism Behavior Checklist*. Austin, TX: Pro-Ed.

Lord, C., and R. Paul
1997   Language and communication in autism. Pp. 195-225 in *Handbook of Autism and Pervasive Developmental Disorders (2nd ed.)*. D.J. Cohen and F.R. Volkmar, eds. New York: Riley.

Lord, C., and E. Schopler
1989   The role of age at assessment, developmental level, and test in the stability of intelligence scores in young autistic children. *Journal of Autism and Developmental Disorders* 19:483-499.

Lovaas, O.I.
1987   Behavioral treatment and normal educational and intellectual functioning in young autistic children. *Journal of Consulting and Clinical Psychology* 55:3-9.

Lovaas, O.I., and R.B. Leaf
1981   *Five Video Tapes: Teaching Developmentally Disabled Children*. Austin, TX: Pro-Ed.

Lovaas, O.I., A.B. Ackerman, D. Alexander, P. Firestone, J. Perkins, and D. Young
1981   *Teaching Developmentally Disabled Children: The ME Book*. Austin, TX: Pro-Ed.

Mahler, M.S., F. Pine, and A. Bergman
1975   *The Psychological Birth of the Human Infant.* New York: Basic Books.
Marcus, L., E. Schopler, and C. Lord
2000   TEACCH services for preschool children. In *Preschool Education Programs for Children with Autism*, J.S. Handleman and S.L. Harris, eds. Austin, TX: Pro-Ed.
Marcus, L.M., M. Lansing, C.E. Andrews, and E. Schopler
1978   Improvement of teaching effectiveness in parents of autistic children. *Journal of the American Academy of Child Psychiatry* 17:625-639.
McEachin, J.J., T. Smith, and O.I. Lovaas
1993   Long-term outcome for children with autism who received early intensive behavioral treatment. *American Journal on Mental Retardation* 4:359-372.
McGee, G.G., and T. Daly
1999   Prevention of problem behaviors in preschool children. Pp. 171-196 in *Functional Analysis of Problem Behavior: From Effective Assessment to Effective Support*, C. Repp and R.H. Horner, eds. New York: Wadsworth.
McGee, G.G., P.J. Krantz, and L.E. McClannahan
1985   The facilitative effects of incidental teaching on preposition use by autistic children. *Journal of Applied Behavior Analysis* 18:17-31.
McGee, G.G., H.A. Jacobs, and M.C. Regnier
1993   Preparation of families for incidental teaching and advocacy for their children with autism. *OSERS News in Print* Winter:9-13.
McGee, G.G., T. Daly, and H.A. Jacobs
1994   The Walden preschool. Pp. 127-162 in *Preschool Education Programs for Children with Autism*, S.L. Harris and J.S. Handleman. Austin, TX: Pro-Ed.
McGee, G.G., R.S. Feldman, and M.J. Morrier
1997   Benchmarks of social treatment for children with autism. *Journal of Autism and Developmental Disorders* 27:353-364.
McGee, G.G., M.J. Morrier, and T. Daly
1999   An incidental teaching approach to early intervention for toddlers with autism. *Journal of the Association for the Severely Handicapped* 24:133-146.
2000   The Walden Early Childhood Programs. Pp. 157-190 in *Preschool Education Programs for Children with Autism, 2nd ed.* J.S. Handleman and S.L. Harris, eds. Austin, TX: Pro-Ed.
McGee, G.G., M.C. Almeida, B. Sulzer-Azaroff, and R.S. Feldman
1992   Promoting reciprocal interactions via peer incidental teaching. *Journal of Applied Behavior Analysis* 25:117-126.
Mesibov, G.B.
1993   Treatment outcome is encouraging. *American Journal on Mental Retardation* 97(4):379-380.
1997   Formal and informal measures on the effectiveness of the TEACCH programme. *Autism* 1(1):25-35.
Miller, J.
1981   *Assessing Language Production in Children.* Boston: Allyn and Bacon.
Mundy, P.
1993   Normal versus high-functioning status in children with autism. *American Journal on Mental Retardation* 97:381-384.
Neisworth, J.T., and S. Bagnato
1999   Special issue on autism. *Infants and Young Children* 12.
Newborg, J., J.R. Stock, and L. Wnek
1984   *Battelle Developmental Inventor.* Allen, TX: DLM Teaching Resources.

O'Neill, R.E., R.H. Horner, R.W. Albin, J.R. Sprague, K. Storey, and J.S. Newton
1997   *Functional Assessment and Program Development for Problem Behavior.* Pacific Grove, CA: Brookes/Cole.
Odom, S.L., and P.S. Strain
1984   Peer-mediated approaches to increasing children's social interaction: A review. *American Journal of Orthopsychiatry* 54:544-557.
Ozonoff, S., and K. Cathcart
1998   Effectiveness of a home program intervention for young children with autism. *Journal of Autism and Developmental Disorders* 28(1):25-32.
Palmieri, L.A., L. Valluripalli, R. Arnstein, and R.G. Romanczyk
1998   Use of the Internet for Information Searches: ABA, Autism, and the Web. Paper presented at the 24th annual convention of the Association for Behavior Analysis, Orlando, FL.
Piaget, J.
1966   *Psychology and Intelligence.* Totowa, NJ: Littlefield, Adams.
Rogers, S.J.
1998   Empirically supported comprehensive treatments for young children with autism. *Journal of Clinical Child Psychology* 27:168-179.
Rogers, S.J., and H. Lewis
1988   An effective day treatment model for young children with pervasive developmental disorders. *Journal of the American Academy of Child and Adolescent Psychiatry* 28:207-214.
Rogers S.J., and D.L. DiLalla
1991   A comparative study of the effects of a developmentally based instructional model on young children with autism and young children with other disorders of behavior and development. *Topics in Early Childhood Special Education* 11:29-47.
Rogers, S.J., H.C. Lewis, and K. Reis
1987   An effective procedure for training early special education teams to implement a model program. *Journal of the Division for Early Childhood* 11:180-188.
Rogers, S.J., J.M. Herbison, H.C. Lewis, J. Pantone, and K. Reis
1986   An approach for enhancing the symbolic, communicative, and interpersonal functioning of young children with autism or severe emotional handicaps. *Journal of the Division for Early Childhood* 10:135-148.
Rogers, S.J., T. Hall, D. Osaki, J. Reaven, and J. Herbison
2000   The Denver model: A comprehensive, integrated educational approach to young children with autism and their families. Pp. 95-133 in *Preschool Education Programs for Children with Autism (2nd ed.)*, J.S. Handleman and S.L. Harris, eds. Austin, TX: Pro-Ed.
Romanczyk, R.G.
1984   A case study of microcomputer utilization and staff efficiency: A five year analysis. *Journal of Organizational Behavior Management* 6:141-154.
Romanczyk, R.G., L. Matey, and S.B. Lockshin
1994   The children's unit for treatment and evaluation. Pp 181-223 in *Preschool Education Programs for Children with Autism*, S.L. Harris and J.S. Handleman, eds. Austin, TX: Pro-Ed.
Romanczyk, R.G., S.B. Lockshin, and L. Matey
1998   *The I.G.S. Curriculum—Version 9.* Vestal, NY: CBTA.
2000   The children's unit for treatment and evaluation. Pp. 49-94 in *Preschool Education Programs for Children with Autism (2nd ed.)*, J.S. Handleman and S.L. Harris, eds. Austin, TX: Pro-Ed.

Schafer, D.S., and M.S. Moersch, eds.
   1981   *Developmental Programming for Infants and Young Children.* Ann Arbor: University of Michigan Press.
Schopler, E.
   1995   *Parent Survival Manual: A Guide to Autism Crisis Resolution.* New York: Plenum Press.
Schopler, E., R. Reichler, and M. Lansing
   1980   *Individualized Assessment and Treatment for Autistic and Developmentally Disabled Children: Vol. 2. Teaching Strategies for Parents and Professionals.* Baltimore: University Park Press.
Schopler, E., G.B. Mesibov, and A. Baker
   1982   Evaluation of treatment for autistic children and their parents. *Journal of the American Academy of Child Psychiatry* 21:262-267.
Schopler, E., M. Lansing, and L. Waters
   1983   *Individualized Assessment and Treatment for Autistic and Developmentally Disabled Children: Vol. 3. Teaching Activities for Autistic Children.* Austin, TX: Pro-Ed.
Schopler, E., R. Reichler, and B.R. Renner
   1988   *The Childhood Autism Rating Scale (CARS).* Austin, TX: Pro-Ed.
Sheinkopf, S.J., and B. Siegel
   1998   Home-based behavioral treatment of young children with autism. *Journal of Autism and Developmental Disabilities* 28:15-23.
Smith, T.
   1999   Outcome of early intervention for children with autism. *Clinical Psychology: Science and Practice.* 6:33-49.
Smith, T., P.A. Donahoe, and B.J. Davis
   2000a The UCLA Young Autism Project. Pp. 29-48 in *Preschool Education Programs for Children with Autism.* J.S. Handleman and S.L. Harris, eds. Austin, TX: Pro-Ed.
Smith, T., A.D. Groen, and J.W. Wynn
   2000b A randomized trial of intensive early intervention for children with pervasive developmental disorder. *American Journal on Mental Retardation* 5(4):269-285.
Sparrow, S.S., D.A. Balla, and D.V. Cichetti
   1984   *Vineland Adaptive Behavior Scales. Interview Edition: Survey Form Manual.* Circle Pines, MN: American Guidance Service.
Strain, P.S.
   1987   Comprehensive evaluation of young autistic children. *Topics in Early Childhood Special Education* 7:97-110.
Strain, P.S., and L. Cordisco
   1994   LEAP preschool. Pp. 225-244 in *Preschool Education Programs for Children with Autism,* S.L. Harris and J.S. Handleman, eds. Austin, TX: Pro-Ed.
Strain, P.S., and M. Hoyson
   2000   On the need for longitudinal, intensive social skill intervention: LEAP follow-up outcomes for children with autism as a case-in-point. *Topics in Early Childhood Special Education* 20(2):116-122.
Strain, P.S., M. Hoyson, and B. Jamieson
   1985   Normally developing preschoolers as intervention agents for autistic-like children: Effects on class deportment and social interaction. *Journal of the Division for Early Childhood* Spring:105-115.
Strain, P.S., G.G. McGee, and F. Kohler
   2001   Inclusion of children with autism in early intervention settings: An examination of rationale, myths, and procedures. *Early Childhood Inclusion: Focus on Change,* M.J. Guralnick, ed. Baltimore, MD: Paul H. Brookes Publishing.

Sulzer-Azaroff, B., and G.R. Mayer
   1991   *Behavior Analysis for Lasting Change.* Chicago: Holt, Rinehart, and Winston.
Taylor, B.A., and S.L. Harris
   1995   Teaching children with autism to seek information: Acquisition of novel informa-
           tion and generalization of responding. *Journal of Applied Behavior Analysis* 28(1):3-
           14.
Taylor, J., and R. Romanczyk
   1994   Generating hypotheses about the function of student problem behavior by ob-
           serving teacher behavior. *Journal of Applied Behavior Analysis* 27:251-265.
Taylor, J., M. Ekdahl, R.G. Romanczyk, and M. Miller
   1994   Escape behavior in task situations: Task versus social antecedents. *Journal of
           Autism and Developmental Disorders* 24:331-344.
Thorndike, R.L., E.P. Hagen, and J.M. Sattler
   1986   *Stanford-Binet Intelligence Scale (4th ed.).* Chicago: Riverside.
Venter, A., C. Lord, and E. Schopler
   1992   A follow-up study of high-functioning autistic children. *Journal of Child Psychol-
           ogy and Psychiatry* 33:489-507.
Watson, L., C. Lord, B. Schaffer, and E. Schopler
   1989   *Teaching Spontaneous Communication to Autistic and Developmentally Handicapped
           Children.* New York: Irvington Press.
Wolery, M.R.
   1983   Proportional Change Index: An alternative for comparing child change data. *Ex-
           ceptional Children* 50(2):167-170.
Wolery, M.R., and A.N. Garfinkle
  *2000   Measures in Intervention Research with Young Children Who Have Autism. Pa-
           per presented at the Second Workshop of the Committee on Educational Inter-
           ventions for Children with Autism, National Research Council, April 12, 2000.
Zimmerman, I.E., V.G. Steiner, and R.E. Pond
   1979   *Preschool Language Scale.* Columbus, OH: Merrill.

CHAPTER 13

Gallagher, J.
   1994   Policy designed for diversity: New initiatives for children with disabilities. Pp.
           336-350 in *Implementing Early Intervention*, D. Bryant and M. Graham, eds. New
           York: The Guilford Press.
Hurth, J., K. Whaley, D. Kates, and E. Shaw
  *2000   Enhancing Services for Young Children with Autism Spectrum Disorder (ASD)
           and Their Families: Infrastructure, Training, and Collaborative Funding. Paper
           presented at the Second Workshop of the Committee on Educational Interven-
           tions for Children with Autism, National Research Council, April 12, 2000.
Kirk, S., J. Gallagher, and N. Anastasiow
   2000   *Educating Exceptional Children, 9th Edition.* Boston: Houghton Mifflin.
Lovaas, I.
   1987   Behavioral treatment and normal educational and intellectual functioning in
           young autistic children. *Journal of Consulting and Clinical Psychology* 55:3-9.
Mandlawitz, M.
  *1999   The Impact of the Legal System on Educational Programming for Young Chil-
           dren with Autism Spectrum Disorder. Paper presented at the First Workshop of
           the Committee on Educational Interventions for Children with Autism, National
           Research Council, December 13-14, 1999.

CHAPTER 14

Anderson, S.R., and R.G. Romanczyk
  1999 Early intervention for young children with autism: Continuum-based behavioral models. *Journal of the Association for the Severely Handicapped* 24:162-173.
Council for Exceptional Children
  2000 *What Every Special Educator Must Know: The Standards for the Preparation and Licensure of Special Educators.* Reston, VA: Council for Exceptional Children.
French, N.K.
  1997 Management of paraeducators. In *Supervising Paraeducators In School Settings: A Team Approach*, A. Pickett and K. Gerlach, eds. Austin, TX: Pro-Ed.
Gallagher, J., and R. Clifford
  2000 The missing support infrastructure in early childhood. *Early Childhood Research and Practice* 2(1):1-24.
Harris, S.L., and J.S. Handleman
  1994 *Preschool Education Programs for Children with Autism.* Austin, TX: Pro-Ed.
Hurth, J., K.T. Whaley, D. Kates, and E. Shaw
  *2000 Enhancing Services for Young Children with Autism Spectrum Disorder and Their Families: Infrastructure, Training, and Collaborative Funding. Paper presented at the Second Workshop of the Committee on Educational Interventions for Children with Autism, National Research Council, April 12, 2000.
Lovaas, O.I.
  1987 Behavioral treatment and normal educational and intellectual functioning in young autistic children. *Journal of Consulting and Clinical Psychology* 55:3-9.
Marcus, L., E. Schopler, and C. Lord
  2000 TEACCH services for preschool children. In *Preschool Education Programs for Children with Autism*, J.S. Handleman and S.L. Harris(eds.) Austin, TX: Pro-Ed.
McClannahan, L.E., and P.J. Krantz
  2000 The Princeton Child Development Institute. Pp. 107-126 in *Preschool Education Programs for Children with Autism*, J.S. Handleman and S. Harris (eds.). Austin, TX: Pro-Ed.
McGee, G., M. Morrier, and T. Daly
  1999 An incidental teaching approach to early intervention for toddlers with autism. *Journal of the Association for Persons with Severe Handicaps* 24:133-146.
Office of Special Education Programs
  1999 *Twenty First Annual Report to Congress on the Implementation of the Individuals with Disabilities Education Act.* Washington, DC: U.S. Department of Education.
Pickett, A.
  1996 *A State of the Art Report on Paraeducators in Education and Related Services.* National Resource Center for Paraprofessionals in Education and Related Services, Center for Advanced Study in Education. New York: The Graduate School and University Center, City University of New York.
Powers, M.D.
  1994 Administrative issues involving behavioral approaches in autism. Pp. 39-54 in *Behavioral Issues in Autism: Current Issues in Autism*, E. Schopler and G.B. Mesibov (Eds.). New York: Plenum Press.
Rogers, S.J., T. Hall, D. Osaki, J. Reaven, and J. Herbison
  2000 The Denver model: A comprehensive, integrated educational approach to young children with autism and their families. Pp. 95-133 in *Preschool Education Programs for Children with Autism (2nd ed.)*, J.S. Handleman and S.L. Harris, eds. Austin, TX: Pro-Ed.
Skelton, K.
  1997 *Paraprofessionals in Education.* Albany, NY: Delmar Publishers.

Smith, T., A.D. Groen, and J. Wynn
2000 Randomized trial of intensive early intervention for children with pervasive developmental disorder. *American Journal on Mental Retardation* 105(4):269-285.
Strain, P.S., and M. Hoyson
2000 On the need for longitudinal, intensive social skill intervention: LEAP follow-up outcomes for children with autism as a case-in-point. *Topics in Early Childhood Special Education* 20(2):116-122.

CHAPTER 15

Baird, G., T. Charman, S. Baron-Cohen, A. Cox, J. Sweetenham, S. Wheelwright, and A. Drew
2000 A screening instrument for autism at 18 months of age: A 6-Year follow-up study. *Journal of the American Academy Child Adolescent Psychiatry* 39(6):694-702.
Barlow, D.E., and J. Hersen
1984 *Single Case Experimental Designs: Strategies for Studying Behavior Change, 2nd ed.* New York: Pergamon Press.
Baron-Cohen, S., J. Allen, and C. Gillberg
1992 Can autism be detected at 18 months? The needle, the haystack, and the CHAT. *British Journal of Psychiatry* 161:839-43.
Berument, S.K., M. Rutter, C. Lord, A. Pickles, and A. Bailey
1999 Autism screening questionnaire: Diagnostic validity. *British Journal of Psychiatry* 175:444-451.
Billingsley, F.F., O.R. White, and R. Munson
1980 Procedural reliability: A rationale and an example. *Behavioral Assessment* 2:229-241.
Bryk, A.S., and S.W. Raudenbush
1987 Application of hierarchical linear models to assessment of change. *Psychological Bulletin* 101:147-158.
Burchinal, M.R.
1999 Statistical methods for describing developmental patterns. *Early Education and Development* 10:83-99.
Burchinal, M.R., and M.I. Appelbaum
1991 Estimating individual developmental functions: Methods and their assumptions. *Child Development* 62:23-43.
Burchinal, M.R., D.B. Bailey, and P. Synder
1994 Using growth curve analysis to evaluate change in longitudinal investigations. *Journal of Early Intervention* 18:422-442.
Campbell, D.T., and J.C. Stanley
1963 Experimental and quasi-experimental designs for research on teaching. In *Handbook of Research on Teaching*, N. Gage, ed. Chicago: Rand McNally.
Cohen, J.
1988 *Statistical Power Analysis for the Behavioral Sciences, 2nd ed.* New York: Academic Press.
Cole, K.N., P.S. Dale, and P.E. Mills
1991 Individual differences in language delayed children's responses to direct and interaction preschool instruction. *Topics in Early Childhood Special Education* 11:99-124.
Cook T.D., and D.T. Campbell
1979 *Quasi-Experimentation: Design and Analysis Issues for Field Settings.* Chicago: Rand McNally.

Dunst, C.J., and C.M. Trivette
  1994   Methodological considerations and strategies for studying the long-term effects of early intervention. Pp. 277-313 in *Developmental Follow-Up: Concepts, Domains, and Methods,* S.L. Friedman and C.H. Haywood, eds. San Diego: Academic Press, Inc

Fenske, E.C., S. Zalenski, P.J. Krantz, and L.E. McClannahan
  1985   Age at intervention and treatment outcome for autistic children in a comprehensive treatment program. *Analysis and Intervention in Developmental Disabilities* 5:49-58.

Filipek, P.A., P.J. Accardo, S. Ashwal, G.T. Baranek, E.H. Cook, Jr., and G. Dawson
  2000   Practice parameter: Screening and diagnosis of autism. *Neurology* 55(4):468-479.

Fombonne, E.
  *1999   Epidemiological Findings on Autism and Related Developmental Disorders. Paper presented at the First Workshop of the Committee on Educational Interventions for Children with Autism, National Research Council, December 13-14, 1999.

Garbarino, J., and B. Ganzel
  2000   The human ecology of early risk. In *Handbook of Early Intervention, 2nd Edition,* J. Shonkoff and S. Meisels, eds. New York: Cambridge University Press.

Gilliam, J.E.
  1995   *Gilliam Autism Rating Scale.* Austin, TX: Pro-Ed.

Goldstein, H.
  *1999   Communication Intervention for Children with Autism: A Review of Treatment Efficacy. Paper presented at the First Workshop of the Committee on Educational Interventions for Children with Autism, National Research Council, December 13-14, 1999. Department of Communication Sciences, Florida State University.

Guralnick, M.J.
  1997   Second-generation research in field of early intervention. In *The Effectiveness of Early Intervention,* M. Guralnick, ed. Baltimore: Paul H. Brookes Publishing.

Hall, G.S., and S.F. Louchs
  1977   A developmental model for determining whether treatment is actually implemented. *American Journal of Educational Research* 14:263-276.

Harris, S.L., and J.S. Handleman
  2000   Age and IQ intake as predictors of placement for young children with autism: A four and six year follow-up. *Journal of Autism and Developmental Disorders* 30:137-149.

Harris, S.L., J.S. Handleman, R. Gordon, B. Kristoff, and R. Fuentes
  1991   Changes in cognitive and language functioning of preschool children with autism. *Journal of Autism and Developmental Disorders* 20:281-290.

Hatton, D.D., D.B. Bailey, M.R. Burchinal, and K.A. Ferrell
  1997   Developmental growth curves of preschool children with vision impairment. *Child Development* 68:788-806.

Horner, R.H., E.G. Carr, P.S. Strain, A.W. Todd, and H.K. Reed
  *2000   Problem Behavior Interventions for Young Children with Autism: A Research Synthesis. Paper presented at the Second Workshop of the Committee on Educational Interventions for Children with Autism, National Research Council, April 12, 2000. Department of Special Education, University of Oregon.

Hoyson, M., B. Jamieson, and P.S. Strain
  1984   Individualized group instruction of normally developing and autistic-like children: The LEAP curriculum. *Journal of the Division for Early Childhood* 8:157-172.

Jocelyn, L.J., O.G. Casiro, D. Beattie, J. Bow, and J. Kneisz
  1998   Treatment of children with autism: A randomized controlled trial to evaluate a caregiver-based intervention program in community-day-care centers. *Journal of Developmental and Behavioral Pediatrics* 19:326-334.
Kasari, C.
  *2000   Assessing Change in Early Intervention Programs for Children with Autism. Paper presented at the Second Workshop of the Committee on Educational Interventions for Children with Autism, National Research Council, April 12, 2000. Graduate School of Education and Information Studies, University of California at Los Angeles.
Kazdin, A.
  1982   *Single-Case Research Designs: Methods for Clinical and Applied Settings.* New York: Oxford University Press.
Krug, D.A., J. Arick, and P. Almond
  1980   Behavior checklist for identifying severely handicapped individuals with high levels of autistic behavior. *Journal of Child Psychology and Psychiatry and Allied Disciplines* 21(3):221-229.
LEAP Preschool and Outreach Project
  1999   *Quality Program Guidelines.* Unpublished fidelity of treatment checklist. Denver, CO: Author.
Leinhardt, G.
  1980   Modeling and measuring educational treatment in evaluation. *Review of Educational Research* 50:393-420.
LeLaurin, K., and M. Wolery
  1992   Research standards in early intervention: Defining, describing, and measuring the independent variable. *Journal of Early Intervention* 16:275-287.
Lifter, K., B. Sultzer-Azaroff, S.R. Anderson, and G.E. Cowdery
  1993   Teaching play activities to preschool children with disabilities: The importance of developmental considerations. *Journal of Early Intervention* 17:139-159.
Lonigan, C.J., J.C. Elbert, and S.B. Johnson
  1998   Empirically supported psychosocial interventions for child: An overview. *Journal of Clinical Child Psychology* 27:138-145.
Lord, C.
  1997   Diagnostic instruments in autism spectrum disorder. In *Handbook of Autism and Pervasive Developmental Disorders, 2nd ed*, D. Cohen and F. Volkmar, eds. New York: John Wiley.
Lord, C., M. Rutter, and A. Le Couteur
  1993   Using the ADI—R to diagnose autism in preschool children. *Infant Mental Health Journal* 14(3):234-252.
Lord, C., S. Risi, L. Lambrecht, E.H. Cook, B.L. Leventhal, P.C. DiLavore, A. Pickles, and M. Rutter
  2000   The autism diagnostic observation schedule-generic: A standard measure of social and communication deficits associated with the spectrum of autism. *Journal of Autism and Developmental Disorders* 30(3):205-233.
McConnell, S.R.
  *1999   Interventions to Facilitate Social Interaction for Young Children With Autism: Review of Available Research and Recommendations for Future Research. Paper presented at the First Workshop of the Committee on Educational Interventions for Children with Autism, National Research Council, December 13-14, 1999. Department of Educational Psychology, University of Minnesota.

McEachin, J.J., T. Smith, and O.I. Lovaas
   1993   Long-term outcomes for children with autism who received early intensive be-
            havioral treatment. *American Journal on Mental Retardation* 97:359-372.
Minshew, N.J., J.A. Sweeney, and M.L. Bauman
   1997   Neurological aspects of autism. In *Handbook of Autism and Pervasive Developmen-
            tal Disorders, 2nd ed.* D. Cohen and F. Volkmar, eds. New York: John Wiley.
Rogers, S.J.
   1998   Empirically supported comprehensive treatments for young children with au-
            tism. *Journal of Clinical Child Psychology* 27:168-179.
Rogers, S.J., and D. DiLalla
   1991   Comparative study of a developmentally based preschool curriculum on young
            children with autism and young children with other disorders of behavior and
            development. *Topics in Early Childhood Special Education* 11:29-48.
Schopler, E., R. Reichler, and B. Rochen-Renner
   1988   *The Childhood Autism Rating Scale (CARS).* Los Angeles: Western Psychological
            Services.
Schwartz, I.S., and D.M. Baer
   1991   Social validity assessment: Is current practice state of the art? *Journal of Applied
            Behavior Analysis* 24: 189-204.
Schwartz, I.S., S.R. Sandall, A.N. Garfinkle, and J. Bauer
   1998   Outcomes for children with autism: Three case studies. *Topics in Early Childhood
            Special Education* 18:132-143.
Siegel B.
   1998   Early Screening and Diagnosis in Autism Spectrum Disorder: The Pervasive
            Developmental Disorders Screening Test. Paper presented at the NIH State of
            the Science in Autism: Screening and Diagnosis Working Conference, June 15-17,
            National Institutes of Health, Bethesda, MD.
Sigman, M., and E. Ruskin
   1999   Continuity and changes in the social competence of children with autism, Down
            syndrome, and developmental delays. *Monographs of the Society for Research in
            Child Development* 64(1):v-114.
Smith, T., A.D. Groen, and J.W. Wynn
   2000   A randomized trial of intensive early intervention for children with pervasive
            developmental disorder. *American Journal on Mental Retardation* 5(4):269-285.
Stone, W.L.
   1998   Descriptive Information About the Screening Tool for Autism in Two-Year-Olds
            (STAT). Paper presented at the NIH State of the Science in Autism: Screening
            and Diagnosis Working Conference, June 15-17, National Institutes of Health,
            Bethesda, MD.
Stone, W.L., E.E. Coonrod, and O.Y. Ousley
   2000   Brief report: Screening tool for autism in two-year-olds (STAT): Development
            and preliminary data. *Journal of Autism and Developmental Disorders* 30(6):607-
            612.
Strain, P.S.
   2000   Personal Communication to the Committee on Educational Interventions, Na-
            tional Research Council, Washington, DC.
Strain, P.S., and M. Hoyson
   2000   On the need for longitudinal, intensive social skill intervention: LEAP follow-up
            outcomes for children as a case in point. *Topics in Early Childhood Special Educa-
            tion* 20:116-122.

Tanguay, P.E., J. Robertson, and A. Derrick
   1998   A dimensional classification of autism spectrum disorder by social communication domains. *Journal of the American Academy of Child and Adolescent Psychiatry* 37(3):271-277.
Tawney, J.W., and D.L. Gast
   1983   *Single Subject Research in Special Education.* Columbus, OH: Merrill Publishing.
Wetherby, A.M., and C.A. Prutting
   1984   Profiles of communicative and cognitive-social abilities in autism. *Journal of Speech and Hearing Research* 27:364-377.
Willett, J.B., and A.G. Sayer
   1994   Using covariance structure analysis to detect correlates and predictors of individual change over time. *Psychological Bulletin* 116:363-381.
Wolery, M., and A.N. Garfinkle
   *2000   Measures in Intervention Research with Young Children Who Have Autism. Paper presented at the Second Workshop of the Committee on Educational Interventions for Children with Autism, National Research Council, April 12, 2000.
Wolf, M.M.
   1978   Social validity: The case for subjective measurement or how applied behavior analysis is finding its heart. *Journal of Applied Behavior Analysis* 11:203-214.
Yirmiya, N., M. Sigman and B.J. Freeman
   1994   Comparison between diagnostic instruments for identifying high-functioning children with autism. *Journal of Autism and Developmental Disorders* 24(3):281-291.

Biographical Sketches

CATHERINE LORD (*Chair*) is a professor in the Department of Psychology at the University of Michigan and the director of the university's Autism and Communication Disorders Center. The center provides direct assessments to families of children with autistic spectrum disorders and consultations to schools and early childhood programs. She is a clinical psychologist with interests in diagnosis, social and communication development, and intervention in autism spectrum disorders. She is best known for her work in longitudinal studies of children and adults with autism and the development of diagnostic measures used in both practice and research. Previously, she worked at the University of Chicago, the University of North Carolina, the University of Minnesota, the University of Alberta, the London Medical Research Council Child and Adolescent Psychiatry Unit, and Harvard University (Children's Hospital).

MARIE BRISTOL-POWER is Special Assistant for Autism in the Office of the Director of the National Institute of Child Health and Human Development (NICHD) at the National Institutes of Health (NIH). She is also coordinator of the NICHD/NIDCD Network on the Neurobiology and Genetics of Autism: Collaborative Programs of Excellence in Autism (CPEAs), ten sites that involve more than 25 universities and more than 2,000 in research on the etiology, pathophysiology, brain structure and function, and developmental course of autism spectrum disorders. Prior to joining the National Institutes of Health, she was on the faculty of the School of Medicine at the University of North Carolina at Chapel Hill.

Her work has focused on research and clinical care in autism, including policy issues and the integration of research and practice.

JOANNE M. CAFIERO is a special education consultant and augmentative communication and assistive technology specialist. She is a faculty member of the Department of Special Education at Johns Hopkins University. She also consults with several school systems in developing state-of-the-art, eclectic, assistive technology programs for children with autism spectrum disorders, and she supports practitioners and families whose lives involve children with autism. She is currently conducting research on how children with severe communication impairments and autism learn literacy and language, what models for instruction are most effective, and how to apply research data to practice.

PAULINE A. FILIPEK is associate professor in residence of pediatrics and neurology at the College of Medicine at the University of California, Irvine (UCI), codirector of the UCI Autism Research Project. She is a child neurologist who has specific clinical and research interests in the developmental disorders, particularly autism. She codeveloped a method of using magnetic resonance imaging to investigate developmental brain anomalies in developmental disorders, primarily autism, learning disabilities, and attention deficit hyperactivity disorder. She was the chair of the American Academy of Neurology/Child Neurology Society (AAN/CNS) committee that established the Practice Parameter: Screening and Diagnosis of Autism, and will reconvene another AAN/CNS committee in fall 2001 to establish the Practice Parameter: Treatment of Autism.

JAMES J. GALLAGHER is a Kenan professor of education and senior investigator at the Frank Porter Graham Child Development Center at the University of North Carolina (UNC) at Chapel Hill. He was the first director of the Bureau of Education for the Handicapped in the U.S. Office of Education and also Deputy Assistant Secretary for Planning, Research and Evaluation in the U.S. Department of Health, Education, and Welfare. He served for 17 years as director of the Frank Porter Graham Center at UNC-Chapel Hill. He has served as the president of the Council for Exceptional Children and is the senior author of a popular textbook *Educating Exceptional Children*, now in its tenth edition.

SANDRA L. HARRIS is a professor in the Department of Clinical Psychology of the Graduate School of Applied and Professional Psychology at Rutgers University, and the founder and executive director of the Douglass Developmental Disabilities Center at Rutgers. The center provides services for people with autism across the life span. Her primary research and clinical activities involve the treatment of autism and other severe developmental disabilities. In addition to the use of behavioral techniques for the treatment of autism, she also trains the parents and families of children and adolescents with autism in the use of applied behavioral analysis technology and provides family support resources.

ALAN M. LESLIE is a professor of psychology and cognitive science, Department of Psychology and Center for Cognitive Science, at Rutgers University. He directs the Cognitive Development Laboratory at Rutgers, New Brunswick, where his current research focuses on normal and abnormal cognitive development. Formerly, he was a Medical Research Council Senior Scientist at the University of London, England, where he originated the 'theory of mind' impairment hypothesis for autism. He has been a Leverhulme European Scholar, a visiting professor at University of California-Los Angeles, University of Chicago, and the Free University of Madrid. He sits on the editorial boards of several cognitive science journals, and is on the advisory board of the Association for Science in Autism Treatment.

GAIL G. MCGEE is an associate professor of psychiatry and behavioral sciences at the Emory University School of Medicine. Her work emphasizes research and treatment applications of incidental teaching procedures to children with autism and her current research focuses on early autism intervention, language acquisition, and typical and atypical social behavior. She directs the Emory Autism Resource Center, Georgia's statewide autism center, which provides interdisciplinary training, family support, and diagnosis and treatment to children and adults with autism. She also founded and directs the Walden Early Childhood Programs, which offer enriched early education to toddlers, preschoolers, and prekindergarten-aged children with autism who are included with a majority of typical peers.

JAMES MCGEE is a study director and senior research associate at the National Academies' National Research Council (NRC), with the Board on Behavioral, Cognitive, and Sensory Sciences. He also supports other NRC panels and committees in the areas of applied psychology and education. Prior to joining the NRC, he held scientific, technical, and management positions in applied psychology at IBM, RCA, General Electric, General Dynamics, and United Technologies corporations. He has also taught undergraduate and graduate courses in general, developmental, and applied psychology at several colleges; is certified as a secondary education teacher of social studies; and has taught at both the elementary and secondary levels.

SAMUEL L. ODOM is Otting professor of special education in the School of Education at Indiana University in Bloomington. His research has examined approaches to promoting the social competence of young children with autism, classroom ecology in inclusive early childhood settings, and effective practices in early childhood special education. His educational background is in special education, applied behavior analysis, and developmental psychology.

SALLY J. ROGERS is a professor of psychiatry at the University of Colorado Health Sciences Center and adjunct professor of psychology at the University of Denver. The body of her research has focused on the development of cognitive and social processes of infants and young children with developmental disabilities, including autism, mental retardation, and blindness. She has also provided clinical care to families and children throughout her career. Her current research is focused on defining the early phenotype and developmental course of autism, as well as examining effects of early intervention.

FRED R. VOLKMAR is professor of child psychiatry in the child study center of the Yale University School of Medicine. His research is broadly focused on issues of developmental psychopathology in children with severe disturbances of development, including autism and mental retardation. His current research studies include the neuropsychology, family genetics, and neuroanatomical correlates of higher functioning autism and Asperger's syndrome.

AMY WETHERBY is an L.L. Schendel professor of communication disorders at Florida State University and executive director of the Florida State University Center for Autism and Related Disabilities. She has had over 20 years of clinical experience in the design and implementation of communication programs for children with autism and severe communication impairments and is a fellow of the American Speech-Language-Hearing Association. Her research has focused on communicative and cognitive-social aspects of language problems in children with autism, and more recently, on the early identification of children with communicative impairments. She is a coauthor of the *Communication and Symbolic Behavior Scales* (with Barry Prizant).

Index

A

Adaptive behavior, 5, 12, 27, 40-41, 47, 103-114, 116, 184, 212
  see also Generalization of learning; Maintenance of behaviors and skills
  age factors, 104, 105-107, 111-113
  comprehensive programs, 144, 169
  independence, 5, 216, 218
  professional education, 184
  self-help, 5, 162, 167, 216, 218
  toilet training, 103, 105-106, 107, 110, 114
Adults
  see also Parental factors; Teachers
  autistic, 36, 37-38, 43, 48, 71, 104, 106
  behavioral problems, 117, 213
  interactions with, general, 6, 49, 56, 59, 68-69, 70, 73, 76-77, 78, 80, 81, 138, 218, 219
  comprehensive programs, 142, 157
Advocacy, 13, 181-182, 223
  see also Litigation
  parental, 32, 36-37, 39, 146, 214-215, 222
Age factors, 37-38, 71, 76-77, 84, 85, 88, 216
  see also Adults; Developmental theory and approaches; Early intervention, general; Peer interactions

adaptive behavior, 104, 105-107, 111-113
assessment of children, 29, 30, 74
behavior problems, 116, 117-118
communication and symbolic abilities, 50, 54, 123, 160
diagnosis, 3-4, 23, 25, 93, 94, 195-197, 212
interventions, 6, 7, 29, 43, 71, 74, 144-145, 160, 163, 167-168, 169, 170, 171-172, 206, 207, 210, 220, 221
IQ and, 47, 71, 201, 206
older children with autism, 95, 104, 105-106, 116, 144-145
  parents of, 36, 37-38, 78-79
onset of autism, 2, 11, 211
screening, 4, 25, 195-197
sensory/motor deficits, 93, 94, 97, 110
Aggressive behavior, 49, 115, 116, 118, 125, 131, 145, 213
  self-injurious behavior, 49, 115, 116, 117-118, 123, 125, 128-129
  tantrums, 115, 123, 125, 145, 213
Alternative communication, see Augmentative and alternative communication
American Academy of Neurology, 14
American Psychological Association, 14
American Speech-Language-Hearing Association, 62, 188
Americans with Disabilities Act, 179

Applied behavior analysis, 34, 35, 119, 120, 125-126, 131, 142, 148-149, 156, 184, 225
Asperger's Disorder, 2, 24, 29-30, 85, 95, 212
Assessment, 2, 4, 7, 26-30, 156-158, 184-185, 211-214, 220-221
  see also Diagnosis; Outcomes; Screening
  adaptive behavior, 107-110
  age factors, 29, 30, 74
  behavioral problems, 118-132
    applied behavior analysis, 34, 35, 119, 120, 125-126, 131, 142, 148-149, 156, 184, 225
    functional assessment, 15, 27, 48, 120, 122-124, 127, 130, 131-132, 134, 135, 213
  communication and language deficits, 26, 27, 28-30, 51-52, 74, 167
  comprehensive programs, 142, 144, 156-158, 167
  functional, 15, 27, 48, 120, 122-124, 127, 130, 131-132, 134, 135, 213
  growth curve analysis, 207-208, 210
  intelligence, 27-28, 82, 90, 108, 193
    IQ scores, 5, 44, 70, 84-87, 88, 90, 108, 168, 170-171, 172, 184, 201, 217
    mental retardation, 1, 2, 24, 27, 82, 84-85, 104, 105, 106, 125, 129, 176-177, 184
  language factors, 27, 28, 29-30, 31, 52, 138-139, 167, 179, 215-216
  multidisciplinary, 4, 23-24, 28, 30
  parental factors, 27, 28, 29-30, 31, 52, 138-139, 167, 179, 215-216
  siblings of autistic children, 38-39
  videotapes, 94, 155, 156, 157-158, 171
Assessment, Evaluation, and Programming System, 74
Assistive technology, 2, 3, 12, 56-57, 59-63, 103, 136, 184
Association for Persons with Severe Handicaps, 141
Attachment and attachment constructs, 67
Atypical autism, 3, 213
  prevalence, 24
Auditory perception, 30, 31-32, 42, 83, 85, 98, 99-101, 123, 131, 212
Augmentative and alternative communication, 51, 55, 56-63, 136-137
Autism Behavior Checklist, 196

Autism Diagnostic Interview-Revised, 85, 196, 197
Autism Diagnostic Observation Schedule, 197, 198
Autism Screening Questionnaire, 25-26
Autism Society of America, 188, 194, 228
Autistic Spectrum Disorders Support Systems, 223
Aversive approaches, 106, 110-111, 121-122, 123, 128, 133, 134-135, 146, 162, 163, 181

B

Battelle Developmental Inventory, 74
Bed wetting, see Toilet training
Behavioral problems, 5, 11, 12, 15, 49, 68, 69-70, 78, 104, 115-132, 194
  see also Adaptive behavior; Aggressive behavior; Imitation; Maintenance of behaviors and skills; Pivotal behavior
  adults, 117, 213
  age factors, 116, 117-118
  applied behavior analysis, 34, 35, 119, 120, 125-126, 131, 142, 148-149, 156, 184, 225
  assessment, 27, 28, 30-31, 118-132
    applied behavior analysis, 34, 35, 119, 120, 125-126, 131, 142, 148-149, 156, 184, 225
    functional assessment, 15, 27, 48, 120, 122-124, 127, 130, 131-132, 134, 135, 213
  auditory perception and, 30-31
  classification of, 115-116
  clinical practice guidelines, 118-119
  communication deficits and, 49, 55
  comprehensive programs, 116, 119-120, 125, 143, 144-145, 146, 147-149, 150, 157, 163, 169
  developmental approaches, 12, 117, 119, 126
  diagnosis, 2, 3-4, 25, 196, 211-212
  family/parental factors, 3-4, 69-70, 115, 116, 120, 121-122, 123
  functional assessment, 15, 27, 48, 120, 122-124, 127, 130, 131-132, 134, 135, 213
  interventions, general, 6, 40-41, 42-43, 68, 71-73, 78, 79-81, 110-114, 118-137, 139, 194, 195, 210, 218

applied behavior analysis, 34, 35, 119, 120, 125-126, 131, 142, 148-149, 156, 184, 225
aversive approaches, 106, 110-111, 121-122, 123, 128, 133, 134-135, 146, 162, 163, 181
drug treatment, 116, 128-131
functional assessment, 15, 27, 48, 120, 122-124, 127, 130, 131-132, 134, 135, 213
incidental learning, 6, 54, 78, 119, 134, 150, 164, 184
Walden Early Childhood Programs, 79, 112, 136, 145, 146, 148-149, 150, 153, 154, 155, 160, 161-162, 162, 165, 171
naturalistic teaching and learning, 15, 42, 134, 142, 148, 149, 159, 184
professional education, 183, 184
neurobiological factors, 116, 117-118
self-injurious behavior, 49, 115, 116, 117-118, 123, 125, 128-129
self-stimulatory behavior, 55, 105, 111, 213
sleeping, 107-108
toilet training, 103, 105-106, 107, 110, 114
stereotypic behavior, 61, 94, 96, 97, 98, 117, 118, 145, 176-177
tantrums, 115, 123, 125, 145, 213
teachers response to, 116, 130
time factors, 116-117, 119, 120, 123, 134, 163
Boys, *see* Gender factors
Brain, *see* Neurobiological factors

C

CARS, *see* Childhood Autism Rating Scale
Centers for Disease Control and Prevention, 208
Central coherence theory, 89
Checklist for Autism in Toddlers (CHAT), 25, 26, 196
Child-centered approaches, 63
Childhood Autism Rating Scale (CARS), 27, 156, 169, 196, 197
Childhood disintegrative disorder, 3, 12, 213
Children's Unit, 142, 146, 148, 150, 154, 155, 158, 161, 163-164, 165, 167

Classification issues, 2-3, 13, 25, 27-28, 69, 176-177
see also Assessment; Diagnosis
behavioral problems, 115-116
features of autism, 11-12, 212
historical perspectives, 31, 32-33, 47
The Clinical Practice Guidelines for Autism/ Persuasive Development Disorders, 118-119
Clinical trials, 6, 8, 15-17, 90, 131, 194, 197-198, 199-201, 204, 218-219, 222-223
Clonidine, 129
Cognitive deficits, 5, 82-92, 212
see also Communication deficits; Language factors
comprehensive programs, 142, 144, 145, 156-157, 162, 168-169, 172
Denver Model, 80, 142, 145-146, 147, 150, 153, 155-156, 157, 159, 160, 163, 164, 165, 167, 188, 189
executive functioning, 84, 89
intelligence, 27-28, 82, 90, 108, 193
see also Mental retardation
intelligence quotients (IQs), 5, 44, 70, 84-87, 88, 90, 108, 170-171, 172, 184, 201, 217
age factors, 47, 71, 201, 206
interventions, general, 6, 86, 90-92, 220, 229
joint attention and, 83, 89
memory, 57, 83, 85, 88, 89
reading skills, 62-63, 78-79, 83, 91
Collaborative Program for Excellence in Autism, 209
Communication deficits, 1, 5, 12, 47-65, 71, 79, 83, 105, 115, 205
see also Auditory perception; Joint attention; Language factors; Social factors
age factors, 50, 54, 123, 160
assessment, 26, 27, 28-30, 51-52, 74, 167
augmentative and alternative communication, 51, 55, 56-63, 136-137
communication training, 121
comprehensive programs, 142, 144, 149, 160, 162, 167
diagnosis, 25, 26, 47, 212
facilitated communication, 61-62
familial factors, 47

functional communication, 49-50, 61-62, 64-65, 123, 160, 221
  initiation of communication/ spontaneous communication, 6, 41, 47, 48, 49, 53, 54, 55, 64, 70, 71, 161, 169, 204, 221
goals of education, 40-41, 50-51, 72
historical perspectives, 47, 48
nonverbal communication, 3, 5, 25, 30, 47, 48, 58-59, 63-64, 69, 84, 85, 88, 95, 123, 214
  augmentative and alternative communication, 51, 55, 56-63
  comprehensive programs, 142, 144
pivotal behaviors, 53, 55-56
professional education, 184, 185
spontaneous, 6, 41, 47, 48, 49, 53, 54, 55, 64, 70, 71, 161, 169, 204, 221
symbol use, 29, 49, 50, 54, 55-56, 58, 82, 123, 142, 160, 218
symbolic play, 42, 49-50, 70-71, 76-77
voice output communication aid, 59-60, 63
Communication Participation Model, 57
Community factors, 1, 11, 15, 32, 199
Denver Model, 80, 142, 145-146, 147, 150, 153, 155-156, 157, 159, 160, 163, 164, 165, 167, 188, 189
interventions, general, 5, 7, 9, 218
Comprehensive programs, 17-18, 55-56, 133, 140-172, 204-205, 206-207
adaptive behavior, 144, 169
assessment, 142, 144, 156-158, 167
  videotapes, 155, 156, 157-158, 171
behavioral problems, 116, 119-120, 125, 143, 144-145, 146, 147-149, 150, 157, 163, 169; see also Children's Unit; Douglass Developmental Disabilities Center; Young Autism Project
Children's Unit, 142, 146, 148, 150, 154, 155, 158, 161, 163-164, 165, 167
cognitive development, 142, 144, 145, 156-157, 162, 168-169, 172
Denver Model, 80, 142, 145-146, 147, 150, 153, 155-156, 157, 159, 160, 163, 164, 165, 167, 188, 189
communication deficits, 142, 144, 149, 160, 162, 167
cost factors, 153, 155, 172
curricula, 142, 143-145, 149, 158, 159, 165, 189

developmental theory and approaches, 144, 147-148, 149, 164
Denver Model, 80, 142, 145-146, 147, 150, 151, 153, 155-156, 157, 159, 160, 163, 164, 165, 167, 188, 189
Developmental Intervention Model, 142, 145, 147, 148, 150, 152, 153, 156-157, 160-161, 164, 168
discrete trials, 112, 141, 143, 144-145, 147, 148, 150, 163-164, 170
Douglass Developmental Disabilities Center, 112, 143, 146, 148, 150, 151, 153, 154, 160, 164, 165, 167-168
emotional factors, 142, 144, 148, 156-157
familial/parental factors, 142, 143, 144-145, 149, 150, 152-154, 157, 170, 215
funding, 141, 143, 146
historical perspectives, 144, 146-147
individualized attention, general, 142, 159, 164-165
Individualized Support Program, 143, 145, 146, 149, 150, 151, 152, 153, 154, 157-158, 160, 161, 162, 163, 168
language factors, 144, 145, 156-157, 160, 167, 168, 172
Learning Experiences Alternative Program (LEAP), 143-144, 145, 146, 148, 150-155 (passim), 157, 158, 160, 161-162, 163, 168-169, 206-207
local education authorities (LEAs), 165, 178, 182, 213-214, 215-216
peer interactions, 142, 146, 148, 150, 157, 161, 162, 165, 171
Pivotal Response Model, 144, 147-153 (passim), 157, 161, 162, 169
play, 142, 161, 162
preschool programs, 143-144, 145, 146, 161, 165
Denver Model, 80, 142, 145-146, 147, 150, 151, 153, 155-156, 157, 159, 160, 163, 164, 165, 167, 188, 189
Individualized Support Program, 143, 145, 146, 149, 150, 151, 152, 153, 154, 157-158, 160, 161, 162, 163, 168
Learning Experiences (LEAP), 143-144, 145, 146, 148, 150-155 (passim), 157, 158, 160, 161-162, 163, 168-169, 206-207

professional education, 154-156, 158-159, 167, 185, 188-189, 224-225
school-based programs, 147, 157, 162, 165, 169; *see also "preschool programs" supra*
social factors, general, 142, 144, 148-149, 156-157, 161-162, 165, 172
standards, 141, 155
state government role, 146, 165
time factors, 119, 142, 150, 151-152, 153-154, 155-156, 161, 163, 167-168, 170
Treatment and Education of Autistic and Related Communication Handicapped Children (TEACCH) program, 34, 35-36, 60, 80, 136-137, 144, 145, 146, 147, 150, 151, 152, 155, 158, 160, 161, 162, 164, 169-170, 188, 189
Walden Early Childhood Programs, 79, 112, 136, 145, 146, 148-149, 150, 153, 154, 155, 160, 161-162, 165, 171
Young Autism Project, 112, 144-145, 146, 148, 150, 151, 153, 155, 158, 161, 162, 163, 170-171, 187-188, 206
Computer applications
assistive learning technologies, 2, 3, 12, 56-57, 59-63, 91-92, 103, 136, 184
voice output communication aid, 59-60, 61, 63
comprehensive programs, 157, 167
Internet, 214, 215
Core deficits, 5, 43, 47, 48-50, 54, 55-56, 63, 89, 128, 162
see also Communication deficits; Joint attention
Cost and cost-effectiveness factors, 90, 180, 182
committee study methodology, 19
comprehensive programs, 153, 155, 172
family financial support, 153, 222
Council for Exceptional Children, 191
Court cases, *see* Litigation
Creative Curriculum, 158
Cultural factors, familial, 34-35
Cure Autism Now, 194, 228
Curricula, 31, 40-41, 74, 120, 181, 186, 219, 226
comprehensive programs, 142, 143-145, 149, 158, 159, 165, 189

individualized education plans (IEPs), 36, 38, 109, 118, 119, 124, 127, 131, 154, 177-178, 180-181, 182, 207, 215-216, 217, 219-221

D

Delivering Individualized Support for Young Children with Autism, 191
Denver Model, 80, 142, 145-146, 147, 150, 151, 153, 155-156, 157, 159, 160, 163, 164, 165, 167, 188, 189
Department of Education, 141
see also Office of Educational Research and Improvement; Office of Special Education Programs
Department of Health and Human Services, *see* Centers for Disease Control and Prevention; *terms beginning "National Institute..."*
Developmental, Individual Difference, Relationship-Based Model, 158
Developmental Intervention Model, 142, 145, 147, 148, 150, 152, 153, 156-157, 160-161, 164, 168
Developmental theory and approaches, *vii*, *x*, 2-3, 6, 11-12, 13, 19, 82-92, 105-106, 135-136, 203-204, 210, 213, 220
see also Age factors; Cognitive deficits; Language factors; Mental retardation
atypical autism, 3, 24, 213
auditory perception, 31
behavioral problems, 12, 117, 119, 126
communication and symbolic abilities, 50, 51, 53-54
comprehensive programs, 144, 147-148, 149, 164
Denver Model, 80, 142, 145-146, 147, 150, 151, 153, 155-156, 157, 159, 160, 163, 164, 165, 167, 188, 189
Developmental Intervention Model, 142, 145, 147, 148, 150, 152, 153, 156-157, 160-161, 164, 168
pervasive developmental disorders not otherwise specified (PDD-NOS), 2-3, 12, 24, 113, 206, 212, 213
social development, 15-16, 31, 66-69, 71-72, 81, 105
state-funded programs, 23

Diagnosis, 2-4, 11, 13, 16, 23-24, 25-26, 30,
    85, 93, 94, 104-105, 195-197, 210,
    211-214, 227
    see also Assessment; Screening
    age factors, 3-4, 23, 25, 93, 94, 195-197,
        212
    behavioral problems, 2, 3-4, 25, 196,
        211-212
    communication deficits, 25, 26, 47, 212
    language factors, 23, 25, 212, 214
    multidisciplinary, 23, 26, 30, 214
    time factors, 3, 25, 211, 214, 219
*Diagnostic and Statistical Manual of Mental
    Disorders* (DSM-IV), 197
Discrete trials, 6, 122, 133-134, 137, 219
    communication skills, 50, 53, 54, 64
    comprehensive programs, 112, 141, 143,
        144-145, 147, 148, 150, 163-164,
        170
    defined, 133
    professional training, 187
    Young Autism Project, 112, 144-145,
        146, 148, 150
Dopamine, 118
Douglass Developmental Disabilities
    Center, 112, 143, 146, 148, 150,
    151, 153, 154, 160, 164, 165, 167-
    168
Drug treatment, 116, 128-131, 132
DSM-IV, *see Diagnostic and Statistical
    Manual of Mental Disorders*

E

Early intervention, general, *vii*, 6, 7, 9, 12,
    37, 38, 123, 221, 222
    see also Preschool programs
    assessment, 29, 30, 196
    committee charge and methodology, 2,
        13-14, 20
    comprehensive programs, 143-144, 145,
        146-147, 151, 162, 165, 166, 171-
        172
    diagnosis, 4, 23
    drug treatments, 129
    goals of, 41-42, 43
    personnel education, 7, 8, 190
Early Intervention Profile and Preschool
    Profile, 157, 167
Echolalia, 29, 47, 49, 105, 163
Education of All Handicapped Children
    Act, 1, 12

Electroencephalograms, 30
Emotional factors, 1, 61, 66-67, 69, 79
    attachment constructs, 67
    comprehensive programs, 142, 144, 148,
        156-157
    parental, 32, 34, 39, 66-67, 153
Epidemiology
    behavioral problems, 118
    prevalence, 17, 24-25, 125, 212-213
Ethical issues, 6, 8
Ethnicity, *see* Racial and ethnic factors
Executive functioning, 84, 89

F

Facilitated communication, 61-62
Familial factors, 3-4, 6, 32-39, 214-216, 218-
    219, 223
    see also Parental factors
    behavioral problems, 3-4, 69-70, 115,
        116, 120, 121-122, 123
    comprehensive programs, 142, 143, 144-
        145, 149, 150, 152-154, 157, 170, 215
    genetic/neurological, 11, 26, 30, 38-39,
        117
    professional development, 8, 226, 229
    research design and description, 8-9,
        198-199, 205-206, 229
Federal government role, 7, 9, 13, 190-191,
    222-224
    see also Funding; Legislation; *specific
        departments and agencies*
Federal Interageny Coordinating Council,
    222-223
Females, *see* Gender factors
Fidelity of treatment, 8, 9, 91, 194, 206-207,
    209, 210, 227, 228
Functional behavioral assessment, 15, 27,
    48, 120, 122-124, 127, 130, 131-
    132, 134, 135, 213
Functional communication, 49-50, 61-62,
    64-65, 123, 160, 221
    initiation of communication/
        spontaneous communication, 6,
        41, 47, 48, 49, 53, 54, 55, 64, 70,
        71, 161, 169, 204, 221
Functional Emotional Assessment Scale,
    156-157
Funding, 7, 9, 23, 175, 182, 195, 210, 223,
    224, 226, 227-228, 229
    comprehensive programs, 141, 143, 146
    professional development, 8, 187, 188,
        189, 191

G

Gender factors
    IQ scores, 85
    parents of autistic children, 33, 34, 37,
        66, 67, 221
    prevalence of autism, 24
Generalization of learning, 5, 8, 35, 43, 64,
        77, 108, 138, 139, 163-164, 184,
        203, 216, 221
    see also Maintenance of behaviors and
        skills
Genetic factors, 11, 26, 30, 38-39, 117
Gilliam Autism Rating Scale, 196
Girls, *see* Gender factors
Government role, *see* Federal government
        role; Legislation; State
        government role
Governor's Council for Developmental
        Disabilities, 223
Group instruction, 90, 91, 137-138, 159, 217
Growth curve analysis, 207-208, 210

H

Haloperidol, 129
Hearing, *see* Auditory perception
Heterogeneity, 2, 47-48, 69-71, 86, 186, 193,
        197, 201, 207, 208, 211, 217
    see also terms beginning "Individ..."
Hierarchical linear modeling, 207-208, 210
Historical perspectives
    behavioral problems, 120
    cognitive development, 82
    communication deficits, 47, 48
    comprehensive programs, 144, 146-147
    definition/explanation of autism, 31,
        32-33, 47
    litigation, 176, 178, 179, 180-181, 182,
        222, 224
    prevalence of autism, 24
    social development issues, 66, 67, 68

I

IDEA, *see* Individuals with Disabilities
        Education Act
IEPs, *see* Individualized education plans
IFSP, *see* Individual Family Service Plan
Imitation, 25, 42, 44, 50, 54, 56, 58, 69, 72,
        73, 75, 80, 83-84, 95, 163, 218
    echolalia, 29, 47, 49, 105, 163

Incidental learning, 6, 54, 78, 119, 134, 150,
        164, 184
    Walden Early Childhood Programs, 79,
        112, 136, 145, 146, 148-149, 150,
        153, 154, 155, 160, 161-162, 165, 171
Independence, 5, 216, 218
    see also Generalization of learning;
        Maintenance of behaviors and
        skills
    problem solving, 4, 124, 142, 163
    self-help skills, 162, 167
    toilet training, 103, 105-106, 107, 110,
        114
Individual differences, *see* Heterogeneity
Individual Family Service Plan (IFSP), 36,
        178, 180-181, 217
Individual instruction, 31, 73, 83, 90, 91,
        120, 137-138, 139, 142, 149
Individualized attention, 4, 6, 7, 31, 34, 144,
        149, 153, 219, 220, 221
    comprehensive programs, 142, 159, 164-
        165
    drug treatment and, 129
Individualized education plans (IEPs), 36,
        38, 109, 118, 119, 124, 127, 131,
        154, 177-178, 180-181, 182, 207,
        215-216, 217, 219-221, 223
    local education authorities (LEAs), 178,
        182, 215-216
Individualized Support Program, 143, 145,
        146, 149, 150, 152, 153, 154, 157-
        158, 160, 161, 162, 163, 168
Individuals with Disabilities Education Act
        (IDEA), 2, 7, 13, 115, 119, 122,
        124, 127, 132, 138, 176-179, 181-
        182, 216, 222, 229
    see also Individualized education plans
Infants and Young Children, 141
Initiation of communication/spontaneous
        communication, 6, 41, 47, 48, 49,
        53, 54, 55, 64, 70, 71, 161, 169,
        204, 221
Instructional strategies, 17-18, 78-81, 90-92,
        112-114, 133-139, 216-218, 227
    see also Comprehensive programs;
        Preschool programs; School-
        based programs; Teachers; *terms*
        beginning "Individual..."
    group instruction, 90, 91, 137-138, 159,
        217
    incidental teaching/learning, 6, 54, 78,
        119, 134, 150, 164, 184

Walden Early Childhood Programs, 79, 112, 136, 145, 146, 148-149, 150, 153, 154, 155, 160, 161-162, 165, 171
  naturalistic teaching and learning, 15, 42, 134, 142, 148, 149, 159, 184
  peer-mediated, 71, 72, 73-74, 77-78, 80, 81, 91, 109-110, 111, 133, 134, 138, 182, 217, 218, 221
    comprehensive programs, 142, 146, 148, 150, 157, 161, 162, 165, 171
Intelligence, 27-28, 82, 90, 108, 193
  see also Mental retardation
Intelligence quotients (IQs), 5, 44, 70, 84-87, 88, 90, 108, 168, 170-171, 172, 184, 201, 217
  age factors, 47, 71, 201, 206
Interdisciplinary approaches, 4, 7, 219
  assessment of children, 4, 23-24, 28, 30
  committee study at hand, *vii-x*, 14
  diagnosis of autism, 23, 26, 30, 214
Internet, 214, 215
IQ, *see* Intelligence quotients

J

Joint attention, 5, 48, 50, 55-56, 63, 65, 123, 217
  diagnosis of autism, 25
  cognitive development and, 83, 89
  goals of educational services, 42, 44, 73, 77
  social development and, 48, 69, 73, 77, 213

L

Language factors, 1, 2, 3, 5, 12, 42, 44, 47-65, 70, 87-88, 95, 118, 138-139, 205, 217, 219, 220
  see also Auditory perception; Communication deficits; Nonverbal communication
  assessment of deficits, 27, 28, 29-30, 31, 52, 138-139, 167, 179, 215-216
  augmentative and alternative communication, 51, 55, 56-63, 136-137
  comprehensive programs, 144, 145, 156-157, 160, 167, 168, 172
  diagnosis of autism, 23, 25, 212, 214

echolalia, 29, 47, 49, 105
  goals of education, 40-41, 50-51, 72
  IQ and age of language development, 47, 70, 71
  literacy, 62-63, 78-79, 83, 91
  professional education, 184
  reading skills, 62-63, 78-79, 83, 91
  theory of mind, 89
Learning Accomplishment Profile, 74
Learning Experiences Alternative Program (LEAP), 143-144, 145, 146, 148, 150-155 (passim), 157, 158, 160, 161-162, 163, 168-169, 206-207
LEAs, *see* Local education authorities
Legal issues, 14, 175-182
  see also Legislation
  litigation, 176, 178, 179, 180-181, 182, 222, 224
Legislation, 176-179
  Americans with Disabilities Act, 179
  Education of All Handicapped Children Act, 1, 12
  Individuals with Disabilities Education Act (IDEA), 2, 7, 13, 115, 119, 122, 124, 127, 132, 138, 176-179, 181-182, 216, 222, 229; *see also* Individualized education plans
  parental advocacy, 36-37
  Rehabilitation Act, 179
Literacy, *see* Reading skills
Litigation, 176, 178, 179, 180-181, 182, 222, 224
Local education authorities (LEAs), 222, 223
  comprehensive programs, 165, 178, 182, 213-214, 215-216
  diagnosis of autism, 23, 214
  individualized education plans (IEPs), 178, 182, 215-216
  litigation, 180
  parental support by, 38, 215-216
Longitudinal studies, 5, 9, 16-17, 42, 44, 95, 210, 217
  epidemiologic, 17, 24-25, 118, 125, 212-213

M

Maintenance of behaviors and skills, 8, 15, 35, 134, 135, 138, 203, 209, 221, 225, 227, 228
  see also Generalization of learning

adaptive behaviors, 106
comprehensive programs, 161, 163-164
personnel training, 184
problem behaviors, interventions, 115,
    121, 122, 125-126, 127, 128, 131
professional education, 184
social development, 72, 75, 76, 77, 78,
    80, 81
Males, *see* Gender factors
Massed trials, 133
Medical considerations, 30-31, 97, 104, 116
    see also Genetic factors; Neurobiological
        factors
    diagnosis of autism, 26
    drug treatment, 116, 128-131, 132
Memory, 57, 83, 85, 88, 89
Mental retardation, 1, 2, 27, 82, 84-85, 104,
    105, 106, 125, 129, 176-177
    diagnosis, 24
    professional education, 184
Methodology, *see* Research methodology
Michigan Scales, 74
Minorities, *see* Racial and ethnic factors
Motor function, *see* Psychomotor function
Multidisciplinary approaches, *see*
        Interdisciplinary approaches

N

Naltrexone, 129
National Alliance for Autism Research,
    194, 228
National Early Childhood Technical
    Assistance Systems, 141, 191
National Institute of Child Health and
    Human Development, 9, 194,
    209-210, 226, 228
National Institute of Mental Health, 9, 194,
    209, 210, 226, 229
National Institute of Neurological
    Disorders and Stroke, 9, 194, 209,
    210, 229
National Institute on Deafness and Other
    Communication Disorders, 9,
    194, 209, 210, 229
National Institutes of Health, 141, 146, 191,
    214, 222-223
National Resource Center for
    Paraprofessionals, 187
Naturalistic teaching and learning, 15, 42,
    134, 142, 148, 149, 159, 184

Neurobiological factors, *vii*, 1, 11, 13, 30, 68,
    83, 89-90, 211, 214
    see also Psychomotor function; Sensory
        perception
    behavioral problems, 116, 117-118
        psychopharmaceuticals, 116, 128-
        131, 132
    genetic, 11, 26, 30, 38-39, 117
    seizures, 30, 85, 130
New York State Department of Health, 14
Nonverbal communication, 5, 25, 30, 47, 48,
    58-59, 63-64, 69, 84, 85, 88, 95,
    123, 214
    augmentative and alternative
        communication, 51, 55, 56-63
    comprehensive programs, 142, 144

O

Office of Educational Research and
    Improvement, 9, 208, 210, 214,
    228
    prevalence estimates, 25
    professional education, 187, 191, 214,
    226
Office of Special Education Programs, 4, 8,
    9, 194, 212-213, 228
    committee charge, *vii*, 2, 13
Outcomes, 3, 5, 8, 9, 15, 64, 65, 71, 73-80,
    140, 151, 166-172, 193, 201-202,
    205-206, 210, 216-217, 228, 229
    see also Generalization of learning;
        Independence; Maintenance of
        behaviors and skills; Recovery
    clinical trials, 6, 15-17, 90, 131, 194, 197-
        198, 199-201
    goals of education, 40-44
    IQ scores, 5, 44, 70, 71, 84-87, 88, 90, 108,
        168, 170-171, 172, 184, 201, 206,
        217
Overarousal theories, 68-69, 94

P

Paraprofessionals, 7-8, 145, 187, 188, 226
Parental factors, 4, 32-39, 66-69, 76, 105,
    179-180, 181-182, 199, 214-216
    advocacy, 32, 36-37, 39, 146, 214-215,
        222
    assessment of autistic children, 27, 28,
        29, 31, 52, 179, 215-216

behavioral problems, 3-4, 69-70, 115, 116, 120, 121-122, 123
  comprehensive programs, 142, 143, 144-145, 146, 149, 150, 152-154, 157, 170, 215
  drug/nutritional treatment of children, 130
  education of, 1, 12, 219, 226
  emotional factors, 32, 34, 39, 66-67, 153
  gender factors, 33, 34, 37, 66, 67, 221
  litigation by, 176, 178, 179, 180-181, 182, 222, 224
  local education authorities (LEAs) and, 38, 215-216
  older children with autism, 36, 37-38, 78-79
  sensory/motor deficits reported, 97, 105, 107
PECS, *see* Picture Exchange Communication System
Peer interactions, 69, 70, 75, 79, 99, 109, 112, 116, 178-179, 213
  comprehensive programs, 142, 146, 148, 150, 157, 161, 162, 165, 171
  instructional methods, other, 71, 72, 73-74, 77-78, 80, 81, 91, 109-110, 111, 133, 134, 138, 182, 217, 218, 221
Personal independence, *see* Independence
Personnel preparation, *see* Professional education and development
Pervasive development disorder-not otherwise specified (PDD-NOS), 2-3, 12, 24, 113, 206, 212, 213
Pervasive Developmental Disorders Screening Test-II, 26, 196
Pharmaceuticals, *see* Drug treatment
Picture Communication Symbols, 58
Picture Exchange Communication System (PECS), 59, 136, 160
Pivotal behaviors, 34, 42, 112, 122, 134, 144-153 (passim), 157, 160-163, 169
  communication, 53, 55-56
  social development, 69, 73, 76-77, 79
Pivotal Response Model, 144, 147-153 (passim), 157, 161, 162, 169
Play, 6, 28, 29, 38, 41, 42, 48, 49, 70, 74-75, 77-78, 79, 80, 84, 112, 122, 218, 221
  comprehensive programs, general, 142, 161, 162
  Denver Model, comprehensive program, 80, 142, 145-146, 147, 150, 151, 153, 155-156, 157, 159, 160, 163, 164, 165, 167, 188, 189

diagnosis of autism, 25
  symbolic, 42, 49-50, 70-71, 75, 76-77, 82-83, 84
Playschool Model, 142
Policy issues, 7, 12, 19, 165, 175-182, 222-224
  see also Advocacy; Federal government role; Legal issues; Legislation; Litigation; Standards; State government role
Posture, 94, 96, 99, 101, 182
Preschool programs, 2, 12, 74, 89, 112, 146, 217, 219
  see also Early intervention, general committee charge, 2, 13
  comprehensive programs, 143-144, 145, 146, 161, 165
    Denver Model, 80, 142, 145-146, 147, 150, 151, 153, 155-156, 157, 159, 160, 163, 164, 165, 167, 188, 189
    Individualized Support Program, 143, 145, 146, 149, 150, 152, 153, 154, 157-158, 160, 161, 162, 163, 168
    Learning Experiences Alternative Program (LEAP), 143-144, 145, 146, 148, 150-155 (passim), 157, 158, 160, 161-162, 163, 168-169, 206-207
Prevalence, 17, 24-25, 125, 212-213
Problem solving, 4, 124, 142, 163
Professional education and development, 7-8, 72-73, 183-192, 194, 214, 224-226
  clinical practice guidelines, 118-119, 167
  comprehensive programs, 154-156, 158-159, 167, 185, 188-189, 224-225
  curricula, 31, 40-41, 74, 120, 181, 186, 219, 226
    comprehensive programs, 142, 143-145, 149, 158, 159, 165, 189
    individualized education plans (IEPs), 36, 38, 109, 118, 119, 124, 127, 131, 154, 177-178, 180-181, 182, 207, 215-216, 217, 219-221
  medical personnel, diagnostic signs, 30
  paraprofessionals, 7-8, 145, 187, 188, 226
  state government role, 189, 190-191
  teachers, 7, 8, 12, 130, 182, 184-186, 189-190, 224-225
  technical assistance, 8, 141, 146, 152, 184, 185, 190, 191, 223, 226

Professional organizations, 4, 14, 62, 188, 214, 228
Psychomotor function, *x*, 15-16, 30, 83-84, 89-90, 93-102, 104, 109, 117, 163, 212, 218
   see also Sensory perception
   age factors, 93, 94, 97, 110
   posture, 94, 96, 99, 101, 182
   toilet training, 103, 105-106, 107, 110, 114
Punishment, *see* Aversive approaches

Q

Qualitative research, 28, 30, 62, 209

R

Racial and ethnic factors, 35, 39
Reading skills, 62-63, 78-79, 83, 91
Recovery, 43, 114, 166, 171, 216-217
   IQ scores, 85-87
Recreational interventions, 144, 162, 177
Rehabilitation Act, 179
Research methodology, 6, 12-13, 64-65, 75-76, 98, 131-132, 193-210
   clinical trials, 6, 8, 15-17, 90, 131, 194, 197-198, 199-201, 204, 218-219, 222-223
   committee study at hand, *vii*, 13-20, 141, 148
   comprehensive programs, 166-172
   controlled studies, 6, 8, 15
   epidemiology, 17, 24-25, 118, 125, 212-213
   ethical issues, 6, 8
   growth curve analysis, 207-208, 210
   interdisciplinary approaches, *vii*, 14, 214, 219
   longitudinal studies, 5, 9, 16-17, 42, 44, 95, 210, 217
   qualitative research, 28, 30, 62, 209
   sampling, 15, 24-25, 26, 50, 52, 64, 71, 76, 87, 194, 198, 201, 208-209, 229
   single-subject designs, 15, 44, 52, 56, 64, 90, 91, 104, 111, 116, 120, 201-203, 204, 205, 217, 227
   standards, 8-9, 14, 16, 196-197, 198, 199, 209-210
   validity, external, 15, 26, 52, 62, 82
   validity, internal, 15, 26, 28, 52, 98

Research recommendations, 4, 5, 8-9, 19-20, 39, 63-65, 81, 92, 102, 113-114, 131-132, 209-210, 211-229 (passim)
Retardation, *see* Mental retardation
Rett's syndrome, 3, 12
Risperidone, 129

S

Sampling, 15, 24-25, 26, 50, 52, 64, 71, 76, 87, 194, 198, 201, 208-209, 229
Scales of Independent Behavior-Revised, 74
School-based programs, 7-8, 12, 31, 112, 115, 139, 177-179, 183-186, 216-218
   see also Local education authorities; Preschool programs; Teachers
   advocacy, 37
   assessment of children, 31, 222
   committee charge, 2, 13
   comprehensive programs, 147, 157, 162, 165, 169
   curricula, 31, 40-41, 74
   diagnosis, 23, 26
   individual instruction, 31, 73, 83, 90, 91, 120, 137-138, 139, 142, 149
   individualized education plans (IEPs), 36, 38, 109, 118, 119, 124, 127, 131, 154, 177-178, 180-181, 182, 207, 215-216, 217, 219-221, 223
      local education authorities (LEAs), 178, 182, 215-216
   parental involvement, 4, 31, 33, 38, 184, 223
School Psychology Review, 141
Screening, 4, 25-26, 27, 28, 195-197
   see also Diagnosis
   age factors, 4, 25, 195-197
Screening Test for Autism in Two Year Olds, 25, 26, 196
Secretin, 130
Seizures, 30, 85, 130
Self-help skills, 162, 167
Self-injurious behavior, 49, 115, 116, 117-118, 123, 125, 128-129
   tantrums, 115, 123, 125, 145, 213
Self-stimulatory behavior, 55, 105, 111, 213
Sensory perception, *x*, 15-16, 42, 83-84, 89, 93-102, 110, 123, 127, 131, 176-177
   see also Psychomotor function
   age factors, 93, 94, 97, 110

assessment, 30, 212
  auditory perception, 30, 31-32, 42, 83,
    85, 98, 99-101, 123, 131, 212
  visual perception, 57, 62-63, 69, 83, 85,
    90, 94, 95, 96, 98, 100-101, 123,
    131, 137-138, 144, 212; *see also*
    Nonverbal communication
Serotonin, 129
Sign language, *see* Nonverbal
  communication
Single-subject designs, 15, 44, 52, 56, 64, 90,
    91, 104, 111, 116, 120, 201-203,
    204, 205, 217, 227
Sleeping, 107-108
  toilet training, 103, 105-106, 107, 110,
    114
Social factors, 1, 2, 5, 11, 12, 15, 66-81, 83,
    115, 119, 212-213
  see also Adaptive behavior; Behavioral
    problems; Communication
    deficits; Community factors;
    Cultural factors; Familial factors;
    Imitation; Joint attention;
    Parental factors; Peer interactions
  adults, interactions with, general, 6, 49,
    56, 59, 68-69, 70, 73
  assessment, 27, 28, 52, 74-75, 212, 214
  comprehensive programs, 142, 144, 148-
    149, 156-157, 161-162, 165, 172
  developmental theory, 15-16, 31, 66-69,
    71-72, 81, 105
  goals of education, 40-41, 42, 71-75, 212-
    213, 221
  historical perspectives, 66, 67, 68
  incidental learning, 6, 54, 78, 119, 134,
    150, 164, 184
    Walden Early Childhood Programs,
      79, 112, 136, 145, 146, 148-149,
      150, 153, 154, 155, 160, 161-162,
      165, 171
  interventions, general, 6, 31, 71-81, 212-
    213, 216, 217, 218, 229
  maintenance of behaviors, 72, 75, 76, 77,
    78, 80, 81
  pivotal behaviors, 69, 73, 76-77, 79
  professional education, 184, 186, 187
  reading skills and, 78-79, 83
  recreational interventions, 144, 162, 177
Society for Clinical Child Psychology, 14
Socioeconomic status, 35, 39
Spontaneous communication, *see* Initiation
    of communication/spontaneous
    communication

Standards
  see also Outcomes
  assessment instruments, 25-30 (passim),
    74, 75, 85, 88, 91, 96, 108-109, 135-
    136, 156-158, 167, 169, 196-197
  IQ scores, 5, 44, 70, 84-87, 88, 90, 108,
    168, 170-171, 172, 184, 201, 217
  age factors, 47, 71, 201, 206
  attachment process, 67
  behavioral problems, response to, 115,
    118-119, 125
  clinical practice guidelines, 118-119, 167
  committee study at hand, 14, 15
  comprehensive programs, 141, 155
  curricular, 40-41
  fidelity of treatment, 8, 9, 91, 194, 206-
    207, 209, 210, 227, 228
  goals of education, 40-44, 50-51, 71-75,
    77, 212-213, 218, 221
  policy, 175
  professional, 7, 118-119, 187, 191, 224,
    227-228
  research design and description, 8-9, 14,
    16, 196-197, 198, 199, 209-210
State government role, 7, 14, 222-224
  comprehensive programs, 146, 165
  diagnosis of autism, 23
  professional education, 189, 190-191
Stereotypic behavior, 61, 94, 96, 97, 98, 117,
    118, 145, 176-177
Student/teacher ratios, 120, 159, 219, 220-
    221
  individual instruction, 31, 73, 83, 90, 91,
    120, 137-138, 139, 142, 149
Symbol use, 29, 49, 55-56, 58, 82, 218
  see also Nonverbal communication
  age factors, 50, 54, 123, 160
  comprehensive programs, 142
Symbolic play, 42, 49-50, 70-71, 75, 76-77,
    82-83, 84
System for Augmenting Language, 61

T

Tantrums, 115, 123, 125, 145, 213
TEACCH, *see* Treatment and Education of
    Autistic and Related
    Communication Handicapped
    Children (TEACCH) program
Teachers, 1, 4, 31, 114, 133, 157, 179
  assessment of autistic children, 27, 31,
    52

behavioral problems of children, 116, 130
communication interventions, 54-55
diagnosis by, 26
education of, 7, 8, 12, 130, 182, 184-186, 189-190, 224-225
individualized education plans (IEPs), 178
parents as, 35-36, 39, 109, 144-145, 146
student/teacher ratios, 120, 159
    individual instruction, 31, 73, 83, 90, 91, 120, 137-138, 139, 142, 149
Technical assistance, 8, 141, 146, 152, 184, 185, 190, 191, 223, 226
Technology, assistive, *see* Assistive technology
Theory of mind, 83, 88-89
Time factors, 2, 11
    see also Age factors
    behavioral problems, 116-117, 119, 120, 123, 134, 163
    diagnosis, 3, 25, 211, 214, 219
    interventions, duration and time intervals, 6, 35-36, 86, 91, 113, 119, 120, 123, 133, 134, 193, 217, 218, 219, 220
        assistive technology, 63
        comprehensive programs, 119, 142, 150, 151-152, 153-154, 155-156, 161, 163, 167-168, 170
    parental time spent with child, 34, 35-36, 152, 153
    professional training, 155-156
    social deficits, 31
    variability in child over time, 86
Toilet training, 103, 105-106, 107, 110, 114
Transfer of learning, *see* Generalization of learning

Treatment and Education of Autistic and Related Communication Handicapped Children (TEACCH) program, 34, 35-36, 60, 80, 136-137, 144, 145, 146, 147, 150, 151, 152, 155, 158, 160, 161, 162, 164, 169-170, 188, 189

V

Validity, external, 15, 26, 52, 62, 82
Validity, internal, 15, 26, 28, 52, 98
Videotapes, 94, 155, 156, 157-158, 171
Vineland Adaptive Behavior Scales, 74, 108-109, 169
Visual perception, 57, 100-101, 62-63, 69, 83, 85, 90, 94, 95, 96, 98, 100-101, 123, 131, 137-138, 144, 212
    see also Nonverbal communication
Voice output communication aid, 59-60, 61, 63

W

Walden Early Childhood Programs, 79, 112, 136, 145, 146, 148-149, 150, 153, 154, 155, 160, 161-162, 165, 171
Women, *see* Gender factors
World Wide Web, *see* Internet

Y

Young Autism Project, 112, 144-145, 146, 148, 150, 151, 153, 155, 158, 161, 162, 163, 170-171, 187-188, 206